Performances of Injustice

Following unprecedented violence in 2007/8, Kenya introduced two classic transitional justice mechanisms: a truth commission and international criminal proceedings. Both are widely believed to have failed, but why? And what do their performances say about contemporary Kenya, the ways in which violent pasts persist and the shortcomings of transitional justice?

Using the lens of performance, this book analyses how transitional justice efforts are incapable of dealing with how unjust and violent pasts actually persist. Gabrielle Lynch reveals the story of an ongoing political struggle requiring substantive socio-economic and political change that transitional justice mechanisms can theoretically recommend, and which they can sometimes help to initiate and inform, but which they cannot implement or create, and can sometimes unintentionally help to reinforce.

GABRIELLE LYNCH is Professor of Comparative Politics at the University of Warwick, and her research interests include ethnic identities and politics, elections and democratisation, and transitional justice and local reconciliation efforts, with a particular focus on Kenya. She has published numerous journal articles and book chapters. Her first book, *I Say to You: Ethnic Politics and the Kalenjin in Kenya*, was published in 2011. She is an elected member of council for the British Institute in Eastern Africa and wrote a regular column in Kenya's *Saturday Nation* from April 2014 to March 2018.

CAMBRIDGE
UNIVERSITY PRESS

University Printing House, Cambridge CB2 8BS, United Kingdom

One Liberty Plaza, 20th Floor, New York, NY 10006, USA

477 Williamstown Road, Port Melbourne, VIC 3207, Australia

314–321, 3rd Floor, Plot 3, Splendor Forum, Jasola District Centre, New Delhi – 110025, India

79 Anson Road, #06–04/06, Singapore 079906

Cambridge University Press is part of the University of Cambridge.

It furthers the University's mission by disseminating knowledge in the pursuit of education, learning, and research at the highest international levels of excellence.

www.cambridge.org
Information on this title: www.cambridge.org/9781108426213
DOI: 10.1017/9781108575164

© Gabrielle Lynch 2018

This publication is in copyright. Subject to statutory exception and to the provisions of relevant collective licensing agreements, no reproduction of any part may take place without the written permission of Cambridge University Press.

First published 2018

Printed in the United States of America by Sheridan Books, Inc.

A catalogue record for this publication is available from the British Library.

Library of Congress Cataloging-in-Publication Data
Names: Lynch, Gabrielle, author.
Title: Performances of justice : the politics of truth and reconciliation in Kenya / Gabrielle Lynch.
Description: Cambridge, United Kingdom ; New York, NY : Cambridge University Press, 2018. | Includes bibliographical references and index.
Identifiers: LCCN 2017053775 | ISBN 9781108426213 (hardback) | ISBN 9781108444934 (paperback)
Subjects: LCSH: Peace-building – Kenya. | Truth commissions – Kenya. | Reconciliation – Kenya. | Transitional justice – Kenya. | Political violence – Kenya. | Kenya. Truth, Justice and Reconciliation Commission. | Kenya – Politics and government – 2002–
Classification: LCC JZ5584.K4 L96 2018 | DDC 967.6204/3–dc23
LC record available at https://lccn.loc.gov/2017053775

ISBN 978-1-108-42621-3 Hardback
ISBN 978-1-108-44493-4 Paperback

Cambridge University Press has no responsibility for the persistence or accuracy of URLs for external or third-party internet websites referred to in this publication and does not guarantee that any content on such websites is, or will remain, accurate or appropriate.

Performances of Injustice

The Politics of Truth, Justice and
Reconciliation in Kenya

GABRIELLE LYNCH
University of Warwick

CAMBRIDGE
UNIVERSITY PRESS

In loving memory of Berenika Stefanska (1983–2016) and the echo of her voice: 'Come on girl, come on!'

Contents

Acknowledgements	*page* ix
List of Abbreviations	xii
Maps	xiv

Part I Haunted by Violence   1

Prologue: A Time of Violence   3

1 Confronting the Past: Transitional Justice and the Politics of Time and Performance   7

2 Framing the Good Citizen for Orderly Elections: The Prioritisation of Peace   30

3 Enter the International Criminal Court: Performing (In)justice   57

Part II A Post–South African Truth Commission   91

4 The Truth, Justice and Reconciliation Commission: A Sense of Once-Againness   95

5 Public Hearings: Bringing the Audience Back In   124

6 Truth's Grand Narrative (Part I): Of Injustice and Suffering   149

7 'The Story of the Kenyan Woman': Of the Performance of Familiar Gender Roles   183

8 Truth's Grand Narrative (Part II): Of Injustice and Impunity   218

9 'Only Talking Won't Help': Of Justice and Reparations   249

Part III	**Familiar Performances**	275
10	Performed Ruptures: Whither Reconciliation?	279
Bibliography		293
Index		327

Acknowledgements

This book stems from research conducted whilst working at the University of Warwick and the University of Leeds, and builds upon earlier research conducted at Keele University and the University of Oxford. The vibrant research communities at all four universities provided a stimulating work environment, and I benefited immeasurably from participation in the African studies communities at Leeds and Oxford, transitional justice group at Leeds and politics and performance network at Warwick. The analysis in this volume has been further strengthened by participation in numerous seminars and conferences and from feedback received. I also thank Jelke Boesten, Nic Cheeseman, Gregory Deacon, Joost Fontein, Irina Ichim, Yvette Hutchison, Ambreena Manji, Neo Musangi, Lionel Nichols, Naomi van Stapele and Justin Willis for reading and commenting on draft chapters.

The arguments of this book draw upon research conducted between 2008 and 2014 under the auspices of several different research projects. I am particularly grateful for the financial assistance provided by a three-year Economic and Social Research Council (ESRC) First Grant entitled 'Truth and Justice: The Search for Peace and Stability in Modern Kenya'. I thank colleagues from Leeds (particularly Jelke Boesten, Ray Bush, Bina Fernandez, Gordon Crawford, Duncan McCargo and Polly Wilding) for their input into the initial project design, and colleagues from Warwick (particularly Yvette Hutchison and Shirin Rai) for their contribution to the project's later development. I worked with a number of fantastic research assistants on this project – namely, Job Bwonye, Patrick Githinji, Nina Holmes, Carrie Hough, Joseph Kirwa, Keffa Magenyi, Albert Mshonda, Samson Ngengi Njuguna, Jolly Ouko, Moritz Wassum and Cyrus Yuge – who all enriched the analysis through their hard work and critical thinking.

The book also draws upon research funded by a British Academy grant in 2008 to investigate Kenya's post-election violence, and a second grant in 2009 to analyse local reconciliation efforts. Finally, the analysis has benefited from heading – together with Nic Cheeseman and Justin Willis – research projects on Kenya's 2013 and 2017 elections and an ESRC Knowledge Exchange project titled 'Kenya 2013–2017: From Election Monitoring to Longer-Term Reform'. It has also benefited from research conducted with Nic and Justin for another ESRC-funded project on the impact of elections in Kenya, Uganda and Ghana. Throughout these projects, Nic and Justin have provided a never-ending supply of academic insights and firm friendship, and the book draws extensively upon their expertise and support. It has also been informed by the knowledge and analysis of other members of these collaborative projects, namely, Job Bwonye, Neil Carrier, Ngala Chome, Greg Deacon, Alexander Dyzenhaus, Denis Galava, Hassan Kochore, Keffa Magenyi, Amanda Magisu, Godwin Murunga, Hassan Mwakimako, Betty Okero, Adams Oloo, Michelle Osborn, Ralph-Michael Peters, Jacob Rasmussen, Mutuma Ruteere, Hannah Waddilove and Muthoni Wanyeki. I also learnt much from Lydiah Bosire with whom I have co-authored an article on civil society and transitional justice in Kenya.

In conducting the research for this project, I spent months following the Truth, Justice and Reconciliation Commission (TJRC) around Kenya, during which commissioners and staff were unstintingly generous with their time and civil society activists welcomed me into their discussions. Particular mention must go to Philip Barno, Japhet Biegon, Wafula Buke, Job Bwonye, Wesley Chebii, Chris Gitari, Lucas Kimanthi, Keffa Magenyi, Amanda Magisu, Paul Masese, Rosemary Maucha, Pastor Sammy Mbugua, Mary Mwangi, Betty Okero, Mercy Shahale, Ron Slye, Andrew Songa and Wachira Waheire for their assistance, insights and friendship.

The process of conducting research was only made possible by the generosity and willingness of hundreds of Kenyans to answer my questions; to share their memories, fears and hopes; and to correct my many errors and presumptions. In particular I must thank interviewees who talked with me on more than one occasion and who trusted me enough to share traumatic memories and security concerns. In large part, these individuals go unrecorded in this text so as to ensure their anonymity; however, the analysis is dedicated to their lives, tenacity and openness.

As a researcher I have lived a rather nomadic life and owe much to the unstinting hospitality of family and friends. This includes Nadine Beckmann, Tamara Britten, Nic Cheeseman, Lucie Cluver, Olivia Collins, Claire Davies, Greg Deacon, Laura Durrant, Neela Ghoshal, Mira Gratier, Rob Guthrie, Gabe Joselow, Sarah Longair, Katrina Manson, Michael Monaghan, Michelle Osborn, Nicola Pratt, Berenika Stefanska, Steph Wynne-Jones and Michael Wiesmann, who all opened their homes to me and my belongings in the UK, Nairobi, Paris or Warsaw.

In Kenya, Greg Aldous, Claire Beston, Tamara Britten, Greg Deacon, Claire Elder, Nilofer Elias, Nzech Emmanuel, Joost Fontein, Neela Ghoshal, Patrick Githinji, Mira Gratier, Laura Heaton, Jen Huxta, Irina Ichim, Gabe Joselow, Zihan Kassam, Keffa Magenyi, Amanda Magisu, Ambreena Manji, Katrina Manson, Alex Mayeye, Kipkorir arap Menjo, Melissa Menke, Samson Ngengi Njuguna, Kaloki Nyamai, Michelle Osborn, Anneke Osse, Emma Phillips, Lindsey Pollaczek, Els Rijke, Sarah Jane Russell, David Some, Karin Sosis, Elizabeth Spackman, Berenika Stefanska, Radha Upadhyaya, Marcis Vanadzins, Verena Waldhart and many others all helped to ensure that Kenya has come to feel like my second home.

This research project often proved tiring and emotional, while life also threw up its own challenges. Final thanks therefore go to my family – my parents, sisters, brothers-in-law, nieces and nephews – and to all of my friends in Kenya and the UK who, through their endless support and much needed light relief, collectively ensured that the ups always outweighed the downs. I am grateful and honoured to have you all in my life.

Abbreviations

AfriCOG	Africa Centre for Open Governance
AG	Attorney General
AI	Amnesty International
AMP	Adversely mentioned person
AU	African Union
CJPC	Catholic Justice and Peace Commission
CSO	Civil society organisation
DC	District Commissioner
DPC	District Peace Committee
DRC	Democratic Republic of the Congo
ESRC	Economic and Social Research Council
FIDA–Kenya	Federation of Women Lawyers – Kenya
GiZ	*Deutsche Gesellschaft für Internationale Zusammenarbeit*
GSU	General Service Unit
HRW	Human Rights Watch
ICC	International Criminal Court
ICG	International Crisis Group
ICJ–Kenya	International Commission of Jurists – Kenya section
ICPC	International Centre for Policy and Conflict
ICTJ	International Centre for Transitional Justice
ICTY	International Criminal Tribunal for the former Yugoslavia
IDP	Internally displaced person
IOM	International Organisation of Migration
KHRC	Kenya Human Rights Commission
KIC	Kenya Intelligence Committee
KKV	*Kazi kwa Vijana*
KNCHR	Kenya National Commission of Human Rights
MYW	*Maendaleo ya Wanawake*
NCCK	National Council of Churches of Kenya

List of Abbreviations

NCIC	National Cohesion and Integration Commission
NGO	Non-governmental organisation
NLC	National Land Commission
NPS	National Police Service
NSC	National Steering Committee on Peace-Building and Conflict Management
NVSN	National Victims and Survivors Network
ODM	Orange Democratic Movement
OP	Office of the President
OTP	Office of the Prosecutor
PNU	Party of National Unity
PS	Permanent Secretary
PTC	Pre-Trial Chamber
RWPL	Rural Women Peace Link
TJRC	Truth, Justice and Reconciliation Commission
TNA	The National Alliance
TRC	Truth and Reconciliation Commission
UNDP	United Nations Development Programme
UNSC	United Nations Security Council
URP	United Republication Party
USAID	United States Agency for International Development
VPRS	Victims Participation and Reparation Section
VTF	Victims Trust Fund

Maps

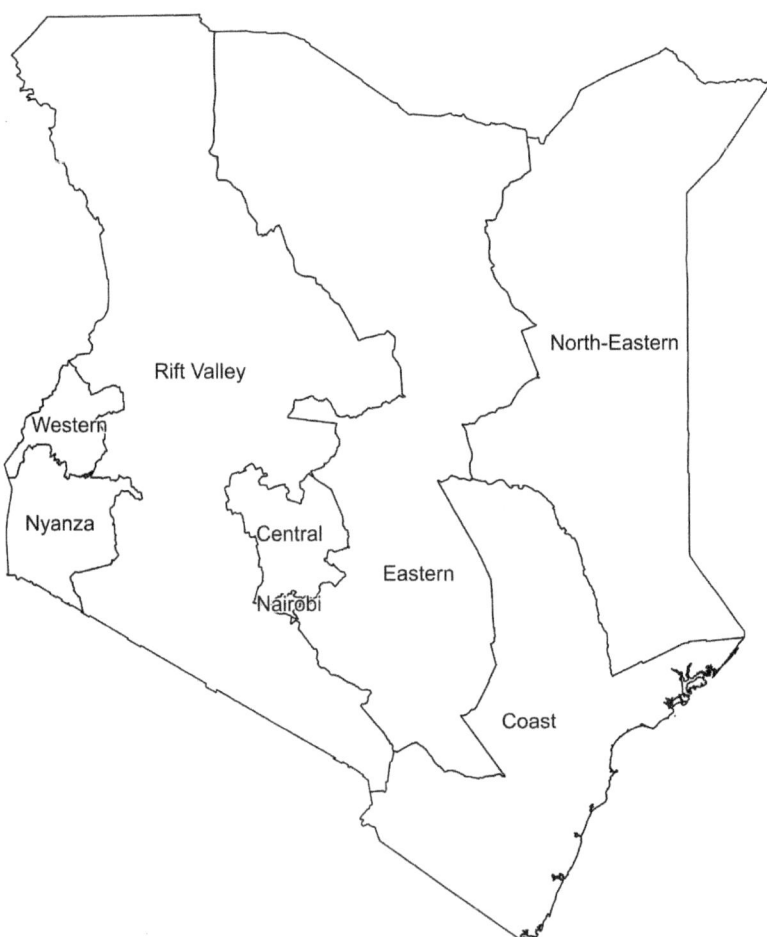

Map 1 Kenya: Provinces, 1963–2010. Source: Alex Dyzenhaus.

Map 2 Kenya; Counties, 2010–to present. Source: Alex Dyzenhaus.

PART I

Haunted by Violence

HAMLET: Let us go in together,
             And still your fingers on your lips, I pray.
             The time is out of joint – O cursèd spite,
             That ever I was born to set it right!
             Nay, come, let's go together.
                             (*Hamlet* Act 1, Scene 5, 186–190)

The present is 'out of joint' because it fuses and incorporates elements of the past and the future, because it is always haunted by ghosts or *revenants* … Hamlet's enigmatic saying that time is 'out of joint' … [is] primarily [an] ethical statement. (Bevernage 2012: 142 & 143)

1

Prologue
A Time of Violence

On 29 December 2007 the friends I was staying with in Nairobi phoned from Kakamega in Western Kenya: they did not know how to get home. They had begun the day's drive back, but supporters of the principal opposition party, the Orange Democratic Movement (ODM), had blocked the road with stones and branches. My friends had decided to turn back after they saw one gang drag passengers out of a *matatu*,[1] demand to see their identity cards and then begin to beat a man whose name must have suggested that he hailed from the 'wrong' ethnic group. In the background they could see a fire with what looked like a man's legs sticking out of the flames.

As I waited for news from my friends, and for the final results from the presidential and parliamentary elections of 27 December, frustration with delays began to provoke scenes like that witnessed by my hosts in pockets across the country, and friends from the opposition heartlands of the Rift Valley (where I had conducted research since 2004) began to call. One man from Eldoret complained of how large numbers of General Service Unit (GSU) personnel – infamous for their repression of opposition activity – were being stationed around the town. In his words, '[W]e're worried [the government's] going to steal the election: what else are the GSU doing here?'

Then, in the early evening of 30 December, the Electoral Commission of Kenya announced – in a closed-door meeting relayed through the state-owned Kenya Broadcasting Company – that the incumbent president, Mwai Kibaki of the Party of National Unity (PNU), had won the election by a little more than 200,000 votes. For a while I sat dumbfounded. The previous day, I had woken to news that the principal opposition candidate, Raila Odinga of ODM (who had enjoyed a marginal lead in pre-election opinion polls), was winning by almost a million votes. It looked like the government had just stolen the presidential election.

---

[1] The name for the ubiquitous private minibuses that ply Kenya's roads.

Within the hour, I was faced with another image televised live to the nation: President Kibaki was being re-inaugurated at State House as the sun went down and late arrivals shuffled around the periphery of the cameraman's gaze. My heart sank.

Almost immediately my friends returned – they had used their credit card to charter a plane back from Kakamega. Over the following days, weeks, months and years, I would hear similar stories of people who had escaped the violence that erupted after Kenya's 2007 election, and which ended with a power-sharing agreement on 28 February 2008. This includes an account by a Kalenjin politician who had campaigned on a PNU ticket in the north Rift Valley (and hence for a party that the majority of his ethnic kin opposed); he relayed how he was driven to Eldoret airport in the trunk of a friend's car in January 2008 so as to avoid angry co-ethnics who regarded him as a traitor to the community (interview, Eldoret, 2 September 2011). Or a Luo flower farm worker who recounted how, later that month, police officers saved him and his family from a gang of Kikuyu youth who had gathered in their Naivasha homestead wielding *pangas*[2] and jerry cans of petrol (interview, Naivasha, 17 December 2012), while an Indian businessman spoke of how police had escorted his family and others across the border from Nyanza into Uganda in early January 2008 (conversation, Nairobi, 5 July 2015).

Unfortunately, I heard many more stories of people who had not managed to escape: who neither had the money to charter a plane nor had benefited from the timely arrival of a brave friend or security personnel. Instead, I heard a litany of harrowing tales of physical violence, loss, destitution and ongoing suffering. A Kikuyu lady described how she was raped by two men in Eldoret town in January 2008 when she left the safety of an internally displaced person's camp to look for her brother's body after she heard that he had been killed by a gang of opposition supporters (interview, Nakuru, 8 March 2011). A Kikuyu man spoke of how his father was murdered by their neighbours and rued the ongoing impact of the patriarch's loss on his extended family (conversation, Molo, 2 August 2009). A Luo woman recalled how her husband had been decapitated during the violence in Nakuru and how, in her shock,

---

[2] A machete-like knife common to most households across the country.

Prologue 5

she had wrapped his head in a *leso*³ and carried it all the way back to Kisumu – almost 150 kilometres away – in a paper bag (TJRC women's hearing, Kisumu, 16 July 2011). A visibly disturbed Luo man testified to the loss of eleven members of his immediate family when a mob set his house ablaze in Naivasha (TJRC public hearings, Kisumu, 14 July 2011). A Kalenjin woman spoke of how her husband had been shot dead by police in January 2008, and of her ongoing struggles to educate their son (TJRC public hearings, Kericho, 21 September 2011). And a Kalenjin man recounted how his property had been destroyed and his family had been forced to flee after being denounced as traitors for supporting Kibaki's re-election bid, and how they had subsequently felt impelled to move from place to place under suspicion of being witnesses at the International Criminal Court (ICC; conversations between 7 August 2011 and 12 April 2015). In *none* of these cases had a perpetrator apologised or been brought to book, or any stolen or destroyed property been returned or replaced. And so the stories of violations and injustice go on.

Collectively these personal narratives, ongoing consequences and examples of impunity comprise some of the realities behind the nameless and conservative statistics: that within two months, more than 1,000 people died and almost 700,000 people were displaced during the post-election violence of 2007–8 (Kenya 2008b: 304; Lynch 2009: 604), with only a handful of low-level perpetrators convicted.

This book does not focus on the post-election violence, which I have discussed in earlier work (Lynch 2011b). Instead, it analyses two of the mechanisms introduced to try to address the violence and its underlying causes so as to confront these realities, assign them to history and facilitate a transition to a more democratic and peaceful Kenya: an international criminal trial and truth commission. Through these mechanisms, many sought to gain justice for the post-election violence, tackle its underlying drivers and kick-start real reforms. However, what should be relegated to 'the past' – or what Kenya was in transition from, and what it should be in transition to – as well as how the past is best confronted and addressed, and what various mechanisms could

---

³ A scarf or piece of cloth.

realistically achieve, were far less clear even to transitional justice's supporters. At the same time, many Kenyans (including many of the political elite) came to prioritise peace and stability over justice. It is the critique that an analysis of these highly public political processes offers of transitional justice's attempts to establish new temporalities in which the present and future are free of violent and unjust pasts, and the window that such an analysis provides onto Kenyan politics, that constitutes the subject matter of this book.

1 Confronting the Past
Transitional Justice and the Politics of Time and Performance

[T]he distancing of past and present does not simply result from the passing of time but is something that must be actively pursued.

(Beverage 2012: 15)

We are in an era of transitional justice (Gready 2011) – a time when it is regarded as standard practice in the face of a recent, or even ongoing, history of authoritarianism or conflict to employ a mix of judicial and non-judicial mechanisms to try and consolidate, or facilitate, a transition to democracy, greater political (and sometimes socio-economic) inclusion, inter-communal cohesion and collective human rights observance. In this era, the common tools of transitional justice include criminal trials, amnesty, reparations, memorialisation, vetting of state officers, lustration (or a ban from holding public office), constitutional and institutional reform (most notably security sector reforms) and a truth commission. The last of these is understood as a temporary state-sanctioned body that investigates a pattern of past abuse, that engages 'directly and broadly with the affected population, gathering information on their experiences' and which aims to conclude with a public report (Hayner 2011: 11–12).

The scope and approach of transitional justice has changed significantly over time. However, the same term can be applied since efforts continue to be motivated by a belief that authoritarian and violent pasts – through traumatic memories, sectional schisms or unjust structures – pose an obstacle to a nation's efforts to move on to a new future. The basic idea is that societies need to be seen to confront and deal with unjust histories if they are to establish a qualitative break between the past, present and future, and, in so doing, render what has occurred 'past' in the 'substantial sense of "passed", "dead", or "over and done with"' (Bevernage 2012: 86).

In this vein, public apologies, to take just one example, become 'transformative rituals [that] always involve time', and which seek to 'mark a temporal transition: wrong done in a time marked as past is recognized as such, and this acknowledgement itself creates or verifies a new temporal plane, a present oriented towards the future' (Trouillot 2011: 458). Proponents of transitional justice thus 'look backwards', not as interested historians, but as a way to 'reach forwards' (Villa-Vicencio & Verwoerd 2000: xiv). Or, as Archbishop Desmond Tutu explained in his foreword to the South African Truth and Reconciliation Commission (TRC) report:

The other reason amnesia simply will not do is that the past refuses to lie down quietly. It has an uncanny habit of returning to haunt one ... However painful the experience, the wounds of the past must not be allowed to fester. They must be opened. They must be cleansed. And balm must be poured on them so they can heal. This is not to be obsessed with the past. It is to take care that the past is properly dealt with for the sake of the future.
(TRC vol. 1 1998: 7 and 22)

Transitional justice is thus motivated by a particular concern with healing and temporality, or with an effort to change people's relationship with time. In short, by trying to mark a break with the past and create new expectations of the future, transitional justice seeks to establish a present and future free from particular complaints, claims and fears that stem from a violent and unjust past.

As a result, transitional justice is propelled, albeit often implicitly, by a recognition of the importance and power of ghosts and hauntings, where the idea of being haunted refers to a sense of 'how that which appears to be not there is often a seething presence, acting on and often meddling with taken-for-granted realities' (Gordon 2008: 8). More specifically, a haunting, or the presence of a ghost, usually represents a loss – either of a life or lives, an aspect of it (such as health or dignity), material stuff, or 'a path not taken' (Gordon 2008: 64). The latter includes any trajectory which seemed possible, but now seems beyond reach – from the diminished opportunities that stem from a child's lost education to the political scepticism and increased ethnic division that can attend nepotistic and ethnically biased leadership. As such, 'the presence of ghosts' reflects a 'double time, a piece of it in the past, another in a future yet to be realised' (Steinberg 2016: 15).

However, when it comes to transitional justice, persistent pasts and possible futures include not only 'seething presences' in the sense of people, material or trajectory 'shaped holes' (cf. Roy 1997: 82), but also continuities, evolutions, echoes and visions, and new or enlivened narratives and repertoires of contention.

Continuities include injustices and violences that did not end with a political transition, such as the economic inequalities and racism that continue to plague South Africa decades beyond the end of political apartheid (Mamdani 2002). While evolutions refer to adaptations – such as the shift of unaccountable elites from repression to grand corruption, the emergence of criminal gangs out of protest politics or the use of excessive force to fight those labelled as 'criminals' – and to the fact that the 'past often affects the present not as straightforward repetition ... but in modified, evolving ways' (Gready 2011: 11; also Hamber 1998a).

The past also persists through echoes and visions. More specifically, traumatic events and experiences have a tendency to revive memories of earlier lived and genealogical pasts, and to suppress other memorial segments, through the evocation of themes, patterns and exceptionalisms (cf. Fontein 2015). As a result, injustice not only enlivens certain memories, but it also helps to shape visions of likely futures. In this way, Kenya's post-election crisis of 2007–8 provided new memories of violence. It also reminded people of earlier periods of election-related violence in the early 1990s and of a more general failure of the state to protect its citizens (Ruteere & Wairuri 2015), and it simultaneously raised the spectre or possibility of repetition.

The implication is that transitional justice needs to address recent pasts, the echoes of more distant pasts that events and analyses have rendered newly vivid and present, and the fear-induced visions of possible futures.

This leads to a final persistence: unjust pasts and their remnants provide memories and stories, and thus codes, tropes and interpretative contexts, which shape actions and responses and which make particular futures thinkable and others feared. They thus haunt the present and future by providing new layers to older or revised narratives of (in)justice, and by helping to shape local repertoires of contention. The latter understood as 'the ways that people act together in pursuit of shared interests' (Tilly 1995), which includes 'not only what people *do* when they engage in conflict with others but *what they know how to do* and what others expect them to do' (Tarrow 2011: 39; emphasis in original). Such repertoires range from strategies of protest (Rolfe 2005) and inter-ethnic violence to the ways in which people speak about (in)justice (cf. Lynch 2011b) and the symbols that they use to evoke status and difference (cf. Horowitz 2000). Such narratives and repertoires of contention are often deemed problematic as they can feed into cycles of violence. Nevertheless, activists often do not want them rendered immediately dead, as the approaches and emotions that they carry constitute powerful political tools for mobilising people against 'others' (cf. Lynch 2011b) *or* against the systemic benefits enjoyed by past perpetrators and ongoing beneficiaries of injustice (Meister 2002).

Collectively, these people or trajectory-shaped holes, continuities, evolutions, echoes, visions, and narratives and repertoires of contention mean that 'the past is not only always with us, it is also always, at least in part, generative of the now and of what comes next' (Fontein 2017: 163). Or, as the anthropologist Nancy Munn has argued, '[P]eople operate in a present that is always infused, and which they are further infusing, with pasts and futures' (1992: 115). As a result:

> We exist ... in the broken middle of time, the 'gap between past and future.' In our present situation we anticipate the future with fear or hope based on remembrance of what was and the knowledge that what has been could be again. Conversely, we remember the past with regret or nostalgia in terms of our imaginative anticipation of the possibilities that the future holds.
>
> (Schaap 2003: 5)

Unfortunately, the idea that one can 'look backwards to reach forwards' downplays these complex ways in which the past actually persists, and possible futures infringe on the now. This is problematic since it can facilitate a politicised assertion of closure that excludes those who do not buy into the absence of the past, the newness of the present, or the desirability of imagined futures; and provides a resource to those who seek to present such 'difficult people' as untrusting, unreasonable, analogue, unpatriotic or even as criminal (Lynch 2015a). An exclusion that unintentionally (and sometimes intentionally) disciplines those who want reform in the broader sense of altered power relations and redistributive justice (cf. Mamdani 2002; Meister 2002; Wilson 2001).

To confront and deal with the presence of the past in the present and future, and render it history in the sense of rendering it largely absent, is thus an extremely ambitious, and, I will argue, an impossible and inherently political endeavour. This is not to say that it is a goal that people should not seek to move towards, but that such efforts need to be considered, cautious, and self-consciously political. It also means that violent pasts cannot simply be confronted and dealt with during short 'transitional' periods (cf. Arthur 2009: 333).

Given the difficulty of producing a new sense of temporality, it is unsurprising that short-term efforts to 'look backwards to reach forwards' have attracted substantial criticism. Controversy has occurred at three broad levels. First, many insist that confrontations with the past are inherently unsettling and dangerous, and that it is better to try and forget, rather than to necessarily seek justice, for the past, and to move on by marking a break in other ways – for example, through a commitment to a new public morality or provision of stability and progress (Apuuli 2011; Rieff 2016).

Second, there are those who believe in transitional justice's rationale; who recognise that it is a beginning, rather than an end point; and who highlight common operational shortcomings, such as insufficient funding, poor leadership and inadequate support. This group tends to call for lessons to be learned and approaches to be improved and updated (Hayner 2011).

Finally, there is a more critical group who agree that it is important to consider and to address aspects of the past – and who do not deny that lessons can be learnt about how this can be best achieved – but who are acutely aware of the fact that life is complicated. This group neither believes that events which belong chronologically to the past can easily be rendered absent and distant from the present, nor that social and structural evolutions fit neatly within a linear distinction between past, present, and future. In turn, many in this school criticise transitional justice's tendency to convert the past's persistent, and the future's intrusive, nature – from people and trajectory-shaped holes to continuities, evolutions, echoes, visions, and narratives and repertoires of contention – into personalised trauma that can be addressed through a Freudian-style talk therapy, punitive justice or acknowledgement. Instead, they emphasise the limited contributions that transitional justice efforts can make to the periodisation of time even in relatively conducive political environments. They also highlight the negative consequences that transitional justice efforts can have as they are undermined, used or reinterpreted by elites, or as they inadvertently (and sometimes intentionally) help to reinforce existing schisms and power relations, and to legitimise the status quo. Finally, scholars in this school tend to view the future as an inherently political arena that should be subject to ongoing debate and disagreement, and which should not be reduced to technocratic notions of reform or anti-political assertions of cohesion and progress (Bevernage 2012; Mamdani 2002; Meister 2002; Payne 2008; Schaap 2006; Wilson 2001; 2011).

This book falls within the last of these three schools. By focusing on the example of transitional justice mechanisms introduced in Kenya following the country's post-election crisis of 2007–8 in the context of international criminal trials and the South African TRC, I suggest that transitional justice institutions can make a contribution to a sense of ending or change through tangible outcomes (such as the provision of compensation to victims of human rights abuses), but also through its performative effects. The latter refers to the ways in which transitional justice can help to enact a break with the past – such as through a displayed commitment to a new human rights regime, or by giving a stage to victim's stories and thus their humanity. At the same time, I argue that these performances are incredibly difficult to get right, since their impact rests not only on their internal design, but also on their evaluation and reception, and thus on their broader contexts. Consequently, I argue that transitional justice is inherently limited; that it can easily be used, manipulated and undermined and that it can inadvertently reinforce or reassert existing power relations and legitimise the status quo. Finally, I criticise an often implicit idea that it is obvious what a desirable shared future would look like – an approach, which, in practice, can all too easily be used to discipline opposing voices and constrain the reach of reforms.

This does not mean that the ideas or approaches of transitional justice should be abandoned. Instead, I simply argue against viewing such mechanisms as tools that can be applied with similar affects in any post-authoritarian or conflict situation, and call for less ambitious goals when they are used – namely, for greater recognition to be given to the extent to which transitional justice's constrained capacities are contingent upon persuasive performances and broader socio-economic, political and historic contexts; for a more complex understanding of the ways in which the past actually persists and possible futures infringe on the present; and for an avoidance of easy assertions of closure.

The next section provides an overview of the evolution of transitional justice. The aim: to highlight how transitional justice enthusiasts have tended to respond to critiques through expansion, rather than (as this book suggests) through an acceptance of inherent limitations. This introductory chapter then moves on to performance as an analytical lens, the Kenyan case study, and notes on research methods.

1.1 The Evolution of Transitional Justice: From Accountability to Democracy Support and Peacebuilding

[Transitional justice] includes that set of practices, mechanisms and concerns that arise following a period of conflict, civil strife or repression, and that are aimed directly at confronting and dealing with past violations of human rights and humanitarian law.

(Roht-Arriaza 2006: 2)

The emergence of transitional justice as a discrete approach can be traced back to the post–World War II era and the decision to establish special courts in Nuremberg and Tokyo to provide accountability for war crimes so as to ensure non-repetition. However, transitional justice only really began to gain coherence as a practical and academic field in the 1980s when truth-telling and reparations were added to criminal trials as recognised methods. At this juncture, transitional justice was generally employed by states in the wake of regime change, as occurred, for example, following the ousting of authoritarian regimes in Latin America when advocates tended to explicitly recognise 'tensions, trade-offs, and dilemmas' between various goals such as peace and justice, or stability and democracy (Lebaw 2008: 98).

During the 1990s and 2000s, the field expanded to embrace efforts to facilitate, or even initiate, a transition from authoritarianism. As a result, common definitions were revised from a 'move from less to more democratic regimes' (Teitel 2000: 5) to 'the full range of processes and mechanisms associated with a society's attempt to come to terms with a legacy of large-scale past abuses, in order to ensure accountability, serve justice and achieve reconciliation' (UN 2010: 2). The Kenyan case falls within this latter epoch: transitional justice mechanisms were introduced after the post-election violence of 2007–8 and formation of a coalition government, but in the absence (at least in the initial stages) of any substantive political reform or transition, and amidst peacebuilding efforts. Similar cases include Uganda and the Democratic Republic of Congo (DRC), where the ICC intervened in the face of competitive authoritarianism and an ongoing crisis and military peacekeeping operation, respectively.

Given such developments, there is now substantial overlap between transitional justice and the fields of political restructuring, democratisation and peacebuilding. Nevertheless, they remain conceptually distinct. First, transitional justice places primary emphasis on an assumed need to look backwards and deal with the past through the provision of justice if one is to move forward and achieve a sustainable transition to a new future. In contrast, democracy promotion efforts tend to place principal focus on the positive changes that can be brought about through institutional strengthening and public confidence (Carothers 1999), while peacebuilding tends to focus on the potential drivers of, and participants in, future conflicts (Lederach 1997). In short, democracy support or peacebuilding efforts are not wedded to the same obsession with questions and performances of temporality.

Second, transitional justice originated in the field of law and human rights, while peacebuilding and democracy promotion are more closely associated with humanitarianism and diplomacy, respectively. As a result, transitional justice prioritises legal processes including judicial and quasi-judicial mechanisms, such as truth commissions and vetting boards, over broad reforms on the basis that, while in 'its ordinary social function, law provides order and stability ... in extraordinary periods of political upheaval, law maintains order even as it enables transformation' (Teitel 2000: 6). In turn, when institutional and constitutional reforms are included in transitional justice packages, they tend to be presented as complementary to judicial and quasi-judicial measures (ICTJ 2009: 1).

A shift from introducing transitional justice after a political transition to employing such mechanisms during or before the same has been accompanied by a conceptual stretching of 'justice' from punitive or retributive justice to reparative, restorative and more recently transformative justice. It has also gone hand-in-hand with more participatory and community-based approaches, and with a presentation of distinct transitional justice mechanisms as compatible and mutually reinforcing. This section provides a brief overview of these evolutions so as to highlight transitional justice's record of responding to criticisms by trying to do more, which provides essential context for this book's call for transitional justice to be less ambitious.

Initially, transitional justice focused first and foremost on punitive or retributive justice. However, criminal prosecutions are not always politically feasible and, in the Latin American transitions of the 1980s, trials were often initially substituted with a truth-telling process that sought acknowledgement and a degree of reparative justice (Hayner 2011). The latter is understood as an effort to address harms suffered by victims of systematic human rights violations through restitution, compensation, rehabilitation, satisfaction and/or guarantees of non-repetition (Adhikari & Hansen 2013: 423). However, with the South African TRC (1995–1998),[1] the emphasis shifted again to restorative justice and the need to heal and reintegrate both the victims and perpetrators of gross human rights violations into their communities and nation-states (Menkel Meadow 2007; Tutu 1999).

These developments encouraged a new package approach whereby discrete processes (such as international criminal trials and truth-telling processes) were increasingly presented as complementary (Crocker 1998; Donald & King 2007; Roht-Arriaza & Mariezcurrena 2006) and established concurrently. This is evident in Kenya, but also in East Timor (Stahn 2001), Rwanda (Clark 2007), Sierra Leone (Lamin 2003) and Tunisia (El Gantri 2015). It is also reflected in the criticism levelled at countries that opted for a single mechanism, such as Cambodia (Ly 2009) and Liberia (Truth and Reconciliation Commission of Liberia 2009).

Greater emphasis also came to be placed on victim participation and the need for justice to be 'rooted in local norms and traditions' (Sharp 2012: 152). However, localism soon attracted criticism of how 'local' mechanisms often ignored due process (Lundy 2009; Sarkin 2001), constituted distinctly modern phenomenon (Ingelaere 2009; Thomson 2011) and reinforced existing narratives, power relations and inequalities (Allen 2008; Branch 2014; Shaw & Waldorf 2010). Such analyses are not against localisation per se, but its romanticisation, and they emphasise how difficult it can be to ensure that interventions enjoy the kind of legitimacy, influence and relevance desired, and how they can be co-opted by elites or Western liberal peacebuilding models (MacGinty 2008).

---

[1] The TRC submitted the first five volumes of its final report in 1998 with the remaining two volumes submitted in 2003.

In this context – and with a focus on both what victims want and need – calls have been made for a more thorough re-conceptualisation of transitional justice so that redress is provided, not only for the direct victims of abuses of bodily integrity rights, but for anyone who has suffered, and continues to suffer, from economic crimes (Carranza 2008), systematic underdevelopment (Duthie 2008) and/or structural inequalities (Miller 2008). In this vein, some propose that transitional justice – which has historically focused on individual perpetrators and individualised violations – should give more attention to ordinary citizens and to their subsistence needs (Sankey 2014), to demands for social justice (Robins 2014) and to the underlying socio-economic problems, which are both cause and effect of gross human rights violations (Laplante 2008). In so doing, many call for transitional justice to be both more explicitly transformative in its consideration and involvement of, and relevance to, local communities *and* in its attention to underlying structural inequalities and causes of violence. In turn, attention has shifted to demands for 'transformative justice' or 'transformative change that emphasizes local agency and resources, the prioritization of process rather than preconceived outcomes, and the challenging of unequal and intersecting power relationships and structures of exclusion at both the local and the global level' (Gready & Robins 2014: 340; also see Esterhuyse 2000; Lambourne 2009).

In part, this is a response to criticisms of the most intensely studied transitional justice mechanism – the South African TRC (1995–2002) – for its limited understanding of injustice, neglect of the majority of apartheid's victims and legitimation of a political transition that replaced a white economic elite with a racially mixed elite in the context of limited retributive or reparative justice, ongoing socio-economic inequalities and high levels of everyday violence (Backer 2010; Feldman 2003; Mamdani 2002; Robins 2014; Stanley 2001; Wilson 2001). For this reason, and given the seminal nature of the South African TRC for future truth commissions, this book views it as instructive to analyse contemporary transitional justice efforts in the context of the myth of the South African TRC (Part II).

Others criticise the broader school of liberal peacebuilding with which transitional justice increasingly falls under or overlaps. These contributions reveal how marketisation and democratisation often fuel tension and provoke conflict (Chua 2003; Sriram 2007) and suggest that transitional justice can become a 'disciplining process' that defines and restricts 'what can be done in the name of justice and how it can be done' (Branch 2014: 612). Indeed, for some, transitional justice is inherently counter-revolutionary in nature (Meister 2002) and only allows for a transition to liberal democracy (Arthur 2009). The idea is that transitional justice forms part of a broader liberal peacebuilding agenda that promulgates 'a particular vision of how states should organise themselves internally, based on the principles of liberal democracy and market-oriented economics' (Paris 2002: 637). According to such views, transitional justice is a successor to neoliberal programmes of structural adjustment, good governance and poverty reduction, which disciplined what could be done (and how) in the name of economic development and democracy (cf. Abrahamsen 2000). Building on these critiques, several analysts have demanded more locally sensitive interventions that re-politicise and re-historicise what justice requires and means (Lu 2002; Shaw & Waldorf 2010: 10), while others call for further rethinking or rejection of transitional justice (Arthur 2009; Meister 2002).

Such critiques link to another, namely, transitional justice's common focus on the individual (be it the perpetrator or victim) to the neglect, and even to the distraction, of structural issues. Indeed, while transitional justice can theoretically consider a range of persistent pasts, it is often employed as a quick-fix solution to quell more insistent and immediate demands. More specifically, and following Freud, there is a tendency to focus on the individual psyche and the need to deal with personal trauma through catharsis, forgiveness and reconciliation to the relative neglect of power relations and contested futures.

As noted, transitional justice enthusiasts have tended to respond to this array of critiques though an expansion of their scope and aims. This is perhaps most evident when it comes to truth commissions, which started as fact-finding bodies that sought to reveal truths, provide acknowledgement and offer recommendations. These bodies then morphed into truth and reconciliation commissions, which were meant to also help restore relations between victims, perpetrators and 'the nation'. More recently still, we have had Kenya's TJRC, which was mandated to promote peace, justice, national unity, healing and reconciliation among the people of Kenya (Kenya 2008d), and Tunisia's Truth and Dignity Commission, which included the restoration of 'dignity' as 'a self-conscious reference to the demand of the Tunisian revolution for "employment, freedom, and national dignity"'

(McRobie 2015). In a similar way, the ICC's Office of the Prosecutor presented itself as contributing to peace in Uganda, retributive justice in the DRC, tackling rebel and state abuses in Sudan and the undermining of a culture of impunity in Kenya (Brown & Sriram 2012; Clark 2008; Nichols 2015; Peskin 2009).

Extended expectations have proved unrealistic, and overburdened mechanisms have fallen short of official mandates (Bosire 2006). In response, those in the transitional justice industry tend to call for improvements and the development of best practice informed by lessons learned (Hayner 2011). In practice, this usually involves an expansion of methods, reach and aims and insistence that, while focused on a short-term 'transition' period, transitional justice can feed through into longer-term and structural reforms.

However, while lessons can clearly be learned, this book builds on a literature which focuses on inherent limitations and the importance of conducive contexts, as well as technocratic processes. More specifically, I argue that transitional justice mechanisms are not always helpful, that they should give even greater consideration to likely responses and interpretations and that they should be less ambitious. Transitional justice mechanisms – as short-term processes that often enjoy limited mandates and political buy-in – are presented as being *incapable* of dealing with the various ways in which violent pasts actually persist. An ongoing political struggle that requires substantive socio-economic and political change that transitional justice mechanisms can theoretically recommend, and which they can sometimes help to facilitate, inform, motivate and enact, but which they cannot implement or create, and can sometimes unintentionally help to reinforce.

In making this argument I draw upon the work of academics such as Richard Wilson, who has shown how the South African TRC was largely concerned with the legitimation of state power and posits that its moralising narrative of earlier 'evil' converted political problems into technical questions in ways that helped to justify limited reforms to the neglect of popular notions of justice and the need for substantive redistribution. In his opinion, TRCs should revert back to truth commissions, which seek to reveal truths about individual abuses and structural violence, and leave other activities (such as the administration of amnesty) to more appropriate bodies (2001: 225–226). Similarly, in later work on international criminal trials, Wilson outlines how the principal function of such bodies is to determine 'individual criminal responsibility for violations of international humanitarian law'. He reminds us of how criminal trials are 'simply not designed ... to fulfill other important tasks such as conflict-resolution, reconciliation, and deterrence' and how they should 'not be overloaded with too many dissimilar and potentially contradictory functions' (Wilson 2011: 17 and 16). In the same vein, Lars Waldorf argues that transitional justice mechanisms are 'already over-stretched and under-funded' and that, instead of expanding their domain to transformative justice, they 'should focus on accountability for gross violations of civil and political rights' and leave other critical policy areas – such as socio-economic inequalities – to the arenas of democratic politics and distributive justice (2012: 179; also Bosire 2006; Wachira & Kamungi 2010).

Building on such arguments, this book presents transitional justice mechanisms as interventions that are potentially, but not inherently, helpful and calls for greater attention to be given to what a particular mechanism can likely achieve in a specific context, the possible tensions and conflicts between different processes, the supportive work that needs to be done to ensure that positive impacts are maximised and negative ramifications minimised, for greater awareness of the ways in which the past persists, and for recognition of the dangers of insisting upon a clear and rapid distinction between the past, present and future. In making these arguments, transitional justice efforts are presented and analysed as inherently performative; their self-conscious decision to be overtly public regarded as something that can help us to understand their approach, strengths, limitations and perverse consequences.

1.2 Transitional Justice and the Politics of Performance

[P]olitics cannot be analysed seriously without a sophisticated understanding of its performances.

(Reinelt & Rai 2015: 2)

A number of transitional justice scholars focus on the politics of ritual and performance (Bevernage 2012; Bozzoli 1998; Cole 2010; Hutchison 2013; Kelsall 2005; Osiel 2000; Payne 2008). In this literature, performance is understood in a broad sense to include a range of public appearances, from theatrical productions to the everyday interactions, through which people embody and enact social norms (cf.

Butler 1988). As a result – and in contrast to everyday discussions where the notions of performance and theatricality are often used in a derogatory sense to denote fakeness or a lack of authenticity – the performance and transitional justice literature does not pre-judge performativity, but instead recognises that performance 'does something' (Palmer 1977 cited in Payne 2009: 230) and attributes significance to the decision of transitional justice practitioners to be so overtly public in their operations (Cole 2010: xiv).

Transitional justice analysts often talk of performance and its principal components – actors, stages, scripts and audiences – for four main reasons. First, this approach recognises how these processes are self-consciously performed in that they are stage managed, loosely scripted, involve different actors and interlocutors and have targeted audiences. Even transitional justice's less theatrical moments are performed in the sense that they embody and enact social norms and can help to reproduce, but also potentially subvert, existing social identities and relationships from generation and gender to class and ethnicity.

Second, understandings of the likely impact of transitional justice mechanisms are increasingly tied to the efficacy of their performance in contributing to tangible and perceived change. The common idea is that, in a time of transition, broad reforms – such as new legislation, a constitution or institutions – require a persuasive performance or enactment of change to become effective (Cole 2010: xi; also Payne 2008: 5). More specifically, transitional justice mechanisms are valued, at least in part, because of their ability to embody transition and thus for their role in helping to change popular perceptions of the state and associated political regimes and institutions, as well as for their potential role in the public articulation, acceptance and internalisation of new shared narratives and ideals and thus for their contribution to nation-building. At the same time, they are often criticised for staging an illusion – namely, a clean and clear break with the past – that distracts from persistencies, continuities and evolutions (Meister 2002).

In this vein, international criminal proceedings have been presented as 'spectacles of legality' that seek to render crimes and 'the sweeping neutral authority of the rule of law' visible to affected and international audiences (Lawrence Douglas cited in Cole 2010: 1), which 'when effective as public spectacle, stimulate public discussion in ways that foster the liberal values of toleration, moderation and civil respect'

(Osiel 2000: 2). However, as history has shown, such spectacles of legality can also be rejected as illegitimate (Peskin 2008) and be hijacked by domestic elites to further vested interests in the national or international sphere (Subotić 2009). The force of public apologies is similarly linked to 'their *ritual convention* and their *ritual form*', which, when successful as 'arousing and collective emotional activities, manage to exert power on the affective level' (Horelt 2012: 348 and 367; emphasis in original), but which are often met with scepticism and claims of insincerity (Wohl, Hornsey & Philpot 2011).

Third, a focus on performance helps to bring the multiplicity of actors and audiences, and thus the complexity of local politics, to the fore. More importantly, it helps to cast light on different understandings, motivations and goals, and on how people might seek to (ab)use political processes in ways 'which may be productive, tragic, and/or banal' (Brassett & Vaughan-Williams 2015: 47). As James Brassett and Nick Vaughan Williams note, 'to recover this contingency (re)politicizes' terms such as 'transitional justice' and guards against a tendency to present them as technocratic and obviously useful, appropriate or necessary (Brassett & Vaughan-Williams 2015: 47). An underlying assumption of this book is thus simply that an analysis of the performative aspects of these processes can enhance our understanding of their politics, efficacy and impact.

This is not to say that an analysis of performance tells the whole story. On the contrary, even a powerful performance that engages a wide audience and which helps to reframe people's perceptions of institutions, processes and/or actors, will require ongoing evidence of transition and transformation through supportive performances and substantive change to sustain and build the semblance of legitimacy and credibility required. Indeed, herein lies a central problem: while transitional justice mechanisms can have tangible impacts – for example, through the incarceration of individuals or lustration and compensation of others – whether or not these are seen or interpreted as justice, and as marking a break with the past, will depend on broader contexts that transitional justice efforts can help to shape, but never determine.

Finally, performances of transitional justice provide excellent insight into political realities and can be used – as Cohen and Odhiambo do in their analysis of a series of public inquiries in Kenya (2004) – 'to read the event as a window onto the complex cultural and social history' of a country or region (Cole 2010: xviii). At one level, this window stems from the opportunities for story-telling and historical overview that public truth-telling and commission reports, but also criminal trials (Wilson 2005) and other transitional justice mechanisms, provide. These processes also provide a less self-conscious window onto contemporary politics through their everyday practices and interactions, the use that others seek to make of them (Ashforth 1990b; Cohen & Odiambo 2004) and the various ways in which people's public engagements embody, enact and (re)produce social norms that can either reinforce or undermine existing inequalities and power dynamics. At the same time, the gaps, omissions, silences and misinterpretations that emerge provide insights into what is deemed politically important and strategic, but also (un)speakable and (un)hearable in a particular context (Blommaert, Bock & McCormick 2006; Krog, Mpolweni-Zantsi & Ratele 2013; Ross 2003a).

These themes inform the approach, analysis and structure of this book: transitional justice mechanisms are performative; performance is central to understanding the politics, efficacy and impact of these mechanisms as processes that are meant to mark a break with 'the past'; 'the past' in question tends to persist in complex ways and an analysis of transitional justice's performances provides excellent insights into contemporary politics. The analysis thus speaks to transitional justice, Africanist, humanities and social science audiences through its critique of common efforts to reproduce transitional justice efforts in widely divergent contexts, but also through an analysis of political and social relations in a particular, but not exceptional, geographical and temporal context. As a result, the book is as much about politics in a modern post-colony as it is a case study and critique of transitional justice in practice.

1.3 Familiar Performances: Transitional Justice in Kenya

With this agreement, we are stepping forward together, as political leaders, to overcome the current crisis to set the country on a new path. (National Accord)

(Kenya 2008a: 9)

Kenya provides an excellent example of the intricacies and difficulties of staging an efficacious performance of transition. The country was subject to a new package approach to transitional justice, where different mechanisms were introduced by domestic and international actors in the absence of substantive political change. In this context, it is perhaps unsurprising that transitional justice efforts met with a lack of political will, intransigence and direct opposition (Hansen 2013; Mueller 2014b), and that Kenyans did not readily accept the narratives presented and transition staged.

Transitional justice has been a subject of discussion in Kenya since the late 1990s. However, it was not until after the 2007–8 post-election crisis that a clear transitional agenda became a reality, as the crisis – together with a history of election-related violence and shadow of forthcoming elections – added a sense of urgency to a much longer struggle for institutional and constitutional reform and criminal and social justice (Hansen 2013; Murunga, Okello & Sjögren 2014; Mutua 2008). In turn, the violence of 2007–8 and inter-election politics of 2008–2013 provide the critical domestic context for the introduction and initial reception of transitional justice.

The post-election violence of 2007–8 can be divided into four broad categories: (a) riots and demonstrations by opposition supporters in urban areas and trading centres across the country; (b) targeted attacks by opposition supporters on co-ethnics and 'others' regarded as pro-government with the aim (at least in part) of disciplining 'traitors' and forcing the displacement of 'outsiders' from disputed land, the epicentre of which was Rift Valley Province; (c) revenge attacks on communities perceived to be opposition supporters by gangs of Kikuyu youth who were quickly labelled as Mungiki (a much feared ethnic militia), which took place towards the end of January 2008 in Nakuru and Naivasha towns in the central Rift Valley and (d) an overzealous state security response whereby an estimated 36 per cent of casualties were shot by the police (Kenya 2008b: 305).

Chapter 2 provides an analysis of peacebuilding efforts introduced between the country's 2008 and 2013 elections. In addition to providing essential context, the chapter reveals how an inter-election peace narrative helped to foster non-violence, but was simultaneously used to counterpose peace and justice. Subsequent chapters then move on to the substance of transitional justice efforts, which emerged out of a political settlement.

The post-election violence came to an end on 28 February 2008 with the signing of a power-sharing agreement, or National Accord, by President Kibaki of the Party of National Unity (PNU) and the principal opposition candidate, Raila Odinga of the Orange Democratic Movement (ODM). During the negotiations, the Panel of Eminent African Personalities, which was chaired by the former United Nations Secretary General Kofi Annan, produced a 'road map' for talks that included four agenda items:

(1) to undertake immediate action to stop violence and restore fundamental human rights and liberties; (2) to take immediate measures to address the humanitarian crisis, promote reconciliation, healing, and restoration; (3) to overcome the political crisis; and (4) to work on long-term issues and solutions, such as poverty, inequality, and unemployment (especially among the youth), as well as the need to confront impunity, tackle land reform, and consolidate national cohesion and transparency.
(Cited in Lindenmayer & Kay 2009: 10)

These four items ensured that the negotiations were informed by a felt need to tackle a troubled past to ensure non-repetition, with negotiations thus paving the way for an ambitious transitional justice agenda. First, PNU and ODM representatives agreed to establish an Independent Review Commission on the General Elections held in Kenya on 27 December 2007, or Kriegler Commission, which was mandated to examine the integrity of the electoral process. The final report, submitted in September 2008, concluded that the election had been a 'resounding failure' due to the widespread violations of electoral laws (Kenya 2008c: 6 and 23) that stemmed from a legacy of one-party rule and a culture of impunity (Tostensen 2009: 432). This analysis is critical since – together with other government and non-government reports and voices (Kenya 2008c; KNCHR 2008) – the Commission's findings contributed to a situation in which impunity, as a frame for understanding the problem, became central to popular analyses and transitional justice responses. Indeed, more than anything else, the notion of a 'culture of impunity' came to shape both transitional justice efforts in Kenya and opposition to it.

Second, the National Accord paved the way for a Commission of Inquiry into the Post-Election Violence, or Waki Commission, which was established in May 2008 and submitted a final report in October. The Commission concluded that at least some of the violence had been organised and recommended that a special tribunal be established to investigate and prosecute those most responsible. Failing that, the Commission recommended that the ICC's Office of the

Prosecutor (OTP) be requested to intervene (Kenya 2008c). After three unsuccessful attempts to establish a special tribunal, the information collected by the Waki Commission was passed on to the OTP, and, in December 2010, the chief prosecutor announced the names of six Kenyans under investigation in two separate cases, with charges confirmed against four in December 2011. This included two prominent politicians – Uhuru Kenyatta and William Ruto – who subsequently came together in the Jubilee Alliance, and who, at least in part, were elected president and deputy president, respectively, in 2013 because of their indictments (Lynch 2014a).

Chapter 3 analyses the ICC's intervention in Kenya up to the final collapse of both cases in April 2016. In so doing, it reveals how the Jubilee Alliance effectively reframed the ICC, at least in the eyes of a significant number of Kenyans, as a familiar performance of injustice, neo-colonialism and impunity. The analysis builds on earlier analyses of international criminal trials to highlight the extent to which such interventions, due to their reliance on state party and international support, are conducted outside of official judicial proceedings through 'virtual trials' (Peskin 2008), which helps these legal processes to be 'hijacked' for vested political ends (Subotić 2009). The chapter therefore reveals how the Kenyan case was both undermined by echoes of a colonial past and proved reminiscent of international trials in other contexts.

Through the National Accord, PNU and ODM representatives also agreed to review long-term issues and to pursue a constitutional review process. This led to the 2008 Constitution of Kenya Review Act and rationalisation of prior constitutional drafts by a committee of experts, which concluded with a national referendum on, and inauguration of, a new constitution in August 2010. Among other things, this document devolved substantive powers to forty-seven new counties and provided for the public vetting of various state officials. This book does not focus on these reforms, although broader conclusions that link the efficacy of such mechanisms to the persuasiveness of their performances and political contexts still apply (for example, see Cheeseman, Lynch & Willis [2016], D'Arcy & Cornell [2016] and Hassan [2015] on devolution; Harrrington & Manji [2015] on the erosion of gains brought by the public vetting of job judges; and Osse [2016] on the failure of police vetting).

Finally, negotiating parties agreed to the need for a TJRC, which was established through an act of parliament in 2008, started work in 2009 and submitted a final report in May 2013. The TJRC was mandated to investigate a wide range of human rights abuses and socio-economic injustices between Kenya's independence on 12 December 1963 and the signing of the National Accord on 28 February 2008; it ultimately made recommendations relating to further investigations, prosecutions, lustration, reparations and institutional and constitutional reforms.

Part II investigates the TJRC through a comparison with the world's most famous and influential truth commission to date: the South African TRC. The aim is to offer insights that are relevant to other post–South African truth commissions (albeit in different ways and to different extents) and to highlight how the TJRC constituted another familiar performance. First, the Commission's credibility crisis and limited media engagement ensured that many dismissed the TJRC as just another commission of inquiry. At the same time, the TJRC's approach, the narratives produced, the non-implementation of its recommendations and a disjuncture between the justice desired and delivered, provided familiar performances of victimhood, gender roles and impunity.

With transitional justice efforts in Kenya having largely performed – not transition, disjuncture or temporal distancing – but familiarity, once-againness and continuity, Chapter 10 turns to understandings of reconciliation and to the implications for transitional justice. More specifically, the chapter provides a critique of a common understanding of reconciliation as the restoration of trust in the motivations and behaviour of others, and highlights the political appeal of an alternative effort to mark a break with the past through a politics of reconciliation that emphasises redemption and unity in the interests of stability and progress. In so doing, the chapter offers an alternative approach to reconciliation, which – drawing upon the work of scholars such as Leigh Payne (2008) and Andrew Schaap (2006) – seeks to address the past, not by asserting closure, but by addressing its more persistent demands and by marking 'newness' through a new respect for difference and debate.

By focusing on peacebuilding, the ICC, the TJRC and reconciliation in Kenya, I am conscious that one cannot generalise to all other political developments in the country, or from Kenya to all cases of transitional justice. However, it is my belief that an analysis of these efforts can help us to better understand contemporary Kenyan politics; both during the years when these transitional justice mechanisms were rolled out and during the years that followed when, for example, another disputed election in 2017, in the absence of a persuasive performance of transition and pervasive sense of once-againness, was met with widespread frustration and anger by opposition supporters. It is also my belief that such an analysis provides unusual insight into the workings of a modern post-colony, and that the similarities between Kenya and many other post-conflict contexts ensures that the ICC's intervention, the story of the TJRC (as a post–South African truth commission) and debates around reconciliation ensure that such an analysis provides important comparable insights. Finally, it is my belief that the Kenyan experience will feed into the ongoing evolution of transitional justice efforts and thus that a critical analysis of the ICC's intervention and TJRC is required to ensure that any lessons learnt are informed and reasoned.

1.4 A Note on Research Methods

The research for this book was conducted over almost ten years (early 2008 to mid-2017) and builds upon earlier research conducted on ethnic politics in the country (2003 to 2008). The arguments rest on a triangulation of different sources. This includes a critical reading of secondary literature, government and non-government reports, media reports and comments on social media; hundreds of formal interviews and informal conversations with TJRC staff, journalists, civil society activists, witnesses and members of the public; an analysis of a range of oral, performed and material culture; and participant observations of political rallies, civil society and peacebuilding meetings, as well as of TJRC public, women's, adversely mentioned person (AMP), and thematic hearings in Upper Eastern, Western, Rift Valley, and Nairobi.

In conducting this research, my interest in performance meant that I was not only interested in what people said, but how they said it, where they said it, what they did not say and with what response. As a result, my fieldwork diaries are filled with descriptions of meeting rooms and interview locations, of people's body language, tone, facial expressions, dress and silences, as well as with notes of what people actually said.

The full transcripts of the TJRC hearings are not currently public. As a result, it has been impossible to crosscheck my hastily written notes for errors in what I heard and wrote down during the public sessions I attended. Nevertheless, given the importance of witness testimony to the analysis, I have included a number of direct quotes from these notes. This clearly raises the possibility of error. However, I hope that the benefit of conveying the colour of witness testimony outweighs any misrepresentations of the particular phrasing used during the TJRC's public hearings that might have ensued.

Given the sensitivity of the research, and the fact that many interviews and conversations were held in cafés and restaurants and outside meeting rooms and hearing venues, I chose not to use a voice recorder in most instances and instead made extensive notes. As a result, limited used is made of direct quotes. Nevertheless, these interactions informed my overall understanding of local situations, fears, concerns, hopes and dreams. When direct reference to interviews is made, interviewees are generally not named; sometimes the place and date are also omitted to ensure anonymity. This is critical given the subject matter and people's understandable fears about the potential repercussions of speaking to a foreign researcher. This was particularly true in the Rift Valley, where, during the course of my research, individuals faced very real threats for not only being an ICC witness, but in the instance of any public perception that they might or could be a witness or that they might have helped the ICC process.

In researching this book, I spoke with many people about the details of the injustices and abuses they had suffered. I also witnessed the ongoing struggles and problems that they faced and was frequently contacted by people who did not know how to cope with life or had been threatened and needed help. As a result, the research process was emotionally draining and difficult, but it also provided a glimpse into the contexts in which people were working and the motivations of transitional justice activists and participants. For example, the experience of sitting through months of TJRC hearings and of interviewing hundreds of victims, community members and civil society activists made me realise the extent to which, and some of the ways in which, the past persists. It also made me realise how hard the Commission staff worked, and the psychological impact of such a job – the toll reflected in cases of high blood pressure, depression and other physical and mental symptoms. I hope that these insights have enriched the analysis, and that attention to the everyday complements and strengthens the book's focus on public performances and their reception and interpretation.

Finally, the fact that most have not forgotten spurs many to continue with their struggle for justice and reform, and most do not want further violence. Real reforms have also occurred. As a result, Kenya remains a vibrant and fast-changing country. This is critical: it ensures an uncertain but exciting future that appears full of opportunity and danger, which acts as a source of both hope and fear. It also ensures the do-ability of the research: the work was only made possible by the kind of country that Kenya continues to be and the openness with which many of its citizens speak.

2 | Framing the Good Citizen for Orderly Elections
The Prioritisation of Peace

> Despite promises from Kenya's leaders to reform, the country's political system remains haunted by the spectre of violence.
>
> (HRW 2013: 5)

The relationship between peace and justice, and the question of whether the struggle for justice endangers peace, or whether justice is necessary for sustainable peace, is a recurring theme in transitional justice debates. However, with the 'justice cascade' of the late twentieth century – or shift 'towards using foreign or international judicial processes to hold individuals accountable for human rights crimes' (Lutz & Sikkink 2001: 2) – and a concurrent increase in historical reparations claims (Anderson 2015; Lynch 2012a), most academics accepted that justice was needed for sustainable peace, and turned their attention to the kind of justice required (for example, Gready & Robins 2014; Lambourne 2009; Wilson 2001).

Yet, just as the academic debate seemed to have moved on, many countries – from post 9/11 America to Ethiopia, Uganda and Kenya – witnessed the return of nationalist narratives that prioritised peace and stability over justice (Desrosiers & Thomson 2011; Jackson 2005; Lynch 2015a; Tripp 2010). Such calls have clearly been pushed, and used, by establishment elites. However, to understand their resonance and power, one must also consider how histories and fears of violence – together with the challenges involved in tackling the underlying causes of violence and in providing redress – produce a sense of precarity and a popular desire for peace – emotions that politicians often fuel and use, but to which they also need to respond.

In Kenya, as in many other places, this has encouraged *familiar performances* of nationalism and patriotic unity, whereby citizens are presented with a stark choice: violence, chaos and economic collapse *or* peace, stability and economic development. However, while familiar, an emphasis on peace during President Kibaki's second term (2008–2013) and President Kenyatta's first term in office (2013–2017) was presented – not as countering colonialism's 'divide and rule' policy, as per Africa's nationalist imperatives of the mid-twentieth century – but as a bulwark against the 'terror of history', or the histories, memories and potentialities of local, national and global violence (cf. Moses 2011).

To take the Kenyan case, in early 2008 the country seemed on the brink of civil war (Anderson 2008; Chege 2008; KNCHR 2008). This experience dented a 'sense of complacency' (Githongo 2010: 9) and served as a reminder of how, with the exception of the country's 2002 election (which is generally perceived to have been largely peaceful), every election since the return to multi-party politics in 1992 has been associated with extensive violence. However, even the relatively peaceful election of 2002 was characterised by a level of electoral violence that would be shocking in most other contexts, with an estimated 325 people killed in political conflicts linked to electoral logics in the year running up to the polls (Mutahi 2005: 73). In this context, and as transitional justice efforts moved at a characteristically slow pace, and the country edged closer to the next general election in March 2013, the spectre of past violence, and a fear of repetition, began to dominate political debate.

Popular concerns focused on potential disputes around the upcoming presidential election of March 2013, which – with President Kibaki at the end of a two-term limit and in the face of new political alliances – came to pit two ICC indictees, Uhuru Kenyatta and William Ruto of the Jubilee Alliance, against prominent opposition leader, Raila Odinga, and former government insider, Kalonzo Musyoka, who had formed the Coalition for Reform and Democracy (CORD). In this context, the widespread fear of repetition was fuelled by another ethnically divided and high stakes election, which, as in 2007, pitted an 'establishment Kikuyu' against an 'opposition Luo' in a country with a history of election-related violence in which few (and no high-level) perpetrators had been brought to justice (HRW 2011; Nichols 2015). These fears were then compounded by the fact that – following the inauguration of a new constitution in 2010 – voters would have to cast six (rather than three) ballots on a single day.[1] Levels of inter-communal mistrust also

---

[1] In previous elections Kenyans had voted for their ward representative, Member of Parliament (MP) and president. However, following the 2010 constitution they had to vote for their member of county assembly (MCA), MP, women's representation, governor, senator and president.

remained high (Kasara 2013; Lynch 2014b); underlying issues (such as historical land injustices) had not been addressed; and delays in security sector reforms meant that the 'very same policing structures blamed by many for serious human rights violations' in 2007–8 remained in place (AI 2013: 6). In this context, many feared that renewed violence could escalate beyond that of 2007–8, as people might take revenge for earlier harms and be better prepared. The widespread fear of repetition, and escalation, was thus not a product of a Freudian mass trauma – although many were still traumatised – but of an informed understanding of what could potentially happen given the country's history and contemporary politics.

Facing the certainty of polls in 2013 and the uncertainty of their trajectory, Kenyans from every walk of life – from musicians, actors, artists and clergy to businesspeople, traditional and social media personalities, state officials, security officers and politicians – campaigned for peace. The common message was the need for citizens to live in harmony with neighbours; to vote in peace, and to go home and await (and accept) election results in peace; and to actively participate in a culture of non-violence. Collectively, these campaigns created a pervasive 'peace narrative' that individualised responsibility by framing a particular understanding of the 'good citizen' (cf. Pykett, Saward & Schaefer 2010) as someone who prioritised non-violence, interethnic cohesion and national unity (Cheeseman, Lynch & Willis 2014). However, while this narrative was cultivated and used by establishment politicians ahead of the 2013 elections, it was ultimately the product of a much more diverse, reactive and populist campaign; a campaign that resonated with widespread fears, and with religious and psychoanalytical understandings of the world.

This chapter analyses the emergence of this peace narrative between the 2008 and 2013 elections. In so doing, the aim is not to provide an exhaustive account of peacebuilding efforts or of political campaigns, but to provide essential context for parallel transitional justice efforts. More specifically, it sets out popular understandings of peace, and reveals how practical peacebuilding initiatives came to increasingly emphasise the role that individuals could and should play in ensuring non-repetition. The chapter then turns to campaigns for a peaceful election as well as to how a similar approach of individualised responsibility drew from, and was reinforced by, Christian and medical narratives of individual salvation and trauma. Finally, the chapter turns to the political campaigns and to the revival of a familiar 'ideology of order', whereby the spectre of instability and individualisation of responsibility for peace was used to justify unity and delegitimise dissent (cf. Atieno-Odhiambo 1987).

2.1 Peace as the Absence of Violence

Few words are so often used and abused – perhaps, it seems, because 'peace' serves as a means of obtaining verbal consensus – it is hard to be all-out against peace.

(Galtung 1969: 167)

Peace, according to Johan Galtung's seminal definition, is the absence of violence, with the kind of peace that one enjoys depending on the violence that one is free from (1969). In this vein, Galtung distinguishes between negative and positive peace: where the former refers to the absence of direct or personal violence, which includes actual bodily and threatened harm, and the latter refers to the absence of structural violence or the presence of social justice. However, while the absence of actual or threatened violence is a common state for many, it is everywhere troubled (albeit to wildly different degrees) across lifetimes and lives. In contrast, positive peace in the Galtung-ian sense – where no individual or group suffers an avoidable harm that is removed from the agency of particular perpetrators, such as poverty, ignorance and disease (Galtung 1969: 168) – remains an ideal state that only relatively wealthy societies with an 'egalitarian distribution of power and resources' approach (Galtung 1969: 183).

In practice, however, most people tend not to regard avoidable harms as violence per se, and instead often justify them as the result of personal shortcomings, fate or the influence of the spiritual world. At the same time, people often distinguish between different kinds of Galtung's negative peace. Between the mere absence of immediate and actual bodily harm (particularly on a substantive scale), which many interviewees termed as a 'negative', 'cosmetic', 'surface' or 'shallow peace', and the simultaneous absence of an immediate or looming threat of violence, which many Kenyans in the inter-election period referred to as a 'substantive' or 'positive peace'.

This difference between Galtung's and everyday uses of the term 'positive peace' is an area of conceptual confusion, but it also hints at the possibility of a sliding scale between the two definitions on the basis of an oft-assumed relationship between social injustice and poverty *and* direct violence. In short, while injustice is the basis of indirect or structural violence and thus an obstacle to Galtung's positive peace, it can also be a source of grievance, anger and hatred that can facilitate incitement and the organisation of mass violence (Cramer 2003; Lynch 2011b). In such contexts, direct violence can either erupt or remain a looming shadow and an ever-present threat; with injustice thus standing as an obstacle to both lay understandings of 'positive peace' and Galtung's 'negative peace'. In turn, absolute poverty is evidence of the absence of Galtung's positive peace, but it also produces a group of people who (it is often assumed) can be incited and organised to engage in mass violence with relative ease, and who are thus often seen as a threat to negative peace.

This logic is important as it provides multiple paths to sustainable peace, including justice and development. These two paths are not mutually exclusive and are often closely interwoven, but they can present alternatives especially in the short-term – if, for example, the search for justice is seen as a potential trigger of mass violence. Facing this dilemma, transitional justice proponents tend to accept the need for compromises in the kind of justice sought so as to avoid a return to violence, but to simultaneously insist that sustainable peace requires justice to be considered so as to facilitate a transition to a new future. In contrast, peacebuilders tend to focus on conflict prevention and resolution. In so doing, they try to create a context in which direct violence is avoided; where people can live together without fear; economic development can proceed unhindered by disruptive conflicts; and the likelihood of further conflict is gradually undermined (Lederach 1997). However, this characterisation begs the question of what kind of conflicts transitional justice enthusiasts try to avoid, and peacebuilders try to prevent or resolve? In Kenya, the answer during the time period under study was principally election-related violence. In turn, this chapter looks at peacebuilding and peace messaging efforts between the 2008 and 2013 elections, before subsequent chapters turn to parallel efforts to address the past, whilst avoiding violence.

2.2 Peacebuilding in Practice, 2008–2013

[In 2007/8 we] didn't have structures on the ground apart from the provincial administration, but now structures [are] owned by the people themselves ... People [are] beginning to realise that [they] need to change and go against any political manipulation.

(Interview, coordinator of the Rift Valley Provincial Peace Forum, Nakuru, 8 March 2011)

The fear that a disputed election could trigger further violence – together with the new funding opportunities that flowed from Kenya's geopolitical importance to the international community – motivated a wide range of transitional justice and peacebuilding initiatives in the years between the 2007 and 2013 elections. The former included the TJRC and prosecutions. However, while the TJRC did not submit a final report until after the 2013 election, only a handful of low-level perpetrators were convicted of post-election crimes (HRW 2011; Nichols 2015), and investigations of those deemed most responsible were limited to the ICC, which postponed the onset of trials until after the 2013 election (Chapter 3). Nevertheless, the Court's intervention rendered the consequences of ethnic incitement and the organisation of violence increasingly uncertain, and fostered a sense amongst supporters of the new Jubilee Alliance that a rejection of violence would help Kenyatta and Ruto's cases at The Hague (Elder, Stigant & Claes 2014: 11). More significant was the inauguration of a new constitution in 2010, the appointment of prominent human rights activist Willy Mutunga as Chief Justice in 2011, the vetting of judges in 2012 and the establishment of a new electoral commission in 2011. Collectively these reforms helped to boost public confidence in key institutions, reduce perceptions of politics as a zero-sum game and foster some hope that longstanding grievances, such as historical land injustices, would at some point be addressed, for example, through the work of a new National Land Commission (NLC; Cheeseman, Lynch & Willis 2014).

At the same time, numerous peace projects were introduced by local, national and international actors, many of which focused on the former and potential hotspots of Rift Valley, Coast, Western, and Nyanza provinces and Nairobi. This section does not seek to offer an exhaustive discussion of these initiatives. Instead, it provides a brief overview of some representative examples from Rift Valley and Nyanza provinces – the heartlands of the Jubilee and CORD alliances, respectively – as essential context for parallel transitional justice efforts.

In terms of national efforts, three months after a power-sharing agreement was signed in February 2008, the government launched Operation Urijani Mwema (or 'Operation Good Neighbourhoods') to foster peace and reconciliation, the central plank of which was the use of administrative *barazas* (or public meetings) and district peace committees (DPCs) for early warning and conflict prevention. According to administrative regulations, each provincial official – from the local headmen to assistant chiefs, chiefs, district commissioners and provincial commissioners – should hold a minimum of two *barazas* per month.[2] A colonial hangover, these meetings had long been used to inform, direct and admonish local subjects (Haugerud 1997). Moreover, while there was meant to be a shift from directive to interactive public meetings during Kibaki's first term in state house (2002–2007), this new policy did not necessarily filter down to administrative practice. In turn, many interviewees complained of how *barazas* were still one-way lectures through which people were told about problems, ways forward and their own duties. This top-down dynamic limited the potential for *barazas* to act as a forum for conflict mitigation and prevention, and also contributed to an emergent message that it was largely up to individuals to deter violence. The same was true of 'peace caravans', a new initiative in potential hot spots, which saw members of the provincial administration, security services and peace actors (including musicians and theatre groups) traverse rural areas preaching the benefits of peace and costs of violence.

More systematic was the establishment of DPCs across the country. The idea was born in the 1990s when committees headed by provincial administrators, but involving community members, were formed at the village to district level in the cattle-rustling prone areas of northern Kenya. Widely regarded as a community-based model that had been found to work, DPCs were rolled out across the country in 2008 under the stewardship of the National Steering Committee on Peace-Building and Conflict Management (NSC) – an inter-agency body formed in 2001, which brought together various government offices and civil society organisations (CSOs; Chuma &

---

[2] Following the 2010 constitution, the provincial administration was restructured as the national administration, with district commissioners renamed deputy county commissioners and provincial commissioners replaced with county commissioners.

Ojielo 2012: 26 and 29). The NSC directed each district to establish a sub-locational, locational, divisional and district peace committee to be chaired by the assistant chief, chief, district officer and district commissioner (DC); the administrator's position was subsequently relabelled from chair to patron. Committees were meant to meet regularly and to include local security personnel, women, youth, elders and local stakeholders (such as religious leaders, local activists and businesspeople). The idea was that DPCs would provide a forum for administrators to map potential conflicts, and for information to flow up the chain of command so that early warning could prompt centrally coordinated conflict mitigation and prevention efforts. However, they were also meant to provide an institutionalised space in which members of the community could monitor and respond to early warnings, and thus help foster peace and reconciliation (interview NSC official, Nairobi, 8 September 2011).

This approach suffered from a number of shortcomings. First, due to the close association of DPCs with efforts to avoid a repeat of 2007–8 and inter-ethnic tensions, the structures were relatively inactive in areas inhabited mainly by one ethnic group – with residents in Kikuyu-dominated Central Province, for example, failing to see the point of such initiatives in 'their' area (interview, clergyman, Muranga, 6 May 2011). Second, where committees were active, membership was of critical importance with DPC's wholly dependent on representatives for information, ideas and legitimacy. In turn, while guidelines required communities to participate in their formation, administrators often simply selected the 'usual suspects' (focus group discussion, Burnt Forest, 20 May 2011). The fact that most DPCs lacked an office, vehicle or regular funding also meant that their activities were largely determined by the interest, commitment and support of local provincial administrators, which ultimately rendered them 'committees of the DC' (interview, Kikuyu peace activist, Nakuru, 9 March 2011). As a result, even in hot spots, DPC activity was geographically patchy and temporally inconsistent due to the regular transfer of provincial administrative personnel. In addition, the provincial administration's history of politicisation and ethnic bias raised further concerns (Branch & Cheeseman 2006; Hassan 2015). As one peace activist in the north Rift Valley noted: '[Y]ou can't rely on the administration. In this area most of the chiefs and headmen are Kalenjin and they were biased during the post-election violence and now they are against settlement [of Kikuyu IDPs] because "it's our land" ... so how can you expect them to ensure peace?' (interview, Burnt Forest, 20 May 2011).

Mistrust also surrounded the motivations of DPC members who were often cast as attracted by expectations of 'sitting allowances' and other perks, such that, 'when there's no money there's no work' (interview, Kikuyu peace activist, Eldoret, 10 December 2012). More worryingly, some complained of how members were politically biased and openly campaigned for particular candidates and parties (interview, Kalenjin peace activist, Eldoret, 11 December 2012), and of how some were close allies of prominent politicians; the chair of one DPC, for example, appeared at an ICC confirmation of charges hearing in The Hague in September 2011 as one of Ruto's character witnesses.

The majority of DPC activity between the elections was also consumed with the formation, reconstitution and training of committees, which fuelled concerns of how early warning would prompt successful mitigation beyond the fact that administrators would 'now know' and act accordingly. In particular, it was unclear what happened with reports forwarded up the chain of command, while DPCs from neighbouring districts rarely talked to each other. In turn, the fact that critical issues – such as land disputes, socio-economic well-being, the proliferation of small arms and prosecutions – required a national response placed severe restrictions on what DPCs could achieve in isolation.

Peace trainings were not limited to DPC members. On the contrary, in declared hot spots, various community stakeholders – 'peace volunteers' (if organised by the UN), 'peace animators' (if organised by the International Organization of Migration [IOM]) and 'community mediators and conflict monitors' (if organised by the Eldoret-based Centre for Human Rights and Democracy) – were trained by local and national CSOs in the mid-range hotels of various urban centres. However, the effect was limited by the fact that organisations often trained the same limited group of people (Elder, Stigant & Claes 2014: 14). As one peace activist in Eldoret explained: 'I've attended so many courses in peacebuilding ... can't list, but done conflict management, conflict analysis, early warning, do no harm, so many ... been trained by NCCK [National Council of Churches of Kenya] in first place, secondly PeaceNet, the UNDP [United Nations Development Programme], the IOM, also CJPC [Catholic Justice and Peace Commission]' (interview, Eldoret, 10 December 2012). Such extensive training of a handful of individuals raised questions of efficiency (South Consulting February 2009: 20). It also reinforced an emphasis on individual responsibility for peace by assuming that trained monitors would act as 'trainers of trainers' and disseminate knowledge about how individuals could help resolve tensions, prevent conflicts and report troublemakers.

More significantly, the work of DPCs – together with that of other international and national level actors, such as the NSC and National Cohesion and Integration Commission (NCIC) – contributed to a situation in which people knew their public statements might be monitored and recorded. Here are just two examples: as part of the 'Uwaino Platform for Peace', the NSC – together with UNDP, NCIC and civil society – established a short messaging service whereby people could send free messages about any potential conflict to a central operations room (Chuma & Ojielo 2012: 34); while the NCIC monitored political rallies, community radio stations and other platforms for hate speech. Such efforts created a climate of invigilation, which rendered the consequences of irresponsible speech increasingly uncertain and helped to curtail ethnic incitement. Once again, however, this approach laid ultimate blame and virtue with troublesome and peace-loving individuals, respectively.

The NCIC did not only monitor hate speech. Established in 2009, this permanent commission also ran a national civic education and advertising campaign that called for inter-communal cohesion and peaceful elections, conducted research and advocacy on ethnic inequalities (for example, in state employment practices) and held a series of inter-communal events and meetings across the country where officers preached peace and facilitated dialogue between community members. The NCIC was far from alone on the latter, as provincial administrators and DPCs, a variety of CSOs and the Uwaino Platform for Peace held parallel inter-community cultural and sporting events, and intra- and inter-community dialogue meetings across the country. The former sought to bring community members together in a relaxed and informal setting so that they could interact, learn about each other's cultures and become more aware of the things that they have in common – such as a young man's love of football. In contrast, dialogue meetings sought to provide a more structured forum in which issues could be aired and futures discussed.

The most common format for dialogue sessions was for intra-community meetings to be followed by a series of inter-community sessions, such that protagonists could vent their grievances in 'private' before they met with their neighbours to compare notes and discuss potential ways forward. These discussions and interactions played an important role, but they also faced a number of important limitations. Dialogue meetings often enjoyed limited funding and it was impossible to facilitate meetings in all areas and for all actors. Instead, discussions were often cut short (sometimes after the first or second meeting) due to an organisation's inability to fund further events, while participants tended to be self-selecting and composed of the 'usual suspects'. The nature of inter-community dialogue also required that discussions involve members of different communities, and in practice, focused on relatively close neighbours. They therefore neglected an important dimension of the violence, where youth were sometimes imported from other areas. They also ignored post-2008 resettlement patterns, which led to the further concentration of co-ethnics in towns and settlements across the country (Harris 2012; Lang & Sakdapolrak 2015).

Dialogue sessions were also a tried and tested approach. Great efforts were made following the election-related violence of the early 1990s to engage people in this way (for example, by the Catholic Church and NCCK in Rift Valley Province), and – while they no doubt helped cool tempers – they evidently did not ensure long-term peace. Consequently, dialogue meetings were often treated with scepticism as something that was likely to have little impact, and as something that people might attend and publicly endorse, but not necessarily live by.

Finally, and most importantly, the underlying problem with dialogue is that people had long worked together, intermarried and attended the same schools, churches and marketplaces. In turn, the real causes of violence related to issues and narratives that local dialogue could discuss, but not necessarily address. The effectiveness of such meetings and interactions were thus inherently limited and, while important for overcoming individual and collective anger, were always likely to have limited impact in isolation. Moreover, while activists were keenly aware of this problem, and were often frustrated by the broader political and economic context, they tended to resort (at least at the various dialogue sessions I attended in the Rift Valley between 2008 and 2013) to hark back to the role individuals could play if they renounced violence, were vigilant of their neighbours, sought to mitigate conflicts before they occurred and reported any serious issues to the correct authorities.

However, many did also try to link dialogue sessions with more far-reaching programmes. This included efforts to deepen socio-economic interdependence between communities and thus strengthen the bonds of mutual self-interest that bind people together in any given area, to tackle youth underemployment and thus reduce the seeming ease with which young men could be mobilised to engage in violence either through payment or incitement, and to provide innovative solutions to the problem of ethnically divisive electoral politics. In this way, dialogue meetings often set time aside to discuss how violence affects socio-economic interests, and actively sought to facilitate 'connector projects' and inter-community livelihood programmes. Examples include the work of the Catholic Diocese of Eldoret in Yamumbi and Kapteldon villages in Uasin Gishu District where CJPC organised the building of an eight-kilometre road to link 'the two communities, to foster free exchange, movement and communication'. Rather than use machines, local committees 'opted to use manual labour so that the youth would interact and get to know each other as they worked' (Korir 2009: 36). According to one local youth, 'things cooled down in January [2009] after the connector project' as the experience helped to reduce mistrust and build new friendships (interview, Eldoret, 17 July 2009). Well-intentioned, these projects were nevertheless small in nature and number, and often displayed clear limitations.

Kenya's post-election crisis also drew attention to the large number of unemployed youth who were believed to be 'ready recruits for violent gangs' (Kenya 2008b: 33). In response, programmes often targeted disaffected youth as potential participants in violence, either because they received a small payment or simply because they were angry and had little to lose. A common theme was the need to bring youth together, and give them entertainment and opportunities through sporting events and business projects. For example, following the Catholic Church's connector project in Yamumbi and Kaptwemba, participating youths formed a group – After the Peace Road Project, What? – to support each other through income generating activities and small loans funded by membership fees (Korir 2009: 36–37). The same logic was also evident in the work of better-funded organisations such as the Kenya Red Cross, which consciously opted to employ youths from both communities to construct houses for IDPs across parts of the Rift Valley.

Similar ideas informed national initiatives such as the Youth Enterprise Development Fund and Kazi Kwa Vijana (KKV; or 'Jobs for the Youth'), which were launched in 2006 and March 2009, respectively. The former was set up to support 'enterprise development as a key strategy that will increase economic opportunities for, and participation by Kenyan youth in nation-building'.[3] By October 2009 the Fund had disbursed around KSHS 1.53 billion to 57,075 youth enterprises (South Consulting October 2009: 44). Similarly, KKV was established to create employment opportunities that would contribute to the welfare of local communities and 'channel the skills and energies of the youth to productive activities'.[4] Unfortunately, these projects were undermined by a financial downturn, the sheer number of underemployed youth and widespread allegations of mismanagement. Thus, barely six months in, KKV 'projects – mostly environmental cleanup, road repairs and construction – ground to a halt' (*Standard* 11 October 2009) with many youth left unpaid (*Standard* 25 October 2009) amidst reports of poor management and embezzlement (South Consulting October 2009: 44). These initiatives also assumed that youths' participation in violence could largely be explained by the ease with which they could be used by politicians, which neglected the additional, but arguably more important role of real and perceived grievances and fears of further loss (Lynch 2011b).

In the cosmopolitan Rift Valley, intra- and inter-community peace meetings facilitated by faith-based organisations also bore the idea of zoning the Rift Valley into areas where the Kalenjin or Kikuyu would take the lead in electing political leaders. As one clergyman explained, during peace meetings, groups had 'identified two causes of violence in the region: politics and land'. However, with elections fast approaching, and due to the intractable nature of contested and complex land claims, they decided to focus on the issue of political competition

---

[3] YEDF, *Youth Enterprise Development Fund – About Us*, July 2008, www.youthfund.go.ke/index.php/about-us/about-us-mainmenu-26.html <last accessed 23 March 2015>.

[4] Office of Public Communications, *President, Launch the Kazi Kwa Vijana Programme, Yatta Canal*, 2009, www.communication.go.ke/media.asp?id=829 <last accessed 25 March 2015>.

(interview, Eldoret, 28 March 2013). After further discussions with politicians it was agreed, at least at a mid- to upper level, that Kenyatta's The National Alliance (TNA) would not field candidates throughout the Kalenjin-majority counties. Then, through further discussions, it was agreed – in the interests of Kalenjin and Kikuyu political unity – that Rongai and Kuresoi South constituencies in Nakuru County, where the Kikuyu enjoyed a slight majority, would be regarded as Kalenjin constituencies (Lynch 2014b).

The Rift Valley was not the only site of such deals, which came to be known as 'negotiated democracy' after the NCIC, together with local clergy, elders, peacebuilders and party leaders, made concerted efforts to facilitate such agreements to share posts between ethnic groups in various cosmopolitan counties (Mitullah 2015; Willis & Chome 2014). Dialogue meetings provided a space for the initial discussions that led to these agreements with many constituents then opting – in the context of mistrust and ongoing grievances – to support negotiated democracy as a way, at least in part, to ensure a peaceful election (Lynch 2014a). These agreements provide yet another example of how peacebuilding often reverted to, or resulted in, an emphasis on the contribution that ordinary citizens could make to peace in a context where deeper structural changes seemed unlikely (at least in the short term).

The next section builds on this overview to show how – within a context where peacebuilding efforts frequently reverted to individualised responsibility – a particular framing of the 'good citizen' gained ground in the run-up to the 2013 election. The latter was then reinforced by Christian ideas of salvation and psychoanalytical notions of trauma, and simultaneously used by various actors to emphasise the need for peace and reconciliation, over accountability and justice more broadly speaking.

2.3 Putting Kenya First: Campaigns for Peaceful Elections

Everyone is now preaching peace. Even politicians.
(Interview, civil society activist, Eldoret, 18 July 2008)

As the March 2013 election approached, the various activities previously outlined combined with a pre-election peace drive to produce a pervasive peace narrative. Indeed, in the last year running up to the election, every sector of society – from state institutions, churches, local and international CSOs to theatre groups, musicians, artists, businesspeople and ordinary citizens – participated in peace campaigns. These efforts used every media available from theatre, songs, videos and public art to adverts, rallies, pulpits, social media and text messages (Bowman & Bowman 2016; Bowman & Githaiga 2015; Deacon 2015; Nyairo 2015).

Peace messaging was mainstreamed into preparations for the election. In this way, a national civic education campaign, the Uchaguzi Bora Initiative, or 'Better Elections Initiative', worked with partners across the country and adopted a multi-media strategy to educate people on the electoral process and the importance of participation, but also to promote the importance of peaceful coexistence (Uraia 2013). At the same time, public companies – from Safaricom (the country's largest telecommunications company) to Crown Paints – paid for peace adverts, while others sent peace SMS to their customers (Bowman & Bowman 2016). This corporate decision reflected both how being pro-peace had become a national value, and how the 'spectre of political violence' threatened business investments (Galava 2015: 19). At the same time, politicians from across the political divide competed to display their peace-loving credentials; with televised presidential debates in 2013, for example, transformed into a stage for presidential candidates to publicly commit to peace (Moss & O'Hare 2014).

Peace messaging also became a dominant theme for Kenya's relatively independent, but highly commercial (Wasserman & Maweu 2014), media industry. Kenya's media had been widely criticised in the aftermath of the 2007 election for having either 'contributed to the polarisation of society, or, in other cases, [for not having done] enough to steer the campaign debates in a more enlightening manner' (Gachigua 2014: 63). However, the media's role began to change at the height of the post-election violence with a joint editorial by the major newspapers entitled 'Save Our Beloved Country' (3 January 2008). Conflict-sensitive reporting then became institutionalised in the inter-election period through trainings, new editorial guidelines and disciplined working environments. This included training (largely funded by donors and international organisations) on ethical journalism, which sensitised 'journalists to be careful in what they report so [they] don't arouse passions' (interview, journalist,

Nairobi, 10 April 2013), and instilled a strong sense that individual journalists would 'be the first person to be held responsible' for the consequences of any stories published (interview, newspaper journalist, Nakuru, 3 April 2013). Fifteen media houses and institutions then signed guidelines a year before the elections, which committed to 'reject content that could fuel conflict and violence'; while, just before the polls, 'the Media Owners' Association (MOA) signed a "gentlemen's agreement" pledging to avoid content that could incite ethnic tensions and [to not air] political statements live' (Galava 2015: 13). Finally, while editors killed some stories (for example, by raising the bar on evidence), journalists also self-censored and potential sources often preferred to stay quiet in the interests of stability (Benequista 2015). Collectively, this led to a situation where, '[w]hen polling day arrived in 2013, the Kenyan media was walking gingerly in the shadow of 2007–08, and had been sensitised and trained about peace so much that perhaps peace became everything' (John Warungu in Muriithi & Page 2014: 10–11).

At the same time, others used traditional and social media for peace campaigns. This included the NCIC, which ran a pre-election multimedia campaign titled Kenya Kwanza or 'Kenya First', which emphasised 'individual responsibility to maintain peace ahead of the General Elections' (NCIC 2013: ix) and insisted on the need for Kenyans to place 'service before self'.[5] As the NCIC chairman explained, the Commission's approach was informed by the need to bring about an 'attitude change' or 'a transition to individual responsibility' (interview, Nairobi, 5 May 2011).

Indeed, despite the diversity of messengers, a clear crosscutting theme emerged: the need for individual Kenyans to help maintain peace and prevent violence. This constant reinforcement helped to produce a powerful narrative. As Stuart Croft (2006) has argued with regard to America's 'war on terror', one needs to recognise the extent to which meta-narratives are co-produced, and rarely questioned, by cultural products such as movies, popular songs and evangelical websites to understand their impact. This was clearly true in Kenya, where a pre-election peace narrative gained constant repetition by various actors, but was also rarely questioned by human rights activists,

---

[5] www.cohesion.or.ke/index.php/events/kenya-kwanza <last accessed 26 January 2015>.

opposition politicians or the media due to a shared desire to avoid violence and a generalised fear of being labelled as 'anti-peace'.

This message enjoyed practical appeal given the impossibility of dealing with the array of underlying factors that were generally accepted to have fuelled violence in 2007–8 within a five-year period. However, it also resonated with important frameworks of understanding, most notably, with Christian notions of individual salvation and psychoanalytic ideas of trauma.

Religion and spirituality are central to the majority of Kenyan's understanding of a person's position in the world, while a common theme for many of the country's majority Christian population is a belief in the centrality of individual sin and salvation. This helped to ensure the popular resonance of efforts that individualised responsibility for peace. Particularly important in this regard were neo-Pentecostal ideas and rituals, which pervaded peacebuilding efforts – from the high profile 'prayer rallies' patronised by leading politicians to local church services and dialogue sessions (Deacon 2015; Maupeu 2014; Nyairo 2015).

Neo-Pentecostalism refers to a stream of Charismatic churches that emphasise healing, deliverance, the anointing power of church leaders and prosperity in ways that incorporate the spiritual world as an actor with powers over the material world. As a result, neo-Pentecostalism provides a means to understand, but also to respond to, problems of all kinds through the rituals of repentance and cleansing that welcome Christ in and cast the devil out (Deacon & Lynch 2013). The significance of neo-Pentecostalism was at least three-fold. First, neo-Pentecostalism calls upon 'good' people to change their behaviour, rather than their surroundings per se – an approach to understanding the 'problem' and 'solution', which is consistent with the individualisation of responsibility that characterised much inter-election peace messaging.

Second, from the 1990s, Kenya has witnessed a 'grass-roots Pentecostalizing' of Christian practice (Deacon, Gona, Mwakimako & Willis 2017). This includes the spread of neo-Pentecostal ideas and rituals into mainstream Christian devotional practice, but also the emergence of a 'Pentecostalite style' whereby a clear dichotomy between 'good' and 'evil' – and an ability of individuals to choose the former, but also be ruined by the latter – has, through its incorporation into a wide range of cultural productions, introduced a 'new "atmosphere" into the public sphere' (cf. Meyer 2004: 95). As a result, the core neo-Pentecostalist ideas of rebirth and renewal pervade far beyond those who regard themselves as adherents of neo-Pentecostalist teachings, as Kenyans are presented with particular notions of self-improvement, success and misfortune through church sermons, popular songs, local radio and TV shows, social media debates, self-help books and everyday conversations.

Finally, and in the context of this burgeoning Pentecostalite style, both Jubilee and CORD sought to use neo-Pentecostal rituals and discourse in their efforts to present themselves as cleansed from any allegations of wrongdoing in the 2007–8 post-election violence, and as reborn individuals who could lead the country forward in God's favour (Deacon 2015 and 2016; Deacon & Lynch 2013).

In addition to popular spirituality, an individualisation of responsibility also resonated with, and was further reinforced by, dominant ideas of trauma and healing that stem from the psychoanalytical turn of the twentieth century. This shift is associated with the rise of 'talk therapy', which 'implicitly aims to change not just a person's behaviour but their mind – the way a person construes. Such therapy trades on an ethos of acceptance: it is the person, not the society, that is meant to change' (Summerfield 2002: 1106). In post-conflict situations, the underlying assumption is that distressing experiences trigger 'traumatic symptoms causing dysfunctionalism, leading to cycles of trauma and violence' (Pupavac 2001: 362), which can be broken through psychosocial support. As with neo-Pentecostalism, psychoanalytical notions of 'trauma' and 'healing' helped to shape people's reception of general peace messages, and pervaded peacebuilding efforts as many organisations opted to support psychosocial activities.

More specifically, this framework of understanding led various organisations to support group therapy sessions, which encouraged an emphasis on an individual's power to change his or her situation. One example is a project conducted by RWPL and an international NGO, Feminenza, in Mt Elgon, where women were taken through the 'field of fears' to the 'domain of courage'.[6] As women learnt 'how to bring fears to a standstill; gain deeper insight and understanding of oneself, to be less affected by fear; acquire the means to manage

---

[6] http://rwpl.tumblr.com/post/3326796488/healing-abducted-girls-in-mt-elgon <last accessed 26 January 2015>.

ongoing fears quietly, resolutely; [and to] move on, re-acquire choice, [and] restart a self-determining existence'.[7]

These Christian and psychoanalytical worldviews share an understandable appeal, but also inherent shortcomings. On the one hand, they empower individuals to do something about their past and future, either by welcoming Christ in, or by talking through one's experiences and claiming ownership of one's future. As a result, they have proven extremely popular and are often welcomed by those who feel that they have been able to regain a sense of control (interview, widow of violence on Mt Elgon, Cheptais, 25 February 2011). On the other hand, *if over-emphasised to the neglect of parallel socio-economic and political reforms*, they can distract from broader structural inequalities and injustices that ultimately shape people's realities, understandings and expectations.

In this vein, Gregory Deacon and I have argued that, while neo-Pentecostalism 'can offer defence mechanisms or strategies that assist with survival', they simultaneously 'detract from a class-based identification of, and opposition to structural violence, inequality, corruption, and oppression' (2013: 108). Similarly, many have criticised an over-emphasis on 'trauma healing' in post-conflict settings, on the grounds that healing 'is tied up with wider questions of social justice and normative concerns about what type of society we all want to inhabit ... [which] can only be addressed in the political domain' (Gilligan 2006: 339–340). More specifically, critics argue that, while '[a] person may subjectively experience a memory of an event as overwhelming ... the problem lies in the difficulty he or she experiences in trying to integrate the memory into a framework of meaning, not in the power of the event', since 'individuals reflect on the past from a socially situated location in the present' (Gilligan 2006: 330 and 338). The implication is not that people are never traumatised by the past, nor that talking through experiences is not useful, and perhaps even an essential part of recovery, but that, ultimately, psychological recovery from conflict 'arises from the general conditions and meaning of people's lives rather than from individuals' internal emotional state' (Pupavac 2004: 163; also Summerfield 2002: 1107). What matters, in short, are self-perceptions and the meaning given to past experiences,

---

[7] http://feminenza.org/understanding-and-managing-fear <last accessed 26 January 2015>.

real and perceived changes, and whether people fear, or are motivated to participate in, further violence.

Nevertheless, these common understandings of people's relationship with the world – together with the reality of a limited transition, ongoing fears of further violence and evolution of peacebuilding efforts – help to contextualise the broad-based appeal of an individualisation of responsibility for peace. Since, collectively, they helped to ensure that a focus on the need for people to change their attitudes and behaviour became the focus of short-term peacebuilding efforts, rather than the full implementation of institutional reforms, a redistribution of resources and mass job creation. This is entirely understandable; it also made a significant contribution to ensuring that the 2013 elections were relatively peaceful. However, it simultaneously had the perverse and, for some, the intended, consequence of helping to stifle dissent through a revised 'ideology of order' that bled through into the post-election period and fundamentally shaped the context for parallel transitional justice efforts and political context up to, during and after the next election in 2017.

2.4 The Violence of Peace[8]

At this point in our development and history, Kenya needs strong and united leadership. This is precisely what the [Jubilee] Coalition undertakes to provide.

(The Harmonised Jubilee Coalition Manifesto)[9]

As Kenya approached the 2013 election, the country remained haunted by the spectre of violence on at least two levels. On the one hand, the loss of lives and property raised the spectre of repetition. On the other hand, the ghost of 2007 represented the loss of 'a path not taken' (cf. Gordon 2008: 64): Kenyans had resorted to violence in 2007, when they could have protested results through more peaceful means, or gone home and accepted their fate. Haunted by such ghosts, peacebuilding and messaging campaigns framed the good Kenyan citizen as one who protects and promotes stability, and who shies away from potentially divisive rhetoric and activities.

---

[8] This section draws in part on Cheeseman, Lynch & Willis 2014.
[9] www.mwakilishi.com/content/articles/2013/02/03/viewdownload-the-full-harmonized-jubilee-coalition-manifesto.html <last accessed 18 March 2015>.

This narrative – together with a new political alliance that brought together the previously antagonistic Kalenjin and Kikuyu communities, constitutional reforms and increased public confidence in key institutions, the devolution of substantial powers to new county governments, a better organised and more visible state security presence and a general desire for peace – helped to ensure against mass violence before, during and in the wake of the 2013 election (Cheeseman, Lynch & Willis 2014). With election-related violence limited to a handful of pre-election clashes, such as those that occurred in the Tana Delta in 2012, which were exacerbated by constituency boundary disputes and competition for new county-level posts (Sheekh & Mosley 2012), and localised incidents during the course of the election, as occurred in Nyanza Province during party primaries in January 2013 and following the announcement of the Supreme Court's validation of the presidential results in March 2013, and at the Coast on the eve of the polls (ICG 2013).

The significance of this relative peace should not be underestimated. Every previous multi-party election in Kenya had been characterised by violence in one part of the country or another. At the same time, most of the underlying causes of the 2007–8 post-election violence had not been addressed. Levels of inter-communal mistrust and fear remained high, while partisan support was widely interpreted to reflect the 'tyranny of numbers' enjoyed by the Kikuyu, Kalenjin and allied communities (Lynch 2014b). In addition, hate leaflets were distributed in some areas in the lead-up to the election; debates on social media became increasingly vitriolic; the new technology introduced to safeguard the vote broke down; Kenyatta secured a surprise first round victory with just 0.07 per cent of the vote; and Odinga and CORD initially rejected the presidential result (Barkan 2013; Cheeseman, Lynch & Willis 2014; Elder, Stigant & Claes 2014; Long, Kanyinga, Feree & Gibson 2013). However, rather than call their supporters out onto the streets, as ODM had done in 2007, CORD brought an electoral petition before the Supreme Court and begrudgingly accepted its validation of the results (Harrington & Manji 2015).

For many, the 2013 election was regarded as successful and credible largely because it was relatively peaceful (Long, Kanyinga, Feree & Gibson 2013; Shah 2015). This is particularly true in the historically troubled parts of the Rift Valley where many Kalenjin and Kikuyu were adamant that 'peace was more important this time than anything else' and that now, instead of having to focus on recovering from another bout of election-related violence, the country has an 'opportunity to reflect on promises' (local radio presenter, Nakuru, 3 April 2013) and to 'work on systems' (peace activist, Nakuru, 3 April 2013).

However, credible elections require more than that they be free of mass violence, and many believe that irregularities pushed Jubilee over the 50 per cent plus one vote threshold to win in the first round. As a result, many who did not vote for Jubilee were overtaken by 'a sense of hopelessness' once the results were announced (Chome 2013), while confidence ratings in the electoral commission and Supreme Court fell dramatically (Africog/KPTJ 2013; Harrington & Manji 2015; Otieno 2015). Yet, despite such concerns, many who questioned the credibility of the process did not feel that they were able to protest. Instead they chose 'the path of being quiet. Not because [they're] satisfied, but because [they] don't know what to do next' (interview, civil society activist, Nakuru, 4 April 2013), as many, at least in the short-term, 'resigned themselves to the fate of the numbers game and the apparent violence of proficiency and procedure' (Chome 2013). In part, this sense of hopelessness and resignation can be understood as a product of 'the violence of peace' or a 'productive political violence [that pushes] towards specific possible futures, while cutting off others' (Branch 2014: 609), as an emphasis on peace helped to delegitimise opposition, dissent and peaceful protest as a threat to stability.

First, an idea of peace-at-all-costs 'suppressed frank discussion of critical reform issues' during the campaigns (ICG 2013: 3). The mainstream media avoided reporting contentious issues – from the IEBC's 'lack of preparation and the failure of the electronic voting and vote tallying systems to sporadic violence during the election period and broader issues such as land and ethnicity' (Muriithi & Page 2014: 18 and 19). Indeed, the media stood accused after the 2013 election of extensive self-censorship and of over-emphasising peace to the neglect of reportage and justice (Elder, Stigant & Claes 2014: 13; Gachigua 2014; Galava 2015; Muriithi & Page 2014). The common complaint was that the media had 'gagged itself … for [the] sake of peace' (interview, clergyman, Eldoret, 26 March 2013).

Suppression also went beyond the mainstream media. For example, a month before the election, the Inspector General of Police issued a directive that '[l]and should not be one of the issues on the campaign trail because it is so emotive and can trigger violence. All politicians should... forthwith stop dwelling on issues that will cause tensions and animosities' (cited in Cheeseman, Lynch & Willis 2014: 11). While, at a more general level, many ordinary Kenyans 'feared voicing dissenting opinions, discussing contentious issues, or reporting electoral malpractice' lest they be cast as trouble makers (Elder, Stigant & Claes 2014: 13).

The pre-election peace narrative was also used to justify a range of other repressive measures. This included the strategic location of security forces in CORD strongholds during the announcement of election results and Supreme Court decision on the presidential election; an unconstitutional ban on political meetings and demonstrations in the wake of the elections on the basis that they constituted a 'threat to peace'; and the use of force to quell dissent when it occurred, with six confirmed fatal police shootings during the demonstrations that followed the Supreme Court's validation of the presidential election on 30 March (Cheeseman, Lynch & Willis 2014; ICG 2013: 4). These violent measures were legitimised in the name of peace and order. As a result, they proved reminiscent of the multi-party elections of the early 1960s, when '[t]he extravagant language of control, and the display of uniforms, was coupled with a willingness [by the state] to use force wherever order seemed challenged' (Willis 2015: 106).

At the same time, a number of newspaper columnists, commentators on social media and Jubilee activists demonised vocal members of civil society and the international community as part of a web of 'evil society' that sought to fix Kenyatta and Ruto through the ICC (Chapter 3), which rendered it increasingly difficult for activists to raise concerns lest they face further denigration for undermining the country's sovereignty, and for acting as puppets of Western donors (Opalo 2013).

In this context, many CORD supporters, pro-reform activists and analysts referred to peace as a 'double-edged sword' (Oloo 2015: 256) and complained of a 'tyranny of peace messaging' (Githongo 2013) or 'peace-ocracy' (Shah 2015). Peace was thus prioritised over a competitive and fair election, leading to a negative peace characterised by the absence of violence, but by high levels of inter-ethnic mistrust and a palpable sense of injustice. Pressures to be peaceful also played into the hands of, and were effectively used by, the new Jubilee Alliance – as a pervasive peace narrative became part of a moral campaign that helped to mitigate against violence and a political strategy.

During the campaigns, both Jubilee and CORD struggled to distance themselves from past violence, ethnic divisions and a path not taken, and to position themselves as effective statesmen in waiting. They struggled for different reasons: while Jubilee was widely viewed as an alliance of convenience between two ICC indictees (Lynch 2014b; Gachigua 2015; Mueller 2014a; Wolf 2015); Odinga and CORD retained the opposition label, and thus the mantel of having rejected the results in 2007. In this context, both alliances actively tried to convince people that they were the ones who could manage a state, ensure order and deliver peace.

Ultimately, while ICC indictments linked Kenyatta and Ruto more closely to past violence, they managed to better distance themselves from the spectre of possible future violence. At one level, Jubilee simply ran a slicker and better funded campaign, through which Kenyatta and Ruto were cast – and also appeared – as a forward-looking alliance that wanted to move on, as compared to Odinga and CORD, who were cast as backward-looking, nepotistic, unpredictable and vengeful (Lynch 2014b). At the same time, Jubilee explicitly associated itself with an ongoing struggle for independence from Western dominance by calling upon Kenyans to assert their sovereignty by voting against the ICC. Finally, by bringing together the formerly antagonistic Kalenjin and Kikuyu communities (who had been at the epicentre of election-related violence in the early 1990s and 2007–8), Jubilee offered a more tangible contribution to peace, which was reflected in the party's slogan of *tuko pamoja* or 'we are together'. Indeed, Jubilee's fight against the ICC and an emphasis on 'togetherness' were intricately intertwined. Since, while the ICC publicly justified its intervention on the ground that 'the lack of an orderly democratic transition [was] a state of exception that required a criminal prosecution' (Höhn 2014: 581), Jubilee suggested that it was the 'lack of an orderly democracy that [was] on trial' (Höhn 2014: 580). This framing encouraged indictees and their allies to counter-shame the Court by showing that it was actually through the new Jubilee Alliance that peace could be ensured, rather than through criminal prosecutions at The Hague (Chapter 3).

In contrast, Odinga ran a relatively lacklustre campaign, which sought to present CORD as the alliance that would implement reforms, oversee more equitable development, tackle corruption, address past injustices and promote sustainable peace. In practice, this was undermined by ODM's chaotic party primaries, and by the fact that the new constitution was already in place and reforms were underway. At the same time, a sub-text of the CORD campaign was that the presidency should pass to a different ethnic group after two Kikuyu presidents (Jomo Kenyatta, 1963–1978, and Mwai Kibaki, 2002–2013) and one Kalenjin president (Daniel arap Moi, 1978–2002). Together with poorly timed comments by Odinga suggesting that the election might be rigged, and that this would be rejected by CORD supporters (*Financial Times* 1 March 2013), such positioning brought Odinga's commitment to 'peace first' under question. At the same time, Jubilee's efforts to blame Odinga for 'taking' Kenya to the ICC (Chapter 3) – together with claims that Odinga would seek revenge for the political and economic marginalisation of his father, Oginga Odinga,[10] and Luo community, and that he would target the Kikuyu and Kalenjin communities as unjust beneficiaries of past land grabs in future land reforms – helped to facilitate Jubilee's projection of Odinga as sectional and outward-looking, rather than as patriotic and peace-loving (Lynch 2014b).

This is not to suggest that Jubilee persuaded all Kenyans of their leadership credentials. On the contrary, official results show a close presidential race – with Kenyatta securing 50.07 per cent to Odinga's 43.31 per cent – which, according to exit polls and petition arguments may have involved some malpractice and an unjustified first round victory for Jubilee (Ferree, Gibson & Long 2014; Harrington & Manji 2015). Instead, it highlights how Jubilee's positioning as an alliance for peace proved popular amongst a significant number of Kenyans, and how it was simultaneously interwoven with an emphasis on unity and order that was to provide crucial context for parallel transitional justice efforts during the campaigns and Kenyatta's first term in office.

2.5 Conclusions: The Ideology of Order

Those unwilling to work to unite Kenyans will not have the space to divide them.

(President Uhuru Kenyatta following terrorist attacks in Mpeketoni, Lamu County, 17 June 2014)[11]

---

[10] Oginga Odinga was Kenya's first vice president and a prominent opposition figure from the late 1960s to his death in 1994.

[11] A copy of the public statement was posted on www.facebook.com/myuhurukenyatta/posts/860979340597287 <last accessed 21 March 2018>.

Transitional justice does not work in a vacuum. It is also not quick. In Kenya, transitional justice mechanisms were introduced amidst constitutional reforms, political realignments, daily struggles for advancement and survival, and an array of peacebuilding efforts. They were also introduced in the wake of a disputed election and in the run-up to another election, which was haunted by the spectres of division and repetition. As the 2013 elections loomed, peacebuilding efforts came to fall back on the role that individual Kenyans could play in early warning, peacebuilding and conflict resolution. These efforts then became intertwined with a pervasive peace campaign, which saw every sector of society call upon Kenyans to be good citizens and to cast their vote, return home and to accept the election results in peace. This framing of the good citizen was cultivated through a conjuncture of political, popular and corporate cultures, and was simultaneously reinforced by Christian and psychoanalytical frameworks of understanding. The power of this narrative lay, at least in part, in the difficulty of outright rejection. It is difficult personally (both morally and politically) to be *against* peace, reconciliation and order, or *for* their opposites: violence, division and disorder.

This narrative helped to ensure that the 2013 elections were relatively peaceful. However, it also helped to determine which activities were deemed politically legitimate – as strategically placed security forces, for example, enforced a ban on public demonstrations, and the media engaged in a high level of self-censorship. As a result, and as in the early 1960s, 'elections helped to routinize ideas about legitimate and illegitimate violence, and particularly about the legitimacy of systemic violence which asserted order' (Willis 2015: 102).

This prioritisation of peace did not end with the election's conclusion. Instead, once Kenyatta and Ruto were inaugurated on 9 April 2013, the duo began to adapt the pre-election framing of good citizenship as a central legitimising discourse of Kenyatta's presidency and as a central plank of their 2017 election campaign. More specifically, and in the context of increased terrorist activity by Al-Shabaab (a radical Islamist group based in Somalia) in the first half of Kenyatta's term in office (Anderson & McKnight 2015), the earlier message of 'voting in peace' was modified into a call for Kenyans to unite behind the government in the interests of stability, sovereignty, development and progress, and to refrain from rhetoric and action that could foster division, disunity and chaos. Particularly significant in this regard was the way in which the experience and threat of terrorist attacks were used to justify the need for unity and to oppose criticism as a source of political weakness (Lynch 2015a). Then, in the lead-up to the 2017 elections, Kenyatta and Ruto once again sought to juxtapose themselves – and their slogan of *tuko pamoja* (or 'we are together') – with Odinga (who stood as the presidential candidate for the new National Super Alliance [NASA]). The latter again cast by Jubilee as divisive and pro-violence (Cheeseman, Lynch & Willis 2017).

Critically, Kenya's pre- and post-2013 election peace narrative drew upon, and re-performed nationalist discourses with which Kenyans, and the world, are long familiar. In this vein, Jomo Kenyatta's post-independence rally cry of *Harambee* was interpreted as a need to 'pull together' in the interests of nation-building, while President Moi's reference to *nyayo* or 'footsteps', quickly morphed from a pronounced commitment to follow in his predecessor's footsteps to a state-prescribed holy trinity of 'love, peace, and unity' (Lynch 2011b: 113). Instead of adopting a new political approach, therefore, Uhuru Kenyatta joined his predecessors – specifically his father and Moi, rather than Mwai Kibaki – in drawing upon an 'ideology of order', where an insistence on stability is used to justify the use of state power as an instrument of control (Atieno-Odhiambo 1987: 179). According to this logic, 'political stability is seen as the number one priority and other factors – typically civil liberties and political competition – are sacrificed whenever they threaten to generate instability' (Cheeseman in *Sunday Nation*, 22 June 2014). Or, to put it another way, this logic casts certain forms of systemic violence as a legitimate means to impose order and to thus create an environment in which development and progress are possible (cf. Willis 2015).

Chapters 9 and 10 return to this prioritisation of peace, and to an associated attempt to perform a break with the past – not through transitional justice – but through a circumscribed form of reparative justice and politics of reconciliation. First, however, this book turns to the evolution of parallel transitional justice efforts and to the challenges that they faced in this political context.

3 | Enter the International Criminal Court
Performing (In)justice

> The [ICC's] first decade suggests that it may be possible to design international institutions around power – but not to escape it.
> (Bosco 2014: 189)

In September 2009, and in the wake of election-related violence in Kenya and Zimbabwe, the International Criminal Court's (ICC) Chief Prosecutor, Luis Moreno Ocampo, declared that Kenya would provide 'an example to the world' on 'how to manage past violence and how to create a peaceful [recovery] process' (2009). Fifteen months later, Ocampo announced the names of six Kenyans under investigation by the office of the prosecutor (OTP) and, in January 2012, the ICC's pre-trial chamber (PTC) confirmed charges against four of the accused in two separate cases. Four years later, both cases had collapsed; two of the accused – who had come together in the Jubilee Alliance – had been elected president and deputy president of the country following a campaign that had placed 'their struggle' against the ICC centre stage; and the process had revealed how the rich and powerful could undermine the ICC and strengthened opposition to the Court around the world.

The example given 'to the world' was far from the enactment of international law that Ocampo had envisaged. Instead, and in line with international criminal tribunals and ICC interventions around the world, the Kenyan cases became associated with a 'virtual trial', albeit a particularly successful one, which contested the Court's moral authority and facilitated the politicisation of legal processes for vested interests (cf. Peskin 2008). As a result, the cases provide an example of 'hijacked justice' – or 'the misuse of transitional justice norms' by domestic political elite (Subotić 2009: 6). As elsewhere, 'hijacked

---

This chapter draws directly from Lynch 2014a and 2014b; and Lynch & Zgonec-Rozej 2013.

justice' took a particular form – this time of a new political alliance and reinterpretation of judicial proceedings as an example of injustice and neo-colonialism.

This reinterpretation of the ICC's intervention helps to explain the formation of the Jubilee Alliance in 2012 – which brought together Kenyatta's The National Alliance (TNA), Ruto's United Republican Party (URP) and several smaller parties – and its electoral success in 2013. Thus, while Ruto had campaigned for Kenyatta as the Kenya African National Union (KANU) flag-bearer in 2002, the duo had been on opposing sides in 2007, when Kenyatta (then still in KANU) had backed President Kibaki's re-election bid on a Party of National Unity (PNU) ticket, and Ruto had formed part of the Orange Democratic Movement's (ODM) central campaign team. Not only had Kenyatta and Ruto been on opposing sides in 2007, but, by early 2012, they also faced charges of crimes against humanity in two separate cases before the ICC for their alleged role in organising violence against each other's support bases and communities during the post-election violence of 2007–8. To further complicate the situation, the majority of Kenyatta's Kikuyu and Ruto's Kalenjin communities had supported opposing parties in every multi-party election between 1963 and 2007 (Lynch 2014a: 95–96); while the worst election-related violence – both in the early 1990s and in 2007–8 – had pitted the Kalenjin in the Rift Valley against their Kikuyu neighbours (Lynch 2011b).

Given this history, the Jubilee Alliance, which was only forged in December 2012, was dismissed by many as an 'alliance of the accused'. As one member of the Kalenjin Council of Elders explained, someone 'can't wipe out animosity between Kikuyu and Kalenjin overnight ... this unity is purely The Hague' (interview, 26 February 2013). Nevertheless, Jubilee managed to persuade a significant number of people – including a majority of the Kikuyu and Kalenjin communities (which together comprise about 31 per cent of the population [Kenya 2009]) – to support the duo. This was achieved through a multi-stranded election campaign. First, the Alliance was cast as the best means to ensure peace by bringing together the previously warring Kalenjin and Kikuyu communities behind two god-fearing individuals blessed by local clergy. Second, Kenyatta and Ruto were presented as a youthful, dynamic and modern dyad that was backed by a nationally representative team that could help bring about meaningful change. This was then contrasted with their principal opponent – Raila Odinga of CORD – who was cast as old, isolated, vengeful, unpredictable, dangerous and 'analogue'. Third, it drew upon a reinterpretation of the ICC as a neo-colonial project that constituted a familiar performance of injustice and a threat to the country's sovereignty and stability (Lynch 2014a). As a result, a vote for Jubilee became, at least for some, a vote for Kenya and Africa against neo-colonialism and 'the West' (Burbidge 2014: 218; Lugano 2017; Mwangi 2015); while, for many of the Alliance's opponents, it became a vote for ethnic spokesmen, impunity and isolation (Oloo 2015). The ICC intervention thus provided an incentive for Kenyatta and Ruto to come together to fight the Court (Mueller 2014a), while a reinterpretation of the process became part of a winning campaign strategy that further divided the country into those who voted for Jubilee and against CORD (officially 50.07 per cent of those who voted), and those who voted for CORD and against Jubilee (Lynch 2014a).

This chapter does not focus on Jubilee's 2013 electoral campaign, associated diplomatic efforts to undermine the ICC process or the intricacies of legal arguments and judicial processes – all of which have been discussed elsewhere. Instead, this chapter narrows in on debates about whether the court's intervention constituted a performance of justice and accountability, of injustice and neo-colonialism, or of injustice and impunity; and it highlights how the cases came to constitute a *familiar performance*. In short, it is argued that the Court's intervention reproduced a common scenario of other international criminal trials, whereby efforts to impose international justice are subverted and new forms of injustice arise (Leclercq 2017), as formal proceedings are accompanied by a 'virtual trial', which facilitates the politicisation of legal processes for vested interests (Peskin 2008). In so doing, local scenarios of neo-colonialism and impunity were reproduced, whereby an untouchable or respected elite can mobilise community support to avoid accountability. The analysis therefore helps to explain how and why levels of public support for the Court gradually decreased in Kenya, albeit with significant ethnic differences, and how – as elsewhere in the world – popular evaluations or perceptions were shaped by one's own positioning and understandings of the past, present and likely futures.

To make this argument, the chapter begins with a discussion of some of the challenges that international trials face in providing a convincing example of transitional justice, and some of the ways in which they often become perceived as a performance of injustice. It then moves on to the Kenyan case and to how the intervention came to be seen – at least amongst a significant number of Kenyans, and a majority of Kenyatta and Ruto's co-ethnics – as an enactment of bias, neo-colonialism and threat; and of how the accused's ability to 'beat' the ICC simultaneously provided an example of impunity in action for many Kenyans including some who were nevertheless pleased that the duo had been 'saved'. The aim is to provide a case study of a transitional justice mechanism in practice, to analyse the familiar performances that were reproduced and to set out essential context for a parallel truth commission and insistence on reconciliation as a necessary means to counter the 'terror of history'.

3.1 International Criminal Trials and the Performance of (In)justice

What emerges [from an analysis of the ICC] is a picture of a nascent global institution still defining its identity and purpose, endeavouring to secure the recognition and confidence of the state parties that back it, and sometimes making inconsistent decisions that undermine its legitimacy.

(Clark 2008: 37)

Courts enjoy the power to determine guilt, culpability and punishment, as well as innocence, exemptions and compensation. As such, public prosecutions constitute a performance of power that is meant to be imbued with a sense of righteousness and justice. This performative dimension is particularly significant when it comes to criminal trials of those deemed most responsible for mass violence, where public prosecutions are ideally meant to perform the reach of international law, rejection of organised violence, commitment to accountability and new moral narrative of wrongs committed and suffered.

Thus, in writing of the Nuremberg trials of the 1940s, Lawrence Douglas notes how:

The trial was understood as an exercise in the reconstitution of the law, an act staged not simply to punish extreme cases but to demonstrate visibly the power of the law to submit the most horrific outrages to its sober ministrations. In this regard, the trial was to serve as a spectacle of legality, making visible both the crimes of the Germans and the sweeping neutral authority of the rule of law.

(Cited in Cole 2010: 1)

Building on this logic, Mark Osiel argues that criminal trials in democratic transitions should be evaluated according 'to the kind of public discussion they foster concerning the human rights abuse perpetrated by authoritarian rulers, recently deposed' (2000: 1). In his view,

> the record of these trials suggest that defense counsel will tell the story as a tragedy, while prosecutors will present it as a morality play. The judicial task at such moments, however, is to ... recast the courtroom drama in terms of the 'theatre of ideas', where large questions of collective memory and even national identity are engaged ... To maximize their pedagogic impact, such trials should be unabashedly designed as monumental spectacles.
>
> (Osiel 2000: 3)

In a similar vein, Richard Wilson (2007) discusses the capacity of legal proceedings to provide an historical account of the past, which can help to reshape people's understanding of what happened and why.

Yet, while the potential for trials to enact accountability, prompt discussion, rewrite history and perform change are central to their role in transitional justice, the 'monumental spectacles' that they provide can easily appear as a performance of injustice if the focus, process or findings are believed to be unfair. In this way, whether a trial is held up as an example of justice or not depends on popular interpretations of guilt, history, the legal process and associated politics.

Such evaluations are shaped, at least in part, by the persuasiveness of legal arguments, the performance of various actors, and tone and substance of final judgements. For example, courtroom theatrics can help to construct new historical accounts of wrongs and culpability, but they can also have a negligible or even negative impact on public debate and social cohesion. In this way, Hannah Arendt talks of how the post–World War II trial of Adolf Eichmann became 'bad theatre' due to the scope and scale of the subject matter, the lack of suspense, and an obsession with details and the 'banality of evil' (1963).

Such evaluations of legal proceedings are partly shaped by people's own pre-conceptions, their positioning and group identity, and whether or not, for example, it is 'their' leader who is being held to account (Subotić 2009). This is evident, for example, in the way that Odinga's co-ethnics proved much more critical of the IEBC and Supreme Court following Odinga's unsuccessful election petition in 2013, than Kenyatta's and Ruto's communities (Shah 2015). Such divergence is possible because of the ways in which the 'truths' revealed in judicial records can be accepted, but also refuted, rationalised or distorted. In this vein, Laurel Fletcher and Harvey Weinstein reveal how Bosnian legal professionals did not necessarily accept the International Criminal Tribunal for the former Yugoslavia (ICTY)

> as a legitimate institution capable of rendering impartial judgments. Instead of being 'convinced' that war crimes were perpetrated in their name … participants felt free to disregard any aspect of the judicial 'record' that did not conform to their perspective on the 'truth' of what happened during the war.
> (2002: 600)

Similarly, various studies have shown how people often feel sympathetically towards those on trial for mass violence if they believe that the harms took place as part of a broader tragedy that afflicted their community. In this scenario, an accused can be seen as a hero who helped to protect his or her community, or as someone who committed wrongs as part of the 'normal' horrors of war. In such contexts, prosecutions can be viewed not as justice, but as scapegoating (David 2014; Fletcher & Weinstein 2002; Osiel 2000).

These evaluations are clearly shaped by people's understanding of mass violence and of what happens inside a courtroom, but also by their understanding of the politics around a trial: how and why a trial has come to focus on particular crimes and individuals, why it has been brought before a particular court and judge, and the significance attached to the support offered (or denied) by interested parties. In short, recourse to the courts in the context of unequal power relations can constitute, or can be widely regarded to constitute, a form of 'lawfare' or 'the use of legal means for political and economic ends' (cf. Comaroff & Comaroff 2009: 58). In this way, a perception of 'unbridled discretion' in case selection, for example, can fuel a sense that prosecutions are politically motivated and self-serving (Orentlicher 1991: 2549), with many trials viewed, at least by some, as an enactment of 'victor's justice' (Peskin 2005) or neo-colonialism (Mamdani 2009).

In the case of international trials, such evaluations are complicated by the fact that the convening bodies lack the vestiges of a state, and are thus reliant on state cooperation to 'carry out investigations, locate witnesses, and bring suspects to trial' (Peskin 2008: 5). However, states often do not want to cooperate and may seek to protect individuals or institutions, or to gain political mileage from the use of nationalist arguments regarding the need to protect state sovereignty against external intervention (Peskin 2008: 5). As a result, international trials tend to go hand-in-hand with a 'virtual trial' or 'trial of cooperation' whereby the prosecution seeks to maximise state co-operation, and states seek to justify selective non-compliance (Peskin 2008: 9). In this extra-judicial battle, international courts

> have only the soft power of attraction ... [but] cannot afford to take their moral authority for granted because the actual practice of international justice often falls short of its idealistic goals. The real and perceived failings of the tribunals leave them vulnerable to attack from targeted states seeking to thwart prosecutions.
>
> (Peskin 2008: 7)

As a result, the prosecution will look to negotiate with, but also to shame, states in an ongoing effort to motivate the required cooperation, while targeted states will seek to further their own interests – for example, by using a tribunal or court to deal with their opponents, or by magnifying the body's shortcomings and mistakes in an attempt to counter-shame the court so as to undermine its moral authority and reduce the costs of non- or partial cooperation (Peskin 2008: 11).

Victor Peskin developed this idea of a 'virtual trial' in relation to international tribunals, but later extended it to the ICC (Peskin 2009), where such dynamics are complicated by the Court's permanent nature. The ICC is mandated to 'help end impunity for the perpetrators of the most serious crimes of concern to the international community'.[1] To this end, the ICC can investigate and prosecute the crimes of genocide, crimes against humanity and war crimes committed by individuals since the Court's founding treaty, or Rome Statute, came into force on 1 July 2002. However, it may only exercise this jurisdiction if the accused is a national, or if the crime took place within the territory of a state party or of a state that accepts the Court's jurisdiction, or if the United Nations Security Council (UNSC) refers the situation to the OTP. The ICC is also a court of last resort, which means that it can only investigate and prosecute crimes in situations were the chamber decides that the state

---

[1] www.icc-cpi.int/en_menus/icc/about%20the%20court/Pages/about%20the%20court.aspx <last accessed 25 August 2014>.

in question is incapable or unwilling to bring those most responsible to justice. As a result, the Court is governed by a principle of complementarity, whereby it is intended to complement, rather than to replace, domestic proceedings. It has also adopted a principle of 'positive complementarity' or 'proactive policy of cooperation aimed at promoting national proceedings' (ICC 2010: 5).

This mandate and approach ensures that, like earlier criminal tribunals, the ICC suffers from an operational paradox, which tends to fuel a virtual trial of shaming and counter-shaming. Since

> on the one hand, [the ICC] is expected to intervene in countries that are either unable or unwilling to investigate and prosecute those responsible for the worst crimes, while on the other, by its very nature, it has to rely heavily on the support of those very states to carry out its mandate.
> (Williamson 2006: 26)

However, as a permanent court, these extra-judicial negotiations are coloured by previous, ongoing and potential situations. The Court, on the one hand, seeks to justify its intervention in some situations and not in others, to encourage state cooperation in particular situations, to persuade non-state parties to recognise the court and to inspire sufficient confidence to ensure ongoing financial and diplomatic support from state parties. On the other hand, situation states can use the cases selected (and not selected) over time, together with the problems experienced in all previous or parallel cases – from inadequate witness protection and unsuccessful prosecutions to unmet promises and unintended consequences – in their efforts to counter-shame the Court.

One critical debate in this regard is whether the ICC's focus on Africa – with all eight of its situations and twenty-one cases relating to conflicts on the continent at the time that cases began in Kenya – is justified; problematic, but pragmatic; or the result of Western-bias and neo-colonialism. To argue that this focus is justified, some analysts point to how, since the ICC was established, many of the world's most serious crimes against humanity have occurred in Africa; only African states have referred cases to the ICC; and the largest block of members – 34 of 144 state parties in 2009 – hail from the continent. The implication is that the Court is not anti-African or neo-colonial, but that complaints of the same are touted by those who have been, or who fear that they might be, negatively affected as a way to reduce the costs of non- or partial cooperation (Brown & Sriram 2012; Mueller 2014a; Roth 2014; Vilmer 2016).

While this is true, it is clear that the Court's powers are also 'being tested in parts of the world that are politically and economically of limited significance for the major powers' (Allen 2006: 2). It is also evident that, in the case of Uganda and the DRC, the Court allowed itself to be 'politically instrumentalized' by accepting referrals from states that had their own interest in an ICC-led investigation and by only focusing on rebel leaders (Branch 2007). At a more general level, the Court's case selection seems to have been overly determined by a form of 'pragmatism [that] reflects a new global institution that needs to get legal runs on the board in order to build support among its state parties' (Clark 2008: 44).

Ultimately, a level of pragmatism is inevitable given another operational paradox: the ICC's moral authority stems from its assumed existence as a neutral court that holds those most responsible for serious crimes accountable; yet, the ICC can only assume such authority if it enjoys the support of the international community. The implication is that prosecutorial discretion is influenced by legal considerations regarding the strength and significance of potential cases, as well as by a range of political factors. This includes the likelihood of relatively quick 'wins', the potential deterrence effect or promotion of other valued ends and an assessment of whether interventions will be supported (or blocked) by powerful actors. This puts the Court in an unenviable position. It needs to be political, at least in a minimalist sense, since, if it completely ignores political considerations and investigates cases solely on the basis of the magnitude of crimes and evidence of those most responsible, then it would make little headway and jeopardise its relevance, funding and future. However, by taking political considerations into account, the Court undermines its moral authority as a supposedly neutral body, which facilitates non-cooperation by states, reduces the OTP's ability to win cases and raises questions about the Court's capacity, ability and relevance.

This reality – together with a long history of colonialism and racism – lends plausibility to a more contentious argument that the ICC is not just influenced by a conservative pragmatism in the use of prosecutorial discretion, but is neo-colonial in its intent, with suspects in turn demanding sympathy as victims of political persecution (Mwangi 2015). Purveyors of this line of argument include David Hoile, who posits that Europe, which is the largest financial contributor to the Court, has used the ICC 'as a means of destabilising the African continent – something that then makes the political domination of Africa and the subsequent exploitation of African minerals and resources that much easier' (2014: 199).

Unfortunately for the Court, the potential for pragmatic prosecutorial discretion to fuel claims of political persecution and neo-colonialism is exacerbated by its relationship with the UNSC, and politics of powerful states, which fuel a perception that the Court is unduly influenced by those who have an interest in insisting on justice in some contexts, and not in others (Mwangi 2015). For example, the fact that only the UNSC can refer non-state parties to the ICC is highly problematic given the refusal of two of the UNSC's permanent members – China and the United States of America (USA) – to sign the Rome Statute. This is an issue because these countries can refer cases to the ICC but use their veto power to ensure that no cases are ever brought against them. In this context, the stance taken by the US administration is particularly jarring for the Court's critics. As Tim Allen notes, 'No attempt has been made to disguise the premise that international laws are important to regulate the actions of the rest of the world, but that they do not apply to the USA' (2006: 22). Such hypocrisy makes it easier for targeted states, such as Sudan, to cast the ICC as an 'instrument of pressure and punishment, rather than an independent body' (De Waal 2008: 29). This then strengthens a narrative of bias and persecution that suspects and their allies can draw upon in their efforts to counter-shame the Court, as seen in Uganda, Sudan and Kenya, for example, where governments have cast the Court as neo-colonial in their respective efforts to deter additional cases and justify non-compliance (Lugano 2017; Peskin 2009).

Claims of neo-colonialism are often interwoven with other difficult questions about whether, for example, the ICC has focused on the most important crimes in the situation countries; whether it has helped to promote justice, peace or other stated goals; whether it has been able to build and sustain local support; and whether or not it has learnt from criticisms laid or merely become reactive to the same (Allen 2006; Branch 2007; Clark 2008). For example, the fact that the ICC proved incapable of arresting leaders of the Lord's Resistance Army in Uganda is widely assumed to have influenced the selection of cases in the DRC where 'the major militia leaders were already in custody and significant evidence of crimes had already been gathered by local civilian and military courts' (Clark 2008: 40). In turn, the fact that the Court was subsequently criticised for conveying 'the message that the Court is unwilling to prosecute difficult cases related to crimes committed by senior government and military officials' (Clark 2013: 263) seems to have influenced the Court's more balanced approach with regards to the situation in Darfur and Kenya – where the fact that ODM and PNU were taken in equal number (3/3 and then 2/2) looked 'very political and calculated' (interview, Kikuyu elder, Ndeffo, 6 January 2013).

In Kenya, the story was further complicated by domestic politics since – with President Kibaki scheduled to retire at the end of his second term in 2013 – the accused and their allies felt a strong need to secure office (and to prevent Odinga from gaining office) to strengthen their position in the country's 'virtual trial' (cf. Mueller 2014a). As Ruto noted at a campaign rally in Eldoret in late 2012: '[W]e want to be done with this election in the first round before we embark on defending ourselves' at the ICC (*Standard* 2 December 2012). In turn, while the idea of the 2013 election as a referendum on sovereignty in the context of the ICC (Wangusi in *Pambazuka News* 25 October 2012) is an oversimplification – with Jubilee's election campaign and appeal being about much more than the fate of its leaders (Burbidge 2014; Carrier & Kochore 2014; Willis & Chome 2014) – the Court nevertheless constituted a key strand of Jubilee's winning campaign strategy (Lynch 2014a). However, before turning to the particularities of how the ICC became a performance of injustice for many, the next section provides a brief overview of the two cases from their initiation to collapse.

3.2 The ICC in Kenya, 2009–2016

[T]he Government wanted to do the trials locally as recommended in the Waki Report ... [but] Hon. Members kept on saying that it would be a waste of time ... They said: 'We want the Hague, we want the Hague'. So we said: 'Fine, let us not be vague, let us have the Hague'.

(Odinga in the National Assembly, Hansard 18 November 2009)

In early 2008, the Kenya National Commission of Human Rights (KNCHR) – an independent but government-funded body – began to investigate the ongoing post-election violence; a task that was later taken up by the Waki Commission. The latter concluded that the crimes committed potentially constituted international crimes and recommended that a Special Tribunal be established to investigate and prosecute those most responsible. If this did not occur, the Commission recommended that 'a list containing [the] names of and relevant information on those suspected to bear the greatest responsibility' be forwarded to the OTP, and that the latter be requested to 'analyze the seriousness of the information received with a view to proceeding with an investigation' (Kenya 2008b: 473). For the Waki commissioners, the option of passing cases on to the ICC was regarded as a 'nuclear option' that would help to trigger domestic prosecutions (Bosire 2013: 164). However, after parliament rejected efforts to establish a Special Tribunal – and amidst a rally cry of 'Don't be vague, let's go to The Hague' – a sealed list of names and six boxes of supporting evidence were finally handed over to the OTP in July 2009. Weeks later, the government issued a statement noting that it 'rejected a local tribunal and instead settled on [the] Truth, Justice and Reconciliation Commission (TJRC) to deal with post-election violence perpetrators' (cited in HRW 2011: 23).

Just as the Waki Commission saw the threat of the ICC as a catalyst for domestic prosecutions, it seems that Ocampo – who faced much criticism at the time for having done little to promote complementarity (Schabas 2008) – may have seen Kenya as a potential case of positive complementarity. Certainly, the OTP moved relatively slowly and provided a number of opportunities for Kenya to initiate local processes. However, both parliament and the government failed to take advantage of these openings. Instead, politicians rejected several attempts to legislate for a local tribunal, while the government simultaneously sought to extract the country from the ICC's attention. To this end, establishment elites and their supporters (from politicians, diplomats and emissaries through to businesspeople, professionals, clergy and commentators on traditional and social media) suggested that justice could be provided through the TJRC; challenged the admissibility of the Kenyan case; questioned the OTP's selection of those deemed most responsible; lobbied for the cases to be brought back to Kenya (either to a local tribunal or to a mooted International Crimes Division (ICD) of the High Court), to the East African or African Court, or to be suspended or dropped; and actively sought to discredit the ICC as biased, political and neo-colonial amongst domestic, regional and international audiences (HRW 2011; Lugano 2017; Mueller

2014a; Nichols 2015). At the same time, evidence mounted of how witnesses (both listed and potential) were being intimidated, bribed and killed (Mueller 2014a; Rosen 2015); and the Court complained of the Kenyan government's failure to hand over various documents that were requested. These lobbying efforts and stories of interference ensured that Kenyans were exposed to six years of extra-judicial argument and display that ran alongside the formal judicial proceedings. This section provides a brief overview of these judicial and extra-judicial battles before the final sections narrow in on the reinterpretation of the Court as an example of injustice, neo-colonialism and threat; and of the Kenyan cases as a performance of impunity.

Once the Waki Commission evidence had been handed over to the OTP, Ocampo used his powers of *proprio motu* (or 'on his own impulse') to examine the material as two separate cases. In case one, Ruto, Henry Kosgey (another prominent Kalenjin politician and ODM chairman), and Joshua arap Sang (a radio presenter for the Kalenjin vernacular radio station KASS FM) were named in a case that came to focus on the crimes against humanity of murder, forcible transfer and persecution that had allegedly taken place in parts of Nandi and Uasin Gishu districts in the north Rift Valley between December 2007 and February 2008. According to the OTP, these crimes were carried out by 'Kalenjin warriors' at the behest of a 'Kalenjin network' headed by Ruto against PNU supporters, as part of a plan by ODM politicians to gain power, and to punish and drive out PNU supporters, predominately Kikuyu and Kisii, from parts of the Rift Valley (ICC 2016).

In case two, Kenyatta, Francis Muthaura (the former head of the civil service) and Muhamed Hussein Ali (the former police commissioner) were initially named as indirect co-perpetrators of the crimes against humanity of murder, forcible transfer, rape, persecution and other inhumane acts, which were allegedly carried out by members of Mungiki – a Kikuyu gang that had been formed following the election-related violence of the early 1990s (Kagwanja 2003). The OTP argued that these crimes occurred during planned retaliatory attacks in Nakuru and Naivasha towns in the central Rift Valley towards the end of January 2008. More specifically, it was alleged that Kenyatta had 'paid, armed, instructed and transported Kikuyu members and other pro-PNU youth to the attack sites' where ODM supporters, and in particular Luo and Kalenjin residents, were targeted with the aim of keeping PNU in power, and of avenging the prior attacks against

Kikuyu and PNU supporters. The OTP also argued that the police, under Ali's command, had facilitated and protected the attackers (ICC 2015).

After the OTP's initial presentation of the situation, the PTC ruled on 31 March 2010 that the situation was admissible and authorised a full investigation by a two-to-one decision. As the PTC explained, for the case to go forward the OTP had to show that 'i) an attack [was] directed against any civilian population, ii) a State or organizational policy [was in place], iii) the widespread or systematic nature of the attack, and iv) knowledge of the attack' (cited in Jalloh 2011: 542). From the perspective of jurisprudence, the most controversial issue was 'whether the prosecution's evidence revealed the presence of an *organizational policy* that would raise the underlying acts to the level of crimes against humanity' (Jalloh 2011: 544; emphasis in original). In support of this conclusion, the OTP argued, and two of the judges accepted the possibility, that 'many of the post-election attacks were planned, directed, or organized by a concert of local leaders, businessmen, and politicians affiliated with the two leading parties' (Jalloh 2011: 545). However, the fact that the threshold invoked for an organisational policy was lower than the legal precedent formed the crux of a dissenting opinion by Judge Hans-Peter Kaul, who held that a state or organisational policy should be 'conceived at the high policymaking level either by a state or by a nonstate entity that possesses some of the attributes of a state'. For Kaul, the minimum required was 'a collectivity of persons arranged in some type of hierarchy that is acting together toward a common purpose and is capable of formulating and implementing a policy to attack civilians on a large scale' (Jalloh 2011: 545). Critically, this issue of whether the post-election violence resulted from an organisational policy as argued by Ocampo, or from a level of reactive or defensive local-level organisation as concluded by Kaul, continued to lie at the heart of legal debates. The defence in case one sought to show how, among other things, there was no organised and hierarchical 'Kalenjin Network' that planned and oversaw the violence in Uasin Gishu and Nandi districts. In case two, the defence contested the OTP's construction of a case, which sought to make a connection between Mungiki, the accused, and the state. Critically, these arguments also became central to popular reinterpretations of the Court's intervention, as the OTP's presentation of an institutionalised 'Kalenjin Network' in case one, or idea of a state working through a politician with no state office to oversee violence conducted by an ethnic militia in case two, was widely contested (see Section 3.3).

First, the names of six Kenyans under investigation were announced in two separate cases in December 2010. Days later, Kenya's 'virtual trial' began in earnest with a parliamentary motion to withdraw Kenya from the Rome Statute. The bill was never signed, but its production and debate set the tone for the years that followed. This included an intense period of 'shuttle diplomacy' that saw cabinet ministers and diplomats lobby bi-lateral partners, the African Union (AU) and the UN to have the cases suspended, returned to Kenya or moved to another court. At the same time, establishment elites sought to mobilise domestic constituents against the ICC, and to demonise the Court's supporters as traitors and Western stooges (Nichols 2015).

These efforts failed to bring the cases to an immediate conclusion, but they succeeded in prompting displays of support from the AU, several African leaders and local constituents. This included an AU resolution in October 2013 that the ICC should not commence or continue with charges 'against any serving AU Head of State or Government or anybody acting or entitled to act in such capacity during their term of office' (cited in *Capital FM* 6 October 2014).

The accused were assisted in this extra-judicial battle by wildly different expenditures on communications. On the one hand, the Kenyan establishment invested much time and money into fighting the ICC – from the use of an expensive British public relations company, BTP Advisors, in the 2013 election campaign to the facilitation of dozens of politicians to accompany the 'Ocampo Six' to The Hague in 2011, the organisation of a series of mass 'prayer rallies' between 2011 and 2016, and an intensive social media campaign. In contrast, the Court was supported by a single outreach officer with a limited budget (Hansen & Sriram 2015) who was clearly frustrated by the high cost of sharing information through adverts and news broadcasts in Kenya, and by the security concerns that curtailed her ability to meet with ordinary people (interview, Nairobi, 15 September 2011). The same was true of the Court's efforts to interact with case and situation victims through the Victims Participation and Reparation Section, which was also manned by a single officer; and the common legal representatives who bemoaned how the 'amount of legal aid and support they receive is insufficient to reach out effectively to victims' (AI 2014: 58).

As a lone ICC outreach officer – together with a cluster of politicians, human rights activists, outspoken columnists and international organisations – battled it out in the court of public opinion against the full force of the country's political establishment, the cases stumbled on. On 8 March 2011, the PTC II summoned all six suspects to appear before the Court – a decision that was again opposed by Judge Kaul. The Kenyan government took advantage of this dissent to challenge the admissibility of the cases and to argue that the adoption of a new constitution in August 2010 had opened the way for domestic prosecutions. However, this challenge, and a later appeal of the PTC's decision, was rejected on the grounds that the government had not yet begun investigations into any of the Ocampo Six, while the arguments 'presented "cast doubt on the will of the State to actually investigate the ... suspects" even if it had been convinced that an ongoing investigation existed' (AI 2014: 25).

The PTC II's summons led to an initial hearing of the two cases in The Hague on 7 and 8 April 2011 when the presiding judge warned that arrest warrants would be issued if suspects were deemed to be involved in any incitement of further violence. At the same time, the chamber set the date for two confirmation of charges hearings in September 2011. These initial appearances of the Ocampo Six were aired live on national TV and radio, and absorbed much of the country's press coverage. As a result, they provided a novel opportunity for Kenyans to watch the courtroom dynamics within constrained blocks of time when discussions revolved around two key themes: whether the OTP's evidence was reliable and sufficient, and how the ICC – and its various units – actually worked. At the same time, the extra-judicial theatrics continued apace as the suspects and their allies contested the Court's legitimacy and asserted their own innocence and standing. To this end, the state paid for a delegation of MPs to accompany the suspects to The Hague, who, '[d]ressed with caps in the color of Kenya's flag and in a huge show of disrespect ... danced and sang on the steps of the ICC' (Mueller 2014a: 32). The Six then receiving a 'heroes' welcome' on their return (Brown & Sriram 2012: 257). At the same time, politicians began to organise a series of high profile prayer meetings at which religious leaders from various denominations and faiths blessed the suspects and sought God's intervention for the truth to prevail (Maupeu 2014). Indeed, as the 2013 election approached, prayers for Kenyatta and Ruto became an 'indispensable part of every [Jubilee] rally' (Nyairo 2015: 137), as Jubilee 'campaigned using a narrative according to which the nation was being washed clean, redeemed, and born again' (Deacon 2015: 200).

In January 2012, the PTC confirmed charges against four of the accused, but ruled that there was insufficient evidence against Kosgey and Ali. The decision was again reached by a two-to-one vote as Judge Kaul issued his third dissenting opinion, which prompted another unsuccessful admissibility appeal – this time on the grounds that the alleged crimes did not qualify as crimes against humanity (Lynch & Zgonec-Rozej 2013: 7–9).

With charges now confirmed against four men in two cases – Ruto and Sang in case one and Kenyatta and Muthaura in case two – the OTP and defence team focused on preparing for court. In contrast, the attention of Kenya's political elite turned to the forthcoming elections and the arduous work of campaigning.

The trials were initially scheduled to start on 10 and 11 April 2013, after the general election of 4 March, but within the electoral period if the presidential election went to a second round. However, in February, the cases were delayed until August, while case two never actually made it to trial. First, and just days after the 2013 election, charges were dropped against Muthaura, with the new chief prosecutor, Fatou Bensouda, citing the death, bribery and intimidation of key witnesses (Mueller 2014a: 27). The onset of Kenyatta's trial was then delayed until 12 November 2013, and then to 5 February 2014. However, on 19 December 2013, the OTP requested an adjournment of the case so as to garner new witnesses on the basis that the evidence available following the retraction of statements by two additional witnesses did not 'satisfy the high evidentiary standards required' (cited in Mueller 2014a: 35). In response, the Trial Chamber adjourned the commencement of the trial until October 2014. Following further delays, Bensouda finally withdrew the charges against Kenyatta in December 2014. However, she made it clear that he had not been found innocent, and drew attention to 'an unprecedented campaign on social media to expose the identity of protected witnesses', to the 'concerted and wide-ranging efforts to harass, intimidate and threaten individuals who would wish to be witnesses' and to the fact that charges had been withdrawn 'without prejudice to the possibility of bringing new charges ... should the prosecution obtain sufficient evidence' (*Standard* 6 December 2014). The OTP also continued to compile evidence of witness tampering, which led to a referral of the Kenyan government to the Assembly of State Parties in September 2016 for failing to comply with the OTP's requests to hand over various documents (*Standard* 20 September 2016).

In contrast, the trial for case one began in September 2013. However, while Ruto and Sang travelled regularly to and from The Hague over the next few years, and Kenyans followed the first few weeks of the trial with keen interest, the process soon fell off the front pages and everyday debate. In short, and in contrast to the bursts of theatricality associated with the summons to appear and confirmation of charges hearings in 2011, the trial constituted bad theatre. First, proceedings were slow and fractured: about half of the witnesses were heard *in camera*, appeals by the defence caused various delays and the OTP requested several adjournments following the failure or unwillingness of their witnesses to appear. As a result, by the time the charges against Ruto and Sang were withdrawn in April 2016, the chamber had not begun to hear from defence witnesses. Second, public sessions were jargon-heavy and tended to focus on general contexts, rather than on specific allegations. Finally, by the time the trial began, Kenyatta and Ruto had been elected in large part because of their struggles at the ICC. In turn – and as the charges in case two were dropped, and the number of witnesses willing to testify in case one gradually declined – many lost confidence in the OTP's capacity to secure a prosecution, and came to see the cases as a distraction. As a result, the collapse of the cases met with limited protest and was instead celebrated through a big 'thanksgiving service' at Afraha Stadium in Nakuru – the home of one of the country's largest IDP camps during the post-election violence (Deacon 2016).

This burgeoning sense of scepticism and pragmatism was intimately intertwined – not just with problems with the judicial process – but with the reproduction of a 'virtual trial' that, by drawing upon familiar narratives of neo-colonialism, reinterpreted the Court's intervention as a performance of injustice that threatened peace and stability, and was incapable of tackling impunity – perceptions and debates to which this chapter now turns.

3.3 Reframing the Court's Intervention, 2009–2016

The ICC has been reduced into a painfully farcical pantomime, a travesty that adds insult to the injury of victims. It stopped being the home of justice the day it became the toy of declining imperial powers.

(President Kenyatta speaking at an African Union special summit on the ICC, cited in *BBC News* 12 October 2013)

The ICC initially enjoyed high levels of public support in Kenya. However, things began to change after the names of the six Kenyans under investigation were announced in December 2010 – from a high of 68 per cent of people supportive of the process in October 2010 to 56 per cent in August 2011 and 39 per cent in June 2013 (Ipsos Synovate 4 November 2011; Maliti 31 July 2013). Indeed, by February 2014, 58 per cent of Kenyans dismissed the cases as a waste of time and money (*The Star* 1 February 2014), while many who still supported the process believed that the accused were innocent and would ultimately be vindicated (*The Star* 18 November 2013).

There are two important caveats to this overarching picture, which suggests that popular support was shaped by evaluations of the fairness of the process and fate of preferred leaders. Regarding the former, it is notable that there was a marginal increase in levels of public support – from 56 per cent of Kenyans in July 2011 to 59 per cent in October 2011 – following the confirmation of charges hearings in September 2011 (Ipsos Synovate 4 November 2011). This was likely due to a widespread perception that one's side was winning the legal argument – with those opposing the OTP's account impressed by the arguments put forward by the defence, and vice versa – and to greater public awareness of the intricacies of the Court, and of how the judges, for example, could disagree with, and even reprimand, the OTP.

Second, national averages hide significant ethnic differences, which map on to the fate of ethnic spokespeople and voting patterns. In short, co-ethnics of those indicted were the most critical, with support for the Court falling from 57 to 28 per cent amongst Kenyatta's Kikuyu community between December 2010 and February 2013, and from 29 to 22 per cent amongst Ruto's Kalenjin community. Clearly, most Kalenjin were sceptical about the Court's intervention from the outset, which was likely due to a widespread perception that 'their' leaders would be targeted on the basis that the Rift Valley had constituted the epicentre of targeted ethnic attacks against those associated with

Kibaki's PNU. However, over the same period, support for the trials increased amongst ethnic groups associated with the political opposition – from 71 to 87 per cent amongst the Luo (co-ethnics of the principal opposition leader, Raila Odinga), 74 to 87 per cent amongst 'Coastals' and 74 to 86 per cent amongst Kambas (Wolf 2015). In turn, when the final charges were dropped in April 2016, the accused and their supporters lauded the development as a sign of God's power to protect the innocent and saved (Deacon 2016), while many others believed, in line with the OTP, that witness tampering and the government's failure to hand over requested records constituted 'insurmountable hurdles' to a successful prosecution (Lynch in *Saturday Nation* 28 March 2015; *East African* 9 April 2016).

This section seeks to explain this drop in overall support levels and significant ethnic differences. It does so by looking at how arguments made as part of a 'virtual trial' reframed the ICC story, at least in the eyes of a significant number of Kenyans – and the majority of Kenyatta and Ruto's co-ethnics – as a performance of injustice. To this end, the section looks at various charges laid against the Court: namely, that it conducted poor investigations, was inept and inefficient, misunderstood events, came under undue influence, was neo-colonial and was focused on punitive justice to the detriment of peace and stability. In so doing, this section highlights how legal proceedings came to constitute a *familiar performance* by reproducing a common international scenario whereby criminal trials are 'hijacked' for vested interests, and local scenario of neo-colonialism and impunity.[2]

First, much was made by the ICC's critics of the OTP's limited investigations and heavy reliance (particularly during the initial phases) on the work of the KNCHR and the Waki Commission. These local processes were alleged to have conducted poor investigations, to have spent limited time collecting evidence and to have been 'hijacked' by a 'clique' of Nairobi-based human rights activists who wanted to pin the blame on some and exonerate their preferred leaders (interview, peace activist, Eldoret, September 1, 2011). This critique was then reinforced by rumours that Odinga's name had been edited out of the first KNCHR report (*Standard* 10 August 2012), and that his name had been included in the list of names that Waki had placed in the sealed envelope that was

---

[2] In so doing this section draws from, and expands upon an argument made in, Lynch 2014a.

later handed over to the OTP. These rumours were interwoven with claims that Odinga – as the leader of ODM, and the man who had rejected the 2007 election results and called people out onto the streets in protest – should be investigated, and that his absence, and the travails of the Ocampo Six, amounted to 'political persecution' (Mwangi 2015).

Dissatisfaction with the initial KNCHR and Waki Commission investigations proved particularly strong amongst Kalenjin in the Rift Valley, where many believed that the processes had demonised the communities as the main perpetrators of the violence without giving them a proper hearing. In this way, people complained of how the Commission had 'just passed along the highway' (interview, human rights activist, Nairobi, 19 August 2011) and only 'got information from Kikuyu and mainly IDPs' (witness at TJRC public hearings, Kericho, 19 September 2011). The implication was that, since 'Waki didn't come here ... whatever [he's argued] couldn't reflect what the community had' (interview, Kalenjin elder, Kericho, 21 September 2011).

Critiques of the ICC's investigations were not only used to question the basis and motivations behind the selection of the six names out of a list of about twenty people handed to the OTP (AI 2014: 53), they were also used to turn the OTP's claims of witness tampering on its head. The problem, it was alleged, was not that witnesses had been bribed and intimidated by the suspects and their supporters, but that witnesses had initially been coached by human rights activists to give false testimony, had then been induced and coerced by the ICC and had only later come to see the error of their ways and retract their statements. In this vein, David Hoile, in his account of the ICC as a stooge of European powers, tells the story of a former ICC witness who was relocated to Nairobi by the KNCHR and the International Medico-Legal Unit, and then to Tanzania and the Netherlands by the ICC. According to Hoile, the witness 'received periodic payments from the OTP', but after 'deep soul-searching' decided

> that his conscience could no longer allow him to stand by his false testimony. The witness subsequently accused the OTP of harassment. He alleged that court officials had made frantic telephone calls trying to get him to stand by his testimony. He further claimed that the evidence he gave was obtained from him through coercion and that some of it was falsified by the prosecutors.
> (2014: 330)

However, while Hoile's book enjoyed some publicity within Kenya, more important were periodic revelations by those who claimed to have proof of the OTP's falsification of evidence. This included a press conference by David Matsanga (a Ugandan human rights activist) in October 2013, where he called for an independent panel 'to look into serious allegations of witness procurement and fixing in Kenya cases by OTP' (*Capital FM* 31 October 2013). More scandalous still was the revelation by the MP for Gatundu South, Moses Kuria, in September 2015 that he had helped to coach witnesses as a way to 'fix' Ruto at the ICC. Kuria apologised for his role and asked others involved to come clean (*Sunday Nation* 27 September 2015).

Yet, there is likely a very different connection between witness tampering and the KNCHR and Waki Commission investigations. In short, these processes provided little in the way of witness protection (beyond the option to speak *in camera* and the anonymisation of sources), and may have 'inadvertently contributed to witness intimidation through indiscreet investigative and reporting practices' (Mahony 2010: 120). As one interviewee explained, the Waki Commission 'submissions [were] done in public with some *in camera*, so suspects and sympathisers know ... So if Waki Commission formed the basis for ICC investigations ... they become an easy target for intimidations' (civil society activist, Eldoret, 20 May 2011). This is implicitly recognised in an OTP pre-trial brief of 26 August 2013 (released to the public in January 2015) that names several former KNCHR and Waki Commission insiders as 'Defence intermediaries' in relation to attempts to bribe and intimidate witnesses in case two – for example, the brief talks of a group of men who approached three Mungiki insiders with plans to 'buy witnesses' with named intermediaries including a lawyer who had attended many of the Waki Commission's hearings (including those held *in camera*) as a victims' lawyer in 2008. The brief also posits that the infamous 'Witness Number 4' in case two – whose withdrawal of testimony prompted the collapse of Mutharua's case in 2013 – was bribed and threatened by a group of men, which included a former KNCHR staff member who had helped to set up the organisation's victims' database in early 2008 (Lynch in *Saturday Nation* 28 March 2015).

The ICC's failure to provide adequate protection for witnesses together with a host of other procedural shortcomings were then exploited by the Court's critics as evidence of ineptitude and inefficiency, as the accused, for example, submitted a series of legal applications and then chastised the Court for its slow progress (Nichols 2015).

In the face of accusations of witness tampering, and counter-accusations of coaching and perjury, ordinary people had to reach their own conclusions as to the quality of the OTP's evidence and procedures. Such assessments were shaped by individual and collective perceptions of the quality of investigations conducted, but also by understandings of the violence and evaluations of whether or not it seemed likely that the OTP was acting with ulterior motives.

Regarding people's understandings of what had occurred, it is important to recognise that the OTP's case was not self-evident. Indeed, many questioned why the Court was in Kenya, which was relatively stable and 'not a failed state' (Bishop Peter Njenga in *Daily Nation* 4 April 2012), whilst many were divided as to whether or not the wrongs committed constituted crimes against humanity, and, if they did, who bore the greatest responsibility. For example, many insisted that the violence, whilst tragic, was not equivalent to atrocities committed elsewhere in the world; that the violence was largely spontaneous or reactive; that, if anyone was to blame, it was either President Kibaki who 'stole' the election or Odinga who had called people out onto the streets; and that it was better to seek peace and reconciliation than to insist on punitive justice (Mwangi 2015).

Critically, such evaluations quickly took on a strong ethnic dimension, as 'memory poles', or divergent collective narratives of the past, as well as likely futures (cf. Payne 2009: 229), tended to support particular conclusions. In this way, the idea that targeted attacks against those perceived or known to support PNU were a spontaneous reaction to a stolen election, and that claims to the contrary were the result of bias and shoddy investigations, proved particularly prominent amongst Kalenjin interviewees in the Rift Valley.

One thing that people, including me, believe is that the violence of 2008 was as a result of what happened with the vote or rigging of the vote. By all indications Raila was winning and people nearly to the last man voted for him. So seemed outrageous that KNCHR and Waki came up with reports that organized.
(Interview, human rights defender, Kabarnet, 12 March 11)

Ocampo says that planned but, if so, where was the government and security? How can you recruit an illegal army and the government doesn't know? ... [Ocampo] didn't come to the ground to collect own evidence but used the witness of people who hate Kalenjin.
(Interview, Kalenjin IDP, Eldoret, 10 August 2011)

In such discussions, the idea of a 'Kalenjin network' – which supposedly linked leading community politicians with media personalities, elders, businesspeople, clergy and youth across large swathes of the region through an organised hierarchy that had been established prior to the 2007 election without attracting a state security response or any media attention – was either implicitly or explicitly dismissed. Instead, an alternative explanation for the violence emerged: that Kalenjin were frustrated during Kibaki's first term in office, angry that the election had been stolen, worried about what 'the Kikuyu' would take next and trained to be 'able to defend territory' as part of their traditional initiation ceremonies (interview, Kalenjin elder, Kericho, 21 September 2011). According to this logic, those named in case one were either innocent or Ruto was a mere 'foot soldier' in violence initiated by Odinga (interview, Kalenjin peace activist, Eldoret, 3 March 2011), while Sang was a 'little fellow from the radio station' in a context where the 'other vernacular radio stations were [just] as bad' (interview, Kalenjin elder, 23 February 2011).

The idea of a 'Kalenjin network' was also presented by Ruto and his allies as an indictment of the whole community, with Kalenjin 'vilified as monsters – as people who caused the violence' (interview, Kalenjin academic, Eldoret, 5 March 2011). As one clergyman explained:

Let me say the Rift Valley is fully behind Ruto as he didn't plan any war. He didn't fund anything ... Shocked that [the court is] believing lies written by liars. For us, the trial of those from the Rift Valley is a trial of the entire Rift Valley ... lie is against the entire community!

(Interview, Nakuru, 20 July 2011)

According to such logic, the community needed to come together behind the accused, and those who supported the ICC were misinformed at best, and traitors at worst. In this context, Kalenjin who were known, or who were suspected, to be helping the ICC – either as intermediaries and civic educators, or as witnesses and registered victims – faced significant harassment and intimidation from other community members and local leaders for their 'betrayal' (for example, see Lynch in *Saturday Nation* 30 May 2015). As one victim in Nakuru noted: 'I don't want to talk directly to the ICC. If you disclose anything about the violence, you could be cut off or killed. They could come to your house and attack you at night' (cited in AI 2014: 59). The result was a situation where alternative voices within the community were largely silenced, and an emergent communal narrative became predominant.

Just as many Kalenjin adhered to, or were silently resigned to, a shared understanding of the violence that absolved Ruto and Sang of blame, many Kikuyu were convinced that Kenyatta faced false charges. This account emphasised how Kenyatta had 'not [been] contesting the presidency' in 2007 (interview, Kikuyu civil society activist, Eldoret, 24 February 2013), while the country had been at war with Kikuyu targeted across the country. The violence in Nakuru and Naivasha towns in turn cast as either spontaneous – and 'a reaction to the IDP situation' (interview, Kikuyu peace activist, Nakuru, 7 March 2011) by an aggrieved community that sought revenge through retaliatory attacks (interview, Kikuyu elder, Ndeffo, 6 January 2013) – or as self-defence. The implication was that if Kenyatta was guilty of helping to organise the attacks, then he came out 'against the war and defend[ed] his people' (Kikuyu peace activist, Eldoret, 10 December 2012), was 'actually the one who caused the clashes to end' by forcing Odinga to the negotiating table (Kikuyu clergyman, Njoro, 16 December 2012) and should be applauded despite the regrettable loss of life (Kikuyu student cited by Burbidge 2014: 220). Once again, such a narrative helped to produce a repressive environment due to an overriding sense that community members should defend 'their son', and that those who supported or contributed to the OTP's case had been conned or paid, or were traitors and troublemakers.

As noted, the idea that Ocampo had relied on poor investigations and had misunderstood events was then interwoven with claims that the OTP was political and had come under undue influence from local human rights organisations, Odinga and/or 'the West'. There were several discreet, but not mutually exclusive, explanations of how this had occurred: Ocampo had been overly influenced by the flawed KNCHR and Waki Commission investigations, local human rights organisations, and influential politicians, and 'himself doesn't know Kenya' (focus group discussion, Burnt Forest, 20 May 2011); Ocampo did not care about the 'truth' and was only interested in making an 'example' out of Kenya and/or in securing a prosecution so as 'to make [the Court] legitimate as a meaningful global institution' (Wainaina in *Guardian*, 10 March 2013); and/or the Court was neo-colonial and had acted at the behest of Western powers and foreign-funded CSOs who wanted to impose an Odinga presidency onto Kenyans (Mwangi 2015).

The latter became a particularly important theme during the 2013 election campaigns, as Jubilee activists and supporters pointed to Odinga's periodic pronouncements of support for the Court, and insisted that he 'had always prayed for the "success" of the ICC process; not for justice to prevail, but as a means of sorting out his political opponents' (Miguna 2012: 394). As one interviewee posited: 'Luos the ones who started the clashes here but not touched, so if started and not on list. So people are very bitter … people see a hidden agenda, see someone that pushing that agenda' (interview with Kikuyu IDP leader, Eldoret, 28 February 2011). In turn, talk arose of the '3 O's' to refer to an alleged connection between Odinga, his co-ethnic and US president, Barack Obama, and Ocampo, as many posited 'that Raila [was] the one who spoke to Ocampo through Obama' (interview, Kikuyu clergyman, Eldoret, 19 May 2011). As the then MP for Makadara, Mike Sonko, declared at a prayer rally in Eldoret in January 2012: 'There is no way that we can let someone with a name that starts with "O" to be helped with his cousin in the US with a name that also starts with "O" to work together with Ocampo to finish our people' (cited in Omwenga in *Pambazuka News* 16 February 2012). Or as one interviewee bemoaned:

[I'm] personally annoyed with Ocampo, people listed are very innocent; when this thing began it was a reaction against the government … If it was Kibaki and Raila fine, but don't go and arrest foot soldiers … Feeling that [the] US government through Obama influenced Ocampo not to arrest anyone from that [Luo] community … Everyone was expecting Anyang[3] or Raila and then go and pick someone like Sang!
(Interview, Kalenjin peace activist, Eldoret, 3 March 2011)

As the election approached this analysis was increasingly extended to the entire Luo community though rumours, for example, of how it was Odinga and the Luo who had given evidence to Ocampo. As one interviewee bemoaned, 'Most of the witnesses Ocampo met he met them in Nairobi and Nyanza and that is the evidence that he went with. So seems the Luo are against the two communities. Why the grudge is

---

[3] Anyang Nyongo's is a prominent Luo politician who played a public role in ODM's rejection of the 2007 presidential result and in calling people out onto the streets to demonstrate in December 2007.

extended to them. That's how people are talking here' (Kikuyu peace activist, Burnt Forest, 24 February 2013). Such perceptions are important, as they reinforced a sense that the Kikuyu and Kalenjin should unite in defence of their leaders against ethnic 'others' who sought to marginalise them.

The idea that Odinga was supported by 'the West' was also linked to the notion of an 'evil society' whereby foreign-funded CSOs, which supported the ICC, were allegedly trying to 'fix' their opponents through the Court. It was also reinforced by ill-timed comments from the international community, as, at the height of the 2013 campaigns, the British High Commissioner, Christian Turner, for example, noted: 'The policy of my government remains that we do not have contact with ICC indictees unless it is essential. That is not only the policy of my government but also the policy of all the European Union and indeed most other international partners' (*The Star* 8 February 2013). A day later, the US Deputy Assistant Secretary of State for Africa, Johnny Carson, warned Kenyans of how 'choices have consequences'. He went on to note how Kenya 'lives in [an] inter-connected world' where 'people should be thoughtful about the impact of their choices on the nation and the world' (*The Star* 8 February 2013). These patronising lectures, which is what they were widely perceived to be – and, more specifically, the sound bites of 'essential contact' and 'choices have consequences' that they provided – were cited ad nauseum during the last month of the campaign to show how the West sought to impose their preferred leaders on the Kenyan people. As one interviewee noted, the 'problem lies with ICC and those comments ... that, if elect these people we won't come in to help you. Shows that campaigning for someone else' (Kikuyu peace activist, Burnt Forest, 24 February 2013). This interpretation was then reinforced by the fact that all of the ICC's cases were in Africa, while the US and UK had both committed atrocities as part of their 'war on terror', and the US had refused to sign the Rome Statute. Together with a history of colonial rule and neo-colonial relations, such hypocrisies lent some plausibility to the idea that the ICC was a neo-imperial body that sought to 'prosecute Africans but not whites' (interview, civil society activist, Eldoret, 24 February 2013).

In this context, the ghosts of colonial rule cast a strong shadow over debates, as events were interwoven with a longer history of domination and violence, struggles for independence, racism and the often hypocritical, patronising and unhelpful interventions of external actors.

These general spectres also took on a more specific form through two direct comparisons: first, between Kenyatta and his late father, Jomo Kenyatta, who had been imprisoned in the late colonial period for leading the Mau Mau rebellion. Kenyatta later went on to become the country's first president, 'father of the nation' and a respected statesman. In turn, for many, 'Uhuru's ordeal [was] a spooky echo of Jomo Kenyatta's trial and detention ... Like father, like son, the narrative went' (Wrong in *New York Times* 11 March 2013). The suggestion was that, just as '[t]he trial of Jomo Kenyatta by the colonialist did not stop him from being president ... [and] the incarceration of Nelson Mandela by the whites never stopped him from being an African leader', Kenyatta would also rise to power and be vindicated (Hon. Eugene Wamalwa cited in *Pambazuka News* 16 February 2012).

The second comparison was between Ruto's struggle and that of another famous Kalenjin, Koitalel Samoei, who had led an armed resistance against colonial rule in the early twentieth century. As Herve Maupeu notes, these 'victimisation accounts and the reference to a mythical past help[ed] build Uhuru and Ruto as heroes ... [who were] rising from the legend and destined to guide their people' (Maupeu 2014: 31).

As a result of such emotive associations, many who had initially been concerned about the implications and 'consequences' of electing ICC indictees, 'turned towards strongly defending and supporting Kenyatta', as 'the ICC debate was increasingly framed by Kenyatta and Ruto's supporters as a case of "Africa versus the West"' (Burbidge 2014: 218). In this context, a vote for Jubilee came to be seen as a way to defend Kenya's sovereignty and the continent's independence against Western interference. This message clearly appealed to a broad range of Kenyans; as one Kikuyu voter wrote on hearing of Jubilee's victory:

The US and Israel aren't even signatories of the Rome Statute, and everyone knows they have committed crimes against humanity – countless times. That's another reason why I am so proud of Uhuruto' s win – it is our voice, and Africa's, telling the West: 'F*** off, stop your double standards and hypocrisy, these are the leaders we want.'

(Cited in Burbidge 2014: 220)

This sense that a vote for the accused constituted an act of standing up against the West was reinforced after the election, as Western governments actively sought to work with the new administration. As a result, 'essential contact' was revealed to have an extremely loose interpretation when Kenyatta, for example, travelled to the UK in May 2013 for an international conference on Somalia. Or when Obama 'personally called Kenyatta after the Westgate attack and "reaffirmed the United States' partnership" with Kenya' (Brown & Raddatz 2014: 55). The implication was that, as a regional hub and neighbour to Somalia (the home of Al-Shabaab), Kenya was just too important to the West as a business, development and security partner to allow ICC indictments, and reports of witness tampering and non-compliance, to trouble bilateral relations.

This links to a final point, namely that, as the cases went on, the ICC's intervention was increasingly presented as a threat – not only to the country's sovereignty, but to regional peace and stability (Mwangi 2015). Thus, in the lead-up to the 2013 election, and amidst widespread fears of a repetition of the post-election violence (Chapter 2), the Jubilee campaign presented Kenyatta and Ruto not as the problem, but as the country's potential saviours who could unite Kenyans (and particularly the previously 'warring' Kalenjin and Kikuyu communities) and ensure peace. This message proved extremely appealing and offered many Kenyans exactly what they wanted – a way for Kenyans to 'come together' in the interests of peace (Lynch 2014a; also Deacon 2015; Mwangi 2015).

This image was then contrasted with a fear of what would happen if the duo were arrested. As one Kalenjin man explained, if Ruto was convicted the reaction

[w]ill be against government and neighbours as saying who stole the vote – a Kikuyu – and now people taken to The Hague because of these Kikuyu and so reaction against Kikuyu and government, and can't reach government so will be straight to Kikuyu ... if Ruto [arrested], people will fight.
(Interview, IDP from Burnt Forest, Eldoret, 10 August 2011)

At the same time, Odinga was presented as unpredictable and violent – as the one who had stirred up anti-Kikuyu sentiment during the 2007 campaigns, promised to reject defeat, and called his supporters out onto the street in 2007, and the person who might do the same in 2013. In this way, one civil society activist explained how,

when [Odinga] stood up [at a meeting in Kericho during the 2007 campaigns,] he said whatever happens we'll take the government ... said be ready, if these people do something with the election then we'll come out in mass action to claim rights ... said we're going to fight it ... even if we die we're going to take the leadership.
(Interview, Eldoret, 24 February 2013)

Given such memories, Jubilee leapt on any controversial comments by Odinga, such as an interview with the *Financial Times* published two days before the polls in which Odinga warned that the public reaction to a contested election could be 'worse than last time' (1 March 2013).

Once Kenyatta and Ruto were inaugurated, it was then argued that the duo needed to focus all their attention on security and development, and should not be distracted by defending themselves against unsubstantiated claims in a foreign court. Particularly significant in this regard was an increase in terrorist attacks and, in particular, the attack on Westgate Mall in downtown Nairobi in September 2013 in which at least sixty-seven people were killed. The attack coincided with the onset of Ruto's trial, whereupon he was permitted to travel back to Kenya to attend to the tragedy. Westgate thus brought the tension between running a country and standing trial into sharp relief – a tension that the duo and their allies continued to take advantage of until the cases collapsed two and half years later. As Kenyatta noted when he temporarily appointed Ruto as the acting president when travelling to The Hague for a Status Conference in October 2014, 'It should be clear, therefore, that this government has enough on its hands fighting poverty, securing the peace and building regional integration to be focused on any other matter' (cited in *Capital FM* 6 October 2014). At the same time, the neo-Pentecostal-inspired prayer rallies that had begun in 2011 continued until the final 'thanksgiving prayers', which followed Ruto and Sang's reprieve in April 2016. These public displays of support, and 'new political language . . . [of] prophetism and redemption' (Maupeu 2014: 33) were critical, as they helped to cast the accused in the popular imaginary as men of God who were saved, cleansed and blessed, and as leaders with the capacity to forge forward with development and peacebuilding (Deacon 2015 & 2016; Maupeu 2014).

The argument that the ICC was a threat to sovereignty, security and development was then linked to a call not for punitive justice, but for reconciliation. As Eugene Wamalwa, a Luhya politician who supported Kenyatta and Ruto noted in early 2012, 'This country has been through difficult times and needs healing. This healing will not come from the International Criminal Court, but from forgiveness and reconciliation' (cited in *Sunday Nation* 1 April 2012). In this, much was made of other countries around the world – most notably South Africa – where governments had opted to focus on reconciliation and forgiveness rather than long-winded, uncertain and divisive prosecutions (for example, Paisley in *The New York Times* 16 March 2012), as Jubilee revived a long-standing peace versus justice debate as a final attack on the ICC's efforts.

3.4 Conclusions: Performances of Injustice and Impunity

With the ICC everything changed when the names came out.
> (Interview, civil society activist, Nairobi, 25 August 2011)

A clear distinction between law and politics is always a difficult illusion to maintain. However, the ICC's intervention in Kenya reminds us of the particular difficulties of staging such a performance when critics can point to prosecutorial discretion in the context of a court that is trying to build itself as a global institution amidst a long history of (neo) colonialism. At the same time, it reveals how an exaggerated attack on such an illusion can be 'hijacked' through a 'virtual trial' and become an effective political tool, as Kenyatta and Ruto's indictments were used as the basis for a new political coalition and successful presidential campaign. This reinterpretation of the ICC as a performance of neo-colonialism, injustice and threat to the country's peace and stability called upon the ghosts of colonialism and recurrent election-related violence to pose a number of arguments. Most notable was the ICC's alleged failure to confront those most responsible because of poor investigations, ineptitude, political influence, bias, vested interests and a misunderstanding of what had occurred, and an over-emphasis on punitive justice to the neglect of peace and reconciliation. This portrait then became part of a broader campaign and a subsequent narrative of regime legitimisation, whereby 'Uhuruto' presented themselves as leaders from the digital generation who would invest in development, protect the country's sovereignty against the ICC and 'the West', and ensure peace and stability.

This interpretation was assisted by the way in which – at different points in time – an increasing number of people became sceptical about the potential outcomes and gains of the Court's intervention. Thus, while many had initially believed that the ICC could help to tackle a culture of impunity and provide some form of justice, attitudes gradually shifted. For some, this came as a result of the names and a feeling that the OTP had focused on the wrong people. For others, it grew as they became increasingly aware of the OTP's legal argument, which did not seem to fit with their own understanding of what had happened. For others, it came after the 2013 election amidst a feeling that the country should face forwards and focus on development and security. And for others, it came as pressure built for a deferral, witnesses fell by the wayside, concern grew that either the cases would collapse or that Kenyatta and Ruto would stop collaborating, and they came to feel that it was better to 'move on' and 'forget' than to continue with such seemingly doomed prosecutions. Critically, this shift included many of those who were initially amongst the ICC's most ardent supporters, which further weakened the OTP's position and reduced the likelihood of sourcing additional witnesses. In this vein, a registered ICC victim with whom I spoke in January 2014 explained how he might have agreed to act as a witness, but would no longer consider it. The reason: '[I]t was the suffering of victims ... me, I've received threats and no-one listens ... I've come to think that it's better that [the cases] end and [that we] move on without hoping for assistance [from the ICC]' (see Lynch in *Saturday Nation* 30 May 2015).

This is important as it means that many Kenyans were unconvinced by Jubilee's reinterpretation of the ICC as a performance of injustice, and continued to believe that Kenyatta and/or Ruto were guilty and that the charges against them had only been dropped because of witness tampering and partial compliance. For these citizens, the collapse of the cases was a performance of impunity in action: the accused had mobilised their communities against the Court and used their position as establishment elites and then as the government to ensure that no-one dared to give witness against them.

Moreover, even Jubilee's supporters were not necessarily convinced by every aspect of the alliance's reinterpretation of the Court's intervention. For example, it was possible for Kenyans to accept that the Court was neo-colonial and that the West was interfering in local politics without thinking that the duo were entirely innocent. As one Kikuyu lady in Nakuru County explained to me two days before the 2013 election, she believed that Kenyatta and Ruto were guilty of organising violence in 2007–8, but she was still going to vote for them as they had been overtaken by 'the devil' at that time and were now cleansed (interview, 2 March 2013). In turn, while many Kikuyu believed that Kenyatta was innocent of crimes against humanity, many did not feel the same way about Ruto, and vice versa for many Kalenjin.

Indeed, popular interpretations of events included a fairly widespread sense that there likely was some intimidation and bribery of actual or potential ICC witnesses. This included a perception that some of the alleged murders of witnesses were 'so brutal to serve as a lesson to others' (interview, journalist, Nairobi, 2 May 2011). The possibility that Kenyatta and Ruto, or their allies, had used their extensive wealth and connections to find, and then effectively bribe and intimidate, witnesses under ICC protection served as a strong reminder – as Joost Fontein has argued with respect to rumours in contemporary Zimbabwe – of the state's 'profound capacity for violence' (2014: 132) – a suggestion of power that reinforced 'the omnipotent presence of [this political elite], and [their] ability to deploy devastating "state power" at will' (Fontein 2009: 388). As a result, rumours of intimidation and bribery not only served to discourage potential witnesses and to help silence those who disagreed with the collective narratives constructed, but they also fostered a sense of an entrenched culture of impunity that even the ICC was powerless to address.

This was a heavy blow for many including those who had seen the ICC as their only hope for punitive and reparative justice (AI 2014). However, not only did the ICC cases collapse, but the process also made domestic prosecutions even more difficult as potential witnesses feared to speak out, and the government sought to 'convey a message to the international community that there were no crimes against humanity' (Asaala 2015: 360). This raised questions about justice for the post-election violence, but also the reality of an ongoing culture of impunity and fears of the possibility of a further instrumentalisation of violence at some point in the future (cf. AI 2014: 48–39).

The Kenyan cases also had a significant impact on the ICC. Shortcomings with the case strengthened calls for changes in the way that the Court works – from better witness protection to the need for the Court to look at cases outside of the African continent (Vilmer 2016). Second, Kenya's offensive against the Court accelerated an 'African rejection' of it (Vilmer 2016: 1322) reflected, for example, in the decision of South Africa, Burundi and Gambia to announce their withdrawal from the Rome Statute in October 2016. Third, the cases provided an example of how the rich and powerful can evade the Court's reach. Indeed, according to Rashid Abdi from the International Crisis Group, 'Kenya has given the world a rulebook on how to beat the ICC': play the 'victimization' card, undertake 'a diplomatic offensive' and interfere with witnesses (summarised in Vilmer 2016: 1326–1327).

The implication is that, even many Kenyans and non-Kenyans who were pleased or relieved when the cases finally came to an end in 2016 – either because they felt that the Court's intervention was unwarranted, neo-colonial, unhelpful or ultimately doomed to fail – watched the way in which the cases fell apart after Kenyatta and Ruto assumed power amidst claims of witness intimidation, and were struck by the way in which power had been effectively wielded to save the duo. For these individuals, together with those who were convinced of the accused's guilt, this series of events constituted a performance of impunity, or of the untouchability of a protected elite. The example to the world was thus not of the reach of international law, but of a reality where power trumps the law. This example came as a surprise to many. However, in fact, such subversion of international justice by domestic elites is a common theme of international criminal trials around the world (for example, see Leclercq 2017; Peskin 2008; Subotić 2009), while, for the majority of Kenyans, the Court's failings sat neatly within a pre-existing worldview of an untouchable elite. The latter then only further reinforced by the way in which the TJRC process played out.

PART II

A Post–South African Truth Commission

While no one seemed to be able to agree on exactly what genre of performance the [South African Truth and Reconciliation Commission] was – ritual, theatre, drama, bioscope, or circus – most seemed to agree that it was a performance.

(Cole 2010: 27)

There have been more than forty truth commissions convened around the world from 1974 to date. Of all these bodies, the South African TRC – which was mandated to investigate gross violations of human rights between 1 March 1960 and 10 May 1994, and which was established by an act of parliament in 1995 and concluded in 2002 – is the best known, and the most discussed in academic texts, novels, films and plays. This notoriety stems from the Commission's much debated role in the facilitation of South Africa's transition from apartheid to multi-party democracy – a debate that is linked (in large part) to the Commission's charismatic leadership; power to offer amnesty for politically motivated crimes in exchange for full disclosure, but only recommend reparations; and contested legacy. However, it is also due to the TRC's innovative use of public hearings.

Early truth commissions did not hold public hearings and were largely fact-finding bodies that 'sought to make leaders morally and politically accountable, to expose abuses that had been obscured by a miasma of lies, and to acknowledge the stories of individuals whose own realities had been denied' (Shaw 2007: 190). In contrast, the TRC largely became known to people through hearings convened by the human rights violations and amnesty committees. These forums provided a stage for victims, perpetrators, parties, organisations and institutions to tell their personal or 'narrative truths'. This process was meant to be cathartic for those who participated, and to contribute to reconciliation and nation-building. The idea was that confrontation of the past through confession, or through a Freudian-style 'talking cure', would help to restore people's humanity and provide 'a means to 'unwrite the future' [by preventing] that future becoming a compulsive repetition of the trauma of the past' (Sey 1998: 7–8). More specifically, it was suggested that public truth-telling – as a form of performed interconnectedness – could help to heal victims and foster a new inclusive sense of South African-ness as a nation in need of reconciliation and committed to constitutionalism, human rights and democracy (Wilson 2001: 13–18). Public truth-telling presented as an event that would help to heal individual victims, restore perpetrators back into a community, facilitate a shift from a society wounded by gross human rights abuses and historical injustices to a human rights conscious state, and deepen a democratic transition (de Gruchy 2002; Tutu 1999).

Most post–South African truth commissions have held public hearings in line with the South African model (Hayner 2011: 219), even as South Africans have become increasingly disillusioned with, and critical of the South African experience, and its legacies (Bevernage 2012; Gibson 2002; Mamdani 2002). This dichotomy between myth and reality is due, at least in part, to the transitional justice industry's need for a success story. But it is also due to the mediatised version of the TRC that was relayed to the world, which provided evidence of trauma, catharsis, apology and forgiveness, and a 'beacon of hope'. The promise: if a truth commission 'can help South Africa to overcome its differences, if a South African phoenix can rise from the ashes of apartheid, if a "rainbow nation" can be successfully created, then ... reconciliation, anywhere, is possible' (Jenkins 2002: 241).[1]

Yet, post–South African truth commissions have not been mere replicas of the TRC. Instead, they have learned lessons and have responded to a dynamic international context, with no post–South African commission, for example, offering amnesty for gross human rights violations (Hayner 2011: 93). National contexts have also ensured that each truth commission has had a different budget, leadership, staff, mandate, structure, working practices, media coverage and impact (Hayner 2011: 256–286).

The Kenyan TJRC was no different. The Commission was clearly informed by the TRC's particular blend of 'church, court, and couch'

---

[1] Catherine Jenkins, who writes on the transfer of this 'model' to East Timor, is herself critical of this 'myth' of the South African example and of the toolkit approach to transitional justice that it has inadvertently encouraged.

(Posel 2008: 136), and by an assumption that 'as long as we do not allow people to vent their grievances, and have them addressed, we're sitting on a time bomb' (interview, TJRC statement taker, Kabarnet, 12 March 2011). However, in contrast to the South African TRC, the TJRC ran parallel to ICC investigations; conducted adversely mentioned persons (AMPs), rather than amnesty, hearings; did more to increase the participation and voice of women; recognised a wider range of injustices, including economic crimes; and pushed for a more comprehensive form of justice (Slye 2017).

Nevertheless, unlike the South African TRC, which is generally accepted to have at least made a short-term contribution to a sense of transition and to have helped limit the range of permissible lies about the past, the Kenyan TJRC was formed following a short (but intense) political crisis and quickly faced a credibility crisis. It is too early to evaluate the long-term impact of the Kenyan TJRC and its final report, and it has often taken years for truth commission recommendations to be acted upon (Hayner 2011: 163). Instead, chapters within Part II analyse the TJRC as an example of a post–South African truth commission, which, while unique, shares many commonalities with recent truth commissions elsewhere in the world. In so doing, this part highlights how the TJRC, as a performative process, failed to live up to the myth of the South African model, revealed a grand narrative of ongoing suffering, was undermined and used, and helped to reproduce some of the factors it was ostensibly designed to counter – from an embedded culture of impunity to common gender roles. In so doing, the analysis reveals common problems with truth commissions, which, while they often have lofty goals, are unable to resolve the issues that they document even in conducive contexts. However, contexts rarely are conducive with subversion by political elites and a lack of public confidence serving to produce familiar performances that can help to sustain the status quo. The final chapter then turns to the implications of such legacies for reconciliation.

4 | The Truth, Justice and Reconciliation Commission
A Sense of Once-Againness

> People are comparing us with South Africa ... but Kenya is completely different ... I don't think we are in a transition; we are still in a struggle.
> (Interview, TJRC statement taker, Kabarnet, 12 March 2011)

On 27 April 1994, South Africa underwent a seemingly miraculous transition after a political settlement heralded the country's first multiracial polls and the election of President Nelson Mandela and the African National Congress (ANC). Not only did the country escape from a 'potential bloodbath' (Boraine 2000a: 174), but Mandela also reached out to all South Africans through the formation of an interim coalition government, new federal structures and his own example of reconciliation (Graybill 2002: 11; Gibson 2004: 145). This 'miracle' was closely associated with the establishment of the TRC, which, 'led by a figure of unquestioned moral authority, former Archbishop Desmond Tutu, was explicitly dedicated to building a culture of human rights and an inclusive "rainbow nation"' (Wilson 2001: 223). As Deborah Posel summarises:

> The rather more troubled realpolitik of South Africa's democratization aside, its mythic resonances in popular imaginations across the globe were celebratory, replete with hope. In a world mired in war and sometimes intractable violence, here was a historical narrative that told of the redemptive power of a human rights agenda animated by a spirit of 'national reconciliation'. And in this story, the South African Truth and Reconciliation Commission (TRC) loomed large, both as historical author and muse and as a figure of the reason and compassion that was written into the story of the country's democratization. (2008: 119)

Over a decade later in Kenya, President Kibaki and opposition leader Raila Odinga signed an agreement that ended a period of unprecedented violence, created a coalition government and paved the way for the formation of a TJRC. The latter was established through an act of parliament in December 2008; commissioners were appointed in August 2009; and the Commission started a two-year mandate in early November 2009. In August 2011, the Commission was awarded a six-month extension and, after successful applications for two further extensions, submitted a final report on 21 May 2013 – just six weeks after Kenyatta and Ruto were inaugurated as the country's new president and deputy president, respectively.

The TJRC was inspired by, and clearly sought to learn from, the South African experience. However, it was born in a very different environment, had a broader focus and mandate, and was immediately mired in controversy. Indeed, the first year of the Commission's initial two-year mandate was almost entirely absorbed by a credibility crisis that surrounded the Commission's chairman, Ambassador Bethuel Kiplagat, which prompted various stakeholders (including the internationally revered Tutu)[1] to call for Kiplagat to resign or for the TJRC to be disbanded. On 2 November 2010 Kiplagat finally stepped aside, paving the way for a special tribunal to investigate allegations of a conflict of interest, and was subsequently summoned before the TJRC as an adversely mentioned person (AMP). However, in January 2012, the embattled chair returned to head the Commission after the tribunal's time had lapsed, whereupon, his fellow commissioners changed the locks to the office and ordered security to deny him entry (interview, TJRC department head, Nairobi, 6 March 2012). Kiplagat finally returned to work after the High Court confirmed his position and it was agreed that he would neither 'be involved in the writing of the final report', nor would he 'be allowed to review those sections of the report in which he had a conflict of interest' (TJRC vol. 1 2013: 139). Kiplagat was then summoned for the second time as an AMP, while the TJRC's final report – which Kiplagat signed and presented to President Kenyatta, but apparently had not read (interview, TJRC department head, Nairobi, 27 August 2013) – recommended he be deemed unfit to hold public office. Kiplagat subsequently questioned the veracity of the report before becoming largely silent on the matter of its implementation

---

[1] http://blog.marsgroupkenya.org/2010/02/25/desmond-tutu-and-other-international-justice-figures-call-on-ambassador-bethuel-kiplagat-kenyan-tjrc-chair-to-step-down/ <last accessed 14 June 2015>.

until his death in July 2017. As Christopher Gitari notes, 'Kiplagat's performance ... turned the process into a farce' (2014: 3).

This sketch of the TJRC as a commission established in the absence of any real transition, of a chairman who stood aside and bore witness before stern-faced colleagues (and was then recommended for lustration), and of a report that was handed over to a president who still faced charges of crimes against humanity, stands in stark contrast to the 'miracle story' of South Africa's democratic transition and of Tutu's strong 'political and spiritual leadership' (Graybill 2002: 178). This chapter analyses these differences. More specifically, it looks at how, while the TRC contributed to an initial sense of transition and raised hopes of possible transformation, the TJRC was widely understood as a *familiar performance* that fell short of the TRC's mythic status. Indeed, like many other truth commissions, the TJRC became *just* another commission of inquiry that helped to confirm the country's long history of impunity – the TJRC thus constituting a sense of 'once-againness' or a scenario, which, rather than being a mere copy or duplication of earlier events, conjured up past situations (Taylor 2003: 32).

This chapter starts with an overview of the establishment of the South African TRC. It then moves on to the TJRC's mandate, Kenya's long history of commissions of inquiry, the context in which the TJRC was initially considered and then introduced, the chairman debacle and, finally, the uneven support provided by prominent civil society organisations (CSOs). The analysis reveals how truth commissions should not be regarded as a discrete tool that can applied in different contexts with the same effect, and how more attention must be given to local political dynamics (Bosire & Lynch 2014: 256). This includes the level of popular political scepticism, commissioners' reputations, and the capacity, concerns and interests of local CSOs. In short, truth commissions are shown to be part confidence trick: some of their objectives are only possible to achieve (or approach) if enough people have sufficient faith in a Commission's impartiality, relevance and power. Subsequent chapters then discuss in more detail how the TJRC, like other truth commissions around the world, fell short of a performance of transformation and actually reproduced some of the dynamics that it was ostensibly designed to counter.

4.1 South Africa's 'Miracle' and the TCR

The story of South Africa's transformation is many things, but above all, it is a story of hope.

(Marks 2000: 181)

Tutu begins his memoir of the TRC by recalling the historic moment that marked the country's political transition. For Tutu, 27 April 1994, 'was the day for which we had waited many long years, the day for which the struggle against apartheid had been waged ... The day had finally dawned ... when we could vote for the first time in a democratic elections in the land of our birth' (1999: 1). Tutu suggests that the long hours South Africans spent queuing to cast their ballot helped them 'to find one another' and to realise 'what we had been at such pains to tell them, that they shared a common humanity' (Tutu 1999: 4).

It is insightful that Tutu opts to start his account in this way. On the one hand, he contextualises the TRC in a history of repression, an uncertain transition and nascent democratisation that is implicitly concerned, first and foremost, with political rights rather than socio-economic conditions. On the other hand, he hints at a shared need for healing and for a reinterpretation of the nation's values from the separation of apartheid to a realisation of common wounds and humanity.

These same ideas were central to Tutu's conceptualisation of ubuntu – a philosophy that 'says I am human only because you are human' and, thus, '[i]f I undermine your humanity, I dehumanize myself' (cited in Wilson 2001: 9) – which emphasised people's intertwined humanity whereby even supporters of apartheid stood as 'victims of the vicious system' (Tutu 1999: 35). Together with Christian confessional and psychoanalytic traditions, these ideas underpinned the TRC's emphasis on public hearings and 'performed witnessing' (Cole 2010: 162). The idea was that '[t]he humanity of the victims and perpetrators who appeared before the TRC was affirmed by the presence of other human beings who were in the hall or listening in on radios or watching on their television sets from home. This experience of national witnessing implicated everyone who experienced it' (Cole 2010: 162). The significance of South Africa's public hearings is discussed in Chapter 5. Suffice it to note here that, while imperfect, they captured public imaginations and contributed to a sense of disjuncture and newness.

The TRC was also the product of the realpolitik of transition: it was born of a negotiated settlement that often looked close to collapse, and which – amidst an upsurge of violence (particularly 'black-on-black' violence between supporters of Mandela's ANC and Buthelezi's Inkatha Freedom Party) – agreed to a political amnesty. In this context, the TRC offered amnesty for politically motivated crimes in exchange for full disclosure, victims were given an opportunity to tell their stories and the TRC's Reparations and Rehabilitation Committee was tasked with designing a reparations programme. However, while truth-telling and reparations in the absence of prosecutions was initially presented as a strategic compromise in an 'imperfect world' (Tutu 1999: 229), with time, it was increasingly portrayed as a superior form of justice (Boraine 2000a: 427). More specifically, the shortcomings of criminal trials in a discredited judicial system were emphasised: they could retraumatise victims, fail due to insufficient evidence and uncover only limited truths (Boraine 2000a: 27–28). At the same time, enthusiasts lauded the benefits of truth-telling as a process that could help acknowledge victims' suffering and the damage done to perpetrators, and encourage popular recognition of people's common humanity (Boraine 2000a; Tutu 1999).

However, even according to these more idealistic framings, the TRC was cast as a beginning rather than as an end point. The hope was that, by acknowledging wrongs done and by recognising a shared humanity of frailty and compassion, the TRC could help foster 'a commitment to coexistence' (Boraine 2000a: 359) and open the doors to further change. As J. W. de Gruchy argued: 'The truth liberates and sets free, the truth heals and restores, but only when the truth is lived and done. Truth serves the cause of reconciliation and justice only when it leads to a genuine *metanoia*, that is, a turning around, a breaking with an unjust past, and a moving towards a new future' (2002: 164). In the post-apartheid context, it was widely accepted that such a *metanoia* hinged on economic justice through reparations and far-reaching redistributive and social justice programmes (Boraine 2000a; Orr 2000; Tutu 1999). In the words of the Commission: 'Reconciliation requires a commitment, especially by those who have benefited and continue to benefit from past discrimination, to the transformation of unjust inequalities and dehumanizing poverty' (cited in Hayner 2011: 190). The Commission clearly failed to initiate such a transformation. Instead, it initiated a slow and limited reparations programme for registered victims, and did little to alter deeply entrenched socio-economic inequalities or to eliminate violence (Gready 2011; Stanley 2001). At one level, the TRC failed due to its narrow focus on individual bodily integrity violations to the neglect of apartheid 'as experienced by the broad masses of the people of South Africa' (Mamdani 2002: 38). At another level, the TRC failed due to the difficulties of bringing about such radical change, limited political will and opposition from key stakeholders (Boraine 2000a: 200; Sarkin 1996).

Despite such problems, there is a general consensus that extensive coverage of the TRC helped to ensure, at the very least, that the vast majority of South Africans learnt of the Commission's work and some of its most startling revelations. It is also clear that the TRC managed to capture popular imaginations, and that it did so, in large part, by offering a vision of a new inclusive South Africa. Such early and guarded optimism drew upon the political transition, Mandela and Tutu's leadership, the extended and participatory discussions that led to the Commission's establishment (Graybill 2002: 3; Hayner 2011: 27–28) and the iconic moments that emerged from the human rights violations and amnesty hearings that were relayed to the country's citizens through print, television and radio media.

This sense of potential was clearly both a product of and a motivation for public engagement, and is thus central to understanding the TRC's achievements and its mythic international status. However, most other truth commissions have not helped to embody a similar sense of transition (for example, see Kelsall [2005] on the Sierra Leonean TRC; Steinberg [2010] on the Liberian TRC). This includes the Kenyan TJRC, which, during its lifespan, more commonly inspired a sense of familiarity, repetition and continuity.

4.2 Kenya's Truth, Justice and Reconciliation Commission[2]

[W]e must as a nation address the past in order to prepare for the future by building a democratic society based on the rule of law.

(Kenya 2008d: 36)

The TJRC Act of December 2008 mandated the Commission to 'promote peace, justice, national unity, healing, and reconciliation among

---

[2] This section and Sections 4.4 and 4.6 draw in part from Bosire & Lynch (2014).

the people of Kenya' (Kenya 2008d: 41). To this end, the TJRC was tasked with establishing an historical record of violations and abuses of human rights and economic rights by both state and non-state actors from the time of the country's independence in December 1963 to the end of the post-election crisis in February 2008. Violations to be investigated included acts of state repression, irregular land acquisition, perceptions of economic marginalisation and causes of political violence and ethnic tension. The Commission was also mandated to record relevant antecedents and contexts, and the 'perspectives of the victims, and motives and perspectives of the persons responsible for commission of the violations' (Kenya 2008d: 42); to conduct research and investigations, collect statements and memoranda, and hold public hearings; and to publish a final report with recommendations. The latter could include prescriptions on the implementation of previous commission of inquiry reports, constitutional and institutional reform, further investigations, prosecutions, lustration, reparations and amnesty for non-gross human rights violations.

This would have been an impossible task for any truth commission. However, the TJRC was soon troubled by a vicious cycle of limited political will, funding delays, a credibility crisis around the chairman, limited support from CSOs, critical media coverage and a sceptical domestic and international audience. However, before turning to this cycle, this section provides an overview of the Commission's makeup, financial situation and principal activities.

The TJRC was initially headed by Ambassador Bethuel Kiplagat, who was supported by a vice-chair (Betty Murungi), three international commissioners (Prof. Ronald Slye [American], Ambassador Berhanu Dinka [Ethiopian] and Judge Gertrude Chawatama [Zambian]), and four national commissioners (Tecla Wanjala, Prof. Tom Ojienda, Margaret Shava and Major General [Rtd] Ahmed Sheikh Farah). Yet, for most of its life, the Commission had only seven commissioners after Murungi resigned in April 2010 and Kiplagat stepped aside between November 2010 and January 2012. Following Murungi's resignation, Wanjala was promoted to deputy chair and then to acting chair for the duration of Kiplagat's absence.

Four of the commissioners were legal professionals: there was a high court judge (Chawatama), three lawyers (Ojienda, Murungi and Shava) and two law professors (Ojienda and Slye). They were joined by others with a peacebuilding background: Kiplagat as a civil servant and practitioner in the East African region, Chawatama as a practitioner in Kenya and Farah as a former navy officer with some relevant training. This legalistic makeup contributed to the TJRC's quasi-judicial approach, which was criticised by some. This included Kiplagat who held that the Commission should have been more informal, focused less on establishing facts, made greater use of traditional conflict resolution mechanisms and prioritised reconciliation (interview, Nairobi, 9 August 2011).

Once appointed, complaints soon arose about the commissioners' backgrounds. In addition to Kiplagat, this included speculation on Shava's appointment, given rumours of her family's connections with the Kikuyu establishment; while Farah's service in the armed forces was a source of further consternation. It was even alleged (rather bizarrely as a naval officer) that Farah had been involved in military operations in northern Kenya. However, the main protagonist later admitted to a case of mistaken identity and publicly apologised to the Commission (TJRC public hearing, Nairobi, 21 March 2012).

Besides Kiplagat (who was soon the focus of a credibility crisis) and Murungi (who resigned before the Commission had hired most of its staff), none of the commissioners were well known. Moreover, besides Murungi, who had long worked on human rights and transitional justice and had worked as a consultant for the Sierra Leonean TRC, and Slye, who had worked as a consultant for the South African TRC and published a number of academic articles on the same (Slye 1997; 1998/9; 2000), commissioners also lacked a background in transitional justice and none of them were known by Kenyans to have suffered for a political cause. This reinforced popular scepticism, especially amongst prominent human rights activists, of the Commission's motivations, capacity and likely impact. It also ensured that the TJRC lacked a clear moral voice. In the words of one peacebuilder: the 'image of success [has] to do with a number of things including the nature of the transition ... and then hav[ing] iconic figures that can inspire people. We don't have that' (interview, Nairobi, 17 March 2011).

The commissioners' personalities nevertheless made their mark. Chawatama was the most explicitly religious in her work and often included references to the Bible and healing power of prayer in her responses to witness testimony at public hearings. Together with Wanjala, she was also the most emotional. In contrast, Farah tended to maintain a more bureaucratic approach, while Ojienda often probed witnesses for further details in a style reminiscent of legal questioning. Indeed, Ojienda was by far the most intrusive, asking outright, for example, for an apology from the man who had brought a conflict of interest case against Farah at a thematic hearing in Nairobi (fieldwork notes, 21 March 2012), and probing a police shooting victim in Kisumu on his wife's response to his consequent inability to 'perform' sexually (TJRC public hearing, 14 July 2011). In turn, Shava and Slye tended to adopt an approach that lay between Chawatama's overt empathy and Ojienda's courtroom manner, while Dinka exuded the quiet confidence of a diplomat and neighbour who appeared particularly unimpressed with Kenyans' ethnically exclusive narratives of autochthonous belonging as true 'locals'.

Besides the commissioners, the TJRC employed 150 staff – significantly less than the 300 and 500 employed by the South African and Peruvian truth commission's, respectively (Hayner 2011: 213) – and 304 statement takers (TJRC vol. 1 2013: 31). However, hiring and training was delayed by financial problems. In the first fiscal year (2009–2010), the government allocated less than 16 per cent of the Commission's budget, while, during the second half of 2010, commissioners were wholly dependent on ad hoc monthly advances from the Ministry of Justice. The financial situation improved in 2011 when the Commission was allocated Ksh 650 million against a proposed budget of Ksh 1.2 billion. However, the Commission still suffered a shortfall, while resources remained under the control of its parent ministry (TJRC vol. 1 2013: 144–146). International donors also proved reluctant to make up for the shortfall; and only the German development agency, GiZ, and the United Nations Development Programme (UNDP) offered substantial technical and financial support during the Commission's lifespan (Bosire & Lynch 2014: 275).

This financial situation had serious implications for the Commission's work. Commissioners initially had to operate with a skeletal staff, enjoying neither a secretary nor a secretariat, with only seventeen support staff seconded to it from the Ministry of Justice (TJRC vol. 1 2013: 30). In February 2010, the Commission started its own recruitment exercise, but most departments – with the exception of communications, which started in early 2010 – only commenced their operations around September 2010 (TJRC vol. 1

2013: 31). This had a knock-on effect on all aspects of the Commission's work.

The Commission had to cut short its provincial outreach and familiarisation meetings after conducting such meetings in only two provinces. The Commission was unable to conduct intensive training sessions for Statement Takers ... The Commission's launch of public hearings was delayed ... [which] had an adverse 'ripple effect' on the general Work Plan of the Commission ... [and] contributed significantly to the Commission's requests for extension[s].

(TJRC vol. 1 2013: 147)

Once hired, staff were divided between eight departments: Finance and Administration, Legal Affairs, Investigations, Research, Civic Education, Communications, Special Support, and Information and Documentation. Staff worked incredibly hard and many displayed physical and psychological symptoms of stress and secondary trauma – from headaches and high blood pressure to depression and heightened anxiety.

One of the first activities was to hire and train statement takers to collect statements and memorandum, while the civic education team later conducted stakeholders' meetings with members of CSOs, elders, and youth and women's representatives across the country. The investigations team expended much of its time and energy looking into potential 'window cases' for the public hearings, with final cases selected by the Commission's legal team. The information and documentation manager ran a small library and burgeoning archive, and oversaw the coding and data entry of statements into a specialised database. The research team provided a series of in-house reports to help inform the selection of 'window cases' that mapped abuses by region, and also led on the writing up the final report. Finally, the communications team responded to inquiries and sought to publicise the Commission's work, while the special support unit helped to develop policies and recommendations for 'vulnerable groups' (operationalised as women, children, the disabled and marginalised communities); provided logistical and psychological support to witnesses who appeared at any of the Commission's hearings; and helped organise thematic hearings on the plight and rights of vulnerable groups (TJRC vol. 1 2013: viii). In addition, TJRC staff ran a number of lower profile events. These included a series of reconciliation workshops and eighty-one focus group discussions on economic marginalisation across the country (TJRC vol. 1 2013: 89 and 116–118).

This work bore fruits. The team 'collected the largest number of statements of any truth commission in history ... over 40,000' (TJRC vol. 1 2013: iii); held a series of hearings at which 'a hunger, a desire, even a demand for the injustices of the past to be addressed' was powerfully expressed (TJRC vol. 1 2013: iii); and produced a final report that runs to more than 2,000 pages. This report provides a detailed overview of historical injustices and a litany of recommendations. It was also relatively well received by transitional justice experts and interested CSOs and victims' groups, many of whom saw the report as a way to lobby the government for full implementation of the new constitution, institutional reforms, and punitive and reparative justice (Chapter 9).

However, almost five years after the report had been submitted, it had not even been discussed in parliament. This was despite the fact that, according to the TJRC Act, implementation was to start within six months, and all recommendations were to be implemented (Kenya 2008d). The rest of this chapter examines the scepticism that surrounded the Commission from the outset – namely, that it represented repetition, continuity and impunity, rather than transition, change and justice. These fears were then reinforced, as subsequent chapters will show, by limited media coverage of the Commission's hearings and final report, the unwillingness of AMPs to admit wrongdoing, and the non-implementation of its recommendations. All of these problems, while different in their precise details, are common to post–South African truth commissions around the world. In turn, these chapters highlight both how truth commissions are not always useful and, when introduced, need to be more realistic in what they can achieve, pay more attention to local contexts and how they will be received and perceived, and recognise the complex ways in which violent and unjust pasts actually persist.

4.3 A History of Commissions of Inquiry

People are still not sure that information [shared with the TJRC] will lead to action because [we have] a history of commissions and nothing's ever done.

(Interview, civil society activist, Nairobi, 18 March 2011)

Kenya has a long history of commissions and committees of inquiry characterised by a standard format. They are established by the government to look into a specific issue or problem; are presented as independent bodies headed by experts who have the capacity to investigate and offer practicable solutions; seek to uncover the facts through investigations, receipt of documents and public hearings; and submit a final report with findings and recommendations.

To date, such public inquiries have investigated, and advised upon, a wide range of problems and crises from rebellious sects and assassinations to election-related violence, corruption and land grabbing (for example, Kenya 1950; 1992; 1999; 2004; 2005). Like commissions of inquiry around the world, they have conducted much of their work publicly to try and establish a particular kind of unbiased, informed and expert authority that would help to legitimise the commission's final report.

The two commissions that immediately preceded the TJRC, namely, the Kriegler and Waki commissions, exemplify this approach. The Kriegler Commission was established in March 2008 to examine the integrity of the electoral process during the country's 2007 election. Commissioners opted to conduct their own research, but to also publicly interview 'all principal stakeholders in Nairobi, especially the [Electoral Commission of Kenya] and its staff'. They also 'went on an extensive five-week fact-finding tour with public meetings at 36 venues throughout the country [through which the] [e]xperiences, concerns, opinions and proposals of over 1,200 respondents of all political persuasions, age groups, walks of life and communities were noted' (Tostensen 2009: 430). These forums were in part 'fact-finding' efforts. But commissioners were also 'conscious that they were not hearing and testing formal evidence ... [and that public] communications were often subjective, ill-informed and/or manifestly unsubstantiated, at times even deliberately untruthful' (Kenya 2008c: 6). More important was the opportunity that such meetings provided for Kenyans to openly convey their 'opinions, comments, factual allegations, complaints, [and] recommendations' (Kenya 2008c: 7). The Waki Commission was similarly self-conscious in its public operations.

However, while many of these commissions compiled 'a truly formidable body of documentation' (Southall 2005: 150), very few of the recommendations made by post-colonial commissions have been implemented (Africog 2007; KHRC 2011b), and none of those named in adverse terms have been successfully prosecuted (Brown & Sriram 2012: 250). This history reflects the fact that official inquiries are often used by states as a means to reproduce and extend their authority and legitimacy (Cohen & Odhiambo 2004: 44).

In this vein, Adam Ashforth characterised commissions of inquiry in colonial and apartheid-era South Africa as 'reckoning schemes of legitimation', or a means by which the state, on the basis of a detailed presentation of findings presented by supposedly impartial experts, can create 'a framework of knowledge' and present itself 'as the embodiment of the "common good"' (1990a: 12). However, while this analysis applies to many of Kenya's colonial-era commissions – where the administration used such authoritative bodies to pinpoint problems and justify solutions (for example, Kenya 1934; 1950; 1962) – it cannot fully explain their popularity in the post-colonial period when successive administrations have regularly undermined, denigrated and even rejected their own investigations.

This paradox was particularly evident during Moi's presidency (1978–2002). For example, following the February 1990 murder of the foreign affairs minister, Hon. Robert Ouko, Moi invited Inspector Troon from London's Scotland Yard to investigate. However, it took nine years for the government to officially accept Troon's report and, even then, Moi continued to reject the main findings and recommendations (Cohen & Odhiambo 2004: 3). Indeed, instead of using Troon's report as a means to justify solutions, the government released a counter report to discredit it (Cohen & Odhiambo 2004: 33). Moi then established a judicial commission of inquiry, which, after thirteen months of public hearings, he abruptly terminated; whereupon the president issued a directive for police to proceed with arrests and prosecutions (Cohen & Odhiambo 2004: 3). The Ouko investigations did not end there; after Kibaki came to power in December 2002, parliament established a select committee, but MPs rejected the committee's report accusing it of 'doing shoddy work and [of] using the committee's investigations to settle political scores' (KHRC 2011b: 36; also see Deacon & Lynch 2013 on the fate of a 1995 report into devil worship in schools).

This tendency for governments to publicly undermine their own inquiries was not limited to the Moi regime. On the contrary, the day that a parliamentary select committee was expected to present a report into the suspicious murder of Hon. J. M. Karuiki in June 1975, President Kenyatta summoned its members and insisted that the name of a close ally, Mbiyu Koinange, be expunged (Cohen & Atieno

Odhiambo 2004: 5). The Kibaki administration continued along similar lines. The president opted not to publish the report of the Presidential Special Action Committee to Address Specific Concerns of the Muslim Community in Regard to Alleged Harassment and/or Discrimination in the Application/Enforcement of the Law (or Sharawe Committee), which Kibaki established in 2007 and which submitted a final report in 2008. More worrying still is the fate of a Judicial Commission of Inquiry into Inter-Communal Violence in the Tana Delta, which was established in September 2012, but which had not officially handed over a copy of its report at the time of this writing, although it concluded in January 2013. Concerns of political interference were fuelled by the fact that the chair, Lady Justice Grace Nzokia, was taken hostage by armed gunmen just days before the report was scheduled to be submitted. The subsequent excuse that the report could not be handed over because Nzokia had been sacked from the judiciary did little to allay suspicions of a government cover-up (*Standard* 11 May 2013). In other instances, such as with the Commission of Inquiry into the Illegal/Irregular Allocation of Public Land, or Ndungu Commission (Kenya, Republic of 2004), the government's response has been more subtle, namely, delegitmisation through silence and occasional questioning of the Commission's neutrality and practicability of implementation (Africog 2009).

Indeed, it has been common for commissions to name state officials as likely perpetrators and beneficiaries, and for their work to be surrounded by rumours of state interference. To a certain extent, this has helped undermine government legitimacy and bolstered demands for democratisation and constitutional reform, which begs the question of why commissions of inquiry remain such a popular means for the government to respond to public criticism and political crises.

In part, the answer lies in the ability of commissions, at least in the short term, to offset public pressure and dampen criticism (Africog 2008: 11–12) through a performed display of the government's commitment to tackle a particular problem in a way that does not actually require a substantive response (cf. McCargo 2010). However, the level of public scepticism in Kenya means that the establishment of a commission of inquiry is increasingly interpreted as a performance of impunity or a conduit for the 'cover-up and entrenchment of the culture of impunity' (KHRC 2011b: 3), rather than as a means to tackle injustice, spearhead reforms or solve problems.

To understand the attraction of commissions of inquiry for Kenya's political elite, one must also recognise how rumours and 'profound uncertainties' can be politically useful 'by reminding people everywhere of [the state's] profound capacity for violence' (Fontein 2014: 116). However, as Joost Fontein has argued with reference to Zimbabwe, this 'is not to suggest that there [is] necessarily a "master plan" to promote [such] ambiguous uncertainty' (2009: 387). Instead, one must separate *'intention* from political *affect'* (Fontein 2009: 388) and recognise the consistently contradictory nature of politics where rumours may help to reify state power, whilst governments can simultaneously crave the kind of legitimacy that manifests 'itself in its attempts to appeal to (some) people's aspirations towards good governance and a functioning, bureaucratic state' (Fontein 2009: 389).

Herein lies the paradox of contemporary commissions of inquiry: the process is a performance of state-ness. More specifically, they have become a performance of a government's capacity to investigate issues, take action and respond to the common good. Simultaneously, they are a performance of impunity whereby the failure to implement recommendations and rumours of state interference and malpractice constitute a spectacle of raw state power, which fuel rumours that help to inadvertently uphold and undermine the same.

Inquiries in the post-colonial period have thus rarely been used as coherent schemes of legitimation that justify state policy in the sense outlined by Ashforth. Instead, commissions of inquiry are better thought of, in Ashforth's more general sense, as a 'theatre of power' (1990b). However, in contrast to Ashforth, who showed how the power performed in South Africa was a capacity to respond to problems on the basis of authoritative frameworks of knowledge, commissions of inquiry in post-colonial Kenya have become a performance of state power in a blunter sense, namely, the power to investigate and respond to problems, but also to dismiss and ignore them if that suits vested interests. In this way, the establishment of a commission of inquiry has become an institutionalised response to crisis and a means by which the state can display its capacity, which helps dampen criticism in at least two ways. First, a glimmer of hope remains that, perhaps this time, the truths revealed and recommendations offered will be of some consequence – a glimmer that is maintained through increasingly strongly worded mandates. Second, the process performs the extent of state impunity and leaves many ordinary citizens feeling powerless in its wake.

This history is critical for understanding popular receptions of the TJRC because it presents a clear paradox whereby a history of human rights abuses and injustice led many people to think that Kenya needed a TJRC, while people's previous experience of commissions of inquiry led many to be inherently suspicious of what such a process was likely to achieve. More specifically, on the one hand, a long history of commissions of inquiry, which have recorded a litany of injustices that have never been adequately addressed, provided an important justification for a truth commission (Kenya 2008d). At the same time, this history rendered Kenyans inherently sceptical about what *another* commission was likely to achieve.

This suspicion was further fostered by the fact that – in contrast to South Africa and a number of authoritarian regimes in Latin America that denied and justified state atrocities – Kenya's history of public inquiries have ensured that many atrocities are well documented, which led many to be suspicious of what new truths a TJRC would reveal. In the words of Father Gabriel Dolan, a well-known Catholic priest: '[T]he truth about the crimes committed by the former regime against Kenyans is fairly well agreed upon and only denied by a couple of perpetrators who have made every effort to distort and conceal the truth. In my opinion truth is not the issue, but rather justice' (cited in Bosire & Lynch 2014: 263).

This links to a second area of scepticism, namely that, in the absence of a political transition, the TJRC would likely replicate previous commissions of inquiry in that it would write a detailed report that would then be relegated to dusty shelves. Commission staff tried to counteract this expectation through reference to the act's promise that '[a]ll recommendations shall be implemented' (Kenya 2008d: 50[2]). For example, at a civic education meeting in Nakuru County, TJRC staff responded to questions regarding the Commission's newness by arguing that, while 'there have been many commissions ... they've never been implemented ... but this one is different as the recommendations are bound to be implemented' (Molo, 21 July 2011). Yet many Kenyans were not persuaded and instead feared (or hoped) that the government would find reasons for non-implementation (for example, through reference to the Commission's credibility crisis) or sensed that the Act might be ignored or changed.

This sense of once-againness was reinforced by the scale of the Commission's mandate, demands for punitive justice, a credibility crisis and limited support. As the Commission set to work, scepticism then further bolstered by other factors – from the broader political context (Chapters 2 and 3) and way in which public hearings were scripted, staged-managed and covered in the media (Chapter 5); the limited number of new truths that were revealed or acknowledged (Chapter 6); the failure of perpetrators to detail or admit wrongdoings (Chapter 8); and politicians' initial response to the Commission's findings (Chapter 10). However, before turning to such dynamics, this chapter considers the timing of the Commission's establishment and associated debates regarding the substance of justice, the chairman debacle and levels of civil society engagement.

4.4 The Establishment of the TJRC: From Transition to Crisis

The government puts up a commission to investigate historical injustices and others ... but then the same government is full of the perpetrators. I've said before that it will be a sham.

(Interview, civil society activist, Nakuru, 9 March 2011)

The idea for a Kenyan truth commission was briefly discussed in 1997 in the wake of election-related violence around the country's 1992 and 1997 elections (Musila 2009: 1). However, the idea was quickly forgotten; the idea of a TJRC was then raised following the general elections of December 2002 in which Mwai Kibaki and the National Rainbow Coalition (NaRC) beat Uhuru Kenyatta (President Moi's chosen successor) and the Kenya African National Union (KANU). This momentous event, which saw the peaceful transfer of power from President Moi (after twenty-four years at State House and forty-seven years in the legislature) and displacement of KANU (the ruling party since independence), prompted a moment of great hope. It was during this honeymoon period that Kibaki appointed a Task Force on the Establishment of a TJRC (TF) to investigate the utility of a Kenyan truth commission. The TF was headed by Makau Mutua, a prominent Kenyan human rights activist and law professor. According to the TF's final report:

The people of Kenya have spoken ... The overwhelming majority of Kenyans, over 90 percent of those who submitted their views to the Task Force, want the government to establish an effective truth commission, a vehicle that will reveal the truth about past atrocities, name perpetrators, provide redress for victims, and promote national healing and reconciliation.

(Kenya 2003: 9)

The report promised that, if established, the TJRC would 'address past abuses, recreate the state, banish impunity, and set Kenya on an irreversible trajectory to democracy and respect for basic freedoms', and thus act as an 'instrument for the reform of the state, and for creating a more perfect nation' (Kenya 2003: 9).

The TF envisaged a new type of truth commission where truth-telling, public acknowledgement and catharsis would go hand-in-hand with reparations, prosecutions and redress for political and economic crimes. The plan was for a '[T]rojan horse' that could push through a broad reform agenda and act as 'a stealth vehicle to open the war on impunity' (TF member cited in Bosire & Lynch 2014: 260). This innovative approach was embedded in a general sense of optimism regarding the NaRC government – a perception that stemmed from the peaceful transfer of power and long-standing connections between prominent CSOs and NARC politicians (Bosire & Lynch 2014: 260–261).

However, while the TF recommended that a TJRC be instituted by July 2004, the government did not establish one until after the next election. As Lydiah Bosire and I have argued (2014), this failure was due to a lack of political will, as politicians who would have been held responsible for human rights abuses (and politicians who relied on alliances with the same) perceived the stakes to be too high. Inaction also came at little immediate cost: the domestic and international gaze had turned to institutional and constitutional reforms, prominent human rights organisations were focused on new (rather than past) injustices and the TF's vision lacked a deep constituency.

Regarding the latter, and as one participant at a TF meeting in northern Kenya recalled, while 'the report put it like a consensus ... there was no consensus' (interview, Nairobi, 26 March 2012). Indeed, the TF's assertion that more than 90 per cent of Kenyans demanded a TJRC obscured the fact that the team had met with around 1,000 people (TF member cited in Bosire & Lynch 2014: 262), while local hearings revealed significant regional differences (Bosire & Lynch 2014: 263). Instead, the TF decided from the outset 'to recommend a TJRC and worked towards that' (interview, TF member cited in Bosire & Lynch

2014: 263), a fact that was reflected in an opinion piece published by Mutua a day before the TF began its countrywide consultative tour:

> [T]here is no doubt that Kenya needs a truth commission, but in our case, we need a truth, justice, and reconciliation commission this year. Reconciliation cannot be achieved without truth and justice ... It must have the mandate to investigate gross human rights violations and economic crimes committed by the KANU Government from December 12, 1964, to December 30, 2002.
> (Cited in Bosire & Lynch 2014: 263)

In this context, public consultations were more about persuading people of a particular vision of truth-telling and legitimising the TF, than gathering people's views (Bosire & Lynch 2014: 263–264). This is not to say that Kenyans were opposed to the idea of a TJRC. On the contrary, many were sympathetic, but it was not a common priority.

In the face of limited political will and popular pressure, the idea of a TJRC moved into the background until early 2008, when this classic transitional justice mechanism was revived during post-conflict mediation efforts. Proponents included Priscilla Hayner, the world's leading expert on truth commissions, who – as a human rights advisor to the Annan team – explicitly advocated for a truth commission (Langeran 2015: 53) and helped to draft some of the TJRC's founding principles (interview, Kenyan transitional justice expert, Nairobi, 3 May 2011). Advocates also included a wide range of civil society groups. This included those who prioritised peace, such as the Concerned Citizens for Peace (CCP) – a group formed during the post-election violence by Kiplagat and a number of other prominent peace-keepers – which from a base at the Serena Hotel in Nairobi, where Annan's team also stayed during the negotiations, pushed for an immediate political solution and reconciliation (Kanyinga 2011). It also included a second group of prominent human rights organisations, organised around Kenyans for Peace, Truth and Justice (KPTJ), who had pushed for a TJRC in 2003. However, while KPTJ actively engaged with debates over the TJRC Act and amnesty provisions, they came to concentrate more on exposing electoral malpractice, documenting human rights abuses and lobbying for criminal trials (Hansen & Sriram 2015; Kanyinga 2011).

Indeed, while the TJRC Act adopted the approach, and much of the wording of the TF report, the situation was now very different. Hope had turned to a moment of soul-searching (Branch 2011). Moreover, while in 2003 a new government with close links to civil society had ousted a regime that was widely castigated as authoritarian, in 2008, the same politicians implicated in electoral manipulation or in the incitement and organisation of post-election violence were positioned to oversee the TJRC. As a result, many feared that the TJRC would be hijacked. These fears reached a peak in mid-2009 when Kibaki's cabinet responded to the passing of the 'Waki envelope' to the ICC's Office of the Prosecutor by insisting that it would address the post-election violence through a strengthened TJRC (Brown & Sriram 2012). As one prominent Kalenjin politician in the coalition government explained, '[A]ny attempt to arrest leaders will be a recipe for chaos' so 'one of the best ways is for the TJRC to deal with differences – it can compensate a few [people] and settle IDPs' (interview, Nairobi, 10 August 2009). The common conclusion was that politicians sought to use the TJRC as a substitute for, rather than as a route to, accountability.

This scepticism was intertwined with a burgeoning sense that Kiplagat's appointment was a purposeful means to control and undermine the TJRC. Yet, Kiplagat was not simply a government stooge: CSOs were involved in the selection process that led to his nomination, Kiplagat then led commissioners in rejecting the government's suggestion that the TJRC could act as a substitute for criminal prosecutions, and government funding increased once Kiplagat had stepped aside (Lanegran 2015). However, this does not mean that Kiplagat's appointment over individuals with stronger human rights credentials was not intentional. Indeed, it seems that Kibaki 'took advantage of the opportunity handed to him ... to appoint a controversial chairman ... [since] it served the government's interest, and is in keeping with Kibaki's decision-making style, to launch a flawed commission and let it flounder, hopefully to eventually capsize' (Lanegran 2015: 66). Certainly, in the absence of a political transition and in the face of the ICC intervention, the crisis that arose around the chairman dealt the Commission a near fatal blow.

4.5 'The Three That Haunted Him':[3] Kiplagat's Ghosts

All of us welcomed the [TJRC] ... but when issues around the chairman came up ... [it] interfered with what we'd expected, and [we've] not seen what the TJRC has achieved.

(Interview, CSO leader, Nakuru, 14 March 2011)

[3] Interview, transitional justice expert, Nairobi, 3 May 2011.

The TJRC's commissioners were appointed through an agreed process. First, the minister of justice established a nine-member panel made up of representatives from different social groups, which included a representative from the KNCHR, the Federation of Women Lawyers (FIDA), and two religious organisations. The panel then interviewed forty-seven people and forwarded a shortlist of fifteen to the National Assembly, which sent a reduced list of nine to Kibaki, who decided on the final six. The three internationals were then appointed through a separate process overseen by Kofi Annan's team (TJRC vol. 1 2013: 23). Commissioners were asked to swear affidavits that they had not been involved in the past abuses examined.

Unfortunately, opposition to Kiplagat – who had a strong reputation as a domestic and regional peacebuilder through the CCP and in Sudan – took time to grow and only really gained ground after the appointments had been announced. At one level, Kiplagat was dismissed simply for having served as a senior civil servant in Moi's government and, by implication, for having been part of the authoritarian establishment. However, more worryingly, Kiplagat was connected to three injustices that the Commission was tasked to investigate. First, Kiplagat had been permanent secretary (PS) in the ministry for foreign affairs when the minister had been murdered, and, while no-one suggested Kiplagat had killed Ouko, many believed that he might harbour relevant information. Second, Kiplagat was named in the Ndungu Commission as someone who had benefited under Moi from irregular allocations of land on a settlement scheme at Situatanga Farm in Trans Nzoia. Finally, it emerged that Kiplagat had attended a government meeting in Wajir in February 1984 at which some say a decision was made to round up all the Degodia men in the area for interrogation. This operation ended in the infamous Wagalla massacre when an unknown number of men died whilst in detention at Wagalla airstrip in northern Kenya. Given this history, many felt that Kiplagat should not chair the TJRC, but instead be summoned to give evidence.

With time, opposition to Kiplagat also grew within the Commission. This was evident from interviews, but also from the twenty pages of the TJRC's final report on the 'credibility and suitability of the chairperson'. The following excerpt captures this frustration, as commissioners and staff came to see 'Kip' as an arrogant *mzee* (or elder) who had lied to his colleagues and put his own name above the Commission's future.

Over the Wagalla Massacre, Ambassador Kiplagat first stated categorically that he had never been to Wajir in his entire life ... A few weeks later, Ambassador Kiplagat told fellow Commissioners and the public that he 'could not remember' if he had ever been to Wajir or not ... As it later became clear, Ambassador Kiplagat had in fact attended a meeting of the Kenya Intelligence Committee [KIC] in Wajir on 8 February 1984 less than forty-eight hours before the start of the security operation that resulted in the Wagalla Massacre. The alleged involvement of the Chairperson in these matters and the fact that documentary evidence had been presented to the Commission linking him to three important areas of the Commission's mandate, created a conflict of interest between him and the Commission ... Recognising the detrimental effect this controversy was having on the work of the Commission, and recognising further that a legal process had now been initiated ... Ambassador Kiplagat agreed to step aside until the tribunal process reached its conclusion ... However, within 24 hours of having signed the letter indicating he would step aside, Ambassador Kiplagat met Commissioners and stated that he would not in fact step aside ... In October 2010, Ambassador Kiplagat gave a nationally televised interview concerning the Wagalla Massacre in which for the first time he publicly admitted that he had been present in Wajir for [the KIC] meeting ... in that same nationally televised interview he stated, in response to a question about government responsibility for the Wagalla Massacre, the following: 'I doubt, I find it extremely difficult, no government worth its salt plans to massacre its people' ... Lessons of history show that far too often governments unfortunately do massacre their own people. By stating a conclusion concerning government responsibility for the Wagalla Massacre Ambassador Kiplagat was engaging in just the sort of activity that had led to the original concerns about the conflict of interest his inclusion in the Commission presented.

(TJRC vol. 1 2013: 126–129)

The Commission did not resign itself to this crisis but fought it through a multi-level strategy. First, staff sought to collect statements and to hold successful hearings so as to prove that Kenyans wanted a truth commission, and that victims wanted to be heard and to receive justice. This was largely successful and, while there are questions regarding the quality of statements collected (Chapter 6), the large number of statements and memoranda and initial public hearings clearly helped to secure the Commission's much needed extensions and to temporarily dampen civil society critics.

Second, the Commission reached out to victims groups – and particularly the National Victim and Survivors Network (NVSN), the country's only national victims association, which enjoyed close links to prominent Nairobi-based human rights organisations – and hired victim-activists as statement takers and civic educators, although they purposefully did not deploy victims to the research, investigations or legal affairs departments. This approach bore mixed results. On the one hand, it helped to strengthen relations between the Commission and key victims groups, which facilitated statement-taking and mobilisation. On the other hand, these appointments were criticised by prominent CSOs for failing to address the Commission's real problems and for undermining its neutrality. The underlying concern was whether the process would be regarded as 'geared towards ... justice for victims' (Malombe 2012: 115), and, more specifically, towards particular kinds of victims. In this vein, questions were raised about whether an ordinary Kalenjin, for example, would want to speak to a statement taker who was an outspoken Kikuyu IDP from the post-election violence about historical land injustices in the Rift Valley. Ultimately, these concerns were borne out by local complaints of ethnically biased statement takers on the ground (Chapter 8).

Third, the Commission sought to show that its work was unhindered by the chair, in large part by expending much of its energy on the three areas where Kiplagat's name had been mentioned: the Wagalla massacre, Ouko's death and Situatanga Farm. This was particularly true of the Wagalla massacre, which the Commission spent more time on, and dedicated more space to, than any other single event or injustice investigated. The Commission also devoted more attention to Ouko's murder and to Situatanga Farm than to any other political assassination and land dispute. According to the Commission, the focus on Ouko was due to the failure of previous investigations to unearth the truth, which raises questions about whether a general commission like the TJRC was ever likely to unearth new evidence, but also because

> the chairman of the Commission is [also] a witness to some of the events leading up to the assassination, and has himself been the subject of some of the inquiries around Ouko's death. The controversies surrounding the chairman's conflict of interest in this matter require us to be particularly thorough and forthright.
>
> (TJRC vol. 2A 2013: 455–456)

The commission also called Kiplagat as an AMP in their investigations of Wagalla and Situatanga. Notably, this was the only massacre and instance of land grabbing that enjoyed AMP hearings, while both occasions were stage-managed to perform a spectacle of the Commission's authority. For example, when Kiplagat first appeared at the Wagalla AMP hearing, he was kept waiting for an entire day (Nairobi, 2 June 2011); when he finally testified, his day-long interrogation was the most detailed and extensive of any AMP. Then, on 22 March 2012, Kiplagat was summoned again – this time regarding Situatanga Farm, where he owned land on a settlement scheme meant for the poor and landless. Kiplagat responded by sending his lawyer, whereupon the presiding chair read out a statement to the assembled media in a carefully stage-crafted rebuke of how the commissioners were 'dismayed and saddened that Ambassador Kiplagat would flagrantly disobey the law' and were unwilling to squander any more time on his 'theatrical tantrums' (Nairobi, 22 March 2012).

Collectively these moments constituted a 'status degradation ceremony', or ritual by which 'ceremonial denunciations' become 'an exercise in public relations' that was 'less about lowering the status of the degradees ... and more about reaffirming the status of the degraders' (Cavende, Gray & Miller 2010: 255 and 256) – in this case, the embattled TJRC. This denunciation worked to a certain extent, and, in particular, helped to dampen opposition from victims of the Wagalla massacre who had initially been amongst the Commission's strongest critics. However, it also led to complaints that the Commission had 'become the Kiplagat Commission' (interview, TJRC department head, Nairobi, 7 September 2011). Certainly, disproportionate attention to personalised issues of interest to the Commission – most notably Wagalla, but also to ethnic violence on Mt Elgon where Wanjala had previously worked – ensured that the Commission appeared rather inward-looking. This is not to say that Wagalla and Mt Elgon did not deserve attention. On the contrary, despite ongoing debate on the number, Wagalla 'remains the largest loss of life in any single atrocity in Kenya's history' (Anderson 2014: 659). It also represents an iconic example of violence at the hands of state security forces. Moreover, unlike other iconic examples of injustices that the TJRC was mandated to investigate, Wagalla had not been the focus of any previous commission of inquiry. Instead, there had been a concerted effort to cover up Wagalla as a 'wall of silence' was 'slowly but inexirably ... constructed around the operation' (TJRC vol. 2A 2013: 291; also vol. 1 2013: 101). Similarly, the

TJRC was right to argue that the violence on Mt Elgon between 2005 and 2008 provides an excellent 'case study of a conflict that sits at the intersection of three volatile trends that dominated the mandate period,' namely, 'ethnic identity and land and electoral politics' (TJRC vol. 3 2013: 39).

Nevertheless, the disproportionate focus on these issues and associated AMPs distracted the Commission from issues and individuals which may have better captured the interest of various publics. Thus, while it was important for the TJRC to summon Kiplagat, it would also have been important for it to have publicly questioned a former president and other high-level politicians. In the end, while the TJRC summoned Kiplagat twice, the highest profile AMP who spoke in public was the former cabinet minister, G. G. Kariuki (Chapter 8).

The Kiplagat issue also periodically reared its head in ways that undermined gains made. For example, in mid-2011, the TJRC's relations with prominent CSOs had thawed, as the latter came to recognise the high number of statements collected, relatively good turnouts at public hearings, and reality of a forthcoming report (KPTJ strategy meeting, Naivasha, 29 to 30 August 2011). However, six months later, Kiplagat returned to work. According to a TJRC civic educator, this 'was the beginning of the end for the Commission' (interview, Nairobi, 3 August 2012). The damage was initially limited by a deal, which ensured Kiplagat's absence from the last public hearings, barred him from contributing to parts of the report where he might have a conflict of interest, and brought a much-needed three month extension (Bosire & Lynch 2014). However the situation changed, when – just days before the expected submission of the Commission's final report – Kiplagat announced that they needed a further extension to finish the report, conduct further investigations into AMPs, open an amnesty process, clarify its recommendations on reparations and conduct further reconciliation efforts (Bosire & Lynch 2014: 272). In response, the minister for justice awarded a final nine-month extension. However, prominent CSOs, which had begun to work with the Commission (such as the KHRC and International Commission of Jurists [ICJ]), along with many of the Commission's long-standing friends who had not been consulted (such as NVSN and the KNCHR), publicly queried whether the report was to be 'cooked up' (interview, Nairobi, 7 August 2012) and/or to be delayed until after the

2013 election. As one activist explained at a civil society press conference specifically organised to reject the extension:

There is no justification for the 9 months [extension requested] ... If we give them 9 months ... then vetting for elections will be done ... We say they've already done the report and so we want it tomorrow. An extension is supposed to give space to perpetrators of impunity.

(Nairobi, 5 August 2012)

Vocal critics included several former employees of the TJRC from NVSN, such as the civic educators Wafula Buke and Wachira Waheire, who further fuelled civil society suspicions by claiming that their colleagues 'didn't say that a lot of work was pending' when their contracts had expired in May (interview, Nairobi, 3 August 2012).

Questions over Kiplagat's role then came back to the fore in May 2013 when two foreign commissioners – Chawatama and Slye – refused to sign volume 2B of the final report; and all three foreign commissioners issued a dissenting opinion. The latter, which was omitted from the final report in conflict to the Commission's own procedures, detailed how they had all stood by the final report, which had been produced at the end of their operational period on 3 May, but had subsequently found out (on 17 May) that 'the final draft of the Land Chapter in the Report would include changes ... motivated in part by the Office of the President' (OP; Chawatama, Dinka & Slye 2013: 1). The opinion goes on to provide substantial detail about how the Commission was pressured into giving an advance copy of the report to the Ministry of Justice and OP, how commissioners received phone calls from a senior official in the OP and how the land chapter had subsequently been changed with entire paragraphs cut, including those that made direct reference to certain land holdings by the Kenyatta family. The final blow came after the report was handed over to President Kenyatta on 21 May when Kiplagat insisted that, with regard to Ouko's murder, the Wagalla massacre and land 'findings and recommendations do not tally' and the 'Commission will have a difficult time proving their case in court' (*Capital FM* 23 May 2013). The Kiplagat debacle thus undermined the Commission's work from start to finish. In part, this was because of the detrimental impact that it had on the TJRC's relationships with key CSOs.

4.6 Civil Society's (Dis)engagements[4]

One of the milestones [of this meeting] – which would have sent shivers down our spines six months ago is the decision to re-engage with the TJRC.

(Round-up of KPTJ strategy meeting, Naivasha, 30 August 2011)

Civil society is often presented as a key factor in the success or failure of truth commissions, which are said to 'rely on moral suasion, pressure from civil society and the international community, and the political will of politicians to see most of their impact realised' (Brahm 2007: 28–29). Yet, civil society support is not a given and was largely absent in Kenya, where one might have assumed that a relatively active and outspoken civil society, which had played a key role in pushing for a TJRC in 2003, would have facilitated an influential truth commission. In contrast, while the TJRC's final report recognised the importance of civil society support in statement-taking and other areas, it also noted how most CSOs had been 'extremely reluctant to provide support, including in-kind support, for the Commission's activities ... which exacerbated the Commission's financial problems ... and hindered the implementation of its ambitious work plan' (TJRC vol. 1 2013: 154).

In short, the credibility crisis that surrounded Kiplagat's appointment, his refusal to stand down and ultimate return – together with a lack of a political transition, the ICC factor and questions regarding the quality of the TJRC's work – fuelled a negative reinforcing cycle, which prompted many CSOs and donors to walk away from the Commission. This cycle also allowed the government to step back from a process that had initially been pushed by CSOs and foreign mediators, and which discouraged the country's profit-making media houses from paying the TJRC much attention.

Yet, civil society's disengagement was far from complete. At one end of the scale, there were groups that worked fairly closely with, and which supported the Commission for most of its lifespan. This included the Kisumu-based Civil Society Organizations Network, the Truth Be Told Network in northern Kenya, some local CJPC offices, the Nairobi-based *Kituo cha Sheria* and NVSN. This support made a significant difference to the Commission's ability to collect statements

---

[4] See Bosire & Lynch (2014) for a more extensive discussion of civil society's (dis) engagement with the TJRC.

and mobilise audiences for their public events and hearings, although most of these organisations then abandoned the TJRC at the time of the final extension in August 2012.

At the other end of the scale, several organisations remained steadfast in their calls for the Commission's disbandment. These included Kenya Against Impunity (KAI), a coalition of survivors of KANU repression who filed an unsuccessful lawsuit to halt the work of the TJRC in October 2009, and the Constitution and Reform Education Consortium (CRECO) and International Centre for Policy and Conflict (ICPC), which monitored, and publicly criticised, the Commission's work (for example, Wainaina in *Pambazuka News* 29 January 2009; *Daily Nation* 3 September 2010).

Finally, there were those who vacillated between disengagement and partial engagement. This included prominent organisations within KPTJ – such as the KHRC and ICJ – who started and ended the Commission's term at a distance due to the Kiplagat issue, but which, in the interim, helped draft the Commission's reparations and implementation frameworks (interview, Nairobi, 6 August 2012), and which subsequently played a critical role in lobbying for implementation of the same (Chapter 9).

Overall, however, the message received from prominent CSOs by ordinary citizens and donors was overwhelmingly negative as organisations and their leaders (many of whom have columns in the major newspapers) opted to support the Commission in only limited ways, at strategic moments and quietly, or to openly voice their opposition to the process, with some organisations fluctuating between the two at different points in time (Bosire & Lynch 2014).

4.7 Conclusions: A Haunted Body

I think someone has sent [Kiplagat to the TJRC] ... some people need to cover up something ... [The TJRC] had very good objectives but I don't think it will achieve them – not like the South African did.

(Interview, theatre for development activist, Nairobi, 5 April 2012)

A key lesson from people's reception of the TJRC – and of the ICC – is that publics do not approach these performative processes 'uniformly or in a political vacuum', but 'bring to them backgrounds, experiences, political perspectives, and vested interests that shape interpretations'

(Payne 2008: 27). In this vein, a powerful political elite drew upon popular fears of a repetition of violence and the ghosts of imperialism and neo-colonialism to help counter-shame the ICC. While, from the outset, the TJRC was haunted by the ghosts of previous commissions of inquiry and their legacy of performed impunity, the atrocities with which Kiplagat's name was associated, an evolving accountability debate whereby the TJRC looked in danger of being hijacked as a means of avoiding punitive justice for those deemed most responsible, and by the persistence of the past in the form of political continuity and the lack of any real political transition. These hauntings highlight how contextually specific a commission's reception is, and how important broader political histories and contexts are for how ordinary citizens, but also CSOs, the media and international community are likely to interpret a commission's motivations and probable impact, and thus (dis)engage with it.

The lesson is that, if a truth commission is to even approach the myth of the South African model, then it has to instil confidence that it is actually part of a broader transition, and that it will simultaneously contribute to the same. However, while a truth commission can seek to cultivate such an image, there are limits to its ability to perform change when the context points to continuity, or when the credibility of the body itself, comes into question. In short, a truth commission is not a tool that can be applied in different environments with the same or predictable effects (Bosire & Lynch 2016), and credible leadership is an essential, if insufficient, factor (Kenya, Republic of 2004: 3). This may seem like an obvious conclusion, but, given a growing tendency to present truth commissions as an almost natural response to authoritarianism and conflict, it is an important one.

As this chapter has shown, a fear that the TJRC would *just* be another commission of inquiry stemmed, in large part, from the Commission's context and makeup. However, it was also informed by an idea of what a TRC should look like, which was shaped by the myth of the South African model where truth-telling is believed to have been characterised by emotional public hearings that brought victims and perpetrators together, facilitated individual and national catharsis, and captured the public imagination in ways that helped shape new national narratives.

5 | Public Hearings
Bringing the Audience Back In

Maybe it's just me, but it's also reflected in audience size, the fact that people are coming in and out, and the number of commission staff who seem to be paying attention: the process has lost some of its energy, while the 'media corner' has been empty all afternoon.
(Fieldwork diary, TJRC public hearing, Kakamega, 28 June 2011)

The [public] gallery upstairs is now empty and there's only a few people downstairs. If there were any media here they've left.
(Fieldwork diary, 6.10 pm, TJRC public hearing, Bungoma, 8 July 2011)

At around 5 pm on Saturday, 9 July 2011, I scanned the town hall where the TJRC was holding public hearings in Bungoma, Western Kenya, and counted five people I did not recognise as commission staff. The hearings continued for another hour and a half, during which time, the sun set, the room grew chilly and the leader of evidence rushed through the final five witnesses – the last two of whom relayed their story to only a handful of commission staff and just one member of the public who had stayed on to give the closing prayer. There was no media present the whole afternoon. Admittedly this was the lowest turnout I witnessed at a TJRC hearing. However, it was not unusual for numbers to be limited and for attendance to decrease as the day and days in any one location progressed. A week and a half previous, I had sat through public hearings in Kakamega town (also in Western Kenya) alongside no more than twenty-five members of the general public, while at a thematic hearing in Nairobi on 12 March 2012, the audience shrank markedly after Maina Njenga (the founder of the infamous Mungiki militia group) finished his presentation. In addition, many sessions started late, as staff sought to mobilise an audience (for example, the women's hearings in Busia, 4 July 2011, and Nakuru, 24 September 2011), while a thematic hearing on injustice and disabled

An earlier version of this chapter was published as Lynch (2015a).

people was postponed in February 2012 – the commissioners apparently 'furious with the small number of participants' (*The Star* 8 February 2012).

Even when public galleries were relatively full, there was often no national and sometimes no local media coverage, which ensured that even the most carefully stage-crafted testimony often went unreported. This included a public hearing on 21 September 2011 in Kericho town, Rift Valley, where – before about 300 members of the public and commission staff – a Kalenjin, Kikuyu and Kisii widow sat together and recounted, in graphic and moving testimony, how their husbands had been killed during the post-election violence and the everyday challenges that they subsequently faced. During the closing ceremony, Commissioner Rev. Lawrence Bomett from the National Cohesion and Integration Commission (NCIC), who had observed the hearings, noted the widows' heartbreaking stories: '[T]hese three should be on TV so people can learn ... I just wish that women like this who we've heard today could be given a national forum to talk to this nation' (Kericho, 21 September 2011). But surely the TJRC was meant to provide exactly that: a national forum. However, in practice, the women's stories were not relayed through the national media until three years later when I wrote an opinion piece summarising their testimony (*Saturday Nation* 8 November 2014).

As I sat through TJRC hearings in relatively empty halls, and listened to deeply moving testimonies that a broader public would never hear, I was struck by a recurring question: who were the witnesses meant to be speaking to? Were they simply talking to commission staff so as to offload assumed trauma and inform a final report? If so, why did the TJRC need to exert so much time and energy holding the hearings in public? Surely individual catharsis (if that was what was needed) could have been better achieved through a series of one-on-one counselling sessions, while testimony would have been more efficiently gathered through statements, memoranda and interviews. Or were witnesses meant to be speaking to their communities, the nation or the world more broadly? In which case, was the publicness of their testimony not rendered entirely ineffective in the face of limited audiences and media coverage, and a paucity of public commentary and debate?

This chapter is motivated by these questions and argues that the main aims of conducting public sessions are lost if there is a limited audience, although public hearings might still help to legitimise a final report as an authoritative account that 'listened' to stakeholders (cf. Ashforth 1990b). The analysis reveals how commission hearings need to be seen as legitimate and politically relevant, or at least as exciting and interesting, if they are to prompt the kind of audience engagement that could even begin to contribute to the transformative process encapsulated in the South African model. The implication is that, to be successful, processes that are partially dependent on the efficacy of their public performances must ensure an engaged and receptive audience. Without one, there is no interactive dimension between performers and audiences, and the significance of *public* forums is diminished or lost entirely.

The chapter starts by outlining the idealised model of the South African TRC hearings, which has informed subsequent truth commissions, and the significance of media coverage. It then turns to the staging of the TJRC's public hearings, key reasons for limited public engagement and to how an unreceptive, and indeed inattentive, public audience ensured that the TJRC failed to perform a sense of national transition.

5.1 The South African TRC: A Media Event

We pick out a sequence. We remove some pauses and edit it into a 20-second sound bite. We feed it to Johannesburg. We switch on a small transistor ... We lift our fists triumphantly. We've done it! The voice of an ordinary cleaning woman is the headline on the one o'clock news ...

For me, the Truth Commission microphone with its little red light was the ultimate symbol of the whole process: here the marginalized voice speaks to the public ear, the unspeakable is spoken – and translated – the personal story brought from the innermost depths of the individual binds us anew to the collective.

(Radio journalist Antjie Krog on the South African TRC [1999: 48 and 358–359])

Pre–South African truth commissions did not present themselves as making a direct contribution to individual or collective reconciliation, and instead focused on uncovering particular truths about the past. The basic rationale was that information and acknowledgement would offer some justice to victims, and simultaneously help to mobilise support for reform. Most did not hold public hearings, and instead relied on research, written statements and other activities, such as the Argentinean commission's 1984 inspections of clandestine detention centres (Crenzel 2008: 184–186). Moreover, commissions that did hold public hearings generally presented these as just another investigatory tool. In this way, the Study Commission for the Assessment of History and Consequences of the Socialist Unity Party Dictatorship in Germany listened to 327 expert presentations at its hearings, which 'had the atmosphere of a political science or sociology congress, rather than a people's tribunal' (Yoder 1999: 72). Yet, this was intentional: the Commission sought to set 'the record straight' rather than to provide 'collective catharsis' (Andrews 2003: 51).

In contrast, the South African TRC included reconciliation within its title and dedicated much of its time to hearings, which were meant to provide a public ritual or 'performance of memory, loss and grief' (Ross 2003a: 15), which was intricately tied to a vocabulary of individual and collective healing. As Priscilla Hayner notes:

> [O]ne of the cornerstones of modern-day psychology is the belief that expressing one's feelings, and especially talking about traumatic experiences, is necessary for recovery and for psychological health. It is often asserted that following a period of massive political violence and enforced silence, simply giving victims and witnesses a chance to tell their stories to an official commission – especially one that is respectful, non-confrontational, and genuinely interested in their stories – can help them regain their dignity and begin to recover. (2011: 146)

In this vein, the TRC sought to uncover factual truths and make recommendations, but to also provide a stage for people to share their personal or narrative truths. This was meant to be cathartic for individual witnesses; it was also meant to help heal a traumatised nation through an interactive process of speaking and listening that enjoined performers and audiences in an articulation of new shared memories or social truths that rejected the abuses of the past. The hope, according to the TRC's final report, was that

> as we listen to those who are not statistics but human beings of flesh and blood, that you and I will be filled with a new commitment, a new resolve that our country will be a country where violations of this kind will not happen, that the context will be inhospitable for those who seek to treat others as if they were nothing.
>
> (Cited in Andrews 2003: 59)

Given this approach, the presence of an engaged citizenry was critical. First, for testimony to have the potential for catharsis, it is often assumed that there has to be a 'sympathetic' (Minow 1998: 70; Young 2004: 153) or 'empathetic' audience (Stein 1998: 455). This is because sharing 'one's tears' is often believed to make 'grief less lonely and terrifying' (Minow 1998: 68), but also because an official acknowledgement is often regarded 'as a kind of public ritual' or 'public marker of these citizens' rightful passage into equal consideration and respect' (Allen 1999: 332), which can help to undermine earlier narratives of criminality or blame (Borer 2003: 1096).

Second, if hearings are to affect a broader public, a large secondary audience has to be struck by witness testimony and react to it in ways that challenge hegemonic scripts (Mazzei 2011: 439) and foster a new, shared understanding of a nation's past and future trajectory. In South Africa, the idea was that, 'through telling these stories the "master narrative" of colonial and apartheid South Africa was undermined, contradicted, and replaced by the story of struggle, suffering, and the "miracle story" of transition to democracy' (de Gruchy 2002: 23).

Given these extensive aims it is unsurprising that the realities of testifying and of bearing witness has prompted significant debate. Critics highlight, for example, how difficult it is to attest to particular harms (Ross 2003a: 127); how speaking can lead to a retraumatisation or even revictimisation of witnesses (Hamber 1999; Krog 1999: 112); how people may feel alienated and used as they lose control of the circulation, interpretation and political appropriation of 'their' story (Ross 2003a); and how a confessional style can leave people feeling 'inhibited in expressing their legitimate rage and anger' (Hamber & Wilson 2002: 48).

Critics also question the TRC's underlying understanding of injustice as trauma that can be healed through speaking (Fields 2011). At one level, they draw attention to the time and support that is usually required to 'master the past' in psychoanalytic practice in contrast to the limited support offered by the TRC (Hamber 1998b). At another level, they highlight how voices can be rendered ineffective if witnesses are limited to discussing bodily integrity rights, as occurred at the TRC (Mamdani 2002) or if no-one seems to listen (Borneman 2002: 295). With any cathartic effect arguably diminished if speaking does not have a clear effect either in the form of reparations (Laplante & Theidon 2007), punishment (Wilson 2011), promotion of the rule of law

(Hamber 1998a; Lessa 2011) or greater equality (Mamdani 2002; Stanley 2001).

Finally, critics point to how speaking might actually distract from broader reforms – for example, if a truth commission dampens criticism through an appearance of 'doing something' (McCargo 2010), or if it leads to a 'new silencing' and 'partial appropriation of what was said by a national discourse' (Bozzoli 1998: 193) that legitimates a new nation-building project to the neglect of more popularly accepted justice mechanisms (Wilson 2001) or redistributive politics (Mamdani 2002; Meister 2002).

Such critiques are central to ongoing debates regarding the TRC's legacy. Nevertheless, there is a general consensus, even amongst the Commission's critics, that extensive coverage helped to ensure that, at the very least, the vast majority of South Africans learnt of the Commission's work and some of its most startling revelations (Chapman & Ball 2001: 35), and that this made it difficult for people to deny the occurrence of widespread apartheid atrocities (Fields 2011: 144; Mamdani 2000: 61). The Commission therefore met Michael Ignatieff's minimalist measurement of success of having reduced 'the number of lies that can be circulated unchallenged in public discourse' (1996).

However, disproportionate attention to the South African case – where TRC hearings were generally well attended and were widely covered by local and international media – has detracted from separate questions about whether (and why) such public forums enjoy an engaged audience, and the implications of audience scepticism and disengagement for efficacy. This is important since, if public hearings are to work according to the idealised TRC model, they have to contribute to a particular kind of transformative interaction that requires an engaged audience. This includes commission staff who manage hearings, deal with victims and perpetrators, and write a final report and offer recommendations; but it also includes a broader public – both in terms of those physically present, as well as those who follow the process through media coverage and public debate (cf. Hutchison 2013: 36).

This need for an extended audience ensures that the mass media served 'as both essential actors in the TRC drama, as well as the stage on which much of the drama was performed' (Krabill 2001: 568). Indeed, for a TRC to help shape collective consciousness – and thus provide 'a moment of common experience' that compels people 'to discuss a common issue' in ways that represent 'the beginnings of a common if contentious understanding of the past' (Krabill 2001: 569, 570 and 571) – hearings have to be widely disseminated and become a 'media event'. To this end, routine broadcasting has to be interrupted, pre-planned events outside of the media have to be aired live and coverage has to be 'presented with reverence and ceremony' and to enthrall 'very large audiences' (Krabill 2001: 569). The South African TRC managed to do this, as 'radio, television and the press worked to mediatise [the TRC]' (McEachern 2002: 33), ensuring that the TRC became 'one of the most mediatised phenomena of the 1990s ... [and] probably [one of] the most mediatised events ever taking place in Africa' (Verdoolaege 2005: 181).

In contrast, the impact of many post–South African truth commissions have been limited – not only by initial mandates, political manipulations and the failure of hearings to perform 'new-ness' or to create 'new' national(ist) narratives – but by extremely limited and relatively disengaged media coverage (Hayner 2011). In this vein, the executive secretary of Ghana's National Reconciliation Commission (NRC), which sat from 2002 to 2004, noted how

[a] key limitation of the NRC was its inability to maintain media interest in its proceedings throughout its lifespan ... Against the backdrop of a politically polarised society, media interest in the work of the NRC ebbed and flowed with the appearance of 'big shots' and so-called 'star witnesses', such as current and past associates of former President Rawlings.

(Attafuah 2009: 197)

Similarly, analysts of the Sierra Leonean TRC recount how both a hope that testimony would give 'access to economic assistance' (Shaw 2007: 184) and 'rather detached and clinical' deliveries led to small, and often bored immediate audiences and to limited media coverage or public debate (Kelsall 2005: 368). Moreover, while Sierra Leone's hearings were aired live on the radio, 'there was very little reuse or rebroadcast of the stories told ... and although all hearings were recorded, the recordings have not been reused except for in a production called "Witness to Truth," which was circulated mainly overseas' (Millar 2010: 485). In the same vein, media coverage of the Peruvian TRC 'was hardly picked up beyond the human rights community, and did not generate a nation-wide debate' (Boesten 2013: 73). Indeed, public hearings convened by most post–South African truth commissions have failed to become a media event, to provide a powerful performance of a new nation or to bring about new national(ist) discourses or imaginaries. This begs two questions: why was the South African TRC relatively successful at attracting media coverage, and why have subsequent TRC's fallen short? The rest of the section looks briefly at the first, while the final sections consider the second with respect to Kenya.

In part, South Africa's particularity was due to a relatively strong sense of political transition and influence of inspirational public figures, which helped to foster a feeling that 'everything was possible' (Krog 2013: 2). In this context – public hearings, which offered an opportunity for ordinary citizens of different races to talk about their experiences and for perpetrators to account for their actions – constituted 'good theatre', which revealed a range of emotional and historical truths that stimulated debate (Cole 2007: 180). Indeed, these revelations provided

> the fundamental paradigm shift at the moral and political core of the TRC as a media event; in *its* terms [previous] state power [that tortured and killed in the certain knowledge that this would be kept concealed] was illegitimate and unlawful and previously immune officers of the state were to be held accountable, at the very least at the level of explaining their part in the apartheid system of domination. As such it clearly signalled a break with the past, even as the past was its focus. This break both authorised claims about the 'newness' of the nation and set in motion the re-interpretation of history.
>
> (McEachern 2002: 41; emphasis in original)

Hearings were self-consciously staged to cultivate this sense of 'newness'. Thus the Commission's deputy chairman, Alex Boraine, explains how with the first hearing,

> [a]t last the curtain was raised; the drama which was to unfold ... had witnessed its first scene ... The ritual, which was what the public hearings were, which promised truth, healing, and reconciliation to a deeply divided and traumatised people, began with a story. This was the secret of the Commission – no stern-faced officials sitting in a private chamber, but at a stage, a handful of black and white men and women listening to stories of horror, of deep sorrow, amazing fortitude, and heroism. The audience was there too, and a much wider audience watched and listened through television and radio. It was a ritual, deeply needed to cleanse a nation. It was a drama. (2000a: 98–99)

This understanding went hand-in-hand with careful stage management: several venues constituted 'reclaimed spaces that had been denied to black South Africans under apartheid' (Hutchison 2013: 29; also Krog 1999: 58), while Archbishop Tutu 'always prayed in English, Xhosa, Sotho and Afrikaans to underscore that the Commission belonged to us all' (Tutu 1999: 85). The Commission also resisted requests for victim cross-examination to provide a safe environment (Tutu 1999: 88) and adapted its staging as it gained a clearer sense of appropriate dramaturgy. Thus, at the first hearing,

> commissioners were arrayed on a stage before the audience while the witness sat at the front of the house, back to the audience, facing the commissioners. This spatial arrangement changed fairly quickly ... for organizers felt it did not accurately symbolize what the commission was about. The new format placed witnesses on the stage adjacent to the commissioners, both seated at tables angled slightly toward each other. This arrangement enabled both the commissioners and the witness to face outward toward the house, making clear who the real audience was for the TRC and for the testimony given.
>
> (Cole 2010: 93)

The media also covered proceedings from the outset. On the first day of human rights violations' hearings, the South African Broadcasting Company (SABC) aired 'an hour-long [television] programme on the meaning of the [TRC] legislation, the origin of amnesty, the workings of the Commission and an interview with the Minister of Justice' (Krog 1999: 39). For the first five days, the entire hearings were broadcast live on television, while for most of the TRC's lifespan, they were aired live on radio.

However, it is not simply the level of coverage that matters, but also the form. As Leigh Payne argues with respect to public confessions:

> Mediatized performances ... are not faithful copies of the originals ... Camerawork can create or diminish emotion ... Because most audiences [miss the live version and witness developments] ... through mediatized accounts, those accounts actually become the confessional event, not an interpretation of it.
>
> (2008: 23)

Critically, live coverage went hand-in-hand with news bulletins of selected sound bites that provided emotional drama, and longer news packages and debates and analysis (Krog 2013: 21). Moreover, while many journalists provided occasional reports, a handful followed the

Commission around the country. This helped to provide linkages between testimonies, contextualise reports and sustain public interest. The most important programme in this regard was the SABC's weekly *TRC Special Report* – an eighty-seven episode series that told the story behind many of the Commission's revelations (Cole 2010: 99–110) – which, in 1996, enjoyed the largest audience of any televised current affairs programme in South African history (Verdoolaege 2005: 191). Such coverage helped to place regular news bulletins in a broader context (although arguably further improvements could have been made [Bird & Garda 1997: 336 and 341]), and ensured that reporting went beyond a simple relaying of opposing narratives, which might have further entrenched existing societal divisions (Laplante & Phenicie 2010: 209 on Peru's TRC).

However, not all media coverage was supportive. The Commission was regularly mocked as the 'Kleenex Commission' (a reference to the popular tissue brand; Cole 2010: 17), while disproportionate attention was given to allegations of impropriety within the Commission, to the intransigent position of key politicians and to the critiques of party leaders. The Afrikaans language press also proved much more critical than the English (Verdoolaege 2005: 188), which fuelled a situation in which many Afrikaners became convinced that the Commission was 'nothing more than a witch-hunt against them' (Meredith 2001: 199). With time, many South Africans also became deeply disappointed with the apparent lies told, the small number of alleged perpetrators who did not apply for amnesty that were prosecuted and the speed with which amnesty was awarded in the face of delayed and nominal reparations. Nevertheless, much media coverage supported the Commission's general approach and collectively contributed to an overarching narrative of apartheid as an evil system that encouraged atrocities by those who defended and opposed it.

Finally, the very act of reporting the TRC became part of a 'performance of change' (McEachern 2002: 27). In short, the media, which had itself been implicated in helping to hold up apartheid,

> provided an official forum for this new inclusiveness ... in new content for television and radio programming, new personnel, new kinds of newspapers and a plethora of internet sites. Here, narratives of self and collectivities previously suppressed or minimised were told; voices, accents and languages previously silenced or marginalised were affirmed as part of

the new South Africa by being heard in the most important public arena. (McEachern 2002: xvii)

Collectively these factors ensured a positive reinforcing cycle as the TRC staged hearings that attracted coverage, and the media covered hearings in ways that helped to sustain and deepen public interest. But how does this differ from the Kenyan experience, and what are the lessons for future truth commissions?

5.2 The TJRC's Public Hearings

He says he's an old man and happy to tell everything and happy to say it in public, but there's no one here so it's as good as *in camera*!
(TJRC staff member at an AMP hearing, Bungoma, 12 July 2011)

The TJRC Act tasked the TJRC to provide 'victims, perpetrators and the general public with a platform for non-retributive truth-telling that charts a new moral vision and seeks to create a value-based society for all Kenyans' (Kenya 2008d: 5[g]). To this end, hearings were meant to provide 'victims of human rights abuses and corruption with a forum to be heard and restore their dignity; [and provide] repentant perpetrators or participants in gross human rights violations with a forum to confess their actions as a way of bringing reconciliation' (Kenya 2008d: 5[h–i]). The act also tasked the TJRC to 'educate and engage the public and give sufficient publicity to its work so as to encourage the public to contribute positively to the achievement of the objectives of the Commission' (Kenya 2008d: 6 [i]).

For the TJRC, public hearings – together with a final report and recommendations – were central to how staff believed that they could meet this mandate. This is reflected in the time and resources dedicated to organising them. Thus, while the TJRC Act required public hearings, unless there were good reasons to hold them *in camera*, no direction was given on how many hearings should be held and where. Nevertheless, between April 2011 and March 2012, and despite an initially tight time frame and limited resources, the Commission organised local hearings (public, *in camera* and women's hearings) in thirty-five locations across the country. It also held AMP and thematic hearings in Nairobi (with the exception of a two-day AMP hearing in Bungoma) – the latter focusing on a wide range of subjects from armed militia groups and prisons and detention centres to children and persons with disabilities (TJRC vol. 1 2013: 114).

The importance of hearings was also expressed in the TJRC's final report, which notes how

> [t]he written word, no matter how poetic, cannot convey accurately the passion with which people demanded to tell their stories and the integrity and dignity with which they related their experiences ... So while this Report is the final product of this Commission ... we know that the work of the Commission is also written in the hearts and souls of each and every person who interacted with the Commission.
>
> (TJRC 2013: iii–iv)

Public hearings were held in a variety of buildings, but were often tucked away in conventional meeting rooms, which did little to detract from a burgeoning idea that the TJRC was just another commission of inquiry. The exception was a two-day hearing on torture, which was held in the basement of Nyayo House (a government administration building in the centre of town) where the public gaze was guided to the open doorways of the infamous Nyayo House torture chambers, which added depth to the testimony of former inmates and to the denials and excuses offered by government officials (Nairobi, 7 March 2012).

Hearings were also often poorly signposted. One example was in Nairobi, where most hearings were held at the NHIF building (an office block on the edge of the central business district), where one had to go up an escalator and a flight of stairs before finding a small sign for the TJRC's 'public hearings'. Together with a handful of newspaper adverts publicising hearing schedules, last minute changes to dates and venues, and a website that was frequently out of date, limited signage ensured that it was often difficult to know where and when hearings would be held even if one read the national newspapers, had reliable internet access and closely followed the Commission's work.

When one entered the venue, the usual format was for commissioners to sit at the front of the room on a small platform on black padded chairs behind a long table facing the audience. Sign language interpreters were then situated down on the floor in front and slightly to the left or right. Also down on the floor, and at a 45 degree angle to the commissioners and public, was a table for the witness, the leader of evidence (who was to guide the witness and ask questions), the hearing clerk (who swore in witnesses and processed any documents submitted) and a member of the special support unit or a trained counsellor (who was there to comfort witnesses if and when necessary). Next to this table a second table was usually situated in the middle of the room facing the commissioners with recording equipment and space for any international observers or 'important visitors'. The exception to this arrangement were venues with fixed furniture, such as the auditorium at NHIF, where commissioners sat at the front facing rows of tiered seats, the front left row substituting for a witness table, and the first few rows on the right for the media, VIP and recording team.

At each venue, people situated in the 'VIP area' were provided with headphones and could choose whether to listen to the proceedings in English or Kiswahili. During closing ceremonies in each location, this area was also occupied by local dignitaries including administrators and elders who – together with politicians – tended to be absent from the rest of the proceedings.

There was then an interpreters booth, which was usually situated opposite the witness table, where TJRC staff ensured, whether the witness was speaking in English, Kiswahili or a local vernacular, that testimony was available in English and Kiswahili, and that, if necessary, any questions posed by the leader of evidence or commissioner were translated into the appropriate language. English was vital as at least one international commissioner attended every public hearing (with the exception of women's hearings), and none of them could speak a local language. English was also the language in which transcripts were recorded. Kiswahili was also necessary, as (with the exception of some hearings in Nairobi) this was the language in which testimony was relayed to any members of the general public in attendance through loud speakers.

Simultaneous interpretation was incredibly difficult: witnesses often spoke quickly about emotional subjects using words that had no direct equivalents, whilst significant gaps, noises and tears were lost. Witnesses also used different modes of speaking and, at the risk of over-generalising, stories in English tended to be more linear and to make less use of idiom and metaphor than their Kiswahili and vernacular counterparts (cf. Cole 2010: 73). Almost inevitably mistakes were made in interpretation, and Kenyan commissioners regularly picked up on mistranslations between Kiswahili and English (often with visible irritation), while many differences between vernaculars, Kiswahili and English probably went unnoticed.

Venues also had a dedicated 'media area' where journalists could zoom in on both witnesses and commissioners, while later hearings also had a 'media tent' where journalists could watch the hearings, access the internet and file reports (interview, TJRC director, Nairobi, 14 September 2011). The media presence varied between locations and during sessions, but the media area often only housed the TJRC cameraman, while other journalists often left as soon as they had secured a story. I did not see any international media at the hearings attended.

Finally, behind the 'witness' and 'observer' tables sat the general public – usually on plastic chairs – who listened to proceedings through loud speakers. The fact that the 'VIP table' usually divided this audience from the rest of the proceedings created a two-tier audience. At the front, there were the commissioners, media and VIPs who could choose which language to listen to the proceedings in through individual headsets, and who could clearly see the witnesses and their expressions and bearing. Members of the public had no such choice, and while they could hear the witness or the interpreter, could often not see them. The exception were hearings – for example, those held in Nairobi and Kisumu – where proceedings were also captured on a big screen at the front of the room.

The experience of 'observers' and 'the public' was thus markedly different – a fact that I became acutely aware of when I moved from the VIP area (where I usually sat listening to testimony through headphones) to the back of the room at public hearings in Kisumu. The difference was stark: I could no longer see the witness and their facial expressions first-hand but instead watched via a big screen, which rendered their testimony both more theatric and distant as the cameraman tended to zoom in at moments of heightened emotion. The poor quality of the sound system, and periodic crackles and volume changes, also made proceedings much more difficult to follow. When I asked TJRC staff about this two-tiered seating arrangement, I was reassured that this was what Kenyans expected from such an official body and that they were simply following protocol. However, one of the commissioners later acknowledged that there had been 'a discussion at the beginning about having the witness in the middle and commissioners off to the side, but the room wasn't conducive at the first hearings'. Apparently the setup they fell back on then became 'the norm', although he also recognised that 'prestige is also part of the story ... that we're the commissioners!' (Nairobi, 27 March 2012).

The decision to use such familiar staging contributed to a prevalent sense of once-againness; the differences in the oral and visual experiences of various participants not only made it harder for the general public to stay focused on proceedings, but also suggested that, as an audience, they were less important than commissioners and visiting dignitaries. This impression was reinforced by the language choices made by witnesses – whereby those who were proficient in English and Kiswahili tended to speak in English (the language of officialdom and elite business) 'to the Commission', with their testimony then translated into Kiswahili (the language of the marketplace and populist politics) for 'the public'.

In terms of protocol, or scripting, public hearings began with the national anthem. The regional coordinator then read out the commission prayer, and people were asked to stand up when commissioners entered and left the room. Sessions ended with an ad hoc prayer by a selected member of the public. Witnesses were sworn in – either by swearing on the Bible, Koran or Kenyan Constitution – whereupon they read out, summarised or were led through their statement or memorandum by the leader of evidence. They were then asked questions by the leader of evidence and commissioners, which tended to be for clarification or for additional information, and as a way for commissioners to offer empathy and promises of assistance or commitment, rather than as a means of cross examination. *In camera* hearings apparently followed a similar structure but without the presence of media, observers, or members of the general public.

Witnesses were selected as 'window cases' by the Commission's legal team, or as people whose statement or memorandum was deemed to be representative of common issues or problems faced. Due to the temporal and thematic scope of the Commission's mandate and limited time available, about half of the witnesses selected were opinion leaders who summarised local histories and specific problems, and, as a result, usually appeared divorced from the abuses and injustices discussed. This was in stark contrast to the testimony of first-hand victims who often offered less useful summative truths, but more emotional personal truths. The overarching and context-setting memoranda were often scheduled first. This was understandable, but rendered it even less likely that hearings captured the popular imagination, and likely contributed to a falling off in audience size and media attendance in various locations. Moreover, on the first day of public hearings in any one location the first few testimonies often lasted for several hours, which led to an increasingly tight programme and ensured that audiences often received an abundance or scarcity of information.

Relatively poor scripting was also reflected in the fact that testimonies tended to jump from one issue to another: one witness, for example, talking about post-election violence, the next about historical land injustices and the next about problems facing disabled residents. This helped to ensure that the Commission covered different aspects of its broad mandate, but also meant that the hearings lacked a clear overarching narrative – besides the fact that many people had suffered (Chapter 6) – which had further repercussions for levels of public interest and media engagement, as a negative cycle of disinterest, disengagement and limited coverage set in.

In addition to public and *in camera* hearings, women's hearings were also held in each location. These women-only events, which are discussed in more detail in Chapter 7, were characterised by a mix of scheduled speakers and open microphone sessions. They were less formal and often more emotional than their public counterparts. However, while they left a strong impression upon many who attended, the immediate audience was limited to an average of sixty women in each hearing (TJRC vol. 1 2013: xvii), whilst most women's hearings received no media coverage and male journalists were turned away.

Hearings for AMPs took place after public, women's and *in camera* hearings – although 'after' could be the next day or several months later. At these hearings a selection of people adversely mentioned in people's statements were summoned to appear before the Commission, where – if they actually appeared – they read out a statement or were led through their testimony by the leader of evidence, and were then 'cross-examined' by the leader of evidence and commissioners. However, while some of these hearings attracted a fairly sizeable audience and some media coverage, the level of engagement was still relatively limited. In part, this was because reports tended to focus on the mere attendance of AMPs with any shock value limited by the fact that no AMP admitted to any wrongdoing and, instead, usually 'did not know', 'could not remember' or suggested that responsibility 'lay elsewhere' (Chapter 8). This was in stark contrast to the dramatic moments provided by South Africa's amnesty hearings and ensured that there was relatively little to report. However, it also stemmed from the disproportionate attention given to the Commission's strategic foci, namely, injustices with which the chair was associated, and the land-related conflict in Mt Elgon where the acting chair had previously worked, to the relative neglect of more famous atrocities and higher profile AMPs.

Finally, thematic hearings were held in Nairobi where experts (often academics or activists) presented memoranda and answered questions. Themes included children's rights, people living with disabilities, ethnic tension and violence, and torture. These general overviews provided some factual truths, but they tended to be fairly dry and to enjoy limited audiences, and collectively initiated almost no public debate.

Indeed, most TJRC hearings failed to attract sizeable immediate audiences or to become a media event. Hearings were aired live on TV twice, and irregularly on the radio. Testimonies rarely made it on to the evening news or to the front pages of the national newspapers, with limited discussion on national and local radio. Indeed, coverage was usually limited to short articles towards the middle of the newspaper, while local media tended to only cover hearings in that particular area. The exception was the Wagalla massacre, where allegations of Kiplagat's potential involvement, the scale of the atrocity and previous cover-ups ensured that revelations attracted unrivalled media attention. This included a series of feature articles in Kenya's leading daily newspapers, and documentaries for Kenya Television News (KTN), Citizen TV and Al Jazeera, which relayed 'personal testimonies of Wagalla survivors', 'the culpability of Kenyan politicians', and set 'Wagalla in a wider context of political oppression and economic neglect' (Anderson 2014: 659). In addition, excerpts from the Wagalla hearings were included in the documentary *Scarred: The Anatomy of a Massacre*, which was directed by Judy Kibinge with the support of several organisations including The Wagalla Massacre Foundation and KNCHR, and which was screened in Nairobi and Wajir in February 2015. The KNCHR also screened recordings of the Wagalla AMP hearings in northern Kenya as part of their outreach programmes. Finally, coverage of Wagalla benefited from the fact that the Commission launched its public hearings in northern Kenya (in Garissa town) and travelled with six journalists for the first few weeks. However, while this helped to provide initial coverage, questions were raised about the cost of facilitating the journalists' movements, and the Commission consequently became reliant

Public Hearings

on local journalists (conversation with member of the TJRC communications team, Kisumu, 10 July 2011).

Besides irregular coverage, the TJRC had a small communications team who responded to media enquiries, produced occasional inserts for the national newspapers and helped to produce 15-minute roundups for TV. However, the fact that the latter were aired at different times on different TV stations during the course of only some of the public hearings minimised their public impact. The team also oversaw the production of a series of eight 30-minute discussion programmes entitled *Kenya's Unheard Truth*, which were broadcast at 10 pm on a Thursday between February and April 2012 (TJRC vol. 1 2013: 116). However, few people with whom I spoke remembered having seen one of these programmes, which seemed to trigger little (if any) public debate.

The TJRC also had a social media presence. However, the fact that a total of 1,420 tweets had been posted by December 2013, while the Commission had attracted only 687 followers, suggests that its impact was negligible. The TJRC also conducted a handful of media training events. According to one journalist, though, this 'basically [involved] reading out the Act ... I don't remember any TJRC training that impressed' (interview, Nairobi, 7 August 2012). This poor communications record is due to a number of factors. This includes the broader political context and problems with scripting and stage management, but also a poor communications strategy. In particular, a number of commission staff bemoaned the fact that this aspect of the TJRC's work was headed by a former news anchor rather than by a more experienced communications officer (interview, TJRC director, Nairobi, 9 March 2012).

To make matters worse, the majority of media coverage that the TJRC received focused on the chairman issue, which served to further undermine public excitement and reinforce a growing sense of once-againness. This focus on problems was particularly pronounced when it came to opinion pieces written by prominent civil society activists in the leading dailies, which enjoy wide readership and sometimes prompt public debate. In turn, newspaper cartoons of the process tended to depict the Commission through images of the troubled chairman who was easily recognisable by his characteristic shock of combed back white hair. In this way, the popular satirical cartoonist, Gado – in his regular contributions to Kenya's leading daily newspaper, the *Daily*

Nation – either ignored the Commission or reduced it to the embattled chair who, in one controversial cartoon, was drawn 'naked, stripped!' (*Daily Nation* 28 May 2010).

The general feeling that hearings enjoyed limited public engagement was supported by informal discussions with residents of towns where local hearings were ongoing, and by interviews and discussions with people during the course of the Commission's life. Typical comments included a dismissal of the TJRC as a 'non-starter' (interview, Kalenjin peace activist, Eldoret, 3 March 2011; Kikuyu peace activist, Nakuru, 7 March 2011); people 'have well founded fears that its time will lapse before it even gets off the ground' (interview, civil society activist, Nairobi, 21 March 2011); the process is 'doomed' (interview, civil society activist, Nairobi, 28 April 2011); if there is 'anything that I've not followed well it's the TJRC' (interview, Kikuyu clergyman, Murunga, 6 May 2011); and there has been a 'lack of sensitisation and ... people don't understand the commission' (participant in TJRC civic education meeting, Molo, 21 July 2011).

This impressionistic account of scepticism and disinterest is supported by parallel research (Backer, Lahouchuc & Long 2010) and opinion polls. For example, in a survey conducted in June 2011, 52 per cent of Kenyans said they were aware of the TJRC, but 45 per cent did not know that it existed (KNDR June 2011: 10). Limited awareness extended to victims of violations under investigation. For example, when ICTJ researchers met with victims in 2011, 23 per cent had never heard of the Commission, 40 per cent knew something about it and 37 per cent said they knew it well, although 80 per cent said that they had had no contact with the Commission (Robins 2011: 44). Moreover, overall levels of awareness declined during the Commission's term. Thus, in an opinion poll conducted by Ipsos Synovate in June 2013 – just a month after the report's release – only 33 per cent knew of 'a commission that recently submitted its report to the President, accompanied by the controversy over a section of the Land chapter', which could only have been the TJRC. And of those who could identify the TJRC, only 16 per cent had 'a lot' of confidence that the report's recommendations would be implemented, 40 per cent 'some', 37 per cent 'none at all' and 6 per cent were 'not sure'.[1]

---

[1] www.ipsos.co.ke/home/index.php/downloads.

Limited media coverage stands in stark contrast to several previous commissions of inquiry such as the 2003 inquiry into the Goldenberg corruption scandal, which 'elicited great public participation and was intensely covered in the media including through daily live broadcasts of the Commission's proceedings in one of the main television stations' (Christine Alai, a prominent human rights activist, cited in TJRC vol. 1 2013: 112). But how can one explain such limited engagement and confidence beyond the problems of stage management and scripting outlined above, and what are the implications for ensuring that future truth commissions stage more effective performative processes?

5.3 The TJRC's Limited Audience

I would be surprised if people know what [the TJRC] is, it's mandate, or even if people turn up. People associate it with normal commissions that have never produced results in the past.

(Interview, retired senior civil servant from Western Kenya, Nairobi, 2 May 2011)

Limited media coverage of, and public engagement with, the TJRC's public hearings stem from a number of different issues that relate both to the broader context in which the Commission was working, and to the Commission's internal wranglings and dynamics. This section does not seek to provide an exhaustive account of these issues – many of which are discussed in more detail in other chapters – but instead provides a brief overview to contextualise conclusions regarding the need for processes that seek to shape public debate to pay greater attention to the presence of an engaged and receptive audience, which depends in large part on the broader political context.

As detailed in Chapter 4, a sense that the TJRC was going to be like previous commissions of inquiry – in that it would write a detailed report that would then be relegated to dusty shelves – was reinforced from the outset by the fact that there was no political transition and by the credibility crisis that revolved around the chairman. This sense of once-againness was then reinforced by the way in which public hearings were scripted and staged-managed, while initial scepticism also discouraged the country's commercial media industry from paying the Commission much attention. This ensured that the TJRC never enjoyed the '[e]xtensive media interest and coverage [which, in the case of South Africa, had] brought this ritual event ... into people's homes and thus made it part of their routine world' (McEachern 2002: 26).

However, one cannot fully understand the failure of the TJRC to become a media event and widespread dismissal of its work without also considering the push for those deemed most responsible for the post-election violence of 2007–8 to be held criminally accountable. At one level, many feared that the TJRC might be used to avoid the ICC (Chapter 3), but the Court's intervention also impacted on the TJRC's work in other ways. First, there was some confusion at the local level about the relationship and difference between the two bodies, which was exacerbated by limited civic education and the similarities between the TJRC statement and ICC victim registration forms. Thus, while interviewees who had heard of these bodies knew that the ICC was an international court that was investigating prominent Kenyans for their alleged role in the post-election violence, and that the TJRC was a government commission of inquiry, many did not know that the TJRC's mandate extended beyond the post-election violence, and were sometimes unsure about whether information collected by the latter would be shared with, or would be used to support proceedings at, the ICC.

The ICC also completely upstaged the TJRC as any development, or hint of a development – at least during the Commission's lifespan – absorbed the focus of local, national and international print, TV and radio media. Thus, while the TJRC was denigrated as just another commission of inquiry, the relative novelty and potential impact of the ICC – which saw leading politicians fly to and from The Hague to sit in a court with legal representatives and stern judges, and then get elected to run the country – meant that its international character and unpredictability rendered it a relevant process that could have significant ramifications for the country's future. In short, for the Court's supporters, the process seemed capable (at least for much of the lifespan of the TJRC hearings) of providing the kind of justice that seemed impossible within Kenya, while the ICC's opponents feared that the Court would remove popular leaders from the local political stage. Journalists also found it 'easier' to get information from the ICC than from the TJRC where there was 'too much officialdom' (interview, newspaper journalist, Nairobi, 7 August 2012).

The ICC was also not the only distraction. The TJRC was simultaneously upstaged by a successful referendum on a new constitution in 2010, an array of subsequent institutional reforms and campaigns ahead of the 2013 elections. The process was further complicated by the emergence of a pervasive peace narrative, which became interwoven with the revival of an old peace-versus-justice debate to the detriment of a truth-telling process that could recommend further investigations, prosecutions and lustrations (Chapter 2). As one clergyman noted, 'the TJRC is going to unearth and create even more problems ... as Christians we preach to forget past sins' (interview, Muranga, 6 May 2011).

Finally, the TJRC faced problems of vested interests within state and private media companies. This became apparent in October 2011 when the state-owned Kenya Broadcasting Company (KBC) 'failed to air' a 15-minute TJRC round-up, which the Commission had paid for. According to the managing director, 'the round-up scheduled for that day "was found unsuitable for transmission based on KBC's editorial programming policy"', but '[i]t appears that the round-up was censored because a witness appearing in that round-up had mentioned President Kibaki in a negative light' (TJRC vol. 1 2013: 112–113). The Commission subsequently opted to pay the private company, KTN, for a slot. However, such self-censorship likely also affected coverage by private media houses, especially as many sought to present themselves as the voices of peace.

This array of challenges was interwoven with problems that stemmed from the Commission's own limited capacity, which, as previously discussed, led to poor advertising of hearings and signposting of venues, and limited communication of changes to hearing schedules, while financial problems curtailed civic education efforts. This was critical since many people, including journalists and other opinion leaders, ended up knowing little about the TJRC's mandate, working practices or aims, which had a detrimental impact on the quality of public debate.

Moreover, even when members of the public and journalists did attend hearings, the performance staged often failed to enthral, leading attendance to fall off with each subsequent day in any one location. The reasons were multiple but included an extensive mandate and short time frame, which led to a heavy reliance on memoranda by community spokespeople who were often divorced from the abuses discussed; the fact that the perpetrators' voices ended up being largely absent from the truths told (Chapter 8); and the lack of a clear overarching narrative as witness testimonies shifted, for example, from the post-election violence of 2007–8 to land disputes and the marginalisation of local minorities in the course of any one hearing. Ultimately, even the time given to public hearings became part of the problem. As one commissioner explained, they had spent so much time in the field attending hearings that they had not given enough thought to how the hearings could constitute a more effective drama and 'to what our story is' (conversation, Bungoma, July 2011).

5.4 Conclusions: Of Audience and Its Engagement

To change society, a collective memory must be proffered, and people must pay attention. In South Africa, the TRC seemed to succeed at both getting the attention of the people and persuading them of its view of the struggle over apartheid.

(Gibson 2006: 419)

According to Eric Brahm, 'the degree to which [a truth] commission's findings are accessible by the public seems more crucial' for its impact, than whether the hearings are public or not (2007: 31). However, while this may be true for the impact of a final report, and the likelihood that a government implements its recommendations, it is not true for the impact of its hearings. Truth commissions opt to hold hearings, in part, because testimony is meant to help establish factual truths that can then feed into a final report and recommendations. However, they increasingly opt to hold these hearings in *public* because the process of telling and listening – or the interaction between performers and audiences – is believed to be able to contribute to personal and national healing by providing a forum for personal narratives to be shared and for new social truths to be constructed and, with luck, officially acknowledged and publicly internalised. In short, the success of post–South African truth commissions depend largely on popular awareness of, and levels of participation in, such self-consciously public processes.

To this end, there needs to be an audience that listens to personal narratives for the purposes of catharsis, which watches the hearings enactment of 'new-ness', and which engages with the overarching social narratives in ways that can produce a new understanding of a country's past and future trajectory. As a result, the media plays a critical role given its ability and capacity to reach out to the masses, but also through its editorial, interpretative and context-setting role, which generates 'the political meaning' around truth commissions (Payne 2008: 24). However, the presence of an audience is not a given; to become a 'media event', routine broadcasting must be interrupted with coverage characterised by pomp and circumstance that enthrals the general public (Krabill 2001: 569). This means that a TRC has to provide good theatre – it has to captivate, excite and stimulate. It also has to conduct its work in an environment where its performances are interpreted as good theatre by a broader public, and as something worth watching.

This clearly did not happen in Kenya. Indeed, while the 2003 TF envisaged a truth commission 'whose public hearings would be aired live on television and radio', the level of media coverage ended up being 'very different' (TJRC vol. 1 2013: 111) – with hearings ultimately characterised by small immediate audiences, limited media coverage, negligible public debate and low levels of public awareness. The process thus lacked the kind of engaged and receptive public that is essential for a transformative interaction between performers and audiences that could potentially lead to catharsis, a sense of a new state or revised national narratives.

The implication is that much greater attention needs to be given to whether an engaged and receptive audience is following such performances – an analysis that points to the importance of a commission's communications strategy, advertising and media coverage, but also to popular interpretations about what such a process is likely to achieve, and thus, once again, to the importance of broader political contexts and the credibility of key actors. In short, while commission staff can ensure that hearings are performed with pomp and circumstance, it is far more challenging, and largely context dependent, whether or not hearings encourage profit-oriented private media houses to interrupt routine broadcasting and ensure continuous live coverage, and whether or not they draw in an engaged and receptive audience.

Moreover, even if citizens are present and engaged, this does not ensure that public hearings will achieve their goals, and it is not obvious that the interaction of performers and audiences would have been transformative in the Kenyan context even if public hearings had attracted larger immediate audiences and become an extended media event. Instead, presence and engagement simply raise secondary questions about the efficacy of performances, and immediate and long-term responses. For example, do witnesses find the experience cathartic, or are they left feeling newly traumatised and victimised? Are trauma and healing really the main issues, or is it, for example, the anger and suffering that results from a history of injustice, which requires substantive change as well (or instead of) cathartic release? Do the hearings embody the idea of transition and perform a new kind of state, or are they interpreted as familiar performances that foster a sense of 'once-againness'? Or, alternatively, do they simply help to legitimise a new state in the context of limited change? Is an overarching narrative produced that is popularly accepted and which contributes to healing and reconciliation, or does public debate simply reveal the level of division and promote further conflict? Or, alternatively, does it distract from other narratives and a more redistributive politics, and thus help to delimit any real transition that takes place?

The presence of an audience is thus only a first step for public hearings to achieve their goal, but it is an important one since, as Ron Krabill argues in the context of South Africa, '[p]eople may vehemently disagree about whether the TRC process has affected the country positively or negatively, but they are talking about it. While this clearly does not lead to reconciliation in and of itself, it does represent the beginnings of a common if contentious understanding of the past' (2001: 571). In contrast, while the Kenyan TJRC played a role as a fact-finding body that has published a report with an array of recommendations that might be implemented, or at least discussed, at some point, the point of holding its hearings in *public* was largely lost. This reality helps to explain how the Kenyan TJRC – but also other post–South African truth commissions – have fallen short of ambitious goals. It also provides important lessons for any future commissions that seek to follow the South African model whereby public hearings are meant to help both stage and achieve a transition to a more just and less violent society.

6 | Truth's Grand Narrative (Part I)
Of Injustice and Suffering

What followed [Kenya's independence from British rule] was a history of political repression, blatant injustices and widespread, systematic violation of human rights.

(TJRC vol. 1 2013: 4)

South Africa's TRC hearings became a media event, but even then, most testimony was quickly forgotten or passed almost unnoticed. In fact, most stories were rendered 'unheard' as, in failing to 'deploy required or expected ... genres, styles, formats', what an individual said or wrote was 'either not noticed, or [was] easily disqualified as meaningless, trivial or nonsensical' (Blommaert, Bock & McCormick 2006: 42). In contrast, a few moments became emblematic as excerpts from some 'heard' testimonies proliferated 'outside the contexts of individual control' (Ross 2003b: 325), and through articulation were transformed 'into "testimony"/"story" and thence into social fact, open to discussion and disputation' (Ross 2003b: 334). Collectively, these disembodied and mediatised extracts helped to construct the TRC's favoured (albeit contested) narrative: apartheid had been an unjust system that had encouraged defenders and opponents to commit gross human rights violations; apartheid had left South Africans traumatised, wounded and in need of healing; but South Africans were nevertheless still capable of surprising acts of forgiveness and reconciliation.

This narrative lies at the heart of debates around the TRC and its achievements and shortcomings. Such debate has questioned the TRC's legacy, but also accepted that the Commission helped to perform a sense of change – either in the positive sense of contributing to the same, or in the negative sense of constituting a distraction – and invigorated further political debate and action.

This chapter introduces this narrative, and – together with the next two chapters – compares this clear (if contested) narrative of the TRC and its embodiment in a few emblematic moments with the messy overarching narrative of the Kenyan TJRC. As discussed, the TJRC was established in a very different context and came to be defined, at least for most of its lifespan, by the chairman debacle and a sense of once-againness, while the hearings attracted relatively little attention. As a result, this analysis does not look to a recognised public narrative, which is yet to be (and may never be) established, but to a narrative which emerges from a close reading of the Commission's hearings, final report and reception. This narrative is the product of both the commissioners and commission staff, as well as of the citizens and civil society activists who engaged with the process. The conclusion: Kenyans, and particularly political activists, women, children and ethnic minorities have suffered, and continue to suffer, from a long history of injustice, and from an embedded culture of impunity. This chapter focuses on the first part of this narrative, namely, that of an ongoing history of violation and suffering.

To summarise, the TJRC revealed how each regime (from the colonial period through the Kenyatta, Moi and Kibaki eras) had overseen widespread abuses through acts of commission and omission and how Kenyans had suffered (and many continue to suffer) as a consequence. According to the Commission's final report, those who have borne the brunt of atrocities include political dissidents, residents of areas wracked by ethnic conflict and land disputes, communities in marginalised areas (namely, North Eastern, Upper Eastern, Coast, Nyanza, Western and North Rift regions), which collectively constitute well over half the country's land mass, and members of vulnerable groups (namely, women, children, marginalised ethnic minorities and the disabled). In addition, the Commission highlighted the harm that had resulted from socio-economic crimes and corruption, and how even relatively developed areas had been marginalised at one point or another.

Whilst near all-inclusive at one level, the Commission's narrative of suffering is also selectively exclusive. Thus, while it recognised pervasive suffering, it also acknowledged the impossibility of providing 'the definitive history of the broad range of violations committed and suffered' during its forty-five-year mandate period (TJRC vol. 1 2013: v). In turn, some victims – for example, those harassed because of their religious identity or sexual orientation, youths shot by police as alleged criminals or members of the country's racial minorities – will find little that relates to their seminal experiences in the final report. Instead, the Commission focused on political dissidence, ethno-regional disparities and ethnic minorities, and women and children. As a result, the process highlights, but also inadvertently reinforces, a focus on political repression to the relative neglect of a more general imposition of order, and on ethnic difference to the relative neglect of class, creed or generation. It also repeats a common assertion that it is the women and children who tend to 'suffer most', whilst failing to fully consider the extent to which it is the poor and politically active who tend to be targeted.

The TJRC also highlighted how much of this widespread suffering belongs, not to a temporally distinct past, but to the present and expected futures. First, the TJRC hearings and final report reveal how the impact of many harms live on in the form of people-shaped holes and lost trajectories. Second, they highlight how many violations – such as economic marginalisation – continue into the present, while a common failure to investigate and acknowledge past wrongs, or to provide recompense and punitive justice, constitute a continuous violation. Third, a close reading provides insights into how past injustice lives on in the form of evolutions and, in particular, how real or potential victims can become the perpetrators of further injustice. Fourth, the Commission's work provides a glimpse of how the past – together with the echoes of earlier pasts revoked – haunt the present through the fears that people harbour regarding likely futures. Finally, people's participation reveals how many talk of traumatic pasts, not in the hope of catharsis, but of gaining reparations or some other form of justice. The very state of 'being a victim' becoming a resource that self-confessed victims can use to lay claims (Beckmann 2010: 201) and which politicians can use to mobilise support (Lynch 2011b).

This narrative of extensive, long-term and ongoing suffering reveals how almost all Kenyans are victims and how 'the problem' is not a particular socio-economic and political regime, but Kenya's socio-economic and political systems more broadly – from a political system characterised by competition between ethnic groups and an entrenched and corrupt elite to uneven economic development and patriarchy.

This narrative is a product of victims' statements, memoranda and testimony, but also of various pre-existing understandings of the problem and solutions, which helped to shape the original mandate; the management of research, investigations and hearings; the selection of witnesses as 'window cases'; the input of various civil society organisations and activists; and the final report. The latter written by the Commission's research team together with the commissioners, a handful of expert consultants hired to draft particular chapters, and a cluster of civil society groups who helped to develop the Commission's reparations framework. As a result of this collective input, the process was shaped by an emphasis on the long-term socio-economic impact of bodily integrity human rights violations (which had informed thinking around a TJRC from the time of the 2003 task force), the widely recognised salience of ethnic identities in Kenyan politics and an assumption that women, children and minority groups are particularly vulnerable. This process of production ensured that the final report fits within a certain genre of human rights writing, whereby complex histories are simplified into clear and powerful overviews, which can help to justify certain courses of action and delegitimise others. This is perhaps unsurprising. But it means that the truth revealed - while it captures the systemic nature of violations and the scale of suffering - often falls into accepted clichés. The outcome is a report that will likely be more useful to those who seek to support claim-making than to historians of Kenya's past.

This chapter provides an overview of the South African TRC's defining moments and associated grand narrative, which, while problematic, proved productive of further action. The chapter then moves on to the first part of the Kenyan TJRC's narrative and to the Commission's main foci and associated gaps and findings, certain particularities of its data management and report writing process, and the ongoing nature of suffering exposed. The aim is threefold: first, to show how, as a result of the TJRC's expansive mandate and prevalent sense of injustice, the narrative that emerged excludes and downplays key groups, but nevertheless presents Kenyans, as a collective, as victims of injustice, albeit in different ways and to varying extents.

Second, the chapter highlights how, beyond the Wagalla massacre, little of the truths voiced seemed particularly new, ensuring that the mere articulation of history did little to perform any sense of transition. Finally, it highlights how most of those affected by violations did not see their suffering as something that belongs to a temporally distinct past, but as something that persists into the present and envisaged futures. Chapter 7 picks up on one particular dimension of this victim narrative, namely, a focus on female suffering to the relative neglect of gendered power relations. Chapter 8 discusses the second half of the TJRC's overarching narrative regarding an embedded culture of impunity, and Chapter 9 turns to some of the early efforts to use the TJRC report and recommendations as a lobbying tool. The aim: to show how the TJRC helped to highlight, rather than to unearth, a history of injustice, which – while in the long term may be used to lobby for reforms – in the short term provided a further performance of injustice as victims continued to suffer, existing gender relations were reproduced, a culture of impunity gained further re-enactment, and political elites largely ignored the Commission's report and recommendations. This story is important for understanding contemporary Kenya, but also for an analysis of comparable truth commissions, which seek closure to complex and persistent pasts in the absence of substantive political change and in the face of limited political will. The lesson: attempts by truth commissions to try and render persistent pasts quickly dead are naïve and often constitute a further injustice as hopes are raised, little substantive change results, and elites seek to undermine and use the process to maintain the status quo.

6.1 Wounded by Apartheid: The TRC's Defining Moments

For many, these public hearings – with their embodied expressions, their weeping, their silences, their demonstrations of 'wet bag' torture techniques, their confrontations between former torturers and those they tortured, the wails, and the moments that transcended language – most defined the commission.

(Cole 2007: 175)

The South African TRC's hearings on human rights violations, amnesty and thematic issues, and associated investigations, provided the defining moments of the TRC's work as victims spoke of (or displayed) their pain; a relatively small number of perpetrators openly spoke of abductions, torture and murder; the majority of leaders and beneficiaries sought to distance themselves from the abuses, which, they argued, had been committed by a few 'bad apples'; and a handful of victims publicly forgave their torturers and assailants. This section discusses four such indicative moments: a widow's wail; a police officer's re-enactment of torture; Tutu's elicitation of an unconvincing apology from one of the struggle's most prominent figures; and a mother's forgiveness of her son's murderer. These moments encapsulated stereotyped (and highly contested) aspects of the Commission's work, namely, the pain and trauma of ordinary citizens, the crimes committed by the apartheid state, a sense of national sickness and the dream of reconciliation, which together helped to produce the TRC's overarching narrative of a wounded, yet hopeful, nation.

The first moment is perhaps the most famous and occurred during the second day of the first human rights violations committee hearing and testimony of Nomonde Calata, one of the widows of the 'Cradock Four': four anti-apartheid activists who had been killed by Security Branch officers in June 1985. The moment came as Mrs Calata, '[r]ecalling ... when she first heard the news about her missing husband ... threw her head back with a wail of such anguish that it sent a shudder throughout the audience' (Meredith 2001: 6). This image and sound became a common media sound bite as an unrehearsed action that 'captured something elemental about the experience of gross violations of human rights' (Cole 2007: 178).

The significance of Calata's wail is evident from commissioner's accounts. Tutu recalled:

At this point in her evidence, Mrs Calata broke down, uttering a piercing wail which in many ways was the defining sound that characterized the Truth and Reconciliation Commission – as a place where people could come to cry, to open their hearts, to expose the anguish that had remained locked up for so long, unacknowledged, ignored and denied. I adjourned the proceedings so that she could recover her composure and when we restarted, I led the gathering in singing '*Senzenina?*' ('What have we done?').

(1999: 114)

Similarly, Dr Alex Boraine, the TRC's vice chair, remembered:

It was that cry from the soul that transformed the hearings from a litany of suffering and pain to an even deeper level. It caught up in a single howl all the darkness and horror of the apartheid years. It was as if she enshrined in the throwing back of her body and letting out the cry the collective horror of the thousands of people who had been trapped in racism and oppression for so long. (Boraine 2000a: 102; also see Orr 2000: 36)

While Mrs Calata's wail became short-hand for victims' trauma and the insufficiencies of language, the questioning of a police officer, Jeffrey Benzien, provided an iconic example of the brutality of the apartheid regime when, halfway through his testimony, the former interrogator re-enacted the 'wet-bag' torture technique. The shocking image that this action provided

> of a black man lying on the floor, his hands behind his back, with a huge man sitting on him gradually pulling a bag over his head and tightening it (until he passed out) has been described by many as the 'seminal moment' of the TRC, the shocking moment of realisation about the past and the jolting of any complaisance.
>
> (McEachern 2002: 51)

Benzien's testimony was seminal as it provided visual evidence of violations suffered that, as a self-confessed perpetrator, was hard to refute. Benzien also offered testimony of how apartheid had dehumanised and victimised the torturer, telling the Commission 'that he could not recognise himself. "What type of person am I?" is the question he asks himself, he said' (McEachern 2002: 54), whilst he also spoke of threats against himself and his family (Payne 2004: 117).

Not all alleged perpetrators were as forthcoming. This included the political elite who generally ignored the Commission's offer of amnesty in exchange for full disclosure. When politicians did give testimony, it was usually as a political party representative, when they catalogued the crimes they had suffered at the hands of their opponents, and distanced themselves from allegations of their own wrongdoing. Former leaders of the apartheid state either disengaged or refused to make constructive contribution's to truth-telling. This led the TRC to initiate legal proceedings against former President P. W. Botha for his failure to comply with a summons, and to widespread criticism of former President F. W. de Klerk for having 'blustered, flustered, objected and denied' his way through questioning following his presentation on behalf of the National Party (NP; Orr 2000: 222).

However, it was leaders of the African National Congress (ANC) who had to oversee the report's implementation and broader nation-building project. In turn, it was the questioning of Nelson Mandela's ex-wife and prominent anti-apartheid heroine, Winnie Mandela, which came to epitomise some of the TRC's major shortcomings, namely, the failure of the country's political elite to fully embrace the process, and the ongoing popularity of those who represented 'black anger'.

Winnie appeared as the head of the Mandela United Football Club, whose members stood accused of the murder, abduction and torture of numerous alleged 'traitors' and 'collaborators' in the late 1980s. This included the murder of a teenager, Stompie Moeketsi, on 1 January 1989, which provided the focus of a nine-day special hearing in 1997. On the eighth day, Winnie took to the stand, when her 'response to the barrage of accusations was to deny everything and to assert that it was all part of a campaign by her political enemies to destroy her reputation before the ANC elections and to eliminate her from the political arena' (Meredith 2001: 225). Winnie also used the opportunity to perform her elite status, as, accompanied by a large crowd of supporters and 'looking glamorous in gold necklaces and an elegant silk suit, [she] made the most of it, shaking her head, laughing, and indicating with a circular movement of her hand [how one of the witnesses] was a lunatic' (Meredith 2001: 258).

The most discussed moment, however, occurred on the last day, when, in response to Tutu's pleas for 'some sign of contrition' (Meredith 2001: 269), Winnie accepted, 'I am saying it is true: things went horribly wrong and we were aware that there were factors that led to it. For that I am deeply sorry' (cited in Krog 1999: 392). To most, Winnie's statement of regret sounded hollow: 'she didn't mean it!' was the angry response (Krog 1999: 392). However, for some, her unconvincing apology underscored the country's desperate need for truth-telling. According to the Commission's vice chair:

Tutu made a desperate appeal to [Botha and Winnie] to acknowledge their own part in our tragedy. Neither responded with genuine remorse. Both continue to claim that they were right and without fault. At opposite poles, repressor and repressed, they sum up the sickness of the soul of South Africa during the years of racial conflict.

(Boraine 2000a: 257)

At the same time, the fact that – despite her political prominence and popularity – Winnie had felt compelled to appear before the Commission and to admit that things went wrong, was interpreted by some as an affirmation of new national values regarding 'the equality and dignity of all people, their rights and duties regardless of their status' (Krog 1999: 392). Indeed, for the South African journalist Antjie Krog – whose account of the TRC became an international bestseller – such moments filled her 'with an indescribable tenderness towards this Commission', as:

[a]gainst a flood crashing with the weight of a brutalizing past on a new usurping politics, the Commission has kept alive the idea of a common

humanity. Painstakingly it has chiselled a way beyond racism and made space for all our voices. For all its failures, it carries a flame of hope that makes me proud to be from here, of here.

(Krog 1999: 422)

Certainly, the sense of hope that the TRC helped to inspire stemmed, at least in part, from the moments of apology and forgiveness that it provided – of which, Winnie's appearance is a highly questionable example. Another more idealistic moment followed a special event hearing into the 'Gugulethu Seven'; seven ANC militants who were killed in a shoot-out in March 1986. Unlike other apartheid-era murders, this shooting had enjoyed extensive investigations with two inquests (in 1986 and 1989) and a criminal trial (in 1987). However, the question of responsibility remained a mystery until the TRC, when investigations 'managed to seize documents and link up evidence in a way that exposed to an unprecedented degree the corrupt inner workings of the apartheid state at a high level' (Cole 2007: 181). The notoriety of the Gugulethu Seven killings, together with the TRC's investigations and extended special hearing, fuelled considerable media interest, which prompted a situation where a meeting between the mothers of the Gugulethu Seven and an amnesty applicant was filmed. During this encounter, the applicant asked the mothers for their forgiveness; initially they refused, but then one forgave the security officer. This scene became central to a widely screened documentary entitled *Long Night's Journey into Day* (2000) as a moment that encapsulated 'the prospect of forgiveness and personal reconciliation' (Castillejo-Cuellar 2007: 24). The moral lesson was clear: 'Encountering an other who has done wrong, even in the most profound ways, is a plausible scenario. In the midst of much fear and resentment, forgiving is possible, embracing is possible' (Castillejo-Cuellar 2007: 29).

In practice, none of these moments provided the clear and unproblematic message of trauma, dehumanisation, sickness and forgiveness that TRC enthusiasts would have liked. Thus, while Mrs Calata's wail became emblematic of victims' trauma, she rejected the apology of one of the policemen responsible, through her pointed response: 'You have teased our grief for nearly twelve years, and you think you can reconcile in fifteen minutes?' (cited in Graybill 2002: 48). In turn, while Benzien's performance revealed truths about the violence committed by the apartheid state, his response to questions from former victims inflicted 'further humiliation ... by reminding them of how they had broken under interrogation, betraying their colleagues, and by refusing to remember details of their ordeal that they were anxious to confirm' (Meredith 2001: 126). Indeed, Benzien's particular combination of memory and forgetfulness turned 'most of his victims back into the roles of the previous relationship – where he has the power and they the fragility' (Krog 1999: 112) as he became 'their interrogator once more' (Sanders 2007: 112). Similarly, while some interpreted Winnie's appearance as evidence of a national sickness and the emergence of new norms, others cited her popularity – which saw her leave the hearings to stand 'amid a crowd of supporters, laughing heartily until a motorcade whisked her away' (Meredith 2001: 270) – as evidence of how '[d]espite her public vilification, Madikizela-Mandela continues to be the national voice of black vengeance, someone who articulates widespread emotions of anger at the continued racialization of privilege in the "new" South Africa and the lack of economic betterment for the majority of black South Africans' (Wilson 2001: 165). These feelings of anger against individual perpetrators and institutionalised violence were also evident during the Gugulethu Seven hearings when one of the mothers threw a shoe across the room striking two of the accused (Cole 2010: 19–25).

Nevertheless, despite such complexities – and in part because of them and the debates they initiated – such moments helped to construct a meta-narrative, albeit a highly contested one: apartheid had not only been unjust, but had dehumanised South Africans and left a wounded nation in need of healing in which forgiveness and reconciliation is a common good and feasible goal.

The TRC's portrait of apartheid as an illness that affected all South Africans has been used and dismissed by the country's political elite. On the one hand, the Commission helped to perform a new human rights conscious nation that embraced South Africans of all colours, which helped to legitimise President Mandela's reconciliatory politics. The Commission also gave different political parties and institutions an opportunity to present their own narrative and dampened (at least in the short to medium-term) pressure for mass prosecutions and radical redistributive policies, which would have tested inter-racial and intra-ethnic relations. On the other hand, political parties and institutions rejected the Commission's analysis of human rights abuses by denying their own alleged involvement and by blaming a few 'bad apples'. Many in the anti-apartheid struggle also criticised the implied moral equivalency between abuses that occurred during the construction and defence of an inherently unjust system and those that occurred during a struggle for dignity and freedom (Asmar, Asmal & Roberts 1997: 44). Finally, Presidents Mbeki and Zuma both dragged their feet in implementing the Commission's recommendations, as they shifted the reparations agenda away from individual compensation to community development projects, and as the state failed to follow up on alleged perpetrators who were denied, or who had never applied for, amnesty (Backer 2010; Colvin 2004; Hamber 2002). In short, the hearings proved much more useful to political elites than the final report – a reality that helped to reinforce the hearings as the Commission's main legacy.

In turn, the major academic criticisms of the Commission's meta-narrative are that, by focusing on suffering linked to the abuse of bodily integrity rights, it neglected other kinds of suffering and action, and thus provided an impoverished account of harm, beneficiaries and responsibility, which silenced certain narratives and presented a medicalised version of the problem that prioritised psychological solutions and delegitimised calls for redistributive or punitive justice (Gready 2011; Lund 2003; Mamdani 2002; Ross 2003a; Stanley 2001; Wilson 2001). In this vein, critics have highlighted how '[t]he hearings became a warning against police torturing people, but were silent about the injustice of allowing people to be poor, exploited, or pushed around' (Graybill 2002: 115). The conclusion: the TRC shed 'remarkably little light on apartheid' (Posel 1999: 23), its ghosts or the ways in which injustices and violence have continued and evolved in the post-apartheid era (Gready 2011). Instead, many posit that the TRC, as 'the product of a social process already in motion', became 'part of, and one of the first symptoms of, a "depoliticising" and liberalising process' (Hamber 2002: 70–71) that ultimately helped to delegitimise (at least in the short to medium-term) demands for more substantive forms of reparative justice, and for redistributive or punitive justice (Mamdani 2002; Wilson 2001). The implication is *neither* that the TRC was irrelevant *nor* that it had no impact, but that it was political in that it helped to enact transition, whilst effectively curtailing the same, and left a problematic legacy.

These critiques have been productive of further action since, by suggesting 'that the issues are not yet resolved', they imply that 'memories cannot be laid to rest' (Hutchison 2013: 81). In turn, a prominent victims group adopted the Commission's genre of storytelling to lobby for further reparations (Colvin 2004); museum exhibitions have explicitly tried to fill the Commission's silences, such as the communal impact of forced resettlements (Grunebaum 2011); and playwrights have used puppets to speak of people's ongoing trauma and to capture the ways in which people are 'spoken through' (Hutchison 2013: 60).

As a result, while the TRC's grand narrative has rightly attracted substantial critique, it is generally accepted to have had an impact. It invigorated debate – both through an acknowledgement that atrocities were committed, and through efforts to counter the Commission's various shortcomings, fill its silences and demand further action – and simultaneously made some contributions to nation building. At the same time, critiques helped to inform subsequent memory work and activism. Indeed, even for the Commission's strongest critics, the problem is *not* that the TRC had no impact, but that it was counter-revolutionary and helped to legitimise the replacement of a white economic and political elite with a racially mixed one. In short, and as the journalist Max du Preez notes, while the TRC's contributions are intangible and contested, 'I cannot even imagine what our society would have been like at the end of 1999 without having had the TRC experience' (in Orr 2000: v). It is significant that no one is yet to express similar sentiments regarding the Kenyan TJRC.

6.2 The Kenyan TJRC: A History of Injustice and a Nation of Victims

The term 'victim' is ... defined in the [TJRC] Act essentially as any person or group who has suffered any harm, loss or damage as a result of a human rights violation

(TJRC vol. 1 2013: 76)

Unlike the TRC, which adopted a fairly narrow interpretation of a limited remit, the TJRC adopted a generous interpretation of an already broad mandate. In large part, this was due to the TJRC's particular ancestry: part product of the optimism of NaRC's 2002 victory and a sense that a truth commission could be used as a '[T] rojan horse' to force through various reforms (Bosire 2013), and part product of the 2007–8 post-election violence and a sense that the crisis was triggered by a disputed election, but fuelled by much more deep-rooted problems. The TJRC's inclusive approach was also informed by critiques of the South African TRC and consequent sense that truth commission's should look beyond politically motivated violations of bodily integrity rights and investigate socio-economic and structural violations, and offer a broader raft of recommendations (Slye 2017).

In terms of its temporal focus, the TJRC decided that the Act's reference to antecedents and precedents enabled it to look at violations that occurred before 1963, while the legal doctrine of continuing violations and a mandate to foster national reconciliation were taken as reasons to consider certain violations that continued beyond, or which even occurred after, the Commission's cut-off date (TJRC vol. 1 2013: 61). The Commission also decided to investigate historical injustices and socio-economic rights in addition to gross human rights violations even though the TJRC Act did not directly refer to either. Commissioners justified their investigation of historical injustices on the basis that they were mandated to inquire into perceptions of economic marginalisation and irregular and illegal acquisitions of public land with historical injustices understood 'to describe issues of marginalisation and dispossession that resulted in disparities of income, wealth and opportunity that lie at the heart of many of the current conflicts in Kenya' (TJRC vol. 1 2013: 69). Similarly, a focus on socio-economic rights was justified by an asserted relationship with gross human rights violations, a mandate to investigate economic crimes and perceptions of economic marginalisation (TJRC vol. 1 2013: 67–68) and an idea that the 'gross-ness' of a harm could 'be at an individual level, [as is the case, for example with] torture, or according to the numbers affected – [the latter being the standard] that we applied to socio-economic rights' (interview, TJRC director, Nairobi, 7 September 2011).

Finally, the Commission investigated the broader experiences of certain categories of 'historically vulnerable populations' – women, children and minority and indigenous people – and put in place specific procedures 'to accommodate' persons with disabilities (TJRC vol. 1 2013: viii). In so doing, the Commission focused on the violations of bodily integrity and socio-economic rights, historical injustices and day-to-day realities of structural violence. Once again, the TJRC

Act did not explicitly require such an approach, but it was justified on the grounds that the Act had 'empowered the Commission to put in place special arrangements and adopt specific mechanisms for addressing the experience of historically vulnerable populations' (TJRC vol. 1 2013: viii).

It is telling that, while the Act referred to 'the experiences of a) women; b) children; c) persons with disabilities; and d) other vulnerable group' (TJRC Act 2008: 27 [1]), the Commission interpreted 'other vulnerable group' to include ethnic minorities and indigenous peoples rather than, for example, residents of informal settlements, the un- or under-employed, youth, refugees, migrants, religious minorities, homosexuals or transgender people. As a result, the Commission is largely silent on the experience of such groups who have long suffered state violence, harassment and everyday discrimination.

The Commission's focus on gender was informed by an understanding of best practice, which assumes that women suffer more (Chapter 7), while a focus on ethnic minorities stemmed from a common understanding of Kenya's history. The salience of ethnic identities then reinforced by the Commission's approach – from a self-conscious decision to select 'window cases' at public hearings that would reflect local ethnic diversity to the inclusion of separate chapters on the experiences of ethnic minorities, land and conflict, ethnic conflict, and the intersection of ethnic, electoral and land politics in the case of Mt Elgon. This approach was encouraged by ordinary citizens, and Kenyans were quick to criticise the Commission when, for example, statement takers did not reflect local ethnic diversity. At the same time, groups of community spokespeople across the country spent months compiling lengthy memoranda outlining the history of injustice suffered by 'their' community, while witnesses often presented their narratives of suffering through an ethnic lens. This approach was understandable given the political salience of ethnic identities, and it provided a relatively good sense of the pervasiveness of ethnic narratives of suffering. However, it ended up saying relatively little about other cleavages – from generation and religion to race and class – as is evident if we look briefly at how the Commission approached such issues.

With regards to generation, the TJRC included a focus on children with a special thematic hearing designed to be 'child-friendly' so as to promote their 'participation and protection' (TJRC vol. 1 2013: xviii) and the dedication of an entire chapter of the final report to the young and their experiences. However, there is little discussion of 'youth', which, as a category in everyday parlance, often denotes poor young men who (among other things) seek to move from a state of 'junior' to 'senior manhood' and to have, and to provide for, their immediate and extended families (van Stapele 2015). Unfortunately, this silence extends to the struggles that many 'youth' face, which – together with the lack of any acknowledgement of wrongdoing at the Commission's hearings (Chapter 8) – ensured that the report is silent on why 'youth' have been the main perpetrators of non-state violence. Just as importantly, the failure to discuss injustices that young poor men tend to suffer – such as violent arrests and fatal police shootings at the hands of the country's security forces on the basis of alleged criminality (van Stapele 2016) – failed to engage with the 'grey areas' in which extreme state violence is often justified on the grounds of imposing order (Chapter 8).

In turn, while representatives from religious minorities were heard at public hearings, the only substantive discussion of religion in the final report comes, not in a dedicated chapter or sub-section, but in the reproduction of a previously unpublished report by the Presidential Special Action Committee to Address Specific Concerns of the Muslim Community in Regard to Alleged Harassment and/or Discrimination in the Application/Enforcement of the Law, or Sharawe Committee, as an appendix to volume 2C. The Sharawe Committee was established by President Kibaki in 2007 to 'look into and address specific concerns raised by the Muslim community with regard to [their] alleged harassment and/or discrimination in the process of the application of the law particularly as regards to security issues' (TJRC vol. 2C 2013: 293). To this end, the Committee held public hearings across the country during the course of 2007; reviewed memoranda and secondary literature; consulted public officers, local leaders and Muslim and human rights organisations; and submitted a final report in 2008. The latter was critical of the Kenyatta, Moi and Kibaki regimes with 'substance [found] in most of the complaints raised by the Muslim community' (TJRC vol. 2C 2013: 295) from serious abuses during state security operations and discriminatory practices in the issuance of national ID cards and passports to problems of regional underdevelopment, the propagation of negative stereotypes in the country's media, and shortage of Islamic religious education teachers (TJRC vol. 2C 2013:

284–366). The Committee recommended, among other things, that 'security forces should not target communities for investigations or arrest on the basis [of] religion, ethnicity, race, and origin'; 'searches by the security forces should be conducted with due regard to human rights'; and that the 'Government should develop a Marshal plan with adequate budgetary provision for predominately Muslim areas to address the historical marginalization and under-development' (TJRC vol. 2C 2013: 335–340). However, while the TJRC endorsed the Sharawe Committee's findings and recommendations, the decision to also reproduce the report, rather than to also integrate the analysis within the main body of the text, leaves religion hanging as a seemingly marginal factor. It also ensured that there is no discussion of other religions, or of the relationship between religions, and of how, for example, evangelical Christianity has come into conflict with Islam, or of how local tensions are influenced, and exacerbated, by regional and global dynamics from the rise of Al-Shabaab, a radical Islamic group based in neighbouring Somalia, to a global 'war on terror'.

The TJRC also said very little about race and, more specifically, about the country's Asian and white minorities. This is perhaps unsurprising given that, for much of the post-colonial period, these communities have been relatively well off and politically inactive. However, this begs the question of how such a reality came about and is sustained, and the implications for these communities and for our understanding of injustice and transition. Again, these are significant gaps at the level of both particular injustices and general analysis. For example, it means that the Commission failed to engage with claims that the Asian community were effectively sidelined from mainstream politics after the assassination of Pio Pinto in 1965. It also downplays the importance of intersections and the question of how many Asians and whites may have been cushioned from the worst excesses of state and non-state violence simply because it has generally not been middle- and upper-class businesspeople and farmers who have been targeted, but the poor and politically active.

This leads to another gap, namely, the Commission's failure to fully confront the issue of class, which led to a version of the truth that is largely devoid of class relations. This was evident, for example, when the Commission adopted the lens of marginalisation to a series of eighty focus group discussions on socio-economic violations. The reason was apparently threefold.

First, economic marginalization (and the perception of economic marginalization) was a part of the Commission's mandate. Second, many Kenyans ... perceived themselves or their region as being marginalized (thus explaining the inclusion of *perceived* economic marginalization as part of the mandate). Third, economic marginalization encompasses many of the other socio-economic rights within the Commission's mandate (from housing to health care to education).

(Slye 2017: 13–14)

While this made sense, it meant that – in the context of popular understandings of economic marginalisation as referring to ethnic or regional marginalisation, the staging of public hearings and structure of the final report – the Commission focused on ethnic and spatial inequalities to the relative neglect of horizontal inequalities.

To list these gaps and relative silences is not to suggest that the TJRC should have covered all of these issues, which, as the Commission itself notes, would have been an impossible task. Instead, it is to highlight how the Commission's approach was shaped by prevailing debates about the significance of ethnic identities and gender relations to the relative neglect of other identities and divisions.

Nevertheless, the range of violations investigated was unprecedented for a truth commission, while the Commission went further than any other in highlighting continuities and evolutions. To this end, the TJRC conducted its own research and investigations, hired expert consultants to write thematic reports, organised months of public hearings, ran a series of community discussions of socio-economic violations and wrote a final report. However, due to the limited audience enjoyed by the TJRC's public hearings, the rest of this section focuses in on the final report as the Commission's main legacy. The following sections and chapters then look back at the performances of victimhood, gender relations and impunity witnessed at public hearings and detailed in the final report, and to the difficulties involved in rendering such a litany of injustices 'past'.

The TJRC's four-volume report reveals how Kenyans have suffered, and continue to suffer, from a range of injustices linked to acts of state commission or omission during the colonial period and through the three post-colonial regimes included within the Commission's mandate.[1] More specifically, the Commission found that all three post-colonial regimes had

---

[1] Namely, President Kenyatta (1963–1978), President Moi (1978–2002) and President Kibaki (2002–2013).

been responsible for gross human rights violations and concluded that state security forces had been 'the main perpetrators of bodily integrity violations of human rights in Kenya including massacres, enforced disappearances, torture and ill-treatment, and sexual violence', with northern Kenya standing as the 'epicenter of gross violations of human rights by state security agencies' (TJRC vol. 1 2013: vii). However, while the Commission found that the first Kenyatta regime (1963–1978) was responsible for the largest number of political assassinations (TJRC vol. 1 2013: xii), the repression of dissent was found to have reached an apex under the one-party state of Daniel arap Moi (1978–1992) (TJRC vol. 1 2013: ix) – when, among other things, Nyayo House (an administrative block in central Nairobi) was 'purposely designed and built ... for torture purposes' – with the judiciary also complicit in such activities (TJRC vol. 1 2013: xiii). In turn, while the Commission recognised the reforms initiated by the first Kibaki regime (2002–2007), it also drew attention to the ongoing problems of corruption, ethnic favouritism and inter-communal violence, and to the collapse of the NaRC coalition and increase in extra-judicial killings, which in its opinion prepared a 'fertile ground ... for the eruption of violence' in 2007–8 (TJRC vol. 1 2013: x; vol. 2A 2013: 28–29).

In contrast to the South African TRC, the TJRC also highlighted the socio-economic effects of gross human rights violations by pointing, for example, to the challenges faced by former political detainees in finishing their education, securing employment and caring for their children (TJRC vol. 2A 2013: 649). At the same time, the report sketches out some of the ways in which socio-economic factors impact upon bodily integrity rights at a more general level through, for example, the relative vulnerability of marginalised people during conflict, and the violations that stem from corruption and bias in the judiciary and security services (TJRC vol. 2C 2013: 2 and vol. 1: xiii).

In terms of inter-communal conflict, the Commission blamed colonial rule and Britain's adoption of a divide and rule strategy and alienation of large tracts of land for the emergence of 'negative ethnicity' – with historical grievances over land cited as the 'single most important driver of conflicts and ethnic tension' (TJRC vol. 1 2013: vii). However, all post-colonial regimes were blamed for the perpetuation of such politics, as, rather than provide redress, successive administrations 'alienated more land from already affected communities for the benefit of politically privileged ethnic communities and the political elite' (TJRC vol. 1 2013: xiv), and simultaneously favoured members of their own ethnic groups in employment and appointment processes (TJRC vol. 1 2013: x). As the Commission revealed, a sense of ethnic difference and competition was then exacerbated by multi-party politics, as '[e]thnicity became an even more potent tool for political [organisation] and access to state resources' (TJRC vol. 1 2013: ix–x), leading to 'a volatile environment [for the 2007 election] in which violence had been normalised and ethnic relations had become poisoned' (TJRC vol. 2A 2013: 29).

The Commission also emphasised the 'pervasiveness of socio-economic violations' across the country (TJRC vol. 1 2013: xv). More specifically, it found that – in addition to the socio-economic impacts of gross human rights violations noted earlier – the 'government's exclusionary economic policies and practices in the distribution of public jobs and services inflicted suffering on huge sections of society at different historical moments' (TJRC vol. 1 2013: xv); with corruption simultaneously linked to everything from abusive state security forces to poor health and education services and transport and communication networks (TJRC vol. 2B 2013: 353–355). Moreover, in terms of spatial inequalities, the Commission found that northern Kenya – taken to consist of former North Eastern, Upper Eastern and North Rift Valley provinces – together with former Coast, Nyanza and Western provinces suffered particularly harsh economic marginalisation as a result of biased or indifferent state policies (TJRC vol. 4 2013: 48). These areas collectively comprise well over half the country's land mass and about half of the country's total population.[2] In addition, the Commission recognised how even residents of regions that were not identified as economically marginalised – namely, former Central, Nairobi, South Rift Valley and Lower Eastern provinces – consider 'themselves marginalised at one time or another' (TJRC vol. 1: xv). The implication was that no single province had escaped economic marginalisation at some point during the country's post-colonial history, with hardships often passed on to subsequent generations through a cycle of limited education and employment opportunities.

---

[2] For details see the district breakdown of the 2009 population census available at www.opendata.go.ke/Population/Vol-1-A-Summary-Population-Distribution-by-Distric/jizy-xanw <last accessed 7 April 2016>.

Women, minority groups and indigenous people were also found to have suffered state-sanctioned discrimination. Minority and indigenous peoples were found to 'have suffered gross violations of human rights on account of their membership in these communities' (TJRC vol. 2C 2013: 281); women were found to have 'suffered unspeakable and terrible atrocities... in the majority of cases... for no other reason than that they are of the female gender' (TJRC vol. 2C 2013: 151); and children were found to have been 'subjected to untold and unspeakable atrocities' (TJRC vol. 4 2013: vii). The Commission did not make any overarching findings regarding persons with disabilities, but emphasised how citizens were particularly susceptible to 'terrible atrocities' when a disability intersected with being female (TJRC vol. 4 2013: xvii); and how, along with other vulnerable groups, persons with disabilities had suffered disproportionately from corruption (TJRC vol. 1 2013: xvi).

In summary, while many Kenyans were found to have suffered gross human rights violations, the vast majority of the population were found to have been touched by injustice at some point in their lifetime – be it as a result of state security operations, election-related violence, corruption, economic marginalisation, historical land injustice, patriarchal traditions and so forth. Indeed, the Commission's overview suggests that very few (if any) Kenyans had not suffered from one (or several) of the injustices that it was mandated to investigate either directly, or as secondary victims, due to the long-standing impact that many injustices had on extended families and communities.

However, while the Commission's narrative suggests that all Kenyans are a victim of injustice in one way or another and to some extent, this does not mean that all Kenyans suffered, or continue to suffer, equally. On the contrary, some individuals were deemed to have suffered more severe harms or from multiple injustices, and some groups were presented as having suffered more than others. Thus, while it was clear that a minority of Kenyans had suffered direct bodily integrity violations at the hands of state operatives, overall, women were said to have suffered more than men, and some regions or ethnic groups to have suffered more than others.

The Commission was also 'not just interested in what happened.... [but] in why things happened the way they did, what was their impact and who was responsible' (TJRC vol. 1 2013: 43). Regarding the why and the impact, the report is of mixed quality, but it is in establishing the who that the TJRC had the least success. Instead, the Commission met a wall of silence, denial and justifications (Chapter 8), and found that the state had historically 'covered-up or downplayed violations committed against its own citizens, especially those committed by state security agencies', and that, for the entire mandate period, 'the state demonstrated no genuine commitment to investigate and punish atrocities and violations committed by its agents against innocent citizens' (TJRC vol. 4 2013: 10).

In this context, the Commission revealed how the underlying causes of violations and contributing factors are neither simple nor uni-polar but complex and multi-dimensional – ranging from centralised power, a culture of impunity and inter-ethnic competition to limited resources, uneven development, under-employment and patriarchy. The implication is not only that all Kenyans had suffered, but that it was Kenya's socio-economic and political systems, and the complex interactions between these various factors, that was ultimately to blame.

Unsurprisingly, these findings fed into wide-ranging recommendations. This includes further investigations, lustration and prosecution of some of those allegedly involved in assassinations, massacres, land grabs and so forth. As well as apologies by the head of state for various atrocities suffered – from the torture and unlawful detention of political dissidents to acts of sexual violence committed by state security agencies during operations and periods of violence, and the state's sanction of discrimination against women. It also included demands for the release of various reports and materials; the implementation of recommendations from previous commissions of inquiry; the fast tracking of ongoing reforms of state institutions, such as the security services and judiciary; and the enactment of key pieces of legislation. The TJRC also set out extensive guidelines for individual, collective and symbolic reparations, which included a framework for individual compensation; development policies to address the historic marginalisation of some regions; and the establishment of public memorials to commemorate particular places, events and people from the Nyayo House torture cells to the lives of those assassinated. It also made many much more specific recommendations, such as the establishment of a 'fully equipped national modern forensic laboratory' (TJRC vol. 4 2013: 29) and 'gender violence recovery center in every county' (TJRC vol. 4 2013: 36). Finally, the Commission recognised how the recommendations of earlier truth commissions and commissions of inquiry had largely been ignored; stressed the mandatory nature of the Commission's recommendations; and set out a clear timeline for implementation together with detailed guidelines for an implementation and monitoring mechanism (TJRC vol. 4 2013). Indeed, the only recommendation that the Commission was empowered to make, which it did not make, was amnesty for non-gross human rights violations (Chapter 8).

The TJRC therefore provided a detailed overview that went beyond any prior inquiry in the country, and any truth commission to date. However, it ultimately offered little in the way of new revelations, whilst a broad mandate, together with the genre of truth commission reports, also encouraged a tendency to offer existing generalisations that emphasised ethnicity and gender over other possible schisms. The report ultimately offered an important and useful, if imperfect, account.

6.3 From the Repertoire to the Archive

Your contribution is not in vain ... rest assured your truth will go into the final report for posterity.

(Closing remarks by the presiding chair, TJRC hearings, Kakamega, 28 June 2011)

Despite a number of omissions, the Commission's final report constitutes the most comprehensive overview of Kenya's troubled past. However, much of the detail was already known. In part, this is because of the country's long history of commission of inquiries. But it was also due to shortcomings with the Commission's approach – from statement taking and data management through to the final report writing process and a lack of incentives to admit wrongdoing.

The TJRC collected an impressive number of statements and memoranda: more than 40,000 and 1,500, respectively. However, commissioners acknowledged that there was a 'wide variety' in their 'detail and accuracy' (TJRC vol. 1 2013: 89). Indeed, while statements were coded with key details submitted into a central database, it is telling how rarely the Commission draws upon its own statistics with only occasional reference made to them in the final report (for example, TJRC vol. 1 2013: xiii and vol. 2A: 712). This, as one senior staff member explained, was because of problems with the process: some of the statements had clearly been made up by statement takers who struggled to meet Commission quotas, while many included material that fell outside of the Commission's broad mandate or included insufficient detail to support the claims made. In this context, a decision was made not to rely on such an unreliable dataset (interview, Nairobi, 15 September 2013). Not only is relatively little use made of the statistics compiled, but also of the details included in the statements and memoranda collected. As one researcher explained, she not only wrote a section 'and then looked at the database', but did not pay so much attention to 'all the statements. There were so many, and some focus on such minor things' (conversation, Nairobi, 14 August 2012).

The extent to which the report refers to statements and memoranda, and to public, women's, *in camera*, thematic, and AMP hearings also varies markedly between chapters. Thus, while some sections, such as those on the Wagalla massacre, Mt Elgon conflict or Robert Ouko's assassination, make substantive use of testimony, archival documents, government and non-government reports and secondary literature, others, such as those on economic crimes and ethnic minorities, could have been written without a truth commission ever having taken place.

At one end of this scale, the section on the Wagalla massacre in chapter 4 of volume 2A intertwines documentary evidence – including previously unreleased archival documents from the Wajir Registry – with vivid testimony from public, women's and *in camera* hearings to provide an overview of the relevant background context, decision-making processes, security operation, massacre, and subsequent cover-up. Sources are also used in a way that captures some of the ongoing emotional, physical and socio-economic impacts of the massacre; the disturbing attitude of government officials; and chains of responsibility. As a result, it is unsurprising that this section has already inspired new academic discussions of the massacre and its historical significance (Anderson 2014).

At the other extreme, chapter 3 of volume 2B on economic crimes and grand corruption does not make direct reference to a *single* piece of testimony, statement or memorandum collected. Instead, there is only an indirect reference to 'informers' in a three-page summary of reports to the commission (TJRC vol. 2B 2013: 416–418). The chapter also does not include a single reference to academic studies – with the exception of a Transparency International publication on grand corruption and third world development (TJRC vol. 2B 2013: 346). Instead, the discussion relies on previous commission of inquiry reports, legal documents, a scattering of press reports and policy-oriented manuals and toolkits. As a result, the chapter captures nothing of the personal narratives shared with the commission and little of the emotions displayed. It also says little (if anything) that an informed reader would not already know. One possible exception is the chapter's analysis of how, with the mixed implementation of the 2010 constitution (which falls outside of the Commission's main temporal mandate), integrity standards have been set higher for appointed than elected officials (TJRC vol. 2B 2013: 394–415).

This variation in the use of statements, memoranda and testimony, and of previously unreleased archival documents, is a product of the report writing process, which saw some sections and chapters (such as those on Wagalla and Mt Elgon) drafted by TJRC researchers, and others (such as those on economic crimes and ethnic minorities) drafted by consultants. This was important since TJRC researchers helped trawl through statements and memoranda; they prepared pre-hearing reports and attended relevant hearings; they went to archives and resource centres, and spent months on writing retreats. In contrast, consultants did not have easy access to statements and memoranda; they generally did not attend public hearings, and they tended to rely on their own knowledge and insights as recognised experts. While understandable, the variation is problematic because it renders parts of the report a simple summary of existing knowledge, which reinforces a sense – which is only further compounded by the Commission's failure to unearth much new documentary evidence or to elicit a single public confession or admission of wrongdoing (Chapter 8) – that the Commission adds little in the way of new truths.

This variation also commits a further injustice to many of those who expended substantial time and energy in making statements to, writing memoranda for, or appearing before the Commission. In short, participants were often encouraged to believe that their contributions would be included (or at least reflected) in the final report and that they would benefit from the consequent recommendations. The fact that many of their voices (even in the sense of representative examples) are entirely absent from the Commission's narrative – together with the fact that little progress has been made in the dissemination of the report's findings or implementation of its recommendations – ensures that many of the promises made, and hopes raised, have so far been betrayed.

This sense of hope betrayed also affected many of those who worked with the Commission who felt that they had let people down, or been left with difficult questions to answer. As one statement taker noted almost a year after the final report had been submitted:

> I'm becoming a victim of the TJRC business because everyone wants to ask me: 'You took my statement and how and when do we get feedback?'. So I'm still on the job without payment ... Thought I was assisting to reduce people's burden ... [but] if I go and tell people [that nothing is happening with the report] then I become a failure although the responsibility's not mine. This burden traumas me.
> (Interview, former TJRC statement taker, Turkana, 18 March 2014)

Such shortcomings highlight some of the ways in which the suffering of victims may continue past, and might even have been exacerbated by, the TJRC process.

6.4 The Past in the Present and Future

In a nutshell, there has been, there is, suffering in the land.
(TJRC vol. 1 2013: iv)

By drawing upon excerpts from the TJRC's public hearings, civic education meetings and final report, as well as interviews, this section briefly explores the five principal (albeit non-exhaustive) ways in which victims and the Commission revealed – either extensively or implicitly – how the past is present in the now and the future. That is through the ghosts of lives, loves and opportunities lost; the continuous or repetitive nature of some harms; the experientially rooted fears or popular angst regarding imminent and more distant futures; the ways in which past violations can potentially motivate future wrongs (either as a means to wreak revenge, protect against further harms or regain status and self-esteem); and the ways in which past experiences shape narratives of injustice, which – due in large part to the pain, anger, fear, hatred and other emotions that they carry – can be politically useful and purposefully kept alive as a way to lay claims or to mobilise support. This is critical as it is central to the overarching narrative produced, whereby injustice and violation is cast as ongoing rather than as something easily discussed in the past tense; it also points to the inherent limitations of transitional justice mechanisms as a means to render such pasts 'dead'.

'I was not born like this'.
(Bernard Ndege, TJRC public hearing, Kisumu, 14 July 2011)

The TJRC's public hearings in Kisumu in July 2011 began with the testimony of an ordinary but well-known Luo man – Bernard Ndege – who, as the head of one victims' organisation, remarked had 'become a poster child for victimhood' following the post-election violence of 2007–8 (interview, Nairobi, 24 August 2011). Ndege's notoriety is reflected in the number of times he has been interviewed by investigatory commissions and journalists, and his photograph used to accompany general stories about the fate of post-election violence victims (for example, Lynch in *Saturday Nation* 16 April 2016).

Ndege's infamy stems, in large part, from the scale of his experience. In January 2008, he watched as a group of Kikuyu youth barricaded and then set fire to his Naivasha home. Ndege managed to escape, but nineteen other people – including eleven members of his immediate family (twelve if one counts his unborn child) – were burnt alive. The number killed, together with the horrific photographs of piles of charred bodies that soon circulated online, ensured that Ndege's story captured the headlines and public imagination. The fact that Ndege insisted that the attackers had been Mungiki (a much feared ethnic militia), that a local MP had organised residents to buy *pangas* (or machetes) prior to the attacks, and that the police had failed to respond to early warnings that were raised, further increased the significance of his story as an example of how some of the post-election violence was organised and of how the state abrogated on its responsibility to protect.

Ndege's infamy was also due to his personification of trauma and ongoing suffering. At the TJRC's public hearings in Kisumu, this was expressed, at least in part, through his body language – as, perched, and visibly shaking, on the edge of his chair; Ndege narrated his story wide-eyed, arms flailing and amidst sobs, which, at one point, led the commissioners to suspend the hearing so that Ndege could regain his composure. As the woman beside me remarked: 'it is almost like he is possessed'.

This personification of trauma was also embodied in Ndege's physical appearance, which is marked by large patches of raw, pink skin. It is unclear whether this affliction is the result of burns, as is often assumed (including during the commissioners questioning), or of a skin problem resulting from stress or some other problem. Either way, these patches – which Ndege almost compulsively felt and picked at as he spoke – provided a clear visual reminder of how victim's lives are forever changed by violence. As Ndege himself emphasised: 'I was not born like this. Look at me!' Or as one of the commissioners noted in response: it is 'sobering and humbling to see the violence inscribed on your body' (public hearing, Kisumu, 14 July 2011).

Ndege's skin provided a marker of the losses that continue to haunt his present and future, an embodiment then reinforced by Ndege's almost manic style of speaking and horrific story. These losses include the lives of his two wives and nine children, and of his health and property. These losses continue to haunt and shape his life. Thus, while the local MP organised a fundraiser to help Ndege build a new house in Nyanza, Ndege complained of how the house remained empty and how, '[f]rom then to now I sleep like a cow'. He also spoke of how his physical condition rendered him unable to work or to be out in the sun, and thus incapable of providing for his new wife and two young children.

Ndege's example of how the present and future were not what they should or could have been was particularly powerful, but it is a theme that ran through the hearings. For example, widows of post-election victims spoke of the loss of a male breadwinner and the difficulties of educating their children (Lynch in *Saturday Nation* 8 November 2014); victims of state torture relayed the difficulty of completing their education or of finding gainful employment (for example, TJRC public hearings, Kisumu, 15 July 2011); and residents of northern Kenya blamed the region's ongoing poverty on strong-armed security operations and biased government policies – the memorandum presented by one such resident aptly titled 'Dying an invisible death and living an invisible life' (public hearing, Isiolo, 9 May 2011).

This fact – that many 'people continue to suffer from the legacy of historical injustices and gross violations of human rights' (TJRC vol. 4 2013: iii) – is also repeated throughout the Commission's final report. To give just two examples: first, in the section on state violence, the Commission asserts:

The majority of torture survivors have remained unemployed, decades later. Those who were university students at the time of their detention and torture had their education and careers abruptly and indefinitely cut short. Their families were thrown into economic hardship for in most cases the suspects were the main family breadwinners. (TJRC vol. 2A 2013: 649)

Similarly, in the section on the Shifta War (1963–1967) – which saw the state fight insurgents across much of northern Kenya – the Commission relays how Borana in Isiolo refer to those years as *Daaba* or 'when time stopped'. According to the Commission, this name 'gives some sense of how profoundly the Shifta War affected the region' (TJRC vol. 2A 2013: 118), as villagisation and other security measures led to the deaths of thousands of people and the loss of the majority of people's livestock (TJRC vol. 2A 2013: 119 and 121). According to the Commission, 'an irreversible chain reaction had been set off' – the idea of *Daaba*, or of a temporal black hole, capturing a 'total and unwelcome rupture between the past and present' (TJRC vol. 2A 2013: 120). For many victims, the ghosts of the past – in the form of lives and trajectories lost – continue to haunt them and to ensure that what has happened, or has been, continues to affect their prospects and likely futures.

> 'I can see my cows and property with my neighbour'.
> (Victim of the 'ethnic clashes' of 1991–2, TJRC stakeholders meeting, Molo, 21 July 2011)

For many, harms suffered also remained a part of their everyday lives for the simple reason that they were not considered an object in the past tense – this was either because of a continuous violation of 'justice denied' or because the original harm continued to be a part of their contemporary realities.

Regarding the former, it is commonly accepted that justice denied – either in the form of a lack of an apology, investigations, prosecutions or reparations – constitutes an ongoing injustice or continuing violation. This sentiment provided part of the original motivation for holding a TJRC, and was clearly evident during the Commission's activities. This included a TJRC stakeholders meeting in Molo in the central Rift Valley, where one lady spoke of how she was incapable of reconciling with her neighbour because they still had the cows and other property that they had looted from her 'twenty years ago!' (21 July 2011). For others, the ongoing injustice came not in the form of a visible daily reminder, but of an invisible one – such as a lack of information. In this vein, a witness at a TJRC public hearing in Kisumu relayed how his wife and children had disappeared during the post-election violence of 2007–8. For him, the fact that he was 'not sure if [his] family [was] thrown into pit latrines or eaten by wild animals in the park' constituted a continuing violation. In his words, and in his failure to find them, 'you see Ndege buried his family, but me {the sentence left unfinished}' (15 July 2011).

At the same time, other violations were revealed to be continuous in the sense that the original injustice was still ongoing. This, as the following chapter will discuss in more detail, was particularly pronounced in the Commission's discussions of patriarchy and gendered power relations. However, it was also evident in other discussions, for example, of ethnic or regional marginalisation and of economic crimes such as corruption and land grabbing.

While recognised, this aspect of continuity was ultimately underplayed due to a sense, or at least a hope, of substantive change. More specifically, parallel efforts to hold people accountable for the post-election violence through the ICC, offered a possibility of criminal prosecutions throughout the Commission's lifespan. While the inauguration of a new constitution and raft of institutional reforms – which included a new bill of rights, promises of a more equitable distribution of resources and redress for historical land injustices, and the devolution of power – led commissioners to often suggest (both at its hearings and in the final report) that many violations would soon come to an end and be addressed. However, as the Commission wound up, much of this optimism faded as two ICC indictees were elected, parliament failed to discuss the Commission's report, the ICC cases collapsed, extra-judicial killings of alleged criminals and terrorists witnessed a resurgence, and a battle between the government and media and human rights organisations picked up speed.

> 'There's that fear'.
> (TJRC women's hearing, Nakuru, 24 September 2011)

For many who spoke before the TJRC, the past continued to haunt the present and future through a fear that, what they had experienced, or something similar and perhaps even worse, might recur. Vivid memories of past atrocities, and visions or fears of their repetition and potential escalation, were particularly pronounced amongst post-election violence victims in the Rift Valley, many of whom had experienced violence on multiple occasions during the clashes of the early 1990s, 1997, 2002, and 2005. As the Commission noted: 'The written word ... cannot convey the traumatic experience of a woman who was raped during the PEV and her fear that the same could happen to her during the 2013 elections' (TJRC vol. 1 2013: iii–iv).

To give just one example, at the TJRC's women's hearing in Nakuru, a lady spoke of how her house had been burnt down by her neighbours in 1997 and how she had been 'left with nothing'. The lady went on to explain how, after some time, residents started preaching peace and she went and rebuilt her house. But, after one year, there 'were more fights and again it collapsed'; her house was destroyed and her property was looted for a third time in 2007–8. The woman went on to explain how she had taken some of those who had stolen her property in 2007–8 to court but, after being threatened, had decided to 'forgive them and let them free'. Nevertheless, she explained how she had not returned to her former homestead as 'there's that fear ... that thing of going back and building and then it's burnt again!' (24 September 2011).

This woman was far from alone. Indeed, from the Commission's work, it was evident that, for many, memories of earlier violence and injustice had never left them and that the experience of the post-election crisis helped to bring echoes and fragments of these pasts to the forefront of people's consciousness (even in places relatively untouched in 2007–8) and to have fostered a sense of a history that had, and could, repeat itself.

> 'We could get angry later'.
> (Resident of Lamu County in a discussion of local land disputes, TJRC vol. 2B 2013: 249)

The TJRC process also provided some insights into the evolution of injustices over time. This was particularly clear through the Commission's recognition of the complex ways in which past injustices could motivate future wrongs – either as a means to wreak revenge, to protect against further harms or to regain status and self-esteem. Many of these moments were intertwined with notions of masculinity and a desire to provide for one's family and to protect one's community (Silberschmidt 2001; van Stapele 2015). As a result, the fact that the Commission focused on gender as women's experiences, meant that the opportunity to tease out these dynamics was largely lost (Chapter 7). Nevertheless, occasional glimpses were still visible.

Most explicitly, the Commission recognised a general connection between injustice and further injustice through cycles of violence. As the final report noted: '[M]any individuals qualify as both victims and perpetrators. In fact for some perpetrators it is their experience as victims which push them to become perpetrators, sometimes in the name of vindicating either real or perceived violations suffered by themselves, their families, or their community' (TJRC vol. 1 2013: 77). This recognition points to the possibility of revenge, but also of pro-active self or community protection. As one man lamented at a TJRC meeting in Lamu: 'We are old now but the youth will not accept the injustice to go on forever. When the war starts, you will start wondering why the conflict has broken out but that is because somebody has gone to Nairobi and managed to get ownership documents [to our land]' (TJRC vol. 2b 2013: 249). As noted, less visible were the ways in which various injustices suffered by men – from witnessing attacks on one's family or community to the hardships that stemmed from economic marginalisation and experiences of sexual violence – might impinge on notions of virility and the responsibilities of provision and protection that are intimately intertwined with understandings of patriarchy and masculinity. This is an important oversight. For one, the urge by some frustrated men to reassert their masculinity and reaffirm the subordinate position of women through violence and aggressive acts of sexual prowess is often understood to help explain an increase in, or continuity of, everyday violence in many ostensibly post-conflict settings (Boesten 2013). As one man who was castrated during the post-election violence of 2007–8 explained to HRW:

> I cannot provide for my family because I was badly injured. They did bad things to me; they killed my manhood. My wife has to work ... I find it problematic because I don't know whether she is going to wash for a man or woman, whether she is going to do other things. You can even decide to kill the woman because you feel she is demeaning you by going out to look for work. You feel emasculated.
> (HRW 2016: 54)

The past is thus continuing into the future as some seek to prevent a repeat, to right, or to counter earlier, ongoing, or possible wrongs.

> **'[People] have skills but because of being L-positive, or Luo-positive, they become unemployable'.**
> (TJRC public hearings, Kisumu, 14 July 2011)

Many witnesses who spoke before the Commission welcomed the opportunity to speak before an official body. However, many were evidently not motivated, at least not primarily, by a desire for catharsis. Instead, and as Rosalind Shaw found in her analysis of the TRC in Sierra Leone, 'a substantial portion of the victims and survivors who testified [did] so in the hope that this would give them access to economic assistance' (2007: 184). Certainly, most requested some form of justice that went beyond an acknowledgement of the truth – be it compensation, prosecutions or radical reform.

Moreover, while this was the first time that many had spoken about their suffering before an official body, for a surprising number, the TJRC was just one avenue they had pursued to try and secure justice. Many who spoke of torture at Nyayo House, for example, had been involved in compensation claims in the national courts (KHRC 2009), and many who spoke of the ramifications of the post-election violence of 2007–8 were registered victims at the ICC, and several who spoke of their suffering as indigenous people had brought cases before the African Commission of Human and People's Rights, the African Court or the World Bank Inspection Panel (Lynch 2012a; Lynch 2016).

For many, these efforts focused on gaining justice for the long-term effects of injustice previously outlined. However, for some, they were also part of a broader political campaign for reforms and redistribution. Perhaps unsurprisingly, this use of narratives of injustice as a means to mobilise support for, or against, particular political agendas or groups, was most evident when it came to the appearance of political activists or politicians who spoke of the suffering of 'their communities'. In this vein, Phoebe Asiyo, a former MP and cabinet minister, presented a joint memorandum in Kisumu with a local professional on the socio-economic and political marginalisation of the Luo people and Nyanza area. The presentation, which was reminiscent of a political rally, provided an overview of the problems of being 'Luo-positive' and of the various reparations and affirmative programmes that the leaders had been struggling for (public hearing, Kisumu, 14 July 2011).

Many of these explicitly political presentations focused on especial suffering, as reflected in the testimony of a representative from the Talai community in Kericho – a Kalenjin-speaking clan that was physically relocated by the British during the colonial period – on how he could not 'think of another ethnic group that's suffered the same level of human rights abuses in Kenya or elsewhere' and how they 'were reduced to useless beggars' (public hearing, Kericho, 19 September 2011).

Another dimension that such presentations shared was a tendency to focus on the need for community reparations broadly speaking. They thus looked backwards to reach forward – not in the transitional justice sense of putting 'the past to rest' – but as politics in the classic sense of determining who gets what, when, how and why. The implications of such performances for the justice sought, and for the disjunctures between people's expectations and outcomes, is a focus of Chapter 9. The important point here is simply that such testimonies point to another persistence, namely, the political utility of the past, and narratives surrounding it, as a means to lay claims and to mobilise support in the present and future. The past persists, at least in part, because it is simplified, relayed and used to protect and promote individual and community interests.

In addition to such narratives of injustice, it is also possible for the past to live on in the form of repertoires of contention. However, due in large part to the tendency of perpetrators to deny wrongdoing, the TJRC provided little insight into this issue. For example, did the political mobilisation of ethnic militias in the early 1990s render ethnically targeted violence and arson a more thinkable and doable act, and thus a more likely outcome during subsequent periods of political tension? Or did the strategy of blocking roads by burning tyres or piling rocks on them during periods of election-related violence, and of pulling up the railway line in 2007–8, feed through into a focus on transport networks as a recognised (and perhaps even default) means of demanding attention from state authorities? My feeling is that such repertoires of contention have evolved in Kenya and that past violence continues to affect the present and future – not just through its contribution to narratives of injustice and a recognised culture of impunity – but through the structures, networks and memories of organised violence that it provides. However, that is an area of speculation that lies beyond the scope of the current analysis.

6.5 Conclusions: The Persistence of Suffering

[After his death] I tell you there was nothing good in the family.
(Relative of a student leader who died in detention in 1988, TJRC public hearings, Busia, 5 July 2011)

The public hearings of the South African TRC took place following a transfer of political power and a moment of great hope and expectation. These hearings were also closely followed by domestic and international audiences, and helped to perform a grand narrative of trauma, abuse, sickness and salvation, and sense of substantive transition and change. This narrative and performance has attracted widespread criticism, especially as those who did not apply for, or were not granted, amnesty in exchange for full disclosure avoided prosecution; and the new ANC government failed to implement the TRC's recommendations on reparations, and simultaneously oversaw economic policies that facilitated the emergence of a small black economic elite. Nevertheless, the TRC's hearings had an impact: they helped to contribute to a sense of change at a critical moment, and to legitimise (for right or wrong) the reconciliatory policies of the new ANC government, while criticisms of their shortcomings and flaws have fed through into subsequent debates and activism.

In contrast, the Kenyan TJRC was introduced following a relatively short but intense period of violence, and soon suffered a credibility crisis. However, despite extensive problems, the Commission compiled a lengthy, albeit imperfect, final report that provides extensive insights into the range and persistence of injustice. The pervasiveness and tenacity of suffering revealed has substantial implications for how one might seek to address such present and looming pasts, and render what has occurred past in the substantive sense. At the same time, the report writing process, the silencing of some voices and the failure to implement the report's recommendations also point to some of the ways in which a truth commission can lead to further injustice. However, before turning to such difficulties and complexities, and to what it means for efforts to achieve justice and reconciliation, Chapters 7 and 8 narrow in on two further aspects of this narrative, namely, that of women's especial suffering and an embedded culture of impunity.

7 'The Story of the Kenyan Woman'
Of the Performance of Familiar Gender Roles

[T]he story of the Kenyan woman is sad, shameful and heartbreaking ... [It is also] triumphant.

(TJRC vol. 2C 2013: 2)

On 23 May 2011, I attended the first day of the TJRC's public hearings in Kapsokwony, a small town on the slopes of Mt Elgon in western Kenya, where hearings were held inside the local Catholic church. The hearing saw male elders present pre-prepared community memoranda on behalf of the Sabaot, Bukusu and Teso communities who constitute the mountain's principal ethnic groups. Presentations were impassioned but general. They were also cast through a lens of ethnic difference and competition, as elders provided an overview of the *longue duree* of their community's experiences and fears of land injustice, political and economic marginalisation, and conflict.

The following day, I attended the local women's hearing – a half-day female only forum at the District Commissioner's office – where, in the absence of scheduled witnesses, women simply raised their hand if they wished to speak. These sessions – which were held in each of the thirty-five locations around the country where the TJRC held public and *in camera* hearings – formed part of the Commission's commitment to gender mainstreaming, whereby the Commission sought to involve women's perspectives across all aspects of its work.

On this particular morning, the first woman to be handed the roving microphone touched on many issues that would form the focus of the session's discussion. In her opinion:

Women were not part of those who started the whole problem [on the mountain] ... Women were beaten up and tortured by the [Sabaot Land Defence Force]. They cut women's ears. They killed our husbands and buried some of them even without heads ... I do not know what to say. We were very innocent. There was harassment from the political leaders. I personally

183

was a victim ... It is very painful because we are widows now. Without a husband in the family, there is nothing you can do. One can only cry ... I am, however, grateful for this hearing. You have decided to come and cry with us ... If, indeed, this is the TJRC, let us know where justice is.

(TJRC vol. 2C 2013: 99)

The woman was followed by others who spoke with similar passion of the murder of their fathers, husbands and sons; of mutilation; of the void left by those who had 'disappeared'; of gang rape; of how men could not provide for their families, while women had been left impoverished to look after children and other dependants; of women's fears of further violence; of their failed efforts to seek assistance and redress from the government and of their requests for some form of justice.

This focus on a particular conflict – endured at the hands of the Sabaot Land Defence Force (SLDF), a local militia which had terrorised the mountain between 2005 and 2008, and subsequent military operation that saw up to 3,000 men 'screened' by police and military in 2008 on suspicion of being SLDF members or supporters (HRW 2011: 6) – was unusual for women's hearings. However, the informal and openly emotional atmosphere was common, as was the gendered nature of experiences described from the principal victims of murder (men) and rape (women) to the ongoing implications of underemployment and widowhood. These performances – together with chapters in the final report on women's experiences and sexual and gender-based violence – also provided an overarching narrative of Kenyan women as victim-heroines who had suffered but who remained strong.

This chapter focuses on this approach to gender as women as an example of a particular turn in transitional justice practice. The chapter introduces a tendency of truth commissions to mainstream gender through a focus on women before turning to the TJRC's operationalisation of the same. It then narrows in on the problematic idea of female-only interactions as 'safe spaces' before turning to the image of women that this approach was informed by, and simultaneously helped to reproduce, namely, of women as victim-heroines who were vulnerable, non-tribal, and who (alongside children) had suffered most, but were nevertheless resilient.

The discussion reveals how the TJRC's focus on women offered relief to some – with the women's hearings in particular greeted with gratitude by many. It also reveals how the Commission's approach helped to highlight general problems and specific injustices that many women had experienced, as well as a continuum of violence – between private and public, peace and conflict, and state and non-state actors – and the lingering and persistent effects of violations of all kinds.

Nevertheless, it is argued that the Commission's approach to gender was inherently problematic. This is due to various practical shortcomings, the unrealistic expectations of assistance raised, and the ways in which hearing women (and men) may have ultimately involved a degree of undue exposure, alienation and exploitation. However, it is also due to the problematic characterisation of women in general as virtuous victims that was informed by existing understandings of gender roles, and which provided an overly homogenous account of women; said little about *why* many women were particularly vulnerable; offered little insight on women's agency and their role, for example, in generational transfers of ethnic narratives of difference or on men's gendered experiences and constructed masculinities; and gave women much responsibility.

Most importantly, the discussion reveals how the TJRC – like other commissions and programmes that have read 'gender to be essentially about women' – did 'not capture the relational nature of gender, the role of power relations, and the way that structures of subordination are reproduced' (cf. Charlesworth 2008: 359). As the tendency to characterise 'men as "the problem"' and 'women-in-general as "the oppressed"' revealed 'nothing of relationships among women and among men, nor of the intersection of gender with other differences such as age, status and wealth' (Cornwall 1997: 8 and 9). It also ignored the pressures and violence that men experience, and 'their behaviour towards those they feel they have power over' (Cornwall 1997: 12). As a result, the TJRC inadvertently reinforced problematic gender binaries and existing power relations, in which women are cast as vulnerable, subordinate, emotional and peaceful, and men as powerful, domineering, uncommunicative and violent. Herein lies the paradox: the TJRC process and final report provides unusual insights into the range and persistence of women's suffering, at the same time that it did little to start a conversation that could really challenge such gendered experiences.

7.1 Truth Commissions and Gender as Women

[I]n practice, gender mainstreaming still favours (or is 'about') women and ... [thus] continues to marginalise men and the workings of masculinity.

(Zalewski 2010: 6)

While gender refers to social perceptions of masculinity and femininity and how they relate to each other, a gendered approach – from political participation and development programming to transitional justice – often focuses on the need to include women. In this vein, in an operational handbook on truth commissions and gender, Vasuki Nesiah accepts that a gendered approach is 'not a straightforward process of simply adding women into the equation' (2006: 2), but nevertheless focuses her discussion of gender sensitivity 'on how transitional justice processes can better engage with women survivors seeking justice and acknowledgment' (Nesiah 2006: 1; also see UN 2006: 22). This section looks at how early truth commissions tended to ignore women, and at four common critiques of later attempts to include them, namely, claims of tokenistic inclusion, a failure to understand why some women (and men) might choose silence over voice, the ways in which women's stories are incorporated into broader narratives of victimhood and responsibility and the neglect of masculinity.

This approach to gender as women is part of a shift in global norms that followed the Fourth World Conference on Women in Beijing in 1995. Among other things, this conference recognised the need to tackle the 'feminization of poverty' and criticised the idea that gender issues could be addressed through specialist women's institutions and programmes, and instead called for women and their issues to be included, or mainstreamed, across all institutions and programmes (Chant 2006; Charlesworth 2005).

The idea of gender (or women) mainstreaming was then reinforced by a sense that early truth commissions had failed to capture the scale and scope of women's suffering (Hayner 2011: 86; Nesiah 2006: 2) and unintentionally favoured men and their stories (Olckers 1996: 62). For example, the 'invisibility' of women from the South African TRC was blamed on the Commission's focus on political violations of bodily integrity rights, which failed to capture the range of women's experiences, such as the gendered impacts of pass books and forced removals;

the failure to recognise rape as a potentially politically motivated violation in a way that now seems impossible given the widespread perception of rape as a common 'weapon of war' (Graybill 2002: 108; Ross 2003a); and the stigma associated with talking about sexual violence, which is a significant part of women's experiences of conflict and repression (Goldblatt & Meintjes 1997).

In response to the latter, the South African TRC tried to encourage women to talk about their experiences of sexual violence by organising three women-only hearings that sought to transform 'women's experiences of harm into a category that could be investigated and about which findings could be made' (Ross 2003a: 25). The Commission also included a chapter on women in its final report. Similarly, the Peruvian truth commission, which was established five years later, set up a gender unit, organised women-only hearings and included separate gender chapters in an effort to 'capture women's experience of violence – generally defined as rape and other forms of sexual violence' (Theidon 2007: 457).

Silence on women's experiences is clearly problematic – not only because women constitute half the population, but also because 'gender-specific experiences ... give rise to gender-specific needs that are unlikely to be addressed without the participation of women' (Bell & O'Rourke 2007: 30). In short, socially constructed understandings of femininity and masculinity have everyday material effects. For example, the fact that men's work is often better remunerated, while women tend to take primary responsibility for the young, old and sick, has clear implications for the differential socio-economic impact of the loss of a male or female relative. However, while it is clearly necessary to include women's voices, the operationalisation of such efforts by truth commissions has proved deeply problematic on at least four levels.

First, truth commissions (and media coverage of them) have often failed to listen to the complexity of women's stories, and instead tended to focus in on particular aspects of women's testimonies – most notably their vulnerability and experiences of sexual violence – to the neglect of their agency and other harms (Foster, Haupt & de Beer 2005: 17; Ross 2003a: 84–91). This is in part a product of their mandates, which have historically focused on politically motivated gross human rights violations, and ignored or downplayed the various ways in which women also suffer from structural violence and the socio-economic consequences of repression (Goldblatt & Meintjes 1997; Graybill 2001). However, it is also due to a failure to really listen to 'what women say about war – and how they say it', by failing to recognise that when women speak of what happened to significant men in their lives and about their 'children's knawing hunger ... they *are* talking about themselves' (Theidon 2007: 474 and 459). In turn, when rape is discussed, there is a tendency to see violations as an almost natural product of conflict or state repression, rather than to analyse why and how it happened, why sexual violence also occurs during peacetime, why it may increase during conflict both because it is used as a weapon and because of the increased opportunities and exaggerated power imbalances that accompany conflict, and why sexual violence might continue at a relatively high level in post-conflict or post-authoritarian societies (Boesten 2013; Buss 2009).

These shortcomings have implications for a commission's ability to capture the range of injustices suffered, but also for its capacity to consider the past's persistent nature. As Fiona Ross has argued, '[a] focus solely on the body and its violation fixes experience in time, in an event, and draws attention away from ways of understanding that experience as a process that endures across bodies and through time' (2003a: 49). The same can be said of the various factors that conjoined to cause an experience. In this way, a failure to understand violations as part of broader power imbalances can ensure that 'the interpretative line' between coercion and consent or protest and disorder 'may become blurred as well' in ways that have significant repercussions for a society's ability to recognise and address peacetime violations (Boesten 2013: 13).

Second, some question whether it is always better to speak out. More specifically, scholars have shown how women's silence on issues such as sexual violence should not just be seen as a problem to be overcome, but as a form of language, which can express the unspeakable and constitute a self-protecting strategy in uncertain contexts (Motsemme 2004; Ross 2003a; Slyomovics 2005). The implication is that transitional justice should analyse silences and consider what people may lose and gain from speaking, the likely motivations for speaking, and what constitutes a 'safe space'. For example, there might be significant costs of talking publicly about sexual violence when perpetrators are powerful or proximate; where women may be disbelieved, blamed or stigmatised; or when women need to maintain relationships with husbands, families, communities, administrators and politicians (Boesten 2013; Ross 2003a). At the same time, studies reveal how women (and men) often see truth-telling as a form of material exchange, which potentially leaves participants feeling exposed if they speak of traumatic experiences and their testimonies enter the public domain without any clear return (Boesten 2013; Ross 2003a; Shaw 2007; Theidon 2007: 474).

Third, questions arise about the contribution that women's testimonies make to broader narratives of victimhood and responsibility. Thus, while there is a general consensus that women and men tend to experience injustice and violence differently, it is clear that transitional justice practitioners and enthusiasts often leap from a position of different experiences to one in which women are principal victims and saviours simply because of their sex. In this way, it is asserted that '[a]s civilians, women suffer disproportionately from armed conflict', while they 'are disproportionately represented in civil society initiatives to sustain communities during conflict and to bring conflict to an end', and to 'predominate as household-heads in many post-conflict societies' (Bell & O'Rourke 2007: 25–26). This idea of women's innocence and potential is usually linked to the idea that they, as actual or potential mothers, are inherently peaceful (Forcey 1994; Ruddick 1989). As a result, such assumptions silence the ways in which women may also contribute to problems and the extent to which their relative innocence may be due to power imbalances, instead of biological factors (Goetz 2007).

The implication is also that, 'as non-combatants', women 'can act as peace catalysts' (Nordström 2013: 6) or as 'political cleaners' if only they are empowered (Goetz 2007).[1] However, such assumptions can easily lead to a 'feminization of responsibility and obligation', whereby women are given few rights and powers, but shouldered with much of the responsibility for securing valued ends – from development and good governance to peace and justice (cf. Chant 2006).

Finally, there are inter-related questions about a gendered approach that focuses on women's experiences, but which ignores the varied impacts of multiple, and often conflicting, notions of

---

[1] Goetz (2007) sets out, but also critiques, this common position with respect to suggestions that female empowerment would help curb corruption because women are less corrupt.

masculinity on their male counterparts (Wanner & Wadham 2015; Zalewski 2010). More specifically, scholars hone in on the problem of delinking sexual identities from power relations, and ways in which an analysis of femininities and masculinities is critical for an understanding of how violence plays out, and how it can transform and persist into the present and future (Boesten 2013; Hamber 2007).

The implication is that an approach to gender 'as women' reproduces many of the problems witnessed in other fields in which a focus on women has downplayed differences between women, unintentionally silenced marginal male voices, and reinforced stereotyped gender binaries (Arora-Jonsson 2011; Charlesworth 2008; Cornwall 1997; Cornwall, Harrison & Whitehead 2007; El Bushra 2007; Goetz 2007; Ross 2003a; Wanner & Wadham 2015; Zalewski 2010). This includes women in development, where women are often said to constitute the majority of the world's poor and to be inherently pro-development (Bhatta 2001); women, environment and development, where women are often presented as suffering most from environmental decay and as being more environmentally friendly than their male counterparts (Enarson 2012); and women in peacebuilding, where women tend to be cast as innocent victims of violence who will almost instinctively contribute to peace if only they are empowered to do so (Fukuyama 1998; Ruddick 1989). In all these contexts, a common argument about women's especial (rather than different) suffering and their virtuous capacities lacks a robust empirical basis (Chant 2006; Marcoux 1998) and stems from assumed differences between the sexes, rather than gender relations per se.

As this chapter will show, the Kenyan TJRC ignored, or seemingly remained largely unaware of, such critiques and instead reproduced a tried and tested approach to gender as women, whereby half of the population were heard 'as women' and the other half were heard as 'victims' or 'adversely mentioned persons' (AMPs). Critically, this dual narrative of women as victim-heroines informed the Commission's approach and was reproduced by it. However, before looking at this narrative in more detail, it is important to provide an overview of the Commission's gender policy, some of its achievements and more technical shortcomings, and the problematic idea of female-only spaces as 'safe spaces'.

7.2 The TJRC's 'Focus on Women'[2]

Men and women experience violations of human rights and injustices differently. Building on the provisions of the TJRC Act, the Commission adopted policies and took measures that ensured that the experiences and violations suffered by women were appropriately and comprehensively covered both in its work and this Report.

(TJRC vol. 1 2013: xvi)

The TJRC made a conscious decision to mainstream gender and to focus 'on the experiences of the female gender' (TJRC vol. 2C 2013: 3). This approach was permitted by the TJRC Act, which allowed for special arrangements to be made to address the experiences of women and other vulnerable groups (Kenya 2008d: sec. 27[1]a). However, it was justified by the idea that women have historically 'been the subject of systematic discrimination and marginalisation' (Kenya 2008d: 3) and 'when compared to men ... are disproportionately susceptible to violations simply on the basis of their gender' (Kenya 2008d: 3). It was also justified by a sense – informed by the experience of previous truth commissions and by the 2003 Task Force on the Establishment of a TJRC – that women tend to shy away from talking about their own experiences (Kenya 2008d: x) and speak more freely 'when fewer or no men were in attendance' (TJRC vol. 2C 2013: 10). Finally, it was influenced by an international environment in which a gendered approach tends to boil down to a focus on women (UN 2006: 22). Thus, in one interview, a senior TJRC staff member referred directly to Christine Bell and Catherine O'Rourke's 'seminal article on feminist theory of transitional justice' (2007) as they explained the Commission's 'need to add women ... so that we have a gender perspective to everything' (interview, Nairobi, 7 September 2011).

In practice, this approach included the gender-balancing of personnel, the selection of women to give testimony at public hearings, the organisation of women's hearings across the country, a special thematic hearing on women in Nairobi and the inclusion of chapters on women's experiences and sexual violence in the Commission's final report. This section looks at these efforts and highlights some of the

---

[2] From the title of the TJRC's gender chapter: 'Gender and Gross Violation of Human Rights: Focus on Women'.

more practical achievements and shortcomings before the next section focuses in on the problematic idea of female-only spaces as 'safe spaces'.

In terms of gender balancing, the CEO, Patricia Nyuandi, and four of eight department directors,[3] and four out of the TJRC's original nine commissioners were women. However, of the commissioners, only Murungi (who resigned in April 2010) had a strong reputation as a gender expert. The Commission's regional offices in Eldoret, Garissa, Kisumu and Mombasa were also headed by a regional coordinator and an assistant 'of the opposite gender' (TJRC vol. 1 2013: 33). Finally, 43 per cent of statement takers and more than 40 per cent of the Commission's employees were female (TJRC vol. 2C 2013: 7 and vol. 1 2013: 33) albeit with unsurprising biases. Thus, while all of the secretaries were female, the Commission's security team and all but one of the commissioners' drivers were male.

The Commission also developed partnerships with Maendaleo ya Wanawake (MYW), the country's largest women's organisation, and with the Gender Violence Recovery Centre of Nairobi Women's Hospital. The aim: 'to increase women's access to its processes as well as to provide additional support to women, particularly those women who were victims of sexual violence' (Slye 2017: 19). This was a good idea. However, the benefits were undermined by MYW's long association with the ruling establishment (Tripp 2001; Wipper 1975), while it is unclear how many women were assisted by the Gender Violence Recovery Centre and how.

The gender policy also 'enjoined the Commissioners and staff to mainstream gender in all operational undertakings including in statement taking, investigations, civic education and hearings' (TJRC vol. 2C 2013: 6). To this end, the statement taking form encouraged women to speak out about violations against them as individuals:

Experience shows that some people, especially women, testify about violations of human rights that happened to family members or friends, but they are less willing to speak of their own suffering. Please don't forget to tell us what happened to you yourself if you were the victim of a gross human rights abuse.

(TJRC statement taking form, TJRC vol. 1: 170)

---

[3] Women headed Finance and Administration, Communications, Special Support, and Information and Documentation, while men headed Legal Affairs, Investigations, Research, and Civic Education.

The Commission also trained statement takers on gender sensitivity and directed that '[a]s far as it was possible, statements from women were taken by female statement takers' (TJRC vol. 2C 2013: 7–8).

Nevertheless, fewer women gave statements – around a third of all statements collected (TJRC vol. 2C 2013: 8) – and practice often fell far short of the Commission's own policies. First, contracted statement takers were trained over a three day period on a broad-ranging curriculum that included gender sensitivity, as well as an introduction to transitional justice and truth commissions, a lesson on how to categorise human rights violations, an overview of the Commission's mandate and powers, an introduction to ethical issues of confidentiality, advise on trauma management and so forth (TJRC vol. 1 2013: 85). It is therefore unsurprising that, while many statement takers spoke highly of their training, none remembered every aspect of it, and several regarded it as inadequate (for example, interview, statement taker, Muranga, 6 May 2011; and Lodwar, 18 March 2014). The director of special support herself recognised how statement takers 'may not have been adequately equipped with [the] skills and knowledge' required to address the different needs of men and women (cited in Alam 2014: 99).

It was also impossible to ensure the availability of female statement takers when 304 statement takers with limited facilitation budgets were spread out across the country. Indeed, in some localities, there were no statement takers at all. In other parts, such as Baringo County, a six-person team tried to cover 11,075 km^2, but failed to reach five entire divisions (interview, statement taker, Kabarnet, Rift Valley, 12 March 2011). Of two statement takers in Turkana Central (almost 5,000 km^2), one noted, '[I had] decided to limit myself to Lodwar [town]' (interview, Lodwar, 19 March 2014); and the local coordinator recognised how he could not 'cover the whole area and so I went to specific – like the IDPs' (interview, Lodwar, 18 March 2014). Indeed, even when it was known that a female statement taker would be required, they were sometimes notable by their absence – as occurred, for example, during the women's hearing in Nakuru, when a lone male statement taker sat outside the venue for much of the session (notes, 24 September 2011).

The TJRC also prepared guidelines for the investigation of sexual violence, recruited experienced investigators and organised a thematic hearing on women's rights in Nairobi on 8 February 2012, where 'experts, academics and women's rights organisations' engaged 'in an analytical discussion on gender issues' (TJRC vol. 2C 2013: 8–9). However, while a small team of investigators focused on those selected as 'window cases' for public hearings, the thematic hearing on women (as with the other thematic hearings) attracted little attention and stimulated negligible debate.

The TJRC also encouraged women to attend public and women's hearings, and – with support from UN Women – covered the cost for some to travel to and from hearing venues. However, facilitation tended to focus on women who were already part of victims groups and networks, so the scope of this assistance was limited.

More significantly, the Commission selected 161 women to speak at its public hearings – although 'this number was significantly low compared to the number of male speakers' (TJRC vol. 2C 2013: 13). Women's testimonies at these hearings fell into two broad categories. First, there were women who presented memoranda and who spoke not of specific harms that they or their loved ones had suffered, but of more general histories and trends. In this way, women presented memoranda on everything from the marginalisation of a particular ethnic group or the troubles faced by disabled persons to the high number of police shootings during the post-election violence. The second category included those who narrated more personal experiences of injustice. As with previous truth commissions, this tended to involve an account of husbands and sons who had been killed by state or non-state actors. Although some women also spoke of their own experiences of violence – including, on occasion, graphic details of sexual violence (for example, TJRC vol. 2C 2013: 104–106). Women also spoke during *in camera* hearings when more personal accounts of violence, including of sexual violence, were relayed (interview, TJRC special support officer, Nairobi, 26 April 2011).

However, at the centre of the TJRC's gender approach were the women's hearings which 'were framed as "conversations with women"' and, as such, were purposefully designed to be less formal than their public counterparts. To this end, female commissioners (and, in their absence, the CEO or the head of special support) were not seated up on a platform, and, where hearings were held in the same room as public hearings, the room was rearranged to bring the commissioner's table down to floor level (for example, Kisumu,

16 July 2011). In addition, while participants were still asked to stand up when commissioners entered and left the room, the proceedings started with an ad hoc prayer (rather than with the commission prayer) and with songs and dancing in which the participation of female staff and commissioners was regarded as 'a gesture that fostered confidence and trust among the women and created an atmosphere conducive for the candid and open conversations that ensued' (TJRC vol. 1 2013: 106). It was also not uncommon for female commissioners to come out from behind their table to personally console women who succumbed to tears when telling their story – an interaction that I never saw at a parallel public hearing. Participants were also not asked to swear on a copy of the Bible, Koran or the Kenyan Constitution, but were instead simply handed a roaming microphone and spoke from where they were seated. This stage management was largely successful and ensured that the women's hearings had a more informal, communal and collegiate atmosphere than the public sessions.

The regional coordinator, or if the coordinator was male, his female deputy, organised these hearings. The coordinator was assisted by female statement takers from the area who used their own networks, with announcements sometimes made through local radios stations and newspapers, or through loudspeakers driven through the town in question. Most participants were either local leaders or activists who worked on victims' issues, or members of loosely organised victims' networks who could be relatively easily mobilised. They thus fell into two broad categories: the relatively educated activist or leader with some access to resources who saw attendance as part of their work or communal duty, and the relatively uneducated and poor farmer or small businesswoman who had come out of curiosity, or who had decided to exchange a loss of earnings (or a visit to another potential patron) because she wanted the government to know about what had happened in her area and/or hoped that, on being heard, some future assistance or redress would be forthcoming.

In some areas, for example, in Bungoma and Busia towns in Western Kenya – a number of women were pre-selected to speak on issues specific to particular groups, such as widows or IDPs. These short presentations were then followed by an open microphone session. In other locations, such as Kapsokwony, the whole meeting was open with women simply asked to raise their hand if they wished to speak.

Either way, the inclusion of an open microphone session during at least part of the session ensured that women had the freedom to choose what they saw as the main issues and stories. Commission staff also encouraged women to go beyond election-related violence or other local experiences of conflict (such as the SLDF or Shifta War) to relay more general problems – from health care provision to experiences of sexual discrimination.

In this way, and in contrast to previous truth commissions, the hearings were fairly effective at eliciting female testimonials that went beyond direct and indirect violations of bodily integrity rights to include structural violence, inequalities, patriarchal cultures and everyday harassment. Moreover, it did so in ways that helped to reveal continuums of violence – between public and private, conflict and peacetime, and state and non-state actors – and the various ways in which the past persists in women's lives, and why many fear the future. To take just one example, at the women's hearing in Isiolo in Upper Eastern Kenya, female participants spoke of the loss of fathers and husbands, and of their own experiences of violence and rape during conflicts. They also spoke of the need for compensation for the ongoing problem of cattle raids by neighbouring communities and forcible acquisitions by government officers; a need for better health, education and water services; and an end to the economic and political marginalisation of their area. At the same time, women were prompted, and used the opportunity, to speak about the patriarchal culture of local societies and of associated problems – from the education of girl children, female circumcision and early marriage to women's limited control over household wealth, the problems faced by women who were widowed, divorced or in polygamous marriages, and the lack of elected female representatives (notes, 10 May 2011).

The unrehearsed nature of these hearings – together with the way in which woman after woman stood up to relay a litany of injustices and abuses that often included scenes of shocking violence accompanied by sobbing and ad hoc singing – also rendered the women's hearings more emotional than their public counterparts. This was then reinforced by an impression of scale, as often every woman in the room seemed to have a story, and an increasingly heart-wrenching story, that they wanted to tell with half a day always proving too short. Such palpable emotions made the hearings more powerful and seemingly cathartic, but they also raised questions about the safety of the space provided, the possibility for retraumatisation and the consequences of having spoken (see Section 7.3).

The TJRC also included narratives of women's suffering throughout its final report with separate chapters on women and on sexual violence. The former outlines the Commission's gender policy and women's experiences of the gross human rights violations that fell within its mandate. This includes a discussion of systematic discrimination, which, according to the Commission, 'finds justification and breeding ground in communities' cultural practices' (TJRC vol. 2C 2013: 19) such as bride price, early and forced marriage, female genital mutilation/cutting and widow inheritance; issues of socio-economic status and the 'feminisation of poverty'; specific employment, educational and land ownership problems; limited political representation and participation; experiences of conflict, sexual violence, forced displacement and state repression; and women's role in peacebuilding. This chapter casts a light on a wide range of injustices over time and sets these in a broader context of patriarchal traditions and customs. However, it says little about differences between women, or about how men may also be affected by patriarchal customs and traditions. The chapter on sexual violence focuses largely on women's experiences of such violations over time.

The final report also offered various recommendations regarding women. On the one hand, there are specific recommendations, such as the need for the President to offer a 'public and unconditional apology for state's sanction of discrimination against women', for the Gender and Equality Commission to increase efforts 'to raise awareness about harmful cultural practices that adversely affect women's enjoyment of human rights', and the need for specific pieces of legislation – such as the Marriage Bill, Matrimonial Property Bill, Family Protection Bill and Equal Opportunities Bill (all initially tabled in 2007) – to be expedited (TJRC vol. 4 2013: 41). On the other hand, the Commission set out a reparations framework, which, if implemented, would help to address a concern that women have borne the brunt of various violations including their longer-term socio-economic implications as widows and primary caregivers. Unfortunately, these recommendations are yet to be acted upon, and will likely never be implemented in full. However, even if they were, there is a disjuncture between the Commission's broad analysis and fairly limited recommendations. In part, this is due to parallel reform processes and the potential redress provided by the country's 2010 Constitution, but it is also due to the difficulty of providing implementable recommendations for the range of injustices analysed.

The final aspect of the Commission's gendered approach relates to its plan for an 'implementation and monitoring mechanism', which includes a provision for the Implementation Committee's Technical Secretariat to have a 'victim participation, gender and minorities unit'. The plan also recommended that each of the five suggested units 'include a gender focal point to ensure equal access to women in the reparations process' (TJRC vol. 4 2013: 79), that the chair and vice chair be 'persons of opposite gender' (TJRC vol. 4 2013: 85) and that 'not more than two-thirds of the [committee's] members [be] of the same gender' (TJRC vol. 4 2013: 86). However, almost five years later, this mechanism is yet to be established.

The Commission's focus on women was welcomed by many. It also helped to highlight direct and structural violations, and the ongoing and persistent nature of women's suffering. At the same time, though, it suffered from various shortcomings of poor planning, limited resources and unmet expectations. The approach was also premised on an idea of 'safe spaces', which assumed, and ultimately helped to perform, familiar gender binaries whilst doing little to start a conversation that might challenge the same.

7.3 Female-Only Spaces as 'Safe Spaces'?

The women's hearings were framed as 'conversations with women'. They were presided over by female Commissioners and staff, and were thus designed to be safe spaces where women could freely talk about violations that were specific to them.

(TJRC vol. 1 2013: xvi)

In terms of both the statement-taking process and public hearings, the Commission presented female-only interactions as 'safe spaces', which would encourage women to speak out. In practice, however, this ideal was troubled by procedural and substantive factors. For one, the women's hearings always ran out of time, which meant that women who spoke towards the end of the morning were often restricted to talking about such painful experiences as gang rape or the murder of loved ones in a few minutes. In part, this is testament to the hearings' success, as an increasing number of women came to realise the range of experiences that they could narrate and saw the commissioners' sympathetic response. However, it was also due to the short time allocated and tendency for the sessions to start late. For example, in Busia, the hearing started late because it was held on the main market day (notes, 4 July 2011), while in Naivasha, the 'morning' session did not start until almost 2 pm because the commissioners first attended an *in camera* hearing (notes, 27 September 2011).

The fact that many women had not prepared themselves to speak – unlike at public hearings where male and female witnesses were pre-selected and briefed – also meant that participants were potentially less prepared for the emotions that might be unleashed. Indeed, it was unclear whether participants had fully considered the implications of relaying personal stories in front of their neighbours to then return home after a short session with a TJRC counsellor. The latter was often limited to just a few minutes since there were usually only two counsellors, and sometimes only one,[4] present.

There was also the question of what people expected from having given a statement or testimony. Significantly, many women voiced their appreciation for the Commission's understanding of gendered dynamics and the need for them to speak separately from men. As one woman in Mt Elgon explained:

> We are grateful that you have separated us from men because yesterday we listened to what the men were saying and we could not talk ... Thank you for the knowledge and the wisdom you used to decide that women should be separated in order for them to say their own things.
>
> (TJRC vol. 2C 2013: 10)

However, such expressions of gratitude were often linked to an expectation that, once women had spoken and been heard, some assistance would be forthcoming. In this vein, the woman cited in the introduction to this chapter linked her gratitude that the Commission had 'decided to come and cry with us' to a call for justice, while a woman with whom I spoke at the closure of the women's hearing in Naivasha explained how she was glad that she had spoken and how, having told her story, the Commission would 'now come in and help' (conversation,

---

[4] As occurred at the women's hearing in Kericho, 20 September 2011.

27 September 2011). Indeed, from listening to women give testimony and from interviews – together with comparative analyses (for example, Shaw [2007] on Sierra Leone; Theidon [2007] and Boesten [2013] on Peru) – it seems that many women gave statements and testimony in the belief, or at least the hope, that their story would be exchanged for some form of assistance or justice. The TJRC both intentionally and inadvertently raised such expectations by highlighting their ability to recommend reparations, and by insisting that their recommendations would be binding. Moreover, while both male and female participants are likely frustrated by the non-implementation of the report's recommendations (Chapter 9), the fact that gross human rights violations often place a particularly heavy socio-economic burden on women as principal caregivers, ensures that the raised expectations of assistance also has a bearing on the practice of the Commission's espoused gender sensitivity.

Not only are there ethical issues that stem from a woman's decision to give testimony in the expectation of assistance that will likely never come, but also from the fact that victims' testimony did not go hand-in-hand with revelations from perpetrators. As Kimberly Theidon argues with regards to the Peruvian truth commission, 'Reparation should include the redistribution of goods and services; it should also include the redistribution of shame to those who earned it' (2007: 475). Unfortunately, this did not happen in Kenya, where AMPs either did not appear or denied or justified their actions, and where many continue to enjoy an elite position (Chapter 8).

Finally, the supposed safety of these hearings rests on the fact that they were female-only spaces and from the implicit assumption that women would care for each other within and beyond the hearings. However, this assumption, which influenced both the statement taking process and women's hearings, is highly problematic.

With regards to the former, on the basis of lessons 'learned from the experiences of other truth commissions that women were less likely to give their statements to male Statement Takers', the TJRC decided that, 'as far as it was possible, statements from women were taken by female statement takers' (TJRC vol. 1 2013: 83). However, the idea that women would feel comfortable speaking to another woman ignores the complexity of local identities and relations. This was something that the Commission tried to minimise through employing people of different ages and from different clans and ethnic groups, and by allowing people to give statements in a language of their choice and to request a different statement taker (TJRC vol. 1 2013: 83). Nevertheless, concerns were still raised about the possibilities of bias and shame, and about the lack of psychosocial support for statement takers and those they interacted with. For example, some spoke of generational barriers and the taboo of talking about things like sexual violence with someone who was young enough to be one's daughter. Others spoke of the statement taker's ethnic identity and personal history, as in Mt Elgon, where one of the statement takers was reported to be former SLDF. Questions were also raised by the relatively relaxed attitude to confidentiality sometimes adopted. As one statement taker explained, he sometimes felt the need 'to take someone else' with him so that he could collect sufficient statements and that, while this meant that the person had 'not taken the oath' or been trained, this was unimportant, 'as these things are known all over' (interview, Murunga, Central, 6 May 2011).

The idea of female-only hearings as inherently 'safe' was also problematic. First, and on a point of procedure, images and information sometimes did circulate beyond the group of women assembled. For example, at the women's hearing in Busia – where participants were reassured that the 'video camera is for the Commission, not from [media houses] … so let us be free' (notes, 4 July 2011) – footage of one woman's testimony was nevertheless included in a televised TJRC summary aired the following week (notes, 13 July 2011). Even before that, the same woman was asked to stand up during the closing ceremony of the local public hearings as an example of someone who had 'come forward and spoke[n] bravely' (notes, 5 July 2011).

Several of the women who spoke in these 'safe spaces' are also referred to by name in the final report. Not only that, but some of the references to *in camera* testimony in the final report provide considerable detail, which means that people who are knowledgeable of local contexts could probably guess the person's identity, and a photograph of one woman's tearful *in camera* testimony is included in the final report.[5] This clearly raises ethical problems as some women were exposed by telling their story in a way that they purposefully chose not to be exposed.

---

[5] I was told about the latter by one of the Commission's researchers. I have not included references to the photo or to quotes from the women's or *in camera* hearings where the person is named or may be easily identified to avoid further exposure of the individuals in question.

The idea that women-only spaces are inherently safe is also naïve. As Kimberly Theidon explains with regards to Peru:

> In the context of civil conflict, one can only assume that the random assembly of a group of women is unproblematic if women are first defined as peripheral to the conflict. By defining women as noncombatants – by assuming women are a homogeneous group of apolitical bystanders or victims – one has the illusion of yielding a group with shared interests based upon their identity as women.
>
> (2007: 463)

In Kenya – while few women have participated in violations as armed combatants or security personnel – women from a different political party, ethnic group, religious community, clan or land-buying organisation (to name just a few possible divisions) can constitute part of the 'other' that is believed to have perpetrated (or supported or benefited from) past violations and who may be feared as a source of future retribution. This was evident, for example, in the women's hearing in Bungoma, where one of the women present (during a session that largely focused on SLDF atrocities) is said to have been an SLDF sympathiser. Certainly, the woman was close to the incumbent MP who many regard as the man most responsible for the violence that occurred in the area between 2005 and 2008. At a more general level, for those who said they were speaking out about their experiences for the first time, there is no reason why others present would not have relayed excerpts to their family and friends. In such contexts, it is unclear whether women who spoke had fully thought through the possible repercussions, whether they chose to nevertheless speak out in the hope of recompense and how they feel after telling their story given the inaction around the Commission's final report.

As noted, the idea of safety in this context rested on a problematic narrative of woman as innocent victims, which the women's hearings and final chapter of the report also helped to reproduce – a narrative to which the final section of this chapter now turns.

7.4 The Women 'Hold So Much in Their Heart'

[Women] hold so much in their heart and they are the ones who suffer most.

(Interview, TJRC special support officer, Nairobi, 26 April 2011)

It is generally accepted that women tend to experience state repression, conflict and other violations differently from men. This is due to gender stereotypes and associated roles, which ensure that men are more likely to suffer from harms such as extra-judicial killings and detention during periods of state repression, while women are more likely to suffer from sexual violence and to be left looking after children and other dependents. For example, of the 1,133 casualties of Kenya's 2007–8 post-election violence recorded by the Waki Commission, 1,048 were male (92.5 per cent), 74 were women (6.5 per cent) and 11 were children (1.0 per cent) (Kenya 2008b: 384).[6] In turn, of the 12,756 Kenyans identified by the TJRC as having been victims of state torture, only 19 per cent were women; and of the 6,095 people identified as victims of unlawful detention, 10 per cent were women (TJRC vol. 2A 2013: 597). In contrast, more women have been victims of sexual violence during periods of conflict, displacement and security crackdowns. Thus, the TJRC's list includes 2,646 female (88.4 per cent) and 346 male victims of sexual violence (11.6 per cent) (TJRC vol. 1 2013: xiii); the Commission also reported that the majority of IDPs were women (TJRC vol. 2C 2013: 108). All of these statistics are estimates: the Waki Commission recognised its 'figures may not fully reflect totals of people killed' (Kenya 2008b: 385); some of the TJRC's statements seem to have been made up by statement takers seeking to cut corners and meet quotas (Chapter 6); sexual violence is usually underreported, especially by men (Leiby 2009); and there is no reason to think that the Commission's figures are all-inclusive or representative. Nevertheless, it is unlikely that more accurate figures would substantively shift the male to female ratio.

The fact that men and women tend to suffer authoritarianism and conflict differently often morphs into a claim that women are relatively powerless, that they suffer more than men and that they are nevertheless resilient and strong (for example, see Ichim's [2008] critique of the Sierra Leonean TRC; or Ryanga [2015] on the Mt Elgon conflict). This was certainly true of the Kenyan TJRC. Thus, according to the final report, 'the story of the Kenyan woman is sad, shameful and heartbreaking' (TJRC vol. 2C 2013: 2). Among other things: 'women constitute the majority of the poor', with poverty having 'become feminized' (TJRC vol. 4 2013: 39 and 40); 'almost without exception,

---

[6] The report does not say whether the children killed were male or female.

they bear the greatest brunt of conflict' (TJRC vol. 4 2013: 85); 'the vast majority' deemed to be 'secondary victims of state repression' (TJRC vol. 2C 2013: 150). At the same time, 'the story of the Kenyan woman' was cast as 'triumphant' with women lauded for 'bringing change into their lives, families, communities and the nation at large' (TJRC vol. 2C 2013: 3).

This section questions this victim-heroine narrative by looking at four interlocking themes, which informed, and were simultaneously reproduced by, the TJRC, namely, women's shared vulnerability, their non-tribal existence, their suffering and innocence relative to men, and their resilience and strength. It is worth stressing that this discussion neither seeks to offer an account of gender relations in Kenya, nor understandings of femininity and masculinity. Instead, this section simply offers a critique of the TJRC's particular focus on gender-as-women by highlighting how this approach downplayed differences between women; presented gender differences as largely self-evident; offered little insight into the construction, contradictions and common impacts of popular notions of femininity and masculinity; and inadvertently helped to reinforce existing gender binaries through an implied contradistinction between vulnerable, suffering and emotional women, and strong, violent and uncommunicative men.

The implication is not that the Commission should not have reached out to women, which was widely appreciated and highly revealing; nor that it should have organised parallel men's hearings, which would have further expanded the Commission's already impossibly large mandate. Instead, it is to suggest that the Commission should have paid more attention to power relations and to the reasons for why violence and injustice occur, and been more reflective on its own gaps and omissions.

7.4.1 'The Things That Affect Us Are All the Same'

After a meeting like that I don't have much to add. I thank the women of Bungoma and Mt Elgon for coming and speaking so frankly ... the things that affect us are all the same.

(Commissioner, closing of TJRC women's hearing, Bungoma, 9 July 2011)

There is a tension in the TJRC's work – evident during its hearings and in its final report – between recognising the differences between women and nevertheless presenting the causes of their suffering as 'all the same'.

On the one hand, the Commission recognised that some women had suffered more than others in the sense that not all had suffered such gross violations as rape, physical violence or displacement. It also recognised that some groups of women were more vulnerable as a result of regional differences and intersecting inequalities. According to the Commission, 'the most vulnerable among women' include 'women in rural and slum areas, internally displaced and refugee women, women with disabilities, women living with HIV/AIDS and women belonging to minority and indigenous groups' (TJRC vol. 2C 2013: 151). However, this means that a majority of Kenyan women fall within the 'most vulnerable' category given that the majority are rural and a majority can claim – due to the fragmented nature of several large ethnic groups and number of small ethnic groups in the country – to belong to an ethnic minority.

At the same time, an unacknowledged bias in the women's hearings towards relatively uneducated rural victims, and brief overview of women's problems in the final report, downplays the impact of women's positionality. As a result, the impact of women's differential abilities, education, wealth, geography, ethnic identity, religion, race or age on their degree of vulnerability is obscured (cf. Arora-Jonsson 2011), while a sense of shared vulnerability ultimately predominates over recognised differences. In this vein, the gender chapter boldly concludes that 'Kenyan women have suffered unspeakable and terrible atrocities, and in the majority of cases, it has been for no other reason than that they are of the female gender' (TJRC vol. 2C 2013: 151).

This assertion that women suffer simply because they are female draws upon a reality of women's subordination to men in a patriarchal society. As the TJRC's gender chapter reveals, patriarchal norms – whereby women are expected to look after and listen to their men, and men are expected to be strong and to provide for, and to protect, their kith and kin (Kabaji 2008; Mutongi 1999; Rasmussen 2010; Silberschmidt 1999; Spronk 2014) – help to shape women's everyday lives. Among other things, patriarchy ensures that women often marry young (TJRC vol. 2C 2013: 22); have limited rights according to 'customary laws' to own land (TJRC vol. 2C 2013: 49); tend to earn less and to be left to look after children when relationships end or break down (TJRC vol. 2C 2013: 40 and 96) and rarely enjoy decision-making powers as politicians or high-ranking state officials (TJRC vol. 2C 2013: 81).

However, while patriarchy is central to an understanding of how women and men's experiences of poverty, conflict and repression often differ, and to how many women are vulnerable to particular injustices and violations, it does not necessarily follow that patriarchy affects different women in the same way; that women are equally vulnerable to injustice and violations; that women do not also enjoy varying levels of agency and power; or that women are always more vulnerable than men. For example, wealthy, educated urban women may be better at negotiating patriarchy than many of their counterparts in rural villages; such negotiations are also shaped by relative power imbalances – for example, of age and economic asymmetries – between women and proximate men (Luke 2005). In turn, more women than men may, for example, find refuge in IDP camps, but it is generally the poor – both men and women – who are displaced. More importantly, the fact that women are 'generally outside mainstream leadership' does not render them, as the TJRC suggests, 'passive actors for whom decisions are made' (TJRC vol. 2C 2013: 75). The vast majority of Kenyans are 'outside the mainstream leadership', but there are still ways in which they can place pressure on leaders or resist and undermine the same.

The presumption of women's shared vulnerability also presents an overly homogenous view of men through an implicit 'other': women are vulnerable because men are relatively powerful and domineering. However, this contradistinction fails to consider how men can also feel powerless; to understand the ways in which poverty, repression or conflict usually weakens 'the position of those who are already without power' (El Bushra 2007: 136); and to recognise the pressures that patriarchy, and associated responsibilities to provide and protect, place on men (see Section 7.4.3). In so doing, it essentialises sexual difference and neglects the real source of marginalisation and vulnerability, namely, power inequalities (Arora-Jonsson 2011: 749).

However, while the idea of women's shared positionality is overly simplistic and rests on problematic gender stereotypes, it became (at least to a certain extent) a self-reinforcing narrative. Thus, according to the TJRC, a focus on women was required as women tend to suffer more; women-only hearings were an appropriate response because women could speak to each other on a level playing field; the safety of spaces lay in the shared sisterhood of female participants and TJRC conveners; and sessions brought together groups of mainly rural female victims. Perhaps unsurprisingly, this approach, which focused on the challenges that certain women face, found that Kenyan women were united in their suffering.

7.4.2 'Your Tribe Is Women'

[Would] like us to think about what it is that we're going to do between now and the next election to make sure that it doesn't happen again ... what happens is because your tribe is women.
>(Commissioner during the TJRC women's hearing in Naivasha, Rift Valley, 27 September 2011)

Women's appearances were also stage-managed to reinforce a sense of common female suffering. In this way, on the third day of public hearings in Kericho, the joint testimony of three widows of the post-election violence was used to emphasise the similarity of their experiences despite their Kalenjin, Kikuyu and Kisii identities. As the leader of evidence noted during her response, it is clear that the 'pain of the widow does not choose the tribe'. In turn, one of the female commissioners recognised how all three had 'lost husbands in situations where [they were] completely innocent', and the acting chair asked the women present to stand up and 'clap for ourselves' and expressed a hope that, while many had not had a chance to speak, 'as these women spoke you could see yourself in their stories' (notes, 21 September 2011).

A sub-text of women's relative vulnerability was that their experiences were the same despite ethnic differences and that – as a result of inter-marriage and subordination – questions of ethnic identity and associated problems of tension and conflict were largely a male concern. This theme was performed through the Commission's hearings when similarities between women were stressed and ethnic differences were purposefully downplayed. However, it was also reinforced by comments from TJRC staff and commissioners, other influential participants and statements in the final report. In this way, the convener of the TJRC women's hearing in Bungoma encouraged women in her closing remarks to seek each other out, form groups, share information and find ways to 'solve your common problems', which are 'not based on tribe' (notes, 9 July 2011). During the TJRC's closing ceremony in Kisumu, an NCIC commissioner noted how, 'as women we're borderless ... we don't have tribes and when there's the conflict we are the ones who suffer most. Us and our children' (notes, July 2011).

However, such comments fail to really listen to female participants, many of whom did see themselves as being members of a particular ethnic group and whose accounts of suffering sometimes focused more on their ethnic identity than on their gender. As a result, many women – as well as men – relayed the common narratives of communal injustice and suffering that lie at the heart of collective demands against, and fears of, ethnic 'others' (Lynch 2011b). One example was the appearance of Hon. Phoebe Asiyo at the public hearings in Kisumu, where the politician's memorandum, which she presented together with a male researcher, focused on how the Luo community had been 'bedevilled with every societal ill languishing at the bottom of the ladder of progress' due to an 'official policy to suppress [and] dehumanize' them (notes, 14 July 2011). However, it was not just leaders who interpreted their problems through an ethnic lens; one woman in Upper Eastern, for example, talked of state violence as a 'child of Isiolo', while another spoke of how local Somali were still behind, do not have wealth and 'don't have a country' (notes, women's hearing, 10 May 2011).

Comments regarding women's tribelessness also suggest that, because of women's 'limited presence in public spaces of influence, they are only marginally, if at all, engaged in the politics and issues that spark conflict' (TJRC vol. 2C 2013: 85), which ignores a broader literature on how women may contribute to a sense of ethnic difference and competition. This can be as mothers and grandmothers who pass down stories of collective traumas that require redress (Volkan 1997) and ethnic stereotypes of the 'other' as lazy, criminal or untrustworthy (Wendo 2016), but also as community members who believe that they deserve assistance or redress (Lynch 2011b).

This blurring of ethnic differences between women is similar to that which occurred with racial, religious, class or generational differences. However, it is particularly problematic given the emphasis placed on the integration of the country's different ethnic groups into a cohesive nation – '[a] critical challenge that Kenya has faced since attaining independence in 1963' (TJRC vol. 3 2013: 2). According to the Commission, ethnic difference has been 'an instrument of division' (TJRC vol. 3 2013: 2), with claims to belong to an area more than 'others' cited as a principal source of ethnic tension and violence (TJRC vol. 3 2013: 9). Given this understanding, the idea that women are, to a certain extent, tribeless and borderless is central to a presentation of them as collectively vulnerable and innocent, and of men as 'the problem'. However, while consistent with the Commission's overarching narrative, this oversimplification ultimately naturalises, and thus reinforces, existing gender binaries of passive, suffering women and powerful, violent men. It also misses out on an opportunity to discuss the ways in which ethnic stereotypes, narratives and tensions are reproduced from the bottom up, as well as from the top down.

7.4.3 'Women Have Suffered the Most'

Everywhere we've been the men may suffer, but the women have suffered the most. Everywhere we've been. Without exception.

(Commissioner, women's hearing, Naivasha, 27 September 2011)

The other side to the claim of women's particular vulnerability and innocence is the idea that they have suffered *more* than men. However, while the idea of differential suffering is broadly accepted, the idea of greater suffering is highly contentious and only makes sense if the harms that women suffer are somehow deemed to be worse; if the impact of harms on women is more far-reaching; if women's suffering is more deserving of sympathy because they are perceived as innocent and thus less culpable; or if they harbour greater fears for the future. Yet, all of these claims are problematic and over simplistic. More specifically, they neglect power relations and assume natural differences between the sexes, and thus inadvertently reinforce unhelpful gender binaries of weak women and powerful men.

First, it can be said that women suffer *more* than men if the harms that they experience with greater frequency, such as sexual violence or the difficulty of being left to look after children, are *worse* than the common harms experienced by men, such as being killed, detained or tortured. Yet, such comparisons make little sense. Instead, each case ultimately depends on the context, details and aftermath. For example, rape is often associated with personal trauma and significant stigma that can lead to the breakdown of relationships, marginalisation and impoverishment. However, detention and torture in 1980s Kenya – as testimony before the TJRC relayed over and again – is also often associated with trauma, namely, of the state's unfettered power and with the stigma that one was anti-government, which meant that 'dissenters' were often unable to finish an education, gain decent employment or secure opportunities for their children (TJRC vol. 2A [ch. 5] 2013).

Thus, rather than simply assume that violation x is worse than y, it is fruitful to listen to people's accounts. In this vein, Fiona Ross's work on the South African TRC reveals how an assumption that an experience of sexual violence constitutes a primary harm is not always evident from women's testimony – from their sense of agency to the pain of other harms inflicted (2003a: 91). Ross's findings resonate with my interpretation of women's testimonies during the TJRC hearings, when – at least for some women – an account of sexual violence seemed secondary to other harms, such as the loss of a male breadwinner and an ongoing struggle to bring up children. The same was also true of some men, whose experiences of the aftermath of political detention often seemed to outweigh the torture itself.

Not only does the idea of sexual violence as a primary harm prejudge interpretations and effects, but the Commission's focus on women meant that men's stories of sexual violence were largely ignored. For example, in the chapter on sexual violence, the testimony is cited of a woman who, during questioning on the location of her husband as a suspected SLDF member, was assaulted by police officers who 'inserted a bottle of beer into my private parts'. However, the women also relayed how she saw police officers at the police station tell

> an 80-year old man: 'Onto your marks'. The old man bent down, and they started to sodomise him. The sodomising went on for 24 hours, up to the morning. In the morning, at 10.00 am, he was left for 15 minutes. Another one bent down and the ordeal went on. Another one was mistreated in a similar way.
>
> (TJRC vol. 2C 2013: 107)

Astonishingly this part of the woman's testimony is ignored entirely in the main body of the report that surrounds the boxed text; the excerpt simply introduced as a narrative that 'presents the experience of a woman who was sexually violated in a police cell' (TJRC vol. 2C 2013: 106).

It is unclear whether men's accounts of gender-based violence, for example, of rape, castration during security operations, nudity and harm to genitalia during detention or forcible circumcisions during election-related violence were recorded as instances of torture/assault and sexual violence, or just as torture/assault. However, comparative cases show that this is often what happens. As occurred in Peru, for example, where men were found to not only be less likely to report sexual violence and to refer to violence as sexual, but also to be more likely to suffer from violations such as sexual humiliation and torture than rape. This is critical since to suggest that women are sexually violated, while men are tortured or assaulted, is to erroneously suggest that rape is about sex, rather than about power and domination.

It can also be said that women suffer *more* than men if the impact of harms tends to be more persistent or far-reaching. Critically, this was often an impression given by women's more emotional testimony. However, while women's tears were taken as evidence of their relative suffering, there are reasons why men may have been reluctant to 'show weakness' and to say that a violation 'just happened' (interview, TJRC special support officer, Nairobi, 26 April 2011). First, women's hearings were intentionally set up to be more emotional. Second, gendered stereotypes of women's reliance on men means that the image of the 'suffering female', and particularly of the 'impoverished widow', is a narrative of victimhood that has strong social resonance in Kenya, and one that women have long used to make claims for assistance on relatives, communities and the state (Mutongi 1999). In contrast, common gender stereotypes cast the ideal male as emotionally reserved (Kabaji 2008: 40). As a result, a 'cool mask' constitutes a sign of self-control and status (van Stapele 2015: 183), with marginal young men in particular often 'very engaged in masking feelings, as to them it [has] become a distinctive way of demonstrating manhood' (van Stapele 2015: 183). Indeed, so strong is such pressure that one interviewee disbelieved men who spoke out about the 'shameful' details of their torture – for example, of having a 'rubber band [tied] on testes by women and being pricked ... and of them mocking you in front of other men'. In his opinion, 'there was a lot that I went through [during my detention] and don't even share with my wife. So, if someone shares, then the chances are then he never experienced it. According to our culture we are not supposed to say' (interview, Kisumu, 5 August 2011). Given such gendered norms, it is surely possible that many men felt the harms inflicted upon them acutely, but simultaneously felt a need to display self-control and a 'cool mask'. If this is the case, it seems that a reiteration of women's need to cry and release their pain threatens to reinforce a binary of emotional women and strong men that inadvertently upholds the structures of patriarchy and subordination that the Commission simultaneously criticised.

Beyond the emotions displayed, a recurring theme in the Commission's work is that women suffer more because of their responsibilities to look after dependents, which suggests that their suffering lasts longer. However, to suggest that women necessarily suffer more from the demands of looking after kith and kin is to ignore male responsibilities – namely, that, according to predominant notions of patriarchy, for a Kenyan male to 'become' and 'be' a man he should be able to act as the main breadwinner and provider for his family (Kabaji 2008; Rasmussen 2010; Silberschmidt 1999; Spronk 2014; van Stapele 2015: 161 and 2016). In short, responsibilities, as well as privileges, come with being a 'patriarch and head of household' (Silberschmidt 2001: 665). The implication is that, if common notions of femininity can leave women suffering as primary carers should men die or abscond, common notions of masculinity can lead men to 'suffer from feelings of inadequacy and lack of self-esteem' and to be 'met with contempt from women who are left with increasing responsibilities' if they are unable to provide for their families (Silberschmidt 2001: 657).

These pressures of masculinity resonate with many accounts before the TJRC and with some of the testimony cited in the final report, which collectively suggest that the persistence of the past for men is often intertwined with cultural notions of the 'good male' who should be able to provide for, and protect, his family and community. In this way, many men had clearly been made desperate by the financial demands placed upon them, while many seemed more affected by primary harms that indirectly impacted their family members than bodily integrity rights violations per se (for example, TJRC vol. 2A 2013: 636). Such pressures were recognised by the Commission. However, in so doing, gender stereotypes were often only further reinforced. For example, at a public hearing in Naivasha, a commissioner consoled a man who had testified about the post-election violence by noting how '[we] have heard the helplessness that you felt and have heard this from many men especially in IDP camps . . . [we have heard your] inability to be the husbands and fathers that God intended' (notes, 26 September 2011).

Finally, it can be said that women suffer *more* than men if they are less able to avoid harms and are thus less culpable and more troubled by fears for the future. This idea of relative innocence is one that came out clearly during both the final report and commission hearings – with one commissioner noting during the closing of the women's hearing in Bungoma, for example, how the women 'need to remember that we are all children' (notes, 9 July 2011). Moreover, while the Commission recognised that not all women were innocent bystanders, their involvement as perpetrators, supporters or beneficiaries was generally portrayed as marginal and peripheral. In this vein, statements of women's responsibility is generally limited to a paragraph or two towards the end of individual sections of the gender chapter. For example, the six pages on 'women and peacemaking' ends with the following:

> But it is not always the case that women support peace initiatives. On the contrary, women may be involved in planning and executing violence. They may also be silent endorsers of the conflict. As a female witness observed in Kitale:
>
> When our elders planned to go and kill somebody and burn people's houses, where do they plan all that? They plan in our houses and we are the ones who cook food for them and the man comes out of that house and goes to participate in clashes. Why are we, as women not convincing our men to stop the conflicts and killings so that we can live in peace? It seems that as women, we support our men.
>
> During the Mt. Elgon conflict, some women were involved in performing chores for members for SLDF. For instance, a women told the Commission that her role included cooking food for SLDF members.
>
> (TJRC vol. 2C 2013: 146)

However, this is where the discussion abruptly ends. There is no analysis of whether and, if so, when, how and why women may be involved in violence beyond supporting 'their men'. This includes any incitement or support, but also direct involvement, for example, in occasions of mob justice or lynchings (van Stapele 2016).

Similarly, the concluding paragraph on 'women and state repression' recognises that

> women were not just victims of state repression; some of them were active agents of the repressive regime. Many male victims of detention and torture indicated that those who tortured them included women. In most cases, they would be required to strip naked before the presence of the female Special Branch officials.
>
> (TJRC vol. 2C 2013: 151)

But again this is where the discussion ends; the complexity hinted at by both sections – of women as part of communities that perpetrate violations and as participants when employed in the security forces – ultimately limited by the association of the marginal roles mentioned with particular female characteristics such as wifely duties to prepare food and as a physical presence that increases the shame of male nudity.

In turn, there is no discussion of whether women's tendency to 'be peaceful' is due to their femininity and realities of motherhood (cf. Ruddick 1989), or because of their limited powers and influence (cf. Charlesworth 2008; Goetz 2007). However, while some have argued – in line with the TJRC's implied thinking – that women, as a group that have biologically evolved to rear children, are less prone to violence (Fukuyama 1998), there is a growing consensus that it is more useful to think about why perpetrators of violence and injustice tend to be men, rather than to simply assume that men are more violent (Baines 2011; Ross 2003a). Such an approach would give greater insight into the nuances of violence and into constructed and contested masculinities – for example, of how military training and culture encourages security personnel to be aggressive and unemotional (Butler 1990) – and thus on how and why violence occurs and persists. More specifically, anthropological literature on Kenya suggests that this would help to complicate a portrait of men as domineering and powerful by highlighting the pressures that men face 'to become' and 'be' males who can provide for their families, protect and contribute to their communities, but who are also able to show self-restraint and control (Rasmussen 2010; Silberschmidt 2001; Spronk 2014; van Stapele 2015 and 2016). This approach might therefore have painted a picture of men who, rather than being 'naturally' violent, feel that they are able or should be violent in certain contexts.

Finally, while women's fears for the future were highlighted by the Commission (for example, TJRC vol. 1 2013: iii–iv), less attention was given to the fears that men may understandably harbour. However, anthropological studies suggest that Kenyan men who feel relatively powerless also fear the future, with young men in informal settlements, for example, harbouring real fears that they may – like so many of their male friends and relatives – fall victim to a police shooting as an alleged criminal or become 'the last man standing' with the associated burden of looking after the women and children left behind (van Stapele 2016: 305). Such omissions are important since they leave the male experience as the undiscussed 'other', and thus inadvertently reinforce implied gender binaries.

7.4.4 'The Strength, Integrity, and Resilience of Kenyan Women'

These women and their stories reveal not only some of the most shameful periods in the nation's history, but also the strength, integrity, and resilience of Kenyan women.

(TJRC vol. 2C 2013: iv)

The idea of women's relative vulnerability and suffering went hand-in-hand with a sense of women's emotional strength and resilience. In this way, women (and poor women in particular) were presented as shy and less able to speak out, but also as displaying an impressive ability to cope and stay strong as mothers, sisters and daughters with duties to care for, and support, those around them. This narrative is far from unique to the TJRC (for example, see Gathumbi 2008: v) or to Kenya. For example, in a discussion of one woman's testimony before the Peruvian TRC, Jelke Boesten shows how, '[i]nstead of highlighting [the woman's] political message – her quest for justice and reparations, her emphasis on the continued suffering that raped women and those who were left behind by the violence experience – the commissioner highlights her mother-love and forgiveness' (Gathumbi 2008: v). I was struck by a similar dynamic during the Kenyan TJRC. Thus, while many women emphasised how they continued to suffer from past violations, systematic discrimination or an area's political and economic marginalisation, and to stress their need for assistance and a desire for justice, the comments of commissioners and Commission staff, together with the final report, tended to recognise women's suffering, but simultaneously emphasise women's capacity to cope and stay strong, and to interpret this ability as 'resilience'.

However, I heard these stories differently. Most did not suggest resilience – or a capacity to reshape, recover or 'bounce back' (Brassett, Croft & Vaughan-Williams 2013) – but instead spoke of survival and of a yearning for justice and assistance. To give one example: at the women's hearing in Kericho, one participant spoke of how she had lost her husband during the post-election violence of 2007–8 and had broken her hand whilst running away from gunshots. She emphasised how she had no father and her mother was far away;

how there was no-one to help her and she did not have the strength to work because of her hand, but still had to care for her children who were 'not learned'; and requested any help from the government and thanked God 'as you've come to listen to our cries' (notes, 20 September 2011). To cast such a story – and many others like it – as one of resilience is to fail to really listen, to downplay day-to-day realities and to undermine women's demands for justice and reparation.

It is also to imply that women should take action so that they can help to ensure the country's peaceful and progressive future. In this way, the presiding chair at the TJRC's women's hearing in Naivasha declared how, '[i]f every woman stood up and said we want peace, you will get the peace you want ... it's time to say enough is enough and that people want peace, national healing and reconciliation' (27 September 2011). The problem, in short, is that a presumption of women's virtue ultimately increases their 'responsibility without corresponding rewards' (Arora-Jonsson 2011: 744), leading to a 'feminization of responsibility and obligation' (Chant 2006).

7.5 Conclusions: The Performance of Familiar Gender Relations

[T]he existing discourse on gender and transitional justice [as a focus on women as victim-heroines] appears to inadvertently reinforce the gender stereotypes which it tries to dismantle.

(Ichim 2008: 7)

The Commission's focus on gender 'as women' encouraged a homogenisation of women as vulnerable, innocent and resilient, and – by implication – of men as domineering, violent and uncommunicative. As a result, and as Irina Ichim has argued with respect to the Sierra Leonean TRC, 'it failed to engage with notions of gender which might have explained the gendered pattern of violence better than women's victimhood ... [and also] risked reinforcing those gender ideals that dictated a gendered pattern of violence in the first place' (2008: 8). For example, while the TJRC recognised that traditional patriarchal assumptions of men 'as strong, assertive and dominant, [and] women on the other hand ... [as] emotional and timid' were one of the main reasons for why 'women are considered generally ill-suited for leadership positions' (TJRC vol. 2C 2013: 78), its approach – and subsequent narrative – ultimately reinforced this very binary.

The implication is not that special efforts should not have been made to encourage women to participate. On the contrary, while gender norms are socially constructed and contested, they do influence people's behaviour and relations in ways that ensure that patriarchy, sexism and the hyper-sexualisation of women is a reality of daily life. In turn, the Kenyan case provides further evidence that women and men do experience injustices differently, that there are gender-specific needs and that many women speak more openly in female-only environments (Kinyanjui 2016). Instead, it is to suggest that more consideration should be given to the complexities of gender identities and to gender, not as a biological category, but as an analytical category that focuses on interactions and relations, and to the practical costs (as well as benefits) of giving testimony. In turn, the analysis suggests that it is time for transitional justice to move beyond an approach to gender as women and a narrative of women as victims and heroines, and to think more carefully about the safety of spaces provided, the differences between women and between men, the relations between men and women, the pressures and difficulties faced by various sectors of society, and reasons for why some people (and a disproportionate number of men) might become violent and commit, or contribute to, other injustices.

8 | Truth's Grand Narrative (Part II)
Of Injustice and Impunity

Have heard victims' stories, but where are the perpetrators? ... Want to see [former President] Moi dragged ... if we see him and [President] Kibaki then that's a truth commission. When the high and mighty face the lawyers of victims then that's a truth commission.

(Interview, civil society activist, Nairobi, 9 August 2012)

The South African TRC started by listening 'to the voices of victims', but there was soon a desire to hear from 'the other. The counter. The perpetrator' (Krog 1999: 84). After six months, this 'second narrative' finally broke 'into relief' (Krog 1999: 85), as the Commission began to hear from self-confessed perpetrators who sought to exchange full disclosure of political crimes for amnesty from future prosecution. This conditional amnesty was the most contentious aspect of the Commission's work and prompted a number of South Africans to go to court to insist on their right to punitive justice. The fact that 75 per cent of applications were convicts seeking to reduce their sentences (Hamber 2002: 64), rather than politicians or security officers, together with the narrow definition of 'political crimes' adopted (Bhargava 2002), also raised questions about the truth heard.

Public confessions were not accepted at face value. Displays of remorse were often rejected as unconvincing and instrumental. Claims to have changed or 'been saved' were met with popular scepticism. Moments of forgetfulness were read as information withheld; and justifications, excuses and claims to victimhood led many confessions to appear hollow and insincere (Payne 2008). In this vein, Jeffrey Benzien's amnesia – and the fact that he could forget the 'acts of brutality [which] had permanent repercussions' for his victims – 'further traumatized' the latter (Payne 2008: 237), while his self-portrait as a victim due to 'the threats he and his family faced' suggested a degree of 'emotional shallowness' (Payne 2004: 117). In turn, former

President de Klerk's failure to acknowledge the evil of apartheid highlighted how deeply divisions still ran (Boraine 2000a: 371).

The TRC's conditional amnesty also became increasingly contentious with time. Thus, while a majority of South Africans initially approved of amnesty as a practical way forward, public support 'fell dramatically' during the 2000s, as the government begrudgingly paid only limited reparations; public prosecutors failed to bring charges against alleged perpetrators whose amnesty applications had been denied, or who had never applied; and a 'sense of the unfairness of amnesty and dissatisfaction with the extent of truth recovery' burgeoned (Backer 2010: 443; also Gibson 2002 and Wachira 2009).

Nevertheless, while far from perfect, South Africa's conditional amnesty brought new information to light, and, more importantly, did so in ways that rendered the details difficult to refute. Thus, while only a small proportion of applicants received amnesty – just 840 of 7,112 (12 per cent) – this included 'some of the most heinous crimes ... [which] were heard in public as the legislation demanded, meaning that South Africans were subjected to the details' (Hamber 2002: 63–64). Moreover, the fact that details came from 'those who committed political violence' made 'it nearly impossible for regime supporters to claim that the violence did not occur' (Payne 2004: 115). Revelations also had a snowball effect, as some of those implicated were prompted to speak out (Meredith 2001). Thus, while politicians and military personnel effectively closed ranks, the Commission succeeded in exposing some of 'the secret world of the security police' (Meredith 2001: 11; also Tutu 1999: 188–189). Hearings not only brought a level of public acknowledgement, they also provided a ritual whereby some victims and perpetrators could appear together. At the same time, thematic hearings provided a stage on which national politicians – such as de Klerk and Mbeki – presented party memoranda, while a special interest hearing brought Winnie Mandela (an icon of the anti-apartheid struggle and ex-wife of President Mandela) under public scrutiny.

These efforts provided many of the Commission's defining moments, as some perpetrators openly admitted to, and on occasion even enacted out, wrongdoing; some came face-to-face with their victims; a few apologised and asked for forgiveness; and politicians sought to justify their policies and public records (Chapter 6). However, as the stories travelled, these rare moments – of revelation, apology and public scrutiny of the rich and powerful – were transformed into a mythical representation, as contestations and complexities moved backstage, and occasional breakthroughs became a norm (Castillejo-Cuellar 2007).

In contrast, the Kenyan TJRC, as Commissioner Slye has argued, had 'the worst of both worlds': 'The amnesty powers of the Kenyan Commission were so severely limited that they were unavailable as a tool ... to entice perpetrator testimony or foster reconciliation, yet their inclusion created an unnecessary source of controversy' (2017: 30). Indeed, so unhelpful were these provisions that the Commission opted to never even open an amnesty process, and instead held a series of hearings at which some individuals adversely mentioned in statements and memoranda were given a chance to respond to the allegations made against them. However, while some victims attended adversely mentioned persons' (AMP) hearings, there was no real interaction between the two, with testimonies characterised by protestations of innocence and displays of elite status. This was perhaps unsurprising. As Leigh Payne has shown in her study of perpetrator accounts, the most common type of account of past violence is *not* remorseful confession, but denial and silence whereby, if 'perpetrators admit to their roles in the past', they 'deny wrongdoing or knowledge of wrongdoing' (2008: 158–159). As Payne goes on to argue, acknowledgement and remorse are likely only when there is evidence of individual involvement, strong incentives to publicly accept responsibility, and people have had reason to re-evaluate their previous justifications of violence or 'vital lies'. However, none of these factors were in place during the lifespan of the Kenyan TJRC; instead, there were strong peer and community pressures to remain silent. This renders an absence of revelatory confessions unsurprising, but it has important implications for the kind of performance staged, the message relayed and the lessons that can be drawn about the importance of local contexts and receptions.

This chapter investigates these AMP performances. It starts with a discussion of the denials of responsibility at AMP hearings and elite displays of peer and community support, before turning to the unwillingness of ordinary citizens to similarly admit wrongdoing. The chapter reveals how, without the carrot of amnesty or fear of future action, and with strong incentives to remain silent, most elites used their (non)appearance before the TJRC to deny individual responsibility and to perform their protected status as members of an elite, while most witnesses used their appearance at public hearings to insist on their innocence and to support their claims for assistance. The process thus confirmed that injustices had happened, but it failed to unearth much that was qualitatively new, to prompt acknowledgement or remorse or to initiate a public debate about when violence used to 'impose order' is immoral and/or illegal. As a result, and despite the concerted efforts of staff and commissioners, and the potential of the Commission's recommendations, the TJRC largely became another commission of inquiry: it confirmed a history of injustice but simultaneously performed and further reinforced an embedded culture of impunity.

8.1 Adversely Mentioned Persons and Responsibility Denied

[AMPs] response to allegations were characterised by denial of involvement and knowledge of violations ... Even when some admitted knowing the existence of the violations, they defended and justified their action and at times blamed others.

(TJRC vol. 3 2013: 98–99)

Between the establishment of the South African TRC in 1995 and the Kenyan TJRC in 2008, the world changed. The establishment of the ICC meant that it was no longer possible for truth commissions to promise amnesty from future prosecution, while the inclusion of 'justice' in the TJRC's title was testament to an idea that truth-telling should facilitate the attainment of justice in a broad sense. In turn, the TJRC Act (2008) could only recommend amnesty and – following amendments demanded by vocal CSOs – only for non-gross human rights violations, such as the socio-economic crimes of land grabbing and grand corruption (Slye 2017). However, in the end, the Commission never opened an application process rendering amnesty the *only* mandated provision that it did not take advantage of.

According to the Commission, this decision was due to two factors:

First, given the broad definition of gross violations of human rights in the Act, the type of acts for which the Commission could recommend amnesty is very limited ... Second, given ... that it could only recommend and not grant amnesty, the Commission did not anticipate that much additional truth would come out of the amnesty process.

(TJRC vol. 1. 2013: 73)

Interviews and interactions with commission staff revealed a third reason: it was felt that few would apply – not only because the amnesty provisions were so limited, but also because future prosecutions for crimes such as land grabbing and grand corruption appeared unlikely. In short, the idea that elites expected impunity led commissioners to decide that there was no point opening a process that would reveal little information, but absorb substantial time and resources.

Instead, the TJRC conducted investigations, gathered testimony and held public hearings. During this process, the term 'AMP' was adopted to refer to 'those who others named as being perpetrators of a particular violation' so as 'not to prejudge whether an individual indeed qualified as a perpetrator with respect to a specific violation' (TJRC vol. 1 2013: 76). However, while the Commission recognised that it 'was not a court of law and therefore the finding it has made in reference to an adversely mentioned person is not a finding of guilt' (TJRC vol. 1 2013: 76), commissioners opted to name hundreds of AMPs in their final report as those deemed most responsible for particular violations on the basis of the evidence collected, and to recommend that many be subject to further investigations, prosecution or lustration. First, however, and in the interests of natural justice and truth-telling, those listed were given a chance to respond to the allegations levied against them either in writing or through an interview, with a small number also called on to attend a public hearing (TJRC vol. 4 2013: 2).

To this end, a series of AMP hearings were held between May 2012 and early 2013, at which some of those named as perpetrators in a statement and/or memoranda were summoned to defend themselves. As discussed in Chapter 4, these sessions spent a disproportionate amount of time on allegations involving the embattled chairman. Those named with regards to the 1984 Wagalla massacre were summoned before the Commission over a series of months, while other violations that were subject to shorter hearings of a day or two included land grabbing on Situatanga Farm, in which Kiplagat was also adversely mentioned, and a number that he was not, namely, torture at Nyayo House, the violence on Mt Elgon and the 1980 Bulla Karatasi massacre.

Despite initial plans to hold these sessions in the areas where the relevant violations had occurred to facilitate public engagement, logistical constraints ensured that most were held in Nairobi (interview,

TJRC director, Nairobi, 19 August 2011). In mitigation, the KNCHR facilitated a group of Wagalla massacre widows to attend relevant hearings in Nairobi; and, together with the TJRC and German Organisation for International Cooperation (GIZ), organised thirteen 'public feedback meetings' in Wajir and Garissa counties in northern Kenya in October 2011 (TJRC vol. 1 2013: 110). Well-attended, subsequent sessions in Mandera (also in the north) were cancelled because of insecurity, while 'time and financial constraints' prevented similar sessions from being held in other parts of the country (TJRC vol. 1 2013: 110–111). As a result, the Commission's bias towards the Wagalla massacre (which took place at an airstrip in what is now Wajir County) was inadvertently reinforced.

One exception to this Nairobi staging, was a two-day AMP hearing in Bungoma town in western Kenya in July 2011, where the former MP for Mt Elgon, John Serut (2002–2007), the then MP, Hon. Fred Kapondi (2007–2013), and prominent local elder and spiritual leader (or *orkoiyot*),[1] Jason Psongoywo Manyiror Tirop, were summoned to account for their alleged role in atrocities committed by the SLDF in neighbouring Mt Elgon District between 2005 and 2008. Given that Bungoma town is a few hours' drive from the mountain's trading centres, a local women's group facilitated about twenty widows of SLDF and military abuses to attend. However, they had to travel back to the mountain the same day and so missed the second half of Kapondi and all of Psongoywo's testimony (interview, Eldoret, 9 August 2011).

AMPs were also occasionally summoned to local public hearings, as occurred in Kericho, where the former district commissioner (DC) submitted a memorandum on the 'situation before, during and after the post-election of 2007/8'. However, due to limited time, the DC was not asked to go through the report in public, or questioned on the same (public hearing, Kericho, 21 September 2011). Problems of insufficient time were commonplace and – together with inadequate preparation – had a direct impact upon the hearings given to AMPs. As one

---

[1] The position of *orkoiik* (pl.) in Kalenjin-speaking areas (or of *laibons* in Maasai areas) refers to men who are believed (at least by some) to enjoy powers of divination, omen interpretation, prophecy and medicine, which gives then significant influence during tense or difficult periods, and especially during conflicts. These powers are inherited along clan lines, but are dependent on reputation (Lynch 2012a: 261).

commissioner explained, he was often reluctant to ask too many questions of AMPs when, as frequently happened, he had not hitherto seen the documents presented and lacked any substantive evidence (conversation, Bungoma, 9 July 11).

Moreover, even when victims did attend AMP hearings, or AMPs attended public hearings, there was no real interaction between the two, and it was not uncommon for participants to bemoan how the TJRC had fallen short of their expectations. In this way, and in response to a question about the value of public hearings, one man (who testified about police brutality at a general hearing in Busia in western Kenya) explained:

It was my first time to appear at such a thing ... I was impressed ... [But] it was my expectation – I thought that they might have done some research to find out who'd done the shooting and that he'd appear and also give a statement. But I think they must have used their wisdom to have my statement first, and then the researchers to find the person to make a statement, and then see how they can bring us together ... [I think the question is] can they be an instrument to bring the people together so they can shake hands? As that's the essence of the TJRC.

(Interview, Busia, 3 July 2011)

Or, as another witness, who had presented a memorandum at the Kisumu hearing, noted in response to the same question:

If you compare, for example with the South African Truth and Reconciliation Commission – it provided an opportunity for alleged victims and perpetrators to speak – but we're seeing a situation where we're just listening to victims ... [But] if you don't offer opportunities to perpetrators then the first casualty is the truth. Then TJRC loses the first – the T – and when removed, you can't have justice, and then can't reconcile.

(Interview, Kisumu, 5 August 2011)

Ultimately however, instead of interactive sessions between victims and perpetrators, the Commission held AMP hearings where men – and all of the AMPs I heard except one were male[2] – gave a presentation that responded to specific allegations communicated to them beforehand. AMPs then answered questions from the leader of evidence and

---

[2] The exception was Hon. Jane Kihara, the MP for Naivasha, who responded to allegations that she had incited and organised post-election violence in Naivasha town in January 2008 (AMP hearing, Nairobi, 29 March 2012).

commissioners with individual hearings lasting anywhere from a few minutes, as in the case of the former DC in Kericho, to a whole day, as in the case of Kiplagat's appearance regarding the Wagalla massacre on 6 June 2011.

The Commission not only failed to bring victims and self-confessed perpetrators together, it also failed to encourage confessions or apologies. Indeed, even when AMPs recognised that 'things went wrong' they were generally reluctant to apologise, or to even recommend that the government offer an apology. This included Kiplagat, who 'began his testimony [on the Wagalla massacre] by acknowledging the enormity of the tragedy that occurred ... Yet even [he] could not be convinced that the government should apologize for the wrongs committed' (TJRC vol. 1 2013: 361). I attended about half of these sessions. This included the AMP hearing in Bungoma, which stood in stark contrast to the local women's hearing that had been held in Kapsokwony two months previous (Chapter 7), and saw Serut, and then Kapondi – in immaculate English and attended by their supporters – deny wrongdoing, blame each other and claim victimhood. In turn, Psongoywo, who spoke last, and in Sabaot, blamed the violence on the 'evil' that he had seen in the government's approach to land allocation in the mountain's Chebyuk Settlement Scheme, which, in his opinion, was what had led local residents to take up arms in 2005 (11–12 July 2011).

These three performances constituted the norm at the weeks of AMP testimony and questioning that I sat through – as the Commission and the accused drew upon different aspects of complex histories to produce alternative accounts of events. As a result, I heard little that was new and *not a single* admission of personal responsibility or guilt let alone anything that could be described as a 'revelatory confession'. Instead, testimonies were characterised by five discursive strands of responsibility denied: denial through a transfer of responsibility, denial through a questioning of sources, denial through amnesia, denial through a reinterpretation of events and an assertion of victimhood and denial that events constituted a wrongdoing. During most testimonies, a mix of two to four of these narrative strands were interwoven within an overarching narrative that provided plausible (in the sense of theoretically feasible) reasons why the individual in question could not be held accountable (cf. Payne 2008: 162), but which simultaneously failed to deny that bad or unfortunate things had happened.

The first, denial through a transfer of responsibility, was the dominant theme of the AMP hearings in Bungoma. In this vein, Serut, who spoke first, claimed that it was actually the incumbent MP, that is, Hon. Kapondi, who had incited and organised the violence that occurred between 2005 and 2008. In turn, Hon. Kapondi denied any involvement and laid the blame squarely with Serut. According to the then MP, the problems could 'be attributed to one person and his ego' (AMP hearing, Bungoma, 11 July 2011).

This transfer of blame to a peer, or, in other cases, to someone further up or down the pecking order, drew upon a sense of plausible deniability. Serut and Kapondi did not deny that the violence in Mt Elgon had a political dimension, which was generally accepted, but drew on the complexity of history and unclear timelines (for example, about when people had acquired guns) to deny that *they* were the politician to blame. This is not to suggest that the Commission or general public were persuaded by such protestations. On the contrary, the Commission laid much of the blame for SLDF atrocities with Serut and Kapondi: 'Without individualizing the Mount Elgon issue, the Commission has attributed much of the animosity, venom and degeneration of the region into a very difficult relationship between two competing politicians who have both represented the constituency in parliament: Fred Kapondi and John Serut' (TJRC vol. 3 2013: 54). The Commission went on to recommend the prosecution of Kapondi, Serut and Psongoywo 'against whom it received evidence of involvement in militia activities in Mt Elgon including financing, planning and instigating violence in the region' (TJRC vol. 4 2013: 60). Given such conclusions, the term 'plausible deniability' is used, not to imply persuasiveness, but to suggest that an individual's version of events is logically and sociologically feasible, and that it would require clear evidence to the contrary to refute.

The claim that responsibility lay elsewhere was a common theme during the AMP hearings. In this vein, a reality of regular transfers of administrative personnel helped officials to blame their predecessor or successor (AMP hearing into the Wagalla massacre, Nairobi, 2 June 2011), while others drew upon recognised chains of command to suggest that the Commission should really be speaking to those who had been on the ground, or to those who had been in charge. In this way, several senior officials emphasised either their effective powerlessness in a highly centralised system – what one former cabinet minister referred to as the 'illusion of power' (G. G. Kariuki during AMP hearing, Nairobi, 17 May 2011) – or their physical distance from events that had occurred far from their Nairobi offices (for example, AMP hearing into the Wagalla massacre, 2 June 2011). In contrast, several of those on the ground used their lowly rank to claim that decisions were made by their seniors and insisted that they had not been there when actual atrocities had taken place (for example, AMP hearing into the Wagalla massacre, Nairobi, 16 May 2011).

Critically, this debate – between what senior officials should be expected to know and take responsibility for, and what directives junior officials actually receive and how they should interpret or resist them – is a recurring theme in contexts where officials stand accused of participation in unjust acts of past violence. It recurs not only because the facts are often unclear, but also because of a moral dilemma on whether, and to what extent, individual blame can be evaluated and attributed to 'big or small collaborators' within a system of oppression (Levi 1986: 43–44). Given the contested nature of this dilemma, it is understandable that AMPs were prone to take advantage of it – not only to resist accountability but to maintain the 'vital lies' that help them to justify, understand and live with their pasts (Payne 2007: 5). It also helps us to understand why such denials appeared plausible to many peers, friends, families and supporters who could imagine a situation where one's seniority or lowly rank could render one distant from critical decisions.

The idea that chronologies of leadership, or an AMPs position in a chain of command, could plausibly exculpate 'them from committing or even knowing about violent acts' (cf. Payne 2008: 162) was often intertwined with a second strand of denial, namely, a dismissal of the Commission's investigations as based on rumour and hearsay. In this way, Serut explained how his problems started when he supported the Kibaki government during the 2005 constitutional referendum (when most of his constituents rejected the government's draft) and competitors used the opportunity to demonise him; while Kapondi dismissed the allegations against him as 'hogwash' and 'nonsense' (AMP hearing, Bungoma, 11 July 2011). Such claims were also made outside of the hearings, as individuals sought to rubbish the commission and clear their name. In this way, Kapondi dismissed the TJRC's allegations against him as 'political' and denounced the TJRC's investigations as 'shoddy' (interview, Nairobi, 15 August 2011). While Kiplagat –

clearly still angry with the Commission's extensive questioning – explained how:

> Three days before I was summoned, I managed to get eight basic documents with minutes and gave them to the Commission and wrote my statement and gave it to them and said here are the facts ... I gave them all the 8 documents and felt that done the work for them ... think they just had the one document. How do you call people for a hearing when you don't have the documents?
> (Interview, Nairobi, 17 August 2011)

Unfortunately for the Commission, the idea that allegations were based on rumour, rather than hard evidence, was strengthened by the state's unwillingness to share official documents. Thus, while the TJRC could demand access to documents relevant to its mandate, state departments and institutions generally refused to hand such documents over, rendering the Commission 'unable to provide clear answers' to many questions (TJRC vol. 1 2013: 151 & vol. 2A 2013: v; also TJRC vol. 3 2013: 74).

Claims of rumour and false information were then often further supported by the trope of the 'jealous neighbour', which is often employed to 'explain multiple and diverse moments of violence' in Kenya (van Stapele 2015: 248). Here are just two examples. In a discussion of Kiplagat's chairmanship of the Commission, one prominent Kalenjin clergyman explained how, the 'civil society existing today was established during the Moi regime and with an anti-Moi strategy'. In his opinion, 'those Kikuyu who established civil society felt threatened by the Kalenjin', and Kiplagat's removal was 'a strategy' by a Kikuyu-dominated civil society to ensure certain aspects of Kenya's past, such as historical land injustices, went unaddressed (interview, Nairobi, 18 August 2011). Similarly, many Jubilee Alliance supporters in the runup to the 2013 election blamed Odinga for 'taking' his political rivals to The Hague (Chapter 3). In both cases, a commonplace fear, and frequent reality, that one's competitors may wish you harm, was scaled upwards to help explain political infighting between elites.

The materiality of the written word – in both what is documented and archived and the sense of uncertainty that surrounds its absence – was used by AMPs to counter allegations of wrongdoing with those of hearsay, but also to question what they could plausibly be expected to remember. This links to a third strand of denial – amnesia – as many

AMPs asserted, in the absence of any documentary evidence, that they simply could not remember, that they would need to see minutes from a particular meeting to jog their memories or that they could not confirm or deny a particular version of events with any confidence. Such denials were supported by the fact that many of the events discussed happened twenty to thirty years ago, although they were sometimes simultaneously undermined when interspersed with moments of clarity (for example, AMP hearing on the Wagalla massacre, Nairobi, 6 June 2011 and 15 August 2011).

Fourth, AMPs often denied a characterisation of themselves as a perpetrator and insisted that they were a victim. In this way, Serut spoke at length about how he had 'missed [SLDF] bullets severally', how a family member and a number of supporters had been killed during the violence on Mt Elgon and how he had been unfairly labelled as one of the instigators (AMP hearing, Bungoma, 11 July 2011). The implicit suggestion: how could he reasonably be regarded as the cause of his own suffering? In turn, Kapondi claimed that he had 'ended up being a victim' of the violence when 'out of the blue [he had been] declared a wanted person' and arrested on trumped up charges of leading the SLDF, and had been 'through hell' (AMP hearing, Bungoma, 11 July 2011). The implicit suggestion: how could he reasonably be regarded as the politician most responsible for organising violence that reached a peak whilst he was languishing in jail? In short, while the Commission recognised that people could be both perpetrator and victim, and that people often became perpetrators because of the injustices they had suffered (TJRC vol. 1 2013: 77), AMPs tended to present these identities as clear alternatives and to claim victimhood.

The final strand of denial was for AMPs to question whether a series of events actually constituted a wrongdoing, and whether violations, whilst unfortunate, were not justified. The clearest example of this was the series of AMP hearings into the Wagalla massacre, when the closest that any AMP came to an admission of wrongdoing was to recognise that it would have been better if the 'administrative response' to insecurity in Wajir had been to talk to male ethnic Degodia rather than to round them up, or to recognise that something 'went wrong' during the security operation (TJRC vol. 2A 2013: 359). However, several AMPs were not even this conciliatory, and insisted – on the basis of the Degodia's asserted involvement in earlier insecurity in the region, which had included deadly attacks on neighbouring Ajuran and state officials, and the firearms discovered – that the security operation in Wajir had been a success. As one AMP maintained: 'After what [the Degodia] did, [the operation] was a success. Other than the incident of people dying, it was a success' (TJRC vol. 2A 2013: 360).

The idea that the imposition of order justified such extreme state violence – namely, the detention and violent interrogation of all adult males from a particular clan at an open airstrip in a semi-arid area at the hottest time of the year – was often intertwined with a suggestion that any excesses should be shouldered by individual officers. Certainly, this was the stance adopted by former President Moi who, in a statement submitted to the TJRC, insisted that '[i]f the commission has received credible evidence of deliberate and heartless actions by officers which exceeded the prevailing circumstances and led to grave violations, then the culprit should take responsibility' (TJRC vol. 2A 2013: 366). In his opinion, '[t]he whole saga [of Wagalla] came to a happy ending. The different warring clans have forgiven each other. I know this through their evident joint regional approaches to various issues of development' (TJRC vol. 2A 2013: 366).

According to the Commission, it was 'shocking, disturbing and unbelievable that President Moi would describe an event that culminated in the loss of at least 57 lives as a saga that "came to a happy ending"' (TJRC vol. 2A 2013: 366). However, while such comments are disturbing, they are entirely believable. In short, state violence in Kenya (as in many places) has long been legitimised and differentiated from illegitimate criminal violence on the basis that, while the former helps to impose and ensure order, the latter threatens chaos and disorder (Atieno-Odhiambo 1987; Berman 1990; Willis 2015). Or, in other words, the threat of instability is often used to justify state violence to deter, resist or counter the threat in question. The issue then becomes about the source and severity of the threat and the level and form of violence justified – a question on which AMPs and the Commission often diverged. For example, according to one AMP, the decision to open fire on unarmed men detained at Wagalla airstrip when they tried to escape was not an example of excessive force: 'I think as he saw people fleeing and he had not finished with them, was he not entitled to restrain them from fleeing?' One of the commissioners rebutted that the officers should have fired warning shots into the air (AMP hearing on the Wagalla massacre, Nairobi, 2 June 2011). However, while the Commissioner's tone suggested that this was an obvious decision, official positions and public opinion on such matters are less clear-cut.

This is reflected in an ongoing public debate around extra-judicial killings by police, which the TJRC's final report discussed as an obvious gross human rights violation (TJRC vol. 2A 2013), but which is often justified by officials and openly supported by many members of the public. For example, in a statement to the Waki Commission in 2008, the then police commissioner justified the use of live bullets during the post-election violence as necessary to instil order:

If similar situations occurred today, I would do exactly what I did. I would not change a thing my Lord ... because in the enforcement of law, and ensuring that law and order is brought about in the protection of lives and properties, there is nothing that we shouldn't do to ensure that our people are safe.

(Cited in Ruteere 2011: 16)

Many ordinary citizens also support heavy-handed policing, as evidenced, for example, when General Service Unit (GSU) officers were videoed beating a line of prostrate University of Nairobi students amidst protests over the country's electoral management body in April 2016. In short, while some criticised the police for their 'lack of "restraint" and "professionalism" ... others supported the officers' actions while referring to the damage caused during the riots, which included stoning of motorists and the resulting traffic jam that lasted for hours' (*Standard* 5 April 2016). Similarly, while human rights activists oppose extra-judicial killings of suspected criminals, residents of crime-ridden areas often reject disciplinary action against police officers accused of the same on the basis that such tactics are necessary to tackle crime (for example, *Daily Nation* 9 September 2014).

This is important since the fact that there is often much popular support for extreme violence by state and non-state actors if it is believed to ward off crime, terrorism and ethnic division has implications for whether or not those responsible should be deemed as perpetrators of wrongdoing. One obvious example is the support garnered by Kenyatta after the post-election violence of 2007–8 amongst co-ethnics who felt that, if he had helped to organise revenge attacks by Mungiki in Nakuru and Naviasha towns in January 2008, he had done so in defence of his community and should be applauded rather than prosecuted, as suggested by the ICC's chief prosecutor (Chapter 3).

This links to a final point regarding these five narrative strands, which is that, while AMPs denied individual responsibility, *none* denied that injustices had occurred. Thus, Serut and Kapondi neither denied that the violence on Mt Elgon had happened, nor that it was politically instigated. They simply denied that they were the politician responsible. Similarly, amidst the denials of responsibility for the Wagalla massacre – and associated memory loss, requests for documents, claims of victimhood and an insistence that the initial security operation was necessary and ultimately successful – no-one denied that men from the Degodia community had been rounded up and gathered together at an airstrip in Wagalla in 1984, and were then indiscriminately fired at when they tried to escape. Instead, AMPs questioned who was responsible for the security operation and for triggers being pulled, whether they should be held accountable and the numbers killed. As a result, while the AMP hearings provided little clarity on how and why a series of reported events may have occurred, they simultaneously drew attention to, and recognised, past injustice. In this way, they provided a public enactment of impunity: Kenya's history was replete with injustice, but AMPs were unwilling to shoulder any responsibility for it.

This unwillingness also extended beyond the AMP hearings. Theoretically, people could acknowledge wrongdoing and responsibility at any of the Commission's public hearings – one of the aims of which was 'to provide repentant adversely mentioned persons with a forum to confess their actions as a way of bringing reconciliation' (TJRC vol. 1 2013: 97). However, no one took advantage of this opportunity. Instead, on the occasion that AMPs appeared at general hearings (to present an individual statement or community memoranda) and commissioners asked them about their alleged involvement in violations, responses were evasive and self-exculpatory. To give just two examples: after presenting a memorandum on behalf of the Sabaot community at the Commission's public hearings in Kapsokwony, Wilberforce Kisiero – a former MP for Mt Elgon (1979–1997) – was asked whether he was 'completely blameless' for the confusion over Chepyuk Settlement Scheme and subsequent formation of the SLDF. His response: 'in those days' an MP or assistant minister was 'almost totally powerless against the government ... [I'm] near blameless' (public hearing, Kapsokwony, 23 May 2011). Similarly, at a thematic hearing in Nairobi, Maina Njenga, the leader of Mungiki – an ethnic gang that is widely believed to have been responsible for extortion and violence in the 1990s and early 2000s, and to have participated in the post-election violence in Nakuru and Naivasha towns towards the end of January 2008 – was asked about the organisation's fearsome reputation. His response: he had formed the organisation to assist the youth only to be 'branded names' by politicians who were scared of the movement's power and influence, and had subsequently faced great victimisation (thematic hearing, Nairobi, 12 March 2012). Thus, while Kisiero took advantage of the 'chains of command' argument to deny responsibility, Njenga relied on a contradistinction between victims and perpetrator, and the common trope of 'jealous neighbours'.

Indeed, besides several vague references to general bureaucratic and executive shortcomings by a handful of AMPs, the *only* substantive admission of direct involvement and responsibility in the 2,000 plus pages of the TJRC's final report comes from a former police officer who admitted to his involvement in the torture of political activists at Nyayo House in downtown Nairobi, and to how, whilst incarcerated, detainees had been kept in inhumane conditions, stripped, denied food and beaten. Among other things, the former interrogator remembered how:

on many occasions when I was interrogating people, we had food together with my interogees but denying people food ... that was also another way to make somebody break down ... To be frank, that one [physical beatings] was [also] there and I even personally beat some of my friends who are here. You use a whip and you get the information. It was there and I cannot hide it.

(TJRC vol. 2A 2013: 644)

Yet, even this lone confessional voice downplayed personal responsibility by stressing how he had been 'just an Acting Superintendent' and orders were clearly 'a political decision' (TJRC vol. 2A 2013: 641 and 643). The former interrogator also spoke *in camera* and so his admission, while valuable, remained nameless and faceless.[3] As a result, the officer's testimony can be regarded as the exception that proves the rule: AMPs used their appearance before the TJRC to deny responsibility. They also used their appearance to perform their

---

[3] In fact, the man's (admittedly, fairly common) surname is included in a boxed text narrating a discussion between him and the leader of evidence, providing another example of how some who spoke to the Commission *in camera* may have been inadvertently exposed through their participation in direct contravention of their desire to remain anonymous (Chapter 7).

protected status as elites, which provided a further performance of, and helped to reinforce, a culture of impunity.

8.2 Giving AMPs 'a Platform'

I would hate to see more time spent with AMPs than victims, as [attendance at AMP hearings] tends to give these people ... a platform where they deny [allegations] and say the wonderful things that they've done.

(Interview, TJRC director, Nairobi, 7 September 2011)

When alleged perpetrators confess to, or deny, past violence, 'not only do they read a carefully prepared script, they also act it out'. In so doing, '[t]hey imbue their performance with political meaning through what they say, how they say it, and where and when they make their confessional performance' (Payne 2009: 227). In this way, AMPs not only dismissed allegations and denied wrongdoing, many also used their (non)appearance as an opportunity to perform their elite status: as someone who cared for and protected their communities, but who also enjoyed the support and protection of state officials, peers and co-ethnics, and were thus untouchable. In so doing, they presented themselves as part of an established elite in the sense of being members of a group that had 'not only attained the means of production, [but had] also assumed the political and institutional capacity to reproduce their dominance' (Branch & Cheeseman 2006: 11). As a result, AMPs not only performed an embedded culture of impunity, but also reinforced the same. At one level, they exemplified how there was no need to confess: officials and politicians could rely on the silence of others and the support of the state, peers and co-ethnics. At another level, their performances carried an implicit threat: those who dared to speak out would be on their own and liable to regime, peer and community sanction.

First, many AMPs simply did not turn up when summoned, whilst others sent junior colleagues who were unable to answer the questions posed, opted to speak in camera or submitted a memorandum. The Commission begrudgingly accepted such uncooperative behaviour and did little to force attendance despite their powers to 'summon any serving or retired public officer to appear in person' (TJRC Act 2008: 7[2]g). Indeed, the Commission only once called for an arrest warrant to be issued to an absent AMP. This was to the Commissioner of Lands in September 2011, when commissioners staged an announcement before the media as a 'warning to anyone else who wishes to waste the time of the Commission and Kenyans' (AMP hearing, Nairobi, 12 September 2011). However, the warrant was soon lifted. As one of the TJRC directors explained, the official had earlier boasted 'that he could not be arrested so when an arrest warrant was issued he was very concerned. He came and spoke to the commissioners and they agreed to remove the arrest warrant, but not to hold a special hearing [for him]' (interview, Kericho, 19 September 2011). The director presented this as a small victory: the Commissioner of Lands would not be given a chance to defend himself. However, my interpretation was different: that it reflected the commissioners' unwillingness to antagonise elites. Certainly, such caution and a preference for gentle encouragement were understandable. Force was unlikely to encourage honesty, and, in the context of the Commission's ongoing credibility crisis, may have further undermined their access to funds and extension requests.

Second, of those that did attend, most displayed their disdain for the Commission through their statements, body language and tone, and performed their assumed position as legitimate spokesmen whose peers and community members would stand behind them. The rest of this section focuses in on these displays – of tone, presentation and support – and the implications for the performance staged.

Serut – amidst his account of the real causes of the Mt Elgon violence – littered his Bungoma presentation with references to his strong performance as a development-conscious and peace-loving leader. In this vein, he spoke of how 'my people are so dear to me'; of a factory that he had built using the Constituency Development Fund to 'empower the community'; of repeated efforts to report the violence to the government and to bring in the army (for which he had 'no apologies'); and of the people's resolve 'to elect me back'. He concluded with a series of recommendations: the government should issue an apology and build a memorial; land should be purchased for the remaining squatters; and the 'boys [still] in cells' should be released (AMP hearing, Bungoma, 11 July 2011). In so doing, Serut outlined his leadership credentials as someone who had worked, and who continued to struggle, to protect and promote the rights and interests of his community, and who had suffered as a consequence.

As Serut spoke, Hon. Kapondi, who was seated at the front of the hall, sat with his arms crossed and a bemused smile on his face, which occasionally broke into a snigger. Then, when the local MP took to the witness table, he not only placed the blame squarely with Serut and denied wrongdoing, but also insisted that he had mobilised political support in the 2007 election – not through violence and fear – but 'because of the massive sympathy' he enjoyed. In his opinion, 'SLDF never created me ... [I was] formidable without [the] SLDF' (AMP hearing, Bungoma, 11–12 July 2011).

The implication was not only that politician A was innocent and politician B was to blame (as previously discussed), but that – in the face of an upcoming election that would once again pit these two rivals against each other – constituents should vote for politician A and against politician B. As one commissioner noted at the end of the first day, 'there's a danger that today we just gave them a platform to criticize each other'.

This distancing from responsibility and assertion of effective leadership was also evident during G. G. Kariuki's testimony – the highest profile politician to appear before the Commission – when the former Minister of State in the OP distanced 'himself from the main centres of decision-making' and passed 'nearly all responsibility' for the security operation that led to the 1980 Bulla Karatasi massacre down 'towards the District and Provincial Security Committees' (TJRC vol. 2A 2013: 216). At the same time, and whilst periodically exchanging a smile with family members and other supporters in attendance, Kariuki presented himself as someone above such petty processes and as a strong and effective leader. The scene captured from my notes at the time:

KARIUKI: I'm not sure you're asking relevant questions ... {minutes later} I don't understand the question ... if you've run out of questions perhaps you should let me go {Smiles at the audience}.

(AMP hearing, Nairobi, 17 May 2011)

Not every AMP was a politician or political aspirant. Nevertheless, many took advantage of the occasion to present themselves as men of status, and as members of the national or local elite. In this vein, and to return to the example of Bungoma, Psongoywo – the non-aspirant of the three AMPs who appeared – explained how, as a spiritual leader, 'God had given [him] the authority to take care of [his] people', to see evil, and to direct people to refuse evil. According to Psongoywo's account, he had warned people of the 'devil' in the government's approach to land allocation at Chepyuk, and it was people's refusal to hear him that had led them to suffer God's wrath (AMP hearing, Bungoma, 12 July 2011). The problem was thus not that he had blessed SLDF violence as alleged, but that people had not listened to his counsel. Whether you believed Psongoywo or not, the impression was of a man of local importance: either he had blessed the SLDF and might still enjoy the capacity to endorse violence; or he was a man with special foresight whose views deserved respect and adherence.

Similarly, while Kiplagat started his testimony by recognising the tragedy of the Wagalla massacre and went on to give an analysis of the documents he had collected, in between he insisted – despite requests from the commissioners to focus on the subject matter at hand – on relaying how he had spent 'a great proportion of his life' saving and protecting lives at great personal risk to himself. In this vein, he outlined how he had helped to achieve the Comprehensive Peace Agreement in Sudan in 2005, persuaded those in Southern Sudan to stop using land mines and founded the Africa Peace Forum to foster better relations between Kenya and Somalia (AMP hearing, 6 June 2011). Critically, this image of a respected *mzee*, or elder, was also predominant when I met the embattled chairman at Nairobi's upmarket Serena Hotel in August 2011. First, and as we started the interview, the former ambassador stressed how the young man I had met him with was a youth leader who had come to seek his counsel. Kiplagat then went on to summarise his national and regional peacebuilding credentials, to criticise the Commission's approach to reconciliation and to dismiss its investigative capacities. He also expressed his resolve to return to the TJRC for reasons of 'pride and dignity, and to show that I'm innocent'. In his words: 'I would have been negating the very purpose of the TJRC – the truth – [if I left] and, if I quit like this, then [it would] encourage the TJRC to continue with allegations without the truth' (interview, Nairobi, 17 August 2011). The impression was of a man who had been wronged, but who nevertheless remained strong, determined and right, and who should return to head the Commission.

Such displays of confidence were intimately interwoven with those of elitism – in the dual sense of an economic and political system that is run by elites, and of a superior attitude amongst elite 'insiders' suggestive of their capacity to protect and sustain their position. More specifically, elitism became embodied, first and foremost, in displays of protected status: as people who could rely on the protection of the bureaucratic-executive state (Branch & Cheeseman 2006), as well as on their peers and ethnic communities.

Official support was reflected in an evident lack of 'political will on the part of the State to give the Commission the support it needed' (TJRC vol. 1 2013: 151). This included the government's failure to intervene over the chairman debacle and to provide the Commission with adequate resources, President Kibaki's refusal to meet with commissioners despite repeated requests for an audience and the unwillingness of state departments to hand over official documents despite multiple applications (TJRC vol. 1 2013: 151–152). It also suffused the AMP hearings. As one commissioner explained, the problem with some of the AMPs was that they seemed to believe that 'they are ok' because they enjoy the President's support; the Commissioner going on to give the example of Kiplagat who seemed to believe that he 'could weather the storm' (conversation, Nairobi, 15 August 2011).

AMP hearings also highlighted the support of peers, as occurred during the hearings regarding the Wagalla massacre. First, several AMPs arrived with documents that the Commission, despite its official powers, had been unable to access, and which AMPs seemed to have been given by friends in relevant offices. Second, no fewer than sixteen of the Wagalla AMPs (including Kiplagat) hired a common lawyer and stuck to a common story, namely, that an official visit to Wajir just days before the massacre – which most of the sixteen had attended, and which is alleged to have prompted the security operation that culminated in the massacre (Sheikh 2007) – was a 'development' tour. As the final report notes:

> It was clear from this testimony [of David Mwiraria, the former Permanent Secretary in the Ministry of Home Affairs] that many of those who testified before the Commission had met 'a few times' to refresh their memories of things that some of them may have 'forgotten completely' ... As Mwiraria made it clear to the Commission, the little he could remember had been aided by the meetings he had attended in his lawyer's office with the other members of the [Kenya Intelligence Committee] prior to the Commission's hearings.
> (TJRC vol. 2A 2013: 348–349)

Here then, was a group of influential men closing ranks.

Some also read the use of a shared lawyer as evidence of regime support. As one man who attended many of the Wagalla AMP hearings reminded me, the attorney hired – Kioko Kilukumi – was the same man that President Kibaki had proposed as the new Director of Public Prosecutions earlier on in the year. According to this man (a businessman who originally hailed from Wajir), many people felt that Kilikumi had been sent by the government to ensure that the truth remained buried (interview, 18 May 2011, Nairobi). It is impossible to corroborate such suspicions. But the fact that such conspiracy theories were shared is critical, since it reflects a public perception of well-connected AMPs as untouchable.

However, not all AMPs were part of such an elite – who could speak to the President, access government documents and come together behind a single (and expensive) lawyer. This included several of the Wagalla massacre AMPs who appeared alone and nervous-looking. Yet, while these mid-level officials insisted that the blame lay with their seniors who ordered for a security operation, or with their juniors who pulled the trigger, they were careful not to implicate anyone in particular. Clearly, without amnesty, there was little incentive for them to do so. However, it also seems that any possible desire that there might have been to speak out – so as to clear one's name, to confess and assuage any sense of guilt, or to contribute to truth, justice and reconciliation – was outweighed by the costs of speaking in a context where the 'big men' seemed set on maintaining a stony silence.

This conclusion is supported by the fact that not even the bitter and isolated spoke out. Once again, perceptions are insightful, as exemplified by periodic references to a well-known interrogator from the days of detention and torture at Nyayo House who was rumoured to have spoken to the Commission *in camera*, but to be unwilling to speak in public. According to one interviewee, the man 'is back in the village, but he doesn't even want to leave home, as some of the people who [he] tortured are from around his place' (interview, clergyman, Kisumu, 30 June 2011). In turn, a former Nyayo House detainee relayed how the man 'is seriously isolated' and lives 'in fear', and how one of his neighbour's 'says that he's someone who's haunted and doesn't want to meet people as he doesn't trust people' (interview, Kisumu, 17 July 2011). The portrait was thus of a man who would have benefited from reconciliation, but who neither wanted to shoulder the blame for a repressive regime, nor was confident in how his account would be received. The implication: mid or low-level perpetrators would retain their silence as long as those at the top retained theirs.

Certainly, given the context at the time, it was understandable that people were wary of implicating themselves or anyone with power and influence. There had been no political transition; the Commission could only recommend amnesty for non-gross human rights violations and could offer no long-term witness protection; while new injustices – from corruption scandals to instances of inter-ethnic violence and ongoing extra-judicial killings by police – suggested that human rights abuses, inter-ethnic conflict, perceptions of economic marginalisation and corruption (to name just a few of the TJRC's areas of focus) were very much part of Kenya's present. At the same time, examples abounded of the ugly fate that might meet witnesses and whistleblowers. To give just two examples: first, parallel rumours of the bribery, intimidation and murder of ICC witnesses – even if exaggerated – painted a lurid and timely picture of what might happen to those who dared to implicate the rich and powerful. Second, there was the example of the whistleblowers of the Goldenberg and Anglo-Leasing corruption scandals of the early 1990s and 2000s: David Munyakei and John Githongo. The former, a clerk at the Central Bank of Kenya, was fired after he raised concerns about suspicious bank transfers and spent the rest of his life impoverished and isolated (Kahora 2009). John Githongo (an anti-corruption tsar) fled to the UK in 2005 after he taped conversations with his colleagues which implicated them in grand corruption, and was vilified by peers and kinsmen as a 'traitor' (Wrong 2009).

This points to another characteristic of elite status that emboldened the rich and powerful, and silenced others – namely, the tendency for co-ethnics to support their leaders and to vilify those who are seen to betray or oppose them. Once again, this finds an example in the embattled TJRC chairman who was periodically defended by politicians and prominent spokesmen from his Kalenjin community. This included a statement issued by 'Rift Valley Leaders' in April 2012 following a meeting of representatives from the Kalenjin, Maasai, Turkana and Samburu communities, or KAMATUSA, which is worth citing at some length:

The Rift Valley has suffered immense historical injustices significant of which relate to land. The community also suffered immense loss of lives and property as a result of successive violence including the post elections violence of 2007/2008. As the Rift Valley we are very concerned about the ongoing process at TJRC because of lack of representation of the interests of Rift Valley region and the community at large ... Going by the manner in which Amb. Kiplagat is treated, the Rift Valley has been placed in a situation of justified fear that the commission does not mean well for its people ... We in Rift Valley maintain a demand that Amb. Kiplagat be reinstated unconditionally to any outstanding proceedings and be involved in the process of writing the Commission's report.[4]

This statement is insightful – not only because its production provides an example of how Kalenjin leaders were willing to come out in Kiplagat's defence – but also because of what it says about top-down and bottom-up political dynamics. On the one hand, the statement reflects a political environment in which Rift Valley politicians, led by William Ruto, were trying to unite the Rift Valley vote ahead of the 2013 election by fostering a sense of communities under attack who should come together in self-defence behind strong leaders (Lynch 2014a). As one of the elder's who helped to organise the KAMATUSA meeting explained, Kiplagat was the 'chief guest', and a number of 'speeches ... [were made] about how he was being pushed out as Kalenjin' (interview, Eldoret, 9 August 2011). However, it also highlights the everyday politics in which many ordinary people view politics as ethnically biased with support for ethnic leaders and against ethnic 'others' becoming a rational means to protect and promote individual and collective interests (Lynch 2011b). As one prominent Kalenjin elder explained:

[People] believe that it's only a Kalenjin chairman who will issue a balanced report on historical injustices in the Rift Valley so when Kiplagat stepped aside we asked for the process to be put on hold until [a] tribunal looked into issues. And if found to be unfit then another Kalenjin should be put in place and, if not, the Kalenjin won't accept, they will reject the TJRC.

(Interview, Eldoret, 2 March 2011)

Critically, such logics of political mobilisation and bottom-up support exemplify the kinds of displays of ethnic support that elites have grown used to relying upon. One example is the Anglo-Leasing scandal of the early 2000s, when – despite Githongo's voice recordings and the well-publicised fact that stories regarding the return of grand corruption were undermining public support for the new NaRC government –

---

[4] http://jukwaa.proboards.com/thread/6808 <last accessed 20 December 2016>.

President Kibaki retained the cabinet members implicated. As Jerome Bachelard explains, such a political calculation only makes sense when one recognises how Kibaki felt that he needed these prominent politicians, and the votes of their ethnic communities, for his re-election (2010: 194).

Thus, while the Commission hoped that even 'where there is no prospect of criminal justice the conduct of rights violators will be held up for close scrutiny' (TJRC vol. 1 2013: 55), AMPs seemed relatively unconcerned about the prospects of being 'named and shamed'. This was understandable: many had already been named as 'persons of interest' in previous commission of inquiry reports, media coverage or public debate with little negative consequence; while, at the time of the AMP hearings in 2011/2012, Kenyatta and Ruto were effectively establishing themselves as the key spokesmen of the Kikuyu and Kalenjin communalities (at least in part) because of the charges levied against them by the ICC. Indeed, while an appearance before the TJRC no doubt caused AMPs some stress, it has not yet ended anyone's career. On the contrary, during the election of March 2013 (which took place after all of the AMP hearings and just two months before the final report was submitted) – not only were two ICC indictees elected president and deputy president, respectively – but G. G. Kariuki was elected the new senator for Laikipia, Serut was re-elected MP for Mt Elgon, Kapondi was later appointed chairman of the board for the Kenya Post Office Savings Bank and Psongoywo remained an influential elder until his death in 2014. In the 2017 election, Kapondi once again replaced Serut as the Mt Elgon MP with a number of other AMPs also (re)elected. Indeed, what the 2013 and 2017 elections revealed was how constituents could be persuaded to vote for politicians despite allegations of wrongdoing if they thought that the leaders in question were best placed to promote and protect their broader interests against ethnic 'others'.

As a result, not only did the 'platform' given to AMPs by the TJRC help to perform continuity, but it also helped to maintain a wall of silence by further diminishing any incentive to admit wrongdoing. Clearly, such effects were minimised by the limited media coverage and public debate that the TJRC hearings enjoyed. However, while few people (if any outside of the TJRC) watched the demeanour and denials of people such as Kapondi and Kariuki as closely as I did, the general public, and, just as importantly, key opinion leaders and potential lobbyists – from journalists and civil society activists to prominent clergy and academics – were aware that AMPs had continued to deny wrongdoing. As one civil society leader surmised: '[U]nfortunately, I believe that the victims are still the ones telling their stories in TJRC, while perpetrators have stubbornly refused' (interview, Nakuru, 14 March 2011).

This is not to suggest that the AMP hearings should not have taken place, but to question their likely legacy given parallel and subsequent developments. Most of the victims with whom I spoke supported the idea of AMP hearings. Indeed, they wanted more of them, for more and higher profile AMPs to be called, more questions to be asked and more documents to be shared. Moreover, while many who attended these sessions were angered by what they saw as the lies and arrogance displayed (for example, conversation following AMP hearing into the Wagalla massacre, Nairobi, 2 June 2011), most had not expected AMPs to admit wrongdoing, while many were encouraged by the fact that commissioners did not seem to believe what the AMPs said (conversation, Nairobi, 18 May 2011). For such individuals, the question was not whether the hearings should have taken place, but whether the TJRC would be able to get past such denials and find sufficient evidence to recommend accountability and, if so, whether their recommendations would be implemented and elites' bluff be called? Looking back, hopes of accountability may look naïve, but hope – by its very essence – is not about realistic predictions, but about a possibility, that perhaps this time things might be different. It is for such possible futures that some Kenyans appreciated the fact that those they believed to be responsible for violations had been summoned and quizzed with the real test lying ahead with the report and its recommendations, and with ordinary Kenyans' response to those named.

8.3 'I Went to Find Milk': The Innocence of Victims

WITNESS (ON EVENTS THAT OCCURRED DURING THE POST-ELECTION VIOLENCE OF 2007–8): ... I went to find milk and heard that the police didn't want to find anyone on the road so I started moving home. I came across a vehicle with military. They were shooting into the air. I started running. Was when they shot me ...

COMMISSIONER DINKA: Thank you very much for your testimony. I empathise. You say you were standing near a petrol station watching the demonstration – at any point that day or the day before, were you in any demonstration?
WITNESS: No

(TJRC public hearing, Bungoma, 9 July 2011)

During the months of public, women's and thematic hearings that I attended, I was struck by how witnesses sought to distance themselves from any hint of culpability with no single individual admitting to anything that might even verge on the suspect or blameworthy. This is important – not because self-identified victims should be expected to take on responsibility for what they have suffered – but because it produced a diminished version of the truth and circumvented public debate on what constituted (il)legitimate political action and violence, and thus what levels and forms of violence are justified to impose law and order. This section provides a brief overview of such shortcomings.

It is notable that assertions of innocence extended to actions that are officially legal but prone to public and official condemnation. This is exemplified by those shot by police during the post-election violence of 2007–8. According to the Waki Commission, 405 of the 1,133 recorded deaths resulted from gunshot wounds, most of whom were deemed to have been shot by the police as a result 'of the indiscriminate firing of live rounds of ammunition into peaceful crowds and in riot situations' (Kenya 2008b: 385–385). However, those who bore testimony to police shootings – either as direct victims or as next of kin – spoke of how they were shot, not as part of a crowd or demonstration, but as someone who was simply in the wrong place at the wrong time. In this way, victims spoke of how they were shot as they cooked near the house, worked at a butchery, or ran an errand for their mothers (TJRC public hearing, Kisumu, 15 July 2011) or as they walked to the marketplace (TJRC public hearing, Kakamega, 28 June 2011) or home from work (TJRC women's hearing, Kericho, 20 September 2011). Indeed, the closest that any victim of police shooting that I heard got to a demonstration or riot was as an observer who was shot while watching 'the going ons ... over the hill' (TJRC public hearing, Kericho, 21 September 2011). This is not to suggest that any particular witness was lying. But it is unlikely that no single police-shooting victim who appeared participated in a demonstration or riot.

Such reticence to admit to participation in even a peaceful demonstration can be explained by official and public perceptions of legitimate action – with protestors often assumed to be predisposed to violence (FIDH & KHRC 2017: 22). In short, protests in Kenya are often characterised by a degree of violence or disruption – such as looting, stone throwing, road blockades or arson – while even those in which the vast majority of participants remain nonviolent, are often labelled as unlawful so as to 'justify a wide range of repressive state measures' (Article 19, April 2016). Moreover, while violence is often strategic and reflects what people have 'learned about how power and politics work' (Cooper 2014: 585), it is often dismissed as the work of selfish delinquents and as a source of disruption and disorder.

As a result, victims of police shootings may have feared to admit to participation in peaceful demonstrations lest their bullet wound be deemed justified, or lest it open them to accusations of being involved in other activities – from the looting of shops and homes to the beating, rape and murder of ethnic 'others'. Victims may also have been wary of indirectly incriminating any friends or relatives that they were with in the context of ongoing calls for a special tribunal to prosecute low and mid-level perpetrators. Finally, but not least, the Commission's powers – namely, an inability to offer amnesty for gross human rights violations and powers to recommend further investigations, prosecutions and reparations – provided strong incentives to present oneself as an innocent victim as a means to avoid sanctions and access assistance.

However, whilst understandable, a felt need to present oneself as an entirely innocent victim produced a diminished version of the truth that was bereft of much complexity and agency. As the Commission recognised, 'for some perpetrators it is their experience as victims which push them to become perpetrators' (TJRC vol. 1 2013: 77). However, such realities were largely absent from the narratives relayed. In turn, little insight was given as to how, for example, protests often turn violent; why ordinary people might loot and burn properties, block roads and displace ethnic 'others'; or the extent to which political violence is sometimes spontaneous, disorganised and highly personal, or whether it is always sponsored, incited and organised by elites. At the same time, no public discussion was prompted about when the use of state and non-state violence shifts from a legitimate use of force that instils order and protects lives, to an illegitimate use of force. With no discussion prompted, for example, on whether police are sometimes justified in beating or shooting protesters, whether police should be able to kill (or ordinary citizens lynch) suspected criminals, whether pastoralists should be allowed to conduct retaliatory cattle raids against their neighbours and so on. The result is one in which the last strand of AMP denial – namely, whether a series of events actually constituted a wrongdoing or not – while discussed in the Commission's final report, was never fully confronted during it's public proceedings.

At the same time, such narratives of innocence were also bereft of agency in a more positive sense. In short, a common focus on reparations encouraged an emphasis on need, desperation, and fears. In this way, one witness at the Kisumu hearings bemoaned how the process had become a 'gospel according to the victim'. He went on to explain how 'most have gone hoping for some monetary compensation. About three quarters are going with the mind of reparations, and if that's the intention then they must design and format the story so that it hurts most ... [They need to make an] argument that appeals to pity' (interview, Kisumu, 5 August 2011). This is not to suggest that witnesses lied or had not suffered. Instead, it is to suggest that the format, and the Commission's powers, encouraged witnesses to select those parts of the story that spoke of their suffering and innocence, and to downplay those parts that spoke of their own activities and agency. This mode of story-telling is not uncommon when victimhood becomes a means to access limited resources (Beckmann 2010) – a dynamic that is well captured by Jonny Steinberg in his discussion of a Somali man's efforts in South Africa to gain asylum to the United States:

Asad told a carefully crafted story about his life. He did not lie; he described faithfully and in great detail the incidents of violence to which he had been subject since coming to South Africa ... But nor did he really tell the truth. For the fuel that burned inside him and that made him Asad Hirsi Abdullahi was drained from the story he related ... leaving only a stick figure, a hapless refugee. That was what was expected, after all. What would an American immigration official do with information about his soul?

(2016: 300)

Similarly selective and drained stories were evident during the life of the TJRC and, whilst understandable, are unfortunate for the diminished truth that they produced, and for the questions and debates that they left undisturbed.

8.4 Conclusions: 'There's No Incentive for AMPs to Come Forward and Talk'

Some said that it's too early for a truth commission. I'm not sure, but know that in other contexts there's been significant change that's provided the right context. But what significant change allows for people to be open and honest? There's no incentive for AMPs to come forward and talk, especially when you're including the ability to recommend prosecutions, which for me flies in the face of encouraging transparency and truth.

(Interview, TJRC director, Nairobi, 7 September 2011)

In contrast to South Africa, where the process of hearing self-confessed perpetrators provided some public acknowledgement, in Kenya, AMPs insisted that they had not been there; the issue in question was the responsibility of someone further up or down the pecking order; the allegations levied were false and a product of poor investigations, groundless rumours or malicious intent; they could not remember things that had happened years ago and did not have access to the relevant documents that might jog their memories; they were actually a victim; or the action in question was legal and, whilst unfortunate, entirely justified. At the same time, many AMPs used the opportunity to present themselves as good and strong leaders. They had suffered due to their involvement in struggles to protect or promote community or national interests, they had special foresight or an ability to make difficult decisions at testing times, and they enjoyed the support of the state, peers, family members and communities. As a result, AMPs performed a sense of continuity, rather than substantive transition: the same elite was still in power and could rely on state, peer and community support.

An unwillingness to admit wrongdoing is not unusual – few people around the world publicly confess to illegal or morally dubious acts unless there is a strong incentive to do so. In Kenya, no strong incentives were provided. Little new information was unearthed as institutions refused to hand over documents. A limited amnesty process was never opened. Political continuity ensured that the same people were in power and had control over key institutions and economic opportunities. One might also not be believed and might face significant sanctions – from being recommended for further investigations, prosecution and lustration to losing out on reparations and being labelled as a traitor or perhaps even killed if one implicated powerful others.

In such a context it is unsurprising that alleged perpetrators failed to admit to wrongdoing or acknowledge responsibility. This was not necessarily a problem if subsequent events undermined the elitism displayed and managed to hold some of those responsible accountable. However, as the process played out, such a legacy appeared increasingly unlikely as AMP denials – in a broader context of political continuity and developments at the ICC – contributed to a political environment in which victims became increasingly sceptical of the possibility of justice in the broad sense, and came to increasingly focus on reparative, rather than punitive, justice, and on political, rather than substantive, reconciliation – troubled legacies to which the final chapters now turn.

9 | 'Only Talking Won't Help'
Of Justice and Reparations

> Yes, we said, but we're now expecting something. Only talking won't help.
> (Interview, TJRC witness, Mt Elgon, 25 February 2011)

On 21 May 2013, Kiplagat handed over a copy of the TJRC's four-volume report to President Kenyatta at an uneventful press conference. The report was contained in a see-through perspex box to denote transparency. Ideally, the ceremony was to mark a moment of transition: the Commission was handing over responsibility for the implementation, monitoring and safekeeping of its records to the executive, legislature and national archives, respectively. However, for some, the moment captured a sense of ending: the 'glass box' suggesting 'only open in case of fire' (interview, transitional justice expert, Nairobi, 21 May 2014); 'the report … now sealed never to be looked at again' (interview, civil society activist, Nairobi, 26 August 2013).

In practice, the report as archive constitutes a place of closure *and* commencement (Derrida 1996: 1). On the one hand, people document and archive the past, at least in part, so that it can be forgotten (Derrida 1996: 7), while the process of selective remembrance and cataloguing helps to edit out some events and interpretations from a collective history. On the other hand, recommendations can prompt further action; the fact that report writing constructs, rather than simply unearths, a collective past (Chapman & Ball 2001: 8) means that it is never passively or uncritically received. Instead, such processes produce 'a sliver of social memory' (cf. Harris 2002b: 135) that becomes part of the 'documentary archives that community members and leaders can draw upon [or ignore] … in their efforts to validate … historical narratives and associated claims' and to (de)legitimise certain courses of action (Lynch 2016: 210). In short, the report as archive is typically neither wholly accepted nor entirely ignored, but is instead (albeit often only periodically and half-heartedly) 'revisited, reread, reappraised, reinterpreted, revised and rewritten' (Harris 2002a: 162).

The TJRC is no different. In the face of limited political will and widespread public scepticism, the Commission's plan for a clear point of commencement – whereby the submission of a final report would prompt public discussion of key findings and the implementation of wide-ranging recommendations – quickly proved optimistic and politically naïve. According to this initial schedule, the public hearings and report merely constituted the initial, albeit critical, stages of a process whereby truth-telling and justice would contribute to a sense of redress and transition, and thus to reconciliation. The latter was understood as the restoration of good relations broadly conceived, and as a long process that needed to occur at various levels. In line with this approach, the Commission emphasised that it had not expected to achieve reconciliation, but hoped to set the country 'on a path to further reconciliation' (TJRC vol. 3 2013: 84).

The path envisioned assumed both 'conceptual and practical links between reconciliation and national healing and justice, which includes redistributive justice, retributive justice and reparative justice'. The idea was that '[t]he goal of reconciliation at various levels will remain elusive unless those who have suffered are restored and repaired; unless those who were excluded are included in meaningful ways; and unless those in dire want as a result of marginalization are materially enabled to move forward' (TJRC vol. 3 2013: 86). To this end, the Commission lauded the legislators' foresight for insisting that the report 'shall be implemented' (TJRC vol. 3 2013: 72), and recommended, among other things, the further investigation, lustration and prosecution of certain named individuals, institutional reforms and reparations.

However, reality soon diverged from this plan. At the time of this writing (almost five years later), the Commission's findings have enjoyed negligible dissemination and popular discussion, while its implementation schedule has long been obsolete. Instead – and in the face of a credibility crisis, claims that the report was doctored, a lack of political commitment, an evolving peace narrative and distractions of everyday politics – most Kenyans continue to be largely ignorant of the truth produced, and sceptical about the Commission's likely impact.

But the Commission's findings and recommendations have not been forgotten. Activists have called for the report to be enacted either in part or in full, while politicians from across the divide have periodically demanded that it be discussed and implemented as an implied panacea for past wrongs and as a means to differentiate themselves from their competitors. On the one side, President Kenyatta issued a general apology in 2015 for past wrongs and directed that a Restorative Justice Fund (RJF) be established; on the other, implementation of the TJRC report – and particularly the idea that it could address land injustices – became a central plank of the opposition's campaign for the presidency in 2017. The report has also contributed to broader debates about justice, reconciliation and reparations and has become part of the historical archives that individuals and communities can draw upon in their efforts to lay claims and justify assistance.

This chapter looks at the most notable aspect of the TJRC's legacy within the first four year's of the report's submission and Jubilee's first term in office (2013–2017), namely, the discrepancy between the kind of justice envisaged and promised by the TJRC and the reparative justice considered by the government. The chapter starts with an outline of the Commission's understanding of the connection between truth-telling and justice and its promises of, and recommendations for, punitive, reparative, social and restorative justice. It then moves on to the response of key stakeholders between 2013 and 2017: from the pragmatic approach taken by leading civil society and victims' groups to the schizophrenic stance of the political elite, a presidential apology for past wrongs and the government's promise of limited reparations.

The analysis highlights the continuity that runs through change, as non-implementation of the report, the establishment of the RJF, and civil society's strategic response – all in the context of the ICC's intervention and evolving peace narrative – collectively ensured that, at the time of this writing, justice has increasingly come to focus on reparations to the neglect of accountability. The TJRC, like the ICC's intervention, has thus contributed, at least in the short term, to a situation where harms and suffering gain some acknowledgement, but not the why, how and by whom. This produces a world of victims without perpetrators – a world in which, at least for the foreseeable future, the political elite are positioned as those with the capacity to assist ordinary citizens, and victimhood becomes a way to try and access scarce resources and meet basic needs at the behest of the same.

9.1 The TJRC's Vision: From Truth-Telling to Justice

You asked about Truth, Justice and Reconciliation but also answered it as we would: that to have reconciliation, one needs justice, and in order to have justice one needs to know the truth.

(Commissioner Slye, TJRC public hearing, Kisumu, 17 July 2011)

For the TJRC, truth-telling provided a limited form of justice, which was capable of making some direct contribution to reconciliation, and an initial stage in a longer-term process whereby truth would help bring justice, reconciliation, healing and national unity.

The argument in terms of truth's direct contribution to justice was twofold. First, truth-telling before a sympathetic official body would provide a forum for 'victims to recount publicly their experiences and to have such experiences acknowledged' (TJRC vol. 1 2013: 50), which would help re-humanise the victim and commence a healing process. Second, by providing a space for the production of a new collective narrative of the past, it was held that truth-telling could help to overcome societal divisions by redrafting 'social understandings of a country's history and rectify past narratives imposed by the state in furtherance of the interests of a powerful few or an intolerant majority' (TJRC vol. 1 2013: 50).

Indeed, it was sometimes implied that speaking could be sufficient, as occurred, for example, during one of the women's hearings when a commissioner bemoaned how, if people's experiences had been discussed earlier, 'the wounds would already have been healed', and spoke of her desire 'to stay here with you all day, two days, three days ... so we exhaust all the weeping' (Nakuru, 24 September 2011). However, while many appreciated the opportunity to speak, the time given clearly fell short of a psychoanalytical model of therapeutic catharsis, and hearings stimulated negligible public debate and failed to prompt agreement on a new shared past (Chapter 5). Moreover, the idea that talking equates with healing suggests that the problem lies largely with individual and communal memories and emotions, rather than a broader history of past, ongoing and potential injustice. In practice, however, a sense of relief in speaking was often, if not always, linked to a hope that on being heard action would be taken.

However, overall – and despite periodic references to the need for people to 'exhaust the weeping' – the TJRC recognised the inadequacy of public testimony alone. More specifically, it realised that only a small number of victims were given the opportunity to speak for a short period of time (TJRC vol. 1 2013: 98) and that the experience could prove newly traumatic (TJRC vol. 1 2013: 48). Commissioners also insisted that it was not just the telling that was important, but the truth that emerged and its effect. For the Commission, truth provided a basis for various recommendations, and thus justice, which was understood to be a necessary bridge to sustainable peace and reconciliation (TJRC vol. 1 2013: 49). As one commissioner explained to a witness in Kisii:

in order to have reconciliation, one needs to have some form of justice ... but, of course, in order to have justice, one needs to know the truth to understand what happened and why it happened, the context in which it happened and who was responsible for this happening.
(Cited in TJRC vol. 3 2013: 85)

This approach – where truth constituted a form of justice and was simultaneously necessary as a basis for justice – informed the Commission's practice. As a result, and in stark contrast to the South African TRC, commissioners and staff rarely asked people about their willingness to forgive. Instead, the leader of evidence and commissioners tended to respond to witness testimony with statements of empathy, requests for further information and recommendations, and statements about how the Commission would study the information given and act on it, and how witnesses had 'come to the right place' (commissioner, TJRC public hearing, Busia, 1 July 2011). Significantly, while witnesses were often asked about traditional or local justice mechanisms during these interactions, there was relatively little interest shown in such approaches. A fact that was then reflected in the absence of any substantive discussion of 'traditional justice' in the Commission's final report.

Instead, the Commission offered a range of 'classic' recommendations, which included punitive justice through further investigations, lustration and prosecution of named individuals; social justice through redress for 'violations of socio-economic rights and the legacy of economic marginalisation' and institutional reforms; and reparative justice through guarantees of non-repetition and a detailed reparations framework (TJRC vol. 1 2013: 46). According to this framework, the victims of gross human rights violations deemed most vulnerable would be eligible for pensions and rehabilitation, while less vulnerable victims would receive standardised symbolic pensions, and groups that had suffered various bodily and socio-economic violations would be eligible for collective reparations (TJRC vol. 4 2013: 105). Restorative justice then presented as something that would be fostered by these collective efforts, as well as by the voice given, and public debate stimulated, by public hearings and the final report.

However, while the Commission called for accountability and punitive justice, it ultimately prioritised reparative and restorative justice. In part, this was a product of the Commission's limited achievements, as perpetrators' unwillingness to confess, and the government's refusal to hand over documents, meant that the Commission revealed relatively little about who had committed past injustices and why. At the same time, interactions with victims helped to justify the prioritisation of a reparations framework; a framework that prominent CSOs had helped to draft and were committed to. However, it was also informed by political considerations and a long-standing debate about whether certain forms of justice are necessary for sustainable peace, or whether an insistence on accountability can undermine peace. This was reflected in a recurring tension between the felt needs of the society as a whole – with fears of future violence encouraging an emphasis on peace, reconciliation and types of justice (such as reparations) that would minimise undue tension – and the demands of victims and civil society groups, which tended to call for a combination of reparations and accountability both in the sense of an acknowledgement of responsibility and punishment. This tension was glossed over in much of the final report through references to the need for different kinds of justice, but is nevertheless evident from the Commission's definition of justice and priorities.

The Commission defined justice in line with a 2004 report of the UN General Secretary as 'an ideal of accountability and fairness in the protection and vindication of rights and the prevention and punishment of wrongs', which 'implies regard for the rights of the accused, for the interests of the victims *and for the well-being of society at large*' (TJRC vol. 1 2013: 44; emphasis added). The Commission recognised that these goals might come into tension, and that some opposed retributive justice as a threat to peace. In response, the final report recommended that retributive justice be 'sensitive to the needs of reconciliation and national unity' (TJRC vol. 1 2013: 51); hoped that, even where prosecutions were absent, naming and shaming would hold perpetrators accountable (TJRC vol. 1 2013: 45); and opted to follow 'in the footsteps of many of its international predecessors in emphasizing an approach to justice that *weighs more towards restorative than retributive justice*' (TJRC vol. 1 2013: 44; emphasis added). Restorative justice was understood as the repair of 'the harm done to the victims and the greater community', and as something that requires acknowledgement of people's suffering and innovative efforts 'to move forward as a nation' (TJRC vol. 1 2013: 45). However, while the Commission's preference for reparative and restorative justice was cast as an issue of balance – with punitive justice playing an important if secondary role – in the post-commission era this weighting was sidelined, as reparative justice, and a limited form of restorative justice, were cast by President Kenyatta as an alternative to punitive justice.

In the meantime, however – and in line with the TJRC Act's stipulation that the Commission provide plans for an implementation mechanism 'to ensure its recommendations are duly and timely implemented' (TJRC vol. 4 2013: 71) – the Commission recommended the establishment of a Committee for the Implementation of the Recommendations of the Truth, Justice and Reconciliation Commission, or Implementation Committee (IC), to be supported by a Technical Committee. In so doing – and cognisant of a tendency for the recommendations of commissions of inquiry and truth commissions to be ignored (TJRC vol. 4 2013: 74) – commissioners emphasised the need for the IC to be empowered through legislation, and for it to be independent and adequately resourced. Commissioners also called for the IC to be established within three months of the report's submission so that it was 'in place before the Commission is dissolved in order to allow for a smooth and direct handover of sensitive documents' (TJRC vol. 4 2013: 76). Once established, responsibilities of the IC were to include the 'management and administration of the Reparations Fund'; 'management and securing of the archives of the Commission, with due regard to the importance of transparency and access to information and consistent with the promises of confidentiality made to specific individuals and organizations'; the facilitation of memorialisation; the monitoring of those recommendations assigned to other bodies; and public awareness (TJRC vol. 4 2013: 77).

These plans for an IC assumed that recommendations 'are, in Parliament's wisdom, of mandatory application and must be complied with by all constitutional, legislative and administrative institutions and bodies' (TJRC vol. 3 2013: 72). Critically, the idea that Kenyans should offer recommendations to the TJRC, and that these would then feed into the Commission's recommendations, which would then be implemented, recurred throughout the Commission's work as – in the face of an ongoing credibility crisis – commissioners and staff sought to encourage people to engage. To this end, the statement taking form asked for general recommendations and for people's views on reparations, while civic educators and statement takers – the latter under substantial pressure to collect as many statements and memoranda as possible – often encouraged people to engage by highlighting how their submissions would be reflected in the final report, which 'the government would have to implement' (interview, statement taker, Lodwar, 18 March 2014). It was also common for commissioners to promise witnesses that their testimony 'would form a part of our records' (commissioner, public hearing, Isiolo, 11 May 2011); that testimony would contribute to 'appropriate recommendations' (commissioner, public hearing, Kakamega, 28 June 2011); and that the Commission's recommendations 'must be implemented' (commissioner, public hearing, Busia, 1 July 2011). In short, while the TJRC was acutely aware of the unrealistic expectations that many victims had of immediate action, and were at pains to tell people that justice and reconciliation were long processes, they also suggested a pre-determined path whereby testimony would inform recommendations, which would then be implemented according to a suggested timeline.

In practice, while the thousands of statements and memoranda collected, and hours of testimony provided, helped to inform wide-ranging recommendations and provided important details and reminders of known problems, the particularities of most stories could not be included, and several of the chapters, and many of the recommendations, could easily have been written without the Commission ever having taken place. At the same time – and given that many of the recommendations drew upon previous commissions of inquiry reports or were recognised responses to known problems, and a group of CSOs drafted the reparations framework – the process of listening proved far more important for a justification of the Commission's recommendations than for the writing of the same.

The promise that recommendations would be implemented was also naïve. According to the TJRC Act, the report was to be tabled in parliament within twenty-one days of being handed over, implementation was to start within six months and 'recommendations shall be implemented' (Kenya 2008d: 50[2]). However, the Act also stipulated that '[t]he Minister [for Justice] shall report to the National Assembly within three months of receipt of the report of the Commission, and twice a year thereafter, as to the implementation of the Commission's recommendations'. Moreover, 'where the implementation of any recommendation has not been complied with, the National Assembly shall require the Minister to furnish it with reasons for non-implementation' (Kenya 2008d: 50[1–2]). Given the Commission's credibility crisis, limited public support and the political nature of the issues covered, many predicted that reasons and means of non-implementation would be found.

9.2 The Politics of Non-implementation, 2013–2017

Stakeholders must recognize that despite the Act's declaration that the recommendations are mandatory, the legal does not control this situation, the political does.

(Former TJRC staff member, ICTJ/GiZ workshop report, October 2013)

The TJRC was ready to present a copy of its final report to President Kenyatta on 3 May 2013, but the President was initially 'too busy'; the volumes were finally handed over almost three weeks later with less than two hours' notice (Chawatama, Dinka & Slye 2013). Inevitably then, the handover was a low-key affair bereft of the pomp and ceremony originally planned, which – together with the fact that the government had known of the 3 May deadline since the Commission's extension of August 2012 – displayed a lack of political commitment.

This delay went hand-in-hand with claims – articulated in a dissenting opinion signed by the three international commissioners – that, between 3 and 21 May, pressure had successfully been applied by officials from the OP to rewrite certain paragraphs of the land chapter, which referred to allegations of land grabbing by the country's first president (and the incoming president's father) Jomo Kenyatta. Then, almost as soon as the report had been handed over, the Chairman, Bethuel Kiplagat, questioned the validity of the Commission's findings, while others called for the report to be thrown out because of what it excluded, for example, because it '[t]otally ignores the coup of 1982, violence in Kisumu [and Kibera] in 2008 . . . and also the coup attempt in 1971' (Omondi in *Africa Review* 21 May 2013). Coming in the wake of a long-standing credibility crisis, these complaints further undermined public confidence in the quality of the Commission's work and likely political response, as the ghosts that had haunted its work continued to haunt its legacy. This proved critical, since – with many ordinary citizens ambivalent about the report's findings and recommendations, and sceptical of the likelihood of implementation, and in the face of a largely disinterested commercial media – the political costs of non-implementation were relatively low from the outset.

The debacle over the land chapter also 'fractured the Commission' and rendered it 'almost impossible to proceed with the full commission on any activity' during the Commission's three-month post-submission period (former TJRC staff member, ICTJ/GiZ workshop report, October 2013). This time was meant to have been used to engage policy makers on implementation and to organise its archive of statements, memoranda, hearing transcripts and supporting documents. However, with the Commission immobilised and no IC on the horizon, lobbying was left largely to the KNCHR, prominent CSOs, victims' groups and a handful of journalists, analysts and backbench politicians, while the Commission's documents were left boxed up in the strong room at the Kenya National Archive with no public discussion of which materials would be made available, and if so, when, how, where and to whom.

The final report was made available. But, again, practice fell far short of the Commission's plan. The TJRC Act stipulated that:

[i]mmediately upon submitting the report to the President, the Commission shall publish the report in the Gazette and in such other publications as it may consider appropriate, and shall make copies of the report, or summaries thereof, widely available to the public in at least three local newspapers with wide circulation.

(Kenya 2008d: 48[3])

However, while the Commission pre-paid the government printers to publish the report in its entirety and summary form, it was only when CSOs threatened to sue the Attorney General (AG) and the government printers that a line was printed in the *Kenya Gazette* stating that the report had been published. As a result, the report was only made available on the TJRC website and in its full form (until the site was later taken down), while it took several months for CSOs to produce a summary that is yet to be widely disseminated and discussed (Hansen & Sriram 2015: 420).

With no IC on the horizon, the report largely unseen and the archive boxed up, the next challenge came through the courts, when the novelist Kiriro wa Ngugi sought to prevent parliament from receiving the report on the basis that 'some sections ... were unconstitutional, inaccurate and incomplete'. However, while the Judge threw out the petition on the grounds that 'Parliament is only performing messenger duties since it has no role in debating or implementing recommendations in the report' (cited in *Daily Nation* 11 June 2013), MPs saw their role differently. Indeed, instead of tabling the document after it was received on 24 July 2013, MPs took advantage of the Act's references to the Minister of Justice – an office which, with the 2010 constitution, no longer existed – to amend the legislation. In this December 2013 amendment, MPs not only replaced all references in the TJRC Act to the minister with the AG; they also removed the requirement that implementation commence within six months and added a requirement that the TJRC report be considered by the National Assembly and only be implemented 'in accordance with [its] recommendations' (cited in AI 2014: 25). In so doing, MPs transformed the report from one that would be recognised by them, to one that lay at their mercy.

By the time of the 2017 elections, MPs had used such powers to ignore the report. Exceptions included a petition brought before parliament by the MP for Wajir South, Hon. Abdullahi Dirie, on behalf of NVSN in December 2015, which requested that the National Assembly adopt the report and allocate 'sufficient budget for the immediate and effective implementation' of its recommendations (cited by Lynch in *Saturday Nation* 12 December 2015). However, while the Hon. Speaker agreed that the report should be prioritised by the House Business Committee when parliament reconvened in February (Hansard 3 December 2015), the National Assembly continued to drag its feet with no further discussion of the report by the time Kenyans returned to the polls in August 2017.

Political will was limited by the far-reaching and complex nature of many of the report's recommendations – including the explosive issue of historical land injustices – and by the fact that individuals from each of the major coalitions were adversely mentioned. This included Kenyatta and Ruto, who were named for their alleged role in organising the post-election violence of 2007–8, as well as Kalonzo Musyoka, Odinga's running mate in 2013 and 2017, who the TJRC recommended be investigated in relation to forceful evictions in 1997 and subsequent land grabbing. Indeed, the fact that the Commission's mandate covered such a wide range of injustices over a long timeframe, together with the ever shifting nature of Kenya's political coalitions, meant that no party or community had an unproblematic relationship with the report.

However, this did not prevent opposition politicians from insisting on their commitment to implementation as a means to differentiate themselves from the ruling Jubille Alliance as leaders committed to justice and accountability. For example, days after the report had been submitted, Odinga called for its implementation on the basis that, '[w]ithout the truth, there can be no justice. Without justice, there is no reconciliation and without reconciliation, there cannot be peace and without peace there is no development' (*Standard*, 27 May 2015). While, at the funeral of the veteran Maasai politician William ole Ntimama in September 2016, Odinga again called for the report, and its provisions on land injustices, to be implemented in line with the ideals that Ntimama had 'fought for all his life' (cited in *Daily Nation* 16 September 2016). In response, Jubilee accused Odinga of misleading Kenyans, as the Deputy President, for example, insisted that 'there was a National Lands Commission (NLC) in place that was dealing with land issues' (*Daily Nation* 4 October 2016) and 'the Leader of Majority ... [insisted that the report] has been tabled and it is waiting discussion because we were waiting for funds to be set aside for its implementation' (*Daily Nation* 17 September 2016).

Such politics picked up ahead of the 2017 elections as prominent opposition politicians – now united behind Odinga and Musyoka in the National Super Alliance (NASA) – made implementation of the TJRC, and, more specifically, claims that such action would help address historical land injustices, a central plank of their campaign. In response, Ruto claimed that implementation of the report's recommendations on land would 'open old wounds' and that Odinga 'believes implementing TJRC means every legitimate land buyer should go back where they came from as a way of dealing with poverty' (*The Star* 18 July 2017). In turn, while NASA's manifesto (NASA 2017) talked at some length about 'coming to terms with our past', Jubilee's simply noted how the government had '[c]losed a painful chapter in our history through the President's apology to the country for historical injustices and the resettlement of Internally Displaced

Persons' (Jubilee Party 2017: 38). However, the fact that NASA politicians had done little to push for the report's implementation as MPs, governors or senators raised questions about whether they were really committed to implementation or were merely engaged in electioneering.

Against such politicking, the judiciary proved relatively supportive of the report. Most notably, on the fiftieth anniversary of the assassination of the political activist Pio Gama Pinto on 25 February 2015, Chief Justice Willy Mutunga recognised that 'the TJRC recommends an apology from the Judiciary for its failure to protect the rights of Kenyans. Let me announce here our apology and our readiness to offer yet another apology when Parliament performs its duty by the report' (cited in Maliti in *International Justice Monitor* 9 April 2015). Then, in June 2015, the High Court rejected merged cases brought by two of Kenyatta's relatives – Ngengi Muigai and Senator Beth Mugo – who sought to quash sections of the report, which referred to their illegal acquisition of land at the Coast and in Karura Forest on the grounds that they had not been given a chance to reply to false allegations. The judge ruled that the report should 'remain intact' – with 'mutilation' of it not in the public's interest – and stressed that the petitioners were free to defend themselves 'before the relevant body' whenever recommendations were implemented (cited in *Nairobi News* 25 June 2015).

While the judiciary defended the report, a group of Nairobi-based human rights organisations and the KNCHR – brought together under the banner of the Kenya Transitional Justice Network (KTJN) – raised public awareness, lobbied for implementation and supported parallel transitional justice efforts. With regards to lobbying, KTJN organised a series of meetings under four broad categories. First, there were closed-door network meetings (at which NSVN tended to be the only victims group in attendance) where members sought to develop a coherent strategy. Second, there were events with victims – most notably an annual NVSN convention in Nairobi – which sought to disseminate information, gather views and mobilise action, when attendees included representatives from a range of organisations such as the IDP Network, Wagalla Massacre Foundation, Mau Mau Veterans Association and Grace Agenda (which supports victims of sexual violence). Third, there were structured workshops with government officials and donors, and finally, small informal meetings to lobby particular individuals.

These meetings were informed by, and simultaneously helped to ossify, a strategic approach that prioritised the Commission's reparations framework. This focus was no doubt influenced by the fact that several KTJN organisations – namely, ICJ-Kenya, KHRC and ICTJ – had helped to draft the TJRC reparations framework. It was also informed by a sense that reparations were a priority for many victims *and* that they were a relatively uncontentious issue (as compared to accountability) on which organisations might gain some political traction. This understanding of political realities was reinforced by interactions with government officials and politicians who tended to emphasise the need for a realistic approach and cited reparations as a possible area for fruitful discussion. To give just one example, in October 2013, ICTJ and GiZ convened a workshop on the implementation of the TJRC Report as a 'first step in engagement between civil society, victims, government and international partners'. At this meeting, the Deputy Solicitor General relayed the AG's hopes that the meeting 'balance the perennial problems of peace versus justice', and made it 'clear that implementation of the TJRC report is important and that the office's main concern is reparations'. In the wake of such comments, workshop conveners noted 'certain areas of potential convergence', namely, '[i]mplementation of reparations for victims … and continuing support for national cohesion and peace building strategies'. The conveners concluded that:

> The workshop discussions made clear that reparations are a shared priority between victims, civil society, and the State. Moreover, reparation is one area in which the TJRC's recommendations were highly detailed and relatively comprehensive. Accordingly, implementation of a fair and comprehensive reparations scheme can be an important starting point for coordinated action.
> (ICTJ/GiZ workshop report, October 2013)

This incremental approach was given new life following President Kenyatta's annual state of the nation address on 26 March 2015 in which he remembered the country's painful memories of past human rights abuses and declared:

> To move forward as one nation I stand before you today on my own behalf, that of my government and all past governments, to offer the sincere apology of the Government of the Republic of Kenya to all our compatriots for all past wrongs. I seek your forgiveness and may God give us the Grace to draw

'Only Talking Won't Help' 263

on the lessons of this history to unite as a people and, together, to embrace our future as one people and one nation.

(Kenyatta, 26 March 2015)

At the same time, the President announced the establishment of a three-year Ksh 10 billion fund for restorative justice.

While the President offered a blanket apology that called for unity in the interests of progress, his words were welcomed by prominent CSOs and victims' groups 'as a major milestone in acknowledging the victims and survivors of the past violations' (KNCHR/ICTJ June 2016). The establishment of the RJF in turn added substance to the apology and reinvigorated civil society's incremental strategy and prioritisation of reparations.

Two and half years later – and as Kenyans returned to the polls – the Fund was still in the process of being established. It was not known whether the Fund would ever actually materialise. And, if it did, for which historical injustices would people receive reparations; how would an individual's status as a victim be determined and verified; would individuals receive financial compensation and, if so, would this vary according to the severity of the abuse and/or victim's current socio-economic status; and would the Fund also oversee symbolic and communal reparations? It was also feared that the Fund had been raided to write cheques for IDP groups during the 2017 campaign period (FIDH & KHRC 2017: 55). As one civil society activist explained, it was unlikely that the government would simply leave the money 'lying idle' (conversation, Nairobi, 17 August 2017).

However, while it is too early to know whether the Fund will become operational, let alone offer an evaluation of it, it seems likely that, if it does come into effect, the Fund will only acknowledge the existence of victims, and not what happened, why and at whose hands. As a result, the idea of reparations as 'restorative justice' – the latter speaking to the need to restore victims, perpetrators *and* beneficiaries into a community – appears to be intentionally misleading.

More specifically, it is important that the Fund was mooted as an alternative to prosecutions in a context where punitive justice was deemed impossible. As Kenyatta explained in his 2015 address, the Director of Public Prosecutions saw 'challenges to obtaining successful prosecutions' for the post-election violence of 2007–8, but '[n]onetheless … recognizes there were victims and recommends that these cases be dealt with using restorative approaches'. In turn, the

President explained how his administration was 'building on the efforts of the last government to advance the resettlement, reconciliation and relief to internally displaced people', and how the RJF 'will provide a measure of relief and will underscore my government's goodwill' (Kenyatta 26 March 2015).

Significantly, the proposed RJF differed from the Commission's reparations framework in both its scope and form. First, while the TJRC envisaged a range of reparations for bodily integrity and socio-economic violations (see Table 9.1), initial discussions suggested that the Fund would only oversee the distribution of financial payments to individual victims of certain bodily integrity right violations (such as the families of those killed during the post-election violence and perhaps the Wagalla massacre and other atrocities) – that is, only to some priority A victims of type 1 and 2 violations. The implication was that justice for other violations would be provided through other means – for example, with historical land injustices addressed through the NLC (*Daily Nation* 4 October 2016) and economic marginalisation through devolution and 'strategic initiatives in marginalised and at-risk regions and populations' (Kenyatta, 26 March 2015).

Table 9.1 *TJRC Reparations Framework*

Category of Violation	Priority A: Most Vulnerable	Priority B: Collective Reparations	Priority C: Non-expedited
1. Right to life	Victims of 1 & 2 eligible for pensions, medical & psychosocial vouchers.	Victim groups in this block are eligible for land reparations, socio-economic measures, government policy interventions, as well as non-material reparations such as restitution of rights, recognition, self-determination measures and memorials.	Victims of 1 & 2 eligible for standardised pensions.
2. Personal integrity			
3. Forcible transfer			
4. Land injustices	If resulted in death, family of victims of 3 can claim as above.		
5. Systematic marginalisation			
	Victims of 4 & 5 only eligible for reparations under priority B.		

Source: TJRC vol. 4 2013: 105.

Second, while the TJRC started with a discussion of who should be eligible for which type of reparations and how, the RJF started with a budget of KSh 10 billion with Ksh 3.4 billion allocated in 2015/16 and another Ksh. 6 billion in 2016/17. This raised questions of how victims would be identified, how much would be awarded and whether additional funds would be sourced.

Third, while the TJRC recommended that the identification of victims and the administration of reparations be overseen by an independent IC, the RJF set out by Jubilee was a government initiative co-opted by the President (Applebaum & Mawby 2016: 48). More specifically, the idea in early 2017 – before people's attention was diverted to the election campaigns – was for the Fund to be managed under the existing Public Finance Management Act (2012) and administered by the AG's office with the registration, verification and payment of victims of historical injustices overseen by a technical committee to comprise of nominees from the AG, OP, treasury, national police service (NPS), KNCHR and ICTJ.

Civil society and victims' groups were keenly aware of the ways in which the RJF proposed differed from the TJRC reparations framework, and voiced concerns, for example, over the inclusion of a representative from the NPS on, and exclusion of a victims' representative from, the proposed technical committee. However, such concerns were trumped by a desire to see victims gain some material assistance, as organisations sought to offer technical advice on how to ensure the process was victim-friendly and conflict sensitive. As one transitional justice expert explained at a civil society meeting in September 2016, we 'need to push on the openings that exist'.

However, while KTJN struggled for the full or partial implementation of the TJRC's report, member organisations lacked the capacity to give this issue consistent and high-profile attention, as they simultaneously tried to respond to new threats, injustices and developments, and to prepare for the 2017 elections. Victims' groups similarly lacked the capacity to maintain a sustained effort, as – with limited funds and personnel – they tried to also respond to the everyday needs of their membership, secure justice through alternative avenues and raise funds. In addition, NVSN, which had been established as a coordinating body, was weakened by the decision of the chair and deputy chair to join politics as members of the ODM secretariat, which left the secretary, Wachira Waheire, to largely carry the NVSN workload.

Civil society was also weakened by the resounding silence of most churches. This was in stark contrast to the early 1990s, when churches had stood at the forefront of popular struggles for multi-party democracy. This is important because it helped to diminish the moral authority of a campaign that was ultimately led by a handful of Nairobi-based and externally funded organisations with little connection to ordinary people in the city or beyond (Hansen & Sriram 2015). The most notable exception was the Catholic Justice and Peace Commission, which – albeit in a rather sporadic and inconsistent manner – continued to discuss the TJRC report with its members.

At the same time, religious leaders and narratives continued to play a central role in an alternative performance of temporal rupture whereby a promised break between the past and present would come – not through the implementation of secular transitional justice mechanisms – but through a neo-Pentecostal discourse and associated rituals of 'repentance and forgiveness ... [that bring] national rebirth and prosperity through divine blessing' (Deacon 2016). This religious discourse of rupture through salvation was intimately interwoven with a political prioritisation of peace and cohesion, which was articulated through a demand for unity and cohesion behind God's chosen leaders in the face of insecurity, poverty and neo-colonialism (Chapters 2 and 3). This was critical as it reinforced references to the need, for example, to 'balance the perennial problems of peace versus justice' (ICTJ/GiZ workshop report, October 2013). The implication was that – while people could discuss compensation – prosecutions and accountability were too divisive and backward-looking.

It is unsurprising that, in this context of public scepticism, a supportive but distracted civil society, weak victim's groups, a dearth of political will, and an alternative (and more immediate) popular performance of temporal rupture through religious renewal, peace, reconciliation, and development that timelines provided by the TJRC Act and the Commission's final report became irrelevant during Jubilee's first term in office. Indeed, it is perhaps surprising that the report was not forgotten altogether. This was due to the efforts of various actors who sought to implement the TJRC's recommendations (or a variation of them) – as civil society and victims groups demanded justice, and NASA and Jubilee looked to present themselves as the alliances for justice and peace respectively. As noted, this conjunction of efforts and political realities led to a strategic prioritisation of reparations between 2013 and 2017, which CSOs and victim's groups hoped would be an opening for further justice, but which the Jubilee government clearly envisioned as a means of closure.

9.3 The Reparations Agenda

Government should assist me so that I can be proud to be Kenyan.

(Victim of police shooting, TJRC public hearing, Bungoma, 9 July 2011)

Prominent CSOs, victims' groups and government officials differ in their reasons for focusing on reparations, but, at this time of writing, they have converged in presenting this as a pragmatic and welcome step in the right direction. Certainly, reparations are a priority for many victims. It was also the obvious area for those seeking justice to apply pressure in the hope of creating 'new openings'. However, while I am sympathetic to this strategic and incremental approach, this section points to some of the possible shortcomings with it, namely, a focus on victims of bodily integrity violations to the neglect of other injustices discussed by the TJRC, a familiar performance of state assistance for victims and impunity for those responsible, and the likelihood that the main audience will not be victims, but other Kenyans who may approve of official efforts to bring closure.

It is clear that many who engaged with the TJRC did so in the hope, at least in part, of securing financial compensation, rehabilitation, restitution or some other form of reparations. In this way, a statement taker reported how most people she had taken statements from 'wanted compensation in terms of monetary or resettlement' (interview, Bungoma, 10 July 2011), while requests for assistance emerged as the dominant theme in people's testimony. More specifically, it was common for witnesses at public hearings to emphasise how 'we are behind others [economically] because of what we went through' (Borana elder, TJRC hearing, Isiolo, 9 May 2011) and to request that the government help them recover their livelihoods, pay their medical bills, educate their children and perhaps even institute 'something similar to a Marshall plan' for their area (resident of Garbatulla, TJRC hearing, Isiolo, 9 May 2011). The TJRC also recognised how 'it was not possible for reconciliation to take place when people lived under conditions that continuously reminded them of the suffering they went through' (TJRC vol. 3 2013: 105), while subsequent frustrations are often articulated as a sense that the hearings 'helped people express their feelings', but even after 'telling they don't see any solution or reparation or reward or compensation. So talked, been heard. So what. What next?' (interview, civil society activist, Lodwar, 20 March 2014).

This prioritisation of reparations has also emerged from other investigatory processes. This includes a 2011 ICTJ study that asked victims of various injustices – from historical land injustices to state repression and election-related violence – 'to articulate in their own terms the needs that arise from their victimization' (Robins 2011: 6). The study found that '[v]ictims of violations of all types prioritized issues of livelihood, demonstrating that almost all violations have economic implications for survivors' (Robins 2011: 7; also see AI 2014; HRW 2016). Similarly, the NVSN's petition, which was brought before the National Assembly in December 2015, explicitly called for sufficient finances to be allocated 'for the immediate and effective implementation of the recommendations contained in the [TJRC] report, in particular reparations of victims' (cited by Lynch in *Saturday Nation* 12 December 2015).

This prioritisation is also not unusual. In Peru, for example, 'the absolute majority [of victim-survivors] explicitly justified their participation [in the TRC] with the hope of some concrete redress from the government' (Laplante & Theidon 2007: 240; also Boesten 2013: 93). Similarly, Rosalind Shaw concluded 'that a substantial portion of the victims and survivors who testified [before the Sierra Leonean TRC] had done so in the hope that this would give them access to economic assistance' (2007: 184). George Wachira and Prisca Kamungi found in a study of truth commissions across Africa that, while proponents 'are prone to cite the broad societal gains such as the consolidation of democratic values', 'victims – variously defined – were motivated by more practical and more specifically material considerations' (2010: 5). In turn, one of the most common criticisms of transitional justice efforts is that they have focused too much on issues of truth-telling and/or accountability to the neglect of people's demands for reparations, assistance and real socio-economic change.

However, while victims tend to prioritise reparations, it is clear that the reparations agenda currently proposed in Kenya is likely to be of limited scale and scope, to be introduced in isolation and to be appropriated by the political elite as a means to dampen calls for other forms of justice *and* to simultaneously perform a commitment to victims in a way that will help mobilise support amongst broader constituencies.

In terms of the scope of the proposed RJF, it is currently unclear – if the Fund ever gets off the ground – which kinds of victims would be compensated and by how much. However, suggestions are that it would be limited to victims of election-related violence and perhaps to some iconic examples of excessive state violence – such as the Wagalla massacre and Nyayo House torture victims. However, it is unlikely that the Fund (or something similar) would include victims of other gross bodily integrity rights violations (such as extra-judicial killings) or communities that, according to the TJRC, suffered as a result of economic marginalisation and historical land injustices. At the same time, this focus on financial payments means that the other reparations recommended by the TJRC – such as the rehabilitation of those injured, the recognition of marginalised communities and memorials for various injustices – as well as the other forms of justice recommended, have largely slipped into the background.

This raises the question of failed promises. It also raises questions about whether a possible focus on certain types of victim would be accepted as 'fair' by those who lost out, and whether it might actually exacerbate tensions given a common perception that certain collective injustices have fuelled individual violations. In short, if reparations

> become too focused on, say, the violence that followed the 2007 elections or the abuses committed by police officials against rival ethnic or political groups, then the reparations measures that follow from those mechanisms may end up ignoring the causes and consequences of those periods of violence and episodes of abuse.
>
> (Robins 2011: 9)

This is particularly important when it comes to land given that '[c]lose to 50 percent of statements and memorandum received by the Commission related to or touched on claims over land' (TJRC vol. 1 2013: vii), the NLC has so far failed to address the vast range of land injustices that fall within its mandate and the TJRC saw 'historical grievances over land ... [as] the single most important driver of conflicts and ethnic tension in Kenya' (TJRC vol. 1 2013: vii).

Moreover, while many hope for some form of compensation or restitution as a way to meet their basic needs and to begin to redress violations suffered, it is clear that the reparations envisaged will be minimal, and that few (if any) victims equate justice with money. Indeed, while money may be valued as a means to meet immediate needs, it is usually only regarded as a form of justice – as the TJRC itself recognised – if it involves a level of acknowledgement, accountability or guarantee of non-repetition.

In practice, acknowledgement is often regarded as key in this regard. As one elder explained at a TJRC community forum in Mandera County: 'Reconciliation can be earned when we see the government taking action to acknowledge the truth of what happened ... When the government recognizes the massacred, admits its lies, and takes the right action that victims want, that is when our trust in government will return' (cited in TJRC vol. 2A 2013: 54). Or as the ICTJ's study of victims' demands concluded:

Truth was perceived as being a prerequisite for the delivery of compensation, but this idea was articulated as 'acknowledgment'. In most cases, victims are well-aware of what they and their communities suffered: what they seek from the government is admission of the harm and clarification of the details and the reason for the violation.

(Robins 2011: 22)

In practice, the relationship between compensation and acknowledgement depends on the statements made (or not made) *and* on local interpretations of meaning and intent. For example, in certain circumstances, the payment of money can be regarded as a sign of acknowledgement and accountability. This includes the Somali tradition of 'blood money' – still practised in parts of northern Kenya – where it is those who are responsible for wrongdoing that are meant to pay compensation to those killed (Robins 2011: 48). However, in other contexts, compensation can be interpreted as an alternative to acknowledgement and accountability. One example is the out of court settlement reached between victims of the Mau Mau Emergency and British government in 2013. In the words of the UK Foreign Secretary William Hague:

The British Government recognises that Kenyans were subject to torture and other forms of ill treatment at the hands of the colonial administration. The British government sincerely regrets that these abuses took place ... this settlement provides recognition of the suffering and injustice that took place ... it is my hope that the agreement now reached will receive wide support, *will help draw a line under these events*, and will support reconciliation. *We continue to deny liability* on behalf of the Government and British taxpayers today for the actions of the colonial administration in respect of the claims, and indeed the courts have made no finding of liability against the Government in this case.

(Cited in *Pambazuka News* 11 June 2013; emphasis added)

This statement shows how reparation can function as a form of redress, but also as a simultaneous attempt at closure or an attempt 'to placate victim demands for criminal justice and regulate the range of political and historical meanings with which the crimes of the past are endowed and through which they are interpreted and acted upon' (Moon 2012).

In addition to the contested symbolism of financial payments, many victims also push for symbolic reparations in the form of public memorials. For some, this is again intimately intertwined with demands for compensation. One example is the Wagalla Massacre Foundation, which has lobbied for a memorial with the names of those killed inscribed, at least in part, because they believe that this will help to identify victims for the purposes of individual compensation, and thus minimise the number of potentially fraudulent claims (interview, Nairobi, 29 September 2016).[1] In contrast, some who call for the basement of Nyayo House in downtown Nairobi to be turned into a museum have already received financial compensation for torture through the courts. In this context, a museum is not about access to money, but the creation of a space in which the past can be acknowledged and discussed so that people can learn from it (interview, Nairobi, 5 October 2016). Or, in other words, the demand is for a 'site of conscience', or a memorial that would 'make a specific commitment to democratic engagement through programs that stimulate dialogue on pressing social issues today and that provide opportunities for public involvement in those issues' (Brett, Bickford, Sevenko & Rios 2007: 1). The implication: even though many victims demand and seek financial compensation, payment of the same is not usually regarded as closure – even if governments may hope otherwise – but as part of a broader process of redress.

This assessment is supported by the fact that most victims and victims' groups seek multi-polar redress. This is evident from those who have brought cases before the national or regional courts. For example, in

---

[1] KNCHR and GiZ actually built a memorial to the Wagalla massacre in Wajir in 2014, but it was soon destroyed in protests over the fencing of the site amidst claims of land grabbing by the new county government (*NEP Journal* 30 April 2014).

a case brought by victims of sexual violence during the 2007–8 post-election violence, which was ongoing at the time of this writing, petitioners sought 'a public apology from the government for their failures to protect citizens during the post-election violence; adequate compensation, psycho-social support and other reparation for survivors; and investigations of cases of sexual and gender based violence and prosecutions of those suspected of responsibility' (AI 2014: 45). In short, while victims have different understandings of justice, it is usually equated with a range of elements – from rehabilitation and restitution to acknowledgement, guarantees of non-repetition and punishment – and most frequently with reparations and accountability (Backer 2010).

Certainly, understandings of justice often include punishment of those deemed most responsible. For example, when victims were asked what they understood by 'justice' in 2011, '49 percent of respondents said prosecutions', while, '[w]hen asked explicitly whether anyone should be prosecuted for the violations they suffered, 82 percent of victims supported prosecutions, either of the actual perpetrators or of those who directed or organized the violations' (Robins 2011: 51). The study concluded that prosecutions are valued as a form of punishment, but also as a form of acknowledgement and deterrence (Robins 2011: 23). Similarly, a study of post-election sexual violence victims found that they perceived 'the prosecution of perpetrators as both a reparative and preventive measure, which would give them the satisfaction that sexual crimes have been acknowledged by the government and provide assurance against ... repetition' (HRW 2016: 78).

At the same time, some oppose prosecutions on the basis that they will likely fail due to insufficient evidence or corrupt courts, because they are divisive or are likely to target the wrong people, and/or to insist that it is better to 'move on'. As one peace activist in Mt Elgon explained, her organisation emphasises 'forgiveness and forget' because SLDF members 'were jailed but then released because judges saying no evidence' (interview, Cheptais, 25 February 2011). In her opinion, if you 'take someone to court ... after jail, they return, and recount [their trauma], and still revenge ... prefer that the community itself through leaders organise the communities to meet, share talks, hear what victims say, and what perpetrators will say, and get a way forward' (interview, Cheptais, 10 August 2012).

Clearly such sentiments are informed by local realities. However, they have also been fostered by the political elite who seek to present prosecutions as impossible and unhelpful. Given this context, the offer of limited reparations is not only potentially problematic because of its limited scope and scale, and because it is offered in isolation, but because it is explicitly introduced as an alternative to punishment and accountability. As a result, it potentially offers another familiar performance whereby a series of victims will receive some financial compensation, but no-one will acknowledge any guilt or be held to account (Robins 2011). Examples of this precedent include the Nyayo House torture victims who have received financial compensation through the courts (KHRC 2009), and the small payouts, patches of land and new houses that were given to some of those displaced during the 2007–8 post-election violence (Lynch 2009). While such payments are welcomed in the context of great hardship, they are also problematic. At one level, they seek closure through the payment of money to the neglect of any other form of justice. At another level, they encourage survivors to present themselves as victims so as to access resources that are distributed by state elites, who then maintain a hierarchical patron-client relationship of exchange.

Finally, such performances are often aimed not so much at the victims, but at a broader constituency. This was clearly evident, for example, in the assistance given by the Kenyan government to IDPs between the 2007 and 2013 elections when limited compensation packages failed to meet IDP demands, but the act of assistance helped to calm complaints amongst Kibaki's Kikuyu co-ethnics of how the government had abandoned its people (Lynch 2009). It is similarly possible, and indeed likely, that plans set out for reparations by the Jubilee government are less about victim demands and more about a performance of a particular kind of state and regime that is committed to reconciliation, peacebuilding and inter-communal cohesion for a broader domestic and international audience.

9.4 Conclusions: Of Closure and Commencement

It is how you follow through on the information that is exposed [by a truth commission] that will determine the project's success.

(Archbishop Tutu on Tunisia's Truth and Dignity Commission)[2]

---

[2] www.ohchr.org/EN/NewsEvents/Pages/TakingOnThePast.aspx <last accessed 13 November 2016>.

By the time of the 2017 elections, MPs had failed to discuss the TJRC report and recommendations, while the executive had offered a blanket apology and promised limited reparations. In so doing, Kenya is different to most transitional justice contexts where the complaint is usually that truth-telling and accountability are prioritised to the neglect of reparations. In Kenya, one sees the opposite. The common theme, however, is the way in which elites can appropriate transitional justice mechanisms for their ends – in this context, as a means to dampen calls for other forms of justice *and* to simultaneously perform a commitment to victims in an effort to mobilise support amongst broader constituencies.

It is too early to say whether the government's efforts to gain closure will be successful, or, as civil society activists hope, that a discussion of reparations will open the door to other forms of justice. However, from the lessons of history and comparative contexts, such efforts are unlikely to satisfy victim demands in the short to medium term. Instead, it seems likely that the TJRC report and its recommendations will be used for the foreseeable future by individuals, communities and politicians as part of the archives that they can deploy to support their claims for assistance and redress, or to mobilise support behind the same.

As a result, the suggestion is not that CSOs have been wrong to take an instrumental and strategic response to reparations. Indeed, this was the only approach that was likely to gain any political traction during the time period in question. Instead, it is to highlight the immediate implications and the possible dangers of it, and the ways in which – at least in the short term – it offers another familiar performance, whereby people are encouraged to present themselves as victims in exchange for assistance, while the possibility of accountability is rejected and a culture of impunity is upheld.

PART III
Familiar Performances

> Before turning the first page of a popular novel, or watching the first scene of a theatrical performance, the 'reader' already occupies a culturally specific receptive position, and each instance of interpretation is likely to be informed by shared preconceptions about the function of literature.
>
> (Newell 1997: 390)

So far, the analysis has focused on some of the efforts introduced in the wake of the post-election violence of 2007–8 to try and ensure that mass violence remained in the country's past – namely, peacebuilding, the ICC's intervention and the TJRC. All these processes fell far short of stated goals and initial expectations, as peacebuilding came to prioritise individual responsibility for non-violence in ways that downplayed structural factors and strengthened the political establishment (Chapter 2), and transitional justice mechanisms failed to perform a persuasive break between a violent and unjust past, a new present and likely futures (Chapters 3–9).

In short, the problem is that such interventions are not received and interpreted in a vacuum, but are read through people's understandings of contexts, political dynamics and likely trajectories; they are open to politicisation; they tend to downplay the myriad and complex ways in which the past actually persists and the future infringes on the now; and they can inadvertently reinforce the status quo. With such realities in mind, the analysis in this volume reveals how – in the context of a continuity of political leadership and limited transition – peacebuilding and transitional justice efforts in Kenya fostered a sense (at least in the short term) of familiarity and once-againness. As an emphasis on the need for peace, unity and cohesion became reminiscent of the approach of presidents Jomo Kenyatta and Moi and many other nationalist leaders around the world. The ICC was reframed as a performance of neo-colonialism, injustice and impunity in ways that echoed other contexts in which international criminal trials have relied on their assumed moral authority to try and enforce state compliance, and states have drawn on histories of colonialism, a sense of tragedy and need for unity to counter-shame such external interventions (Chapter 3). The TJRC in turn was widely dismissed as just another commission of inquiry that would be relegated to the archive's dusty shelves – the body undermined by a credibility crisis around the chairman, a long and unimpressive history of commissions of inquiry, limited media coverage, parallel ICC investigations, little in the way of new truths and no perpetrator confessions, and an overwhelming sense of political continuity (Chapters 4, 5 and 8).

The analysis in this volume also reveals how commissions of inquiry continue to be used to perform a state's capacity to establish authoritative investigations that it can subsequently undermine and ignore (Chapters 4 and 9), as establishment elites display an ongoing ability to draw upon the protection of the state, and peers and co-ethnics try to protect themselves from investigation and prosecution at both the domestic and international level (Chapter 3 and 8). As a result, widespread and ongoing suffering and victimhood gained recognition (Chapters 6 and 7) and reparations were promised (Chapter 9) while acknowledgement or accountability remained elusive in the Kenyan context. Instead, a culture of impunity gained regular performance (Chapters 3, 8 and 9), while processes inadvertently reinforced the salience of ethnic identities (Chapters 3 and 6) and familiar gender roles. The latter was characterised by a representation of women as innocent, suffering but resilient and men simultaneously juxtaposed as political animals who struggle (sometimes violently) against both the state and neighbouring communities (Chapter 7).

In making these arguments, the analysis in this volume underscored the difficulties of staging an effective performance of transition – with popular perceptions shaped by the work of a particular institution, but also by people's understandings of them. The latter, in turn, influenced by an understanding of what was likely to occur, and thus by media coverage and public discussions; the broader political context; a sense of what had changed and remained the same and ideas of likely and feared futures. When taken together with the inherent impossibility of trying to render a violent and unjust history quickly 'past' or absent, this analysis offers an important critique of transitional justice and its increasingly ambitious mandates, and demands that more thought be given to when such mechanisms are introduced: how, why and with what likely effect.

At the same time, the TJRC was shown to have left a report, or documentary archive, of injustices suffered and wide-ranging recommendations, which are being used, and may long be used, to support efforts to push for reform and different forms of justice. For this reason, it may well be that – unlike the South African TRC where public hearings proved more important than the final report - for the TJRC, the final report will prove to be the Commission's most important legacy (Chapter 9).

Finally, efforts to achieve transitional justice were shown to provide an analytic microcosm with respect to state–society, ethnic, gender, class and generational relations (cf. Cohen & Atieno Odhiambo 2004). In this way, people's decisions about which stories to share with the TJRC, and how to present them; the TJRC's decisions about the selection of witnesses for public hearings and limited interest of media editors tells us much about popular perceptions of salient and hearable issues in Kenya. Similarly, the structure, findings and recommendations of the final report tell an interested observer a great deal about the basis and perpetuation of various political identities and associated claims, such as the political salience of ethnic identities and understandings of gender, while performances of a protected elite provide critical insights into the basis of popular political scepticism and an embedded culture of impunity.

However, relatively little has yet been said about reconciliation, which was ostensibly one of the principal goals of both peacebuilding and transitional justice. The final chapter addresses this gap by looking at debates around reconciliation in the context of pervasive peace messaging and failed attempts to secure justice. In so doing, the discussion highlights how a notion of reconciliation as peace and cohesion has been used to try and suppress, rather than address, divisions and frustrations; it proposes an alternative understanding of political or agnostic reconciliation. The implication is that transitional justice mechanisms should be less ambitious. This is to protect against the unrealistic expectations, frustrated hopes, perverse politicisation and reinforcement of existing power relations discussed. It also highlights how a call to 'look backwards to reach forwards' can facilitate too rapid and politicised an assertion of closure that downplays the ways in which the present is a 'broken middle of time' (Schaap 2003: 5) in which people will inevitably disagree about which aspects of the past need to be addressed and how; the details of preferred presents and futures and the ways in which certain trajectories can best be encouraged and others be guarded against.

10 | *Performed Ruptures*
Whither Reconciliation?

> Reconciliation involves the rebuilding, or building, of a relationship in the wake of tension or alienation, often due to actual or perceived wrongdoing.
> (Govier & Verwoerd 2002: 185)

Reconciliation is generally considered to consist of the building or rebuilding of 'good' relations between individuals, groups or nations following a period of estrangement, tension or conflict (for example, Govier & Verwoerd 2002; Lederach 1997; Schaap 2008; Villa-Vicencio 2000). However, while this abstract conceptualisation is broadly accepted, there is far less agreement about what constitutes 'good relations' and how these are best achieved and maintained over time.

For proponents of transitional justice, reconciliation is generally understood to be a long and difficult process that requires truth and a semblance of justice. In this way, the TJRC understood reconciliation as a long-term struggle that required the restoration of good relations at different levels – from an individual's accommodation of 'their situation and circumstances' to the restoration of social relations within and between communities (TJRC vol. 3 2013: 86) – through truth-telling and justice. As a result, the Commission did 'not claim to have achieved reconciliation for the nation', but instead hoped 'that by uncovering the truth, providing a forum for individuals to share their experiences and by providing some accountability, the Commission will have placed the nation on a path to further reconciliation and national cohesion and unity' (TJRC vol. 3 2013: 84).

This idea of reconciliation as a long and difficult process is also a common theme in the academic literature, which tends to present reconciliation not as an event or discrete endpoint, but as an ideal state that one can only ever work towards (for example, Govier & Verwoerd 2002: 182; Lederach 1997: 66). However, in the political realm, various actors – and particularly self-professed nationalist politicians in post-conflict settings – tend to talk of reconciliation as a political imperative (Lynch 2015a). This is certainly true in Kenya where, during the 2013 election campaign and their first term in office, the Jubilee Alliance often cast reconciliation as essential for stability and development, and as something that they would achieve (or had achieved) and were committed to uphold against those who might seek to undermine it. In this vein, and in the wake of terrorist attacks in Mpeketoni in Lamu County in June 2014, President Kenyatta emphasised:

My Deputy and I undertook to make sure that the country will never go the route of ethnic division and political violence. I reiterate that Kenya will not go that route again! ... Reckless rhetoric, incitement and negative propaganda do not constitute responsible leadership. They will not be tolerated ... Fellow Kenyans, We have been victims of terrorism in the past and the threat of terror continues to hang over us ... I ask every one of us to reflect deeply on what each must do to keep our country safe, and to be our brother's and sister's keeper.[1]

In this context, efforts to perform rupture or transition through the provision of justice were usurped by the promise of a more immediate temporal shift through a new political alliance that would bring previously warring communities together (Lynch 2014a); a performance of modernity and promise of development through an increased emphasis on technology and big infrastructure projects[2] and by religious notions of cleansing and renewal (Deacon 2015).

Aspects of this politics have been discussed in previous chapters, and this chapter moves on to look at some common understandings of reconciliation and at some of the implications of this volume's analysis for the future of transitional justice. In so doing, the chapter sets out three broad approaches to reconciliation: good relations as the restoration of trust or friendship, a politicised insistence on cohesion and unity and a political search for common ground amidst an acceptance of disagreement. The discussion is far from exhaustive. Instead, the aim is simply to highlight how a common notion of reconciliation as the

[1] A copy of the public statement was posted on www.facebook.com/myuhurukenyatta/posts/860979340597287 <last accessed 10 September 2016>.
[2] Henry K. Rotich, 11 June 2015, Budget Statement for the fiscal year 2015/2016. Available at http://repository.eac.int/bitstream/handle/11671/356/Budget%20speech%20Kenya%202015-16.pdf?sequence=1&isAllowed= <last accessed 6 March 2018>.

restoration of trust in other people's motivations is ultimately anti-political, and how it also lends itself to the politicisation of reconciliation, whereby the idea often morphs from an ideal state into a political directive.

This chapter supports a third approach to reconciliation of political or agonistic reconciliation, which – drawing on the work of Andrew Schaap (2003; 2004; 2006; 2008) and Leigh Payne (2008) – understands reconciliation as a state of non-violent coexistence in which people can trust that their views and interests will be considered, and that one will retain an ability to speak and be heard. This approach stems from the assumption that, due to the impossibility of achieving fully harmonious relations in the political arena and centrality of difference and conflict to 'normal' politics (Ost 2004: 230), one should not simply assert, or insist, that cohesion exists. Instead, it is argued that one should seek 'contentious coexistence' understood as a 'conflictual dialogic approach to democracy' that 'emphasizes the reality and importance of competition over ideas and conflict over values and goals' (Payne 2008: 3). According to this approach, acceptance of pluralism provides space for different opinions to be aired in ways that invigorate political debate, motivate oversight, enhance accountability and guard against the exclusion of less powerful voices (Mouffe 2000). In short, restoration or establishment of good, healthy or normal relations is understood *not* as cohesion and harmony per se, but as peaceful and lively disagreement and debate between potentially incompatible political outlooks. This analysis – and, in particular, the danger of easy assertions of closure – then feeds into the final section, which provides an overview of some of the implications of the book's principal arguments for transitional justice.

10.1 Reconciliation as Substantive Friendship, Unity or Contentious Coexistence

Reconciliation ... implies the restoration and sometimes the establishment of a hitherto non-existent relationship of trust. This takes time.

(Villa-Vicencio 2000: 208)

Reconciliation is generally considered to consist of the building or rebuilding of 'good' relations between individuals, groups or nations with the quality of relations often evaluated according to the levels of trust that can be said to exist. In this way, John Borneman presents reconciliation as a 'project of departure from violence' where, '[t]o agree to a present that does not repeat requires both to create a "sense of ending" – a radical break or rupture from existing relations – and to create a "sense of beginning" – a departure into new relations of affinity marked not by cyclical violence but by trust and care' (2002: 282).

However, while the idea of restoring trust runs across much of the literature on, and public discussions around, reconciliation, the details of what this would actually entail varies considerably. At least three broad characterisations can be discerned: (i) substantive friendship where people look out for each other's interests; (ii) an insistence on cohesion lest chaos descend and (iii) a commitment to discussion and non-violence, and mutual respect for different opinions and goals. This section briefly discusses these approaches to reconciliation as the restoration of trust and argues that the third should be promoted. In short, while the latter helps to foster meaningful democracy, the first is attractive but inherently apolitical and tends to morph into the second, which encourages the delegitimisation of criticism and dissent.

According to the first approach, the kind of trust that people can place in others following a period of conflict or alienation, and thus the degree of reconciliation that can be said to have been achieved, varies from a high point of substantive friendship to meaningful cooperation to a mere expectation of non-violent coexistence, where individuals, communities or nations 'are able to live alongside each other, barely tolerating each other, not working together, not having common goals or setting themselves common tasks, but nevertheless having a fairly confident expectation that the others will not kill them' (Govier & Verwoerd 2002: 195). For proponents of this approach, and indeed for proponents of all three approaches to reconciliation discussed in this chapter, '[t]o be worthy of the name, reconciliation must involve more than non-violent co-existence' (Govier 2002: 143; also see Lederach 1997: 30). However, for those who point to a sliding scale between substantive friendship and non-violent coexistence, trust is understood as 'an attitude of confident expectation ... that the person, persons, or groups trusted will act, in the context in question, in a competent and acceptably motivated way, so that despite vulnerability, the trusting person or persons will not be harmed' (Govier &

Verwoerd 2002: 183 and 185). To think of this another way, reconciliation as trust that others will act decently towards us allows for a sliding scale of relations. At one end lies an unstable reconciliation, where a minimal but mutual trust of not being violently attacked by the 'other' is associated with Galtung's (1969) negative peace. In this situation, there is calm but strained inter-communal relations and contested demands for social justice. At the other end sits reconciliation as a firm expectation that 'others' will not only restrain from harm, but can be trusted to look after and promote one's interests. The latter fostered by Galtung's ideal state of positive peace (Chapter 2).

For proponents of this approach, substantive reconciliation is generally understood to be a process by which 'final achievement is, in a sense, always beyond our grasp' (de Gruchy 2002: 28), since the 'turnings around' involved require considerable time and political will, and have historically proven impossible to achieve across the board. The reason is twofold.

First, a shift from a state of mistrust to one of substantive trust in the behaviour of others is difficult at any level and is generally deemed most likely when the offender or relevant authority has apologised, those adversely affected have forgiven, a semblance of justice has been provided and both sides recognise mutual obligations and a level of interdependence (for example, see Govier 2002; Theidon 2006; Tutu 1999). This contingent understanding is evident, for example, in John de Gruchy's argument that '[t]ruth serves the cause of reconciliation and justice only when it leads to a genuine *metanoia*, that is, a turning around, a breaking with an unjust past, and a moving towards a new future' (2002: 164). Or in Barbara Misztal's argument of how, 'forgiveness, as a forward-looking act aiming at bringing reconciliation ... is achieved by offering trust for the sake of establishing a new relation based on mutual recognition of each other within a context of justice and a respect for the past' (2011: 39–40).

In stressing the importance of forgiveness for reconciliation, most analysts emphasise the need for bilateral rather than unilateral forgiveness – the idea being that to regard a 'request for forgiveness as sincere and a commitment to repentance and reform as credible is to *trust him*' (Govier 2002: 46; emphasis in original). In contrast, 'unilateral forgiveness' is not considered equal to reconciliation, although by extending goodwill towards the other it may inspire remorse and be 'deemed *therapeutic* for the victim' (Govier 2002: 64; emphasis in original).

However, even a sincere apology is not usually deemed sufficient for reconciliation since forgiveness also 'requires the overcoming of resentment', which can be understood as 'the passion of justice denied' (Govier 2002: 50 and 52). In turn, it is generally believed that if a wrongdoer has had to face up to the suffering inflicted through punishment – or has had to pay compensation for the wrong done or been restored into relevant relationships – then they will be less likely to re-offend, and victims will be more likely to forgive (Theidon 2006; Tutu 1999). Finally, an ability to trust someone else's motivations and actions is deemed easier when people have mutual obligations and where there is a high capacity for internal vigilance, since this will increase the costs of deceit and transgression (Theidon 2006). Clearly such developments are difficult to achieve in practice and cannot be imposed; they take time and are likely to only ever be partial.

Second, trust is a dynamic relationship of degrees that can be bolstered or undermined by new developments and interpretations. Take the example of a cheating spouse: the husband/wife may come to trust his or her partner again, but this trust (if it is not to be naïve) will be undermined by suspicions or evidence of further infidelity (Govier 2002). In turn, community leaders may publicly forgive another community, but years later – for reasons of political opportunism, fear or frustration – they may choose to recall the problematic history in question and the role of the 'others'. As a result, reconciliation as the re-establishment of trust in people's behaviour and motivations is often impossible to achieve even between family members, friends or neighbours and is always subjective, dynamic and unstable.

Nevertheless, reconciliation in this sense is clearly an attractive ideal, which fits with common understandings of the term. However, in addition to the difficulty of achieving such reconciliation in practice, there is also an inherent danger that, if taken too far, it becomes inherently anti-political. The reason is that trust in others – who are everywhere motivated by different values, vested interests and goals to one extent or another – to protect and promote your interests can and should only ever be partial. In short, 'life together is often one in which genuinely good things conflict' (Crocker 2002: 529), and what appears as 'right' or 'just' to one party may look 'wrong' or 'unjust' to others. For example, land claims of 'local' communities may be incompatible with those of existing users or titleholders, and different communities may claim overlapping land rights (Boone 2012; Kanyinga 2000).

Similarly, those borne into privilege may emphasise a simple justice in rewards for hard work, while those more cognisant of existing inequalities may see more justice in efforts to enhance the opportunities of the initially disadvantaged (cf. Rawls 1972). Even in relatively equitable societies, there will be debates about how to distribute expenditure between different budgets – for example, between environmental protection, health, education, infrastructure, communications, foreign aid and defence. As a result, contention, debate and conflict ultimately lie at the heart of 'normal' relations and politics (Ost 2004: 230).

As a result, to suggest that individuals, groups and parties can trust each other to look after and promote each other's interests is inherently anti-political (cf. Ferguson 1990). This is particularly important given that reconciliation can often appear in politics, or can be presented, as essential. Thus, while academics tend to speak of reconciliation as an ideal state that one can only ever approach, it is often presented in the political realm (especially in nationalist or patriotic politics) as something that does or should exist. Indeed, at one point or another, citizens around the world have been encouraged to reconcile and recognise their shared interests, for example, in unity, stability and development, and to accept the 'benevolent' (cf. Desrosiers & Thomson 2011 on post-genocide Rwanda), historically earned (Kriger 2006; Ranger 2004 on post-liberation Zimbabwe) and/or democratically acquired (Jackson 2005 on post–9/11 America) leadership of an incumbent regime. The appeal of such narratives in the face of real or exaggerated security threats is understandable, with citizens often feeling that they face a stark choice between violence, chaos and economic collapse *or* peace, stability and economic development. As one interviewee noted in the runup to the 2013 election in Kenya: the Kikuyu and Kalenjin communities have 'opted to come together, forget the past, and do the necessary so violence doesn't recur' (interview, Kikuyu peace activist from Burnt Forest, Eldoret, 10 December 2012).

However, the practical implication of a political *insistence* on cohesion and unity is a curtailment of dissent, the delegitimisation of political opposition and rearticulation of frustrations through alternative channels. The reason is twofold. First, given different interests and goals, an invocation of the 'common good' inevitably serves to stifle debate and 'legitimate a particular order in which the interests of some are privileged over those of others' (Schaap 2008: 249). In such contexts, 'peace' becomes a 'productive political violence' that pushes 'towards specific possible futures, while cutting off others' (Branch 2014: 609).

Second, efforts to gag criticism tend to 'drive strongly held, but silenced, views underground and beyond the scrutiny and judgement of public debate' (Payne 2008: 291). In short, while some forms of speech (such as hate speech and incitement) require prohibition, for other kinds of speech, 'democracies benefit most from unfettering them, compelling them to compete with better – more democratic – ideas' (Payne 2008: 291–292).

This is evident in Kenya, where an emphasis on reconciliation as peace and cohesion in the runup to the 2013 election was understandable and broadly popular given the memories of the 2007–8 post-election violence and upcoming election in a context where no high-level perpetrators of the violence had apologised or been prosecuted; there had been little justice for victims of the crisis or earlier injustices and the same political elite remained in power. This context fostered a preoccupation with repetition in which 'being peaceful' became a 'good' and 'patriotic' thing to do. However, the flipside was that peace and reconciliation were increasingly cast not as an ideal state approached as a result of a long-term process requiring various interventions and a conducive political context, but as a personal duty. In turn, while an associated peace narrative helped to prevent violence during the 2013 election, it also emphasised individual responsibility to the relative neglect of structural problems and institutional reform and was simultaneously used to delegitimise dissent and protest into the first term of the Jubilee government, as the edicts of peace, order and stability continued to be both a moral campaign and a political strategy – or both an understanding of what was 'right' and a tool of power (Chapter 2). This negative peace has also proved precarious, as, in the face of another disputed election in 2017, a successful presidential election petition and a 'fresh' presidential election on 26 October 2017, many opposition supporters rejected the government's call to 'accept' the election and 'move on'; instead they backed their leaders in a game of brinkmanship that (among other things) involved an enforced boycott of the 'fresh' polls and the unofficial public inauguration of Odinga as the 'People's President' on 30 January 2018 (Lynch in *Saturday Nation* 10 February 2018).

Yet, there is another approach to reconciliation which rejects the idea that it is reasonable for people to trust 'others' to protect their interests in the political realm, or that all 'patriotic' people should unite behind what establishment elites have decided is in the best interests of stability and development. This third approach draws upon an agonistic understanding of democracy, which holds that 'difference, disagreement and discord, directed through channels that guard against a ressentiment revitalize the political field' (Hirsch 2012: 4). In short, agonism holds that certain forms of political conflict – notably disagreement and open debate rather than intimidation or violence – are inevitable in plural societies where the 'objective of unanimity and homogeneity' is always 'fictitious and based on acts of exclusion' (Mouffe 2000: 19). According to this approach:

What is distinctive about democratic politics is not that it seeks to resolve this inevitable conflict... Rather it aims to mediate the conflict in such a way that the other is perceived not as an 'enemy to be destroyed' (or excluded from the political community) but as an 'adversary', i.e. one with whom we disagree vehemently but whose right to contest the terms of our political association we respect. (Schaap 2006: 268)

This emphasis on disagreement and debate distinguishes agonism from a deliberative or participatory approach, which places consensus building and informed participation at the heart of democratic practice (Fishkin 2009). The reason is that '[w]hile participation involves partaking in something, a decision-making process or a discussion, by simply having a say or making a more notable contribution, mobilisation [which is central to a successful agonistic democracy] involves action for or against something' (Tambakaki 2011: 576).

Agonistic democracy is thus characterised by contentious coexistence in which disagreement is embraced as a 'fundamental pillar of democracy' (Payne 2008: 3 and 4). It therefore supports an alternative approach to reconciliation, where 'reconciliation is not about restoring a moral order but initiating a new political order. When conceived in these terms, reconciliation is not about settling accounts but remains an unsettling experience since it seeks to enact a radical break with the social order that underpinned the violence of the past' (Schaap 2006: 272). In other words, 'agnostic reconciliation' is 'predicated on an awareness that community is always not yet ... [such that i]nstead of looking to politics to secure a common identity, reconciliation would depend on founding and sustaining a space for politics within which the emergence of a common identity is an ever present possibility' (Schaap 2004: 538; also Moon 2004).

On the sliding scale of friendship or trust outlined earlier, this form of reconciliation aims for meaningful cooperation rather than non-violent coexistence or full friendship, and while it values agreement and cohesion where and when that emerges, it does not *insist* on these outcomes. It thus supports Alex Boraine's argument that 'reconciliation ought to be viewed as an exchange of ideas in a climate of mutual respect and peaceful coexistence' (2000b: 77).

As an approach that places debate above consensus, agnostic or political reconciliation is liable to be dismissed by some as an inherently un-African concept – with African culture sometimes cast as a realm where unity and consensus is valued over that which creates divisions (Kenyatta 1961; Nyerere 1966), or at least where 'primary emphasis [is placed] on corporate group needs and loyalty', in contrast to an assumed European model of community where 'great stress [is placed] on "individual" interests and values' (Owusu 1992: 376). However, this critique is weak for several reasons. First, the idea of 'African communitarianism' on which it rests, is associated with intra- rather than inter-communal politics. The latter is often characterised historically not by consensus building, but by tension, migration and absorption. Second, pre-colonial or colonial accounts of intra-communal relations reveal a more complex reality than decision-making by consensus building in which community members often disagreed with each other along socio-economic, generational, gender or other lines, and intra-communal decisions were often limited to an older male economic elite, or group of elders, with some voices – such as of those of chiefs or spiritual leaders – carrying more weight than others (Berman & Lonsdale 1992; Peterson 2012; Spear & Waller 1993). Third, while people can learn from pre-colonial pasts, they also have to act in contexts that have been shaped by more contemporary histories – from colonialism's divide and rule to the biased patron-client relations of the post-colonial period and mistrust borne from periods of conflict and authoritarianism. Finally, it is clear that multi-party democracy in Africa is the result of demands from within, rather than simply imposed from without, and that the majority of citizens remain committed to this system as the best way of structuring national politics (Cheeseman 2015; Murunga & Nasong'o 2007).

Contentious coexistence is nevertheless a difficult thing to achieve in practice, and where the political will to embrace such politics is lacking, it is understandable that many choose to 'be reconciled' and to 'be peaceful'. This choice appears particularly prudent where experiences, memories, histories and fears of violence pervade and there are real tensions between 'peace' and 'justice' – for example, where a threat of future prosecution keeps leaders away from peace negotiations or encourages them to incite further violence. In such contexts, protest, disagreement and criticism may feel like an unnecessary luxury that could too easily descend into incitement and disorder. However, this does not mean that *if* there was some political buy-in, that contentious coexistence would not be a better alternative, or that the choice of unity does not involve a trade-off with justice that ultimately reinforces the status quo and temporarily suppresses, rather than addresses, differences and frustrations.

If accepted, the idea of agonistic or political reconciliation also has significant implications for transitional justice. If the aim is to reach not a consensus but an agreement on how people will learn to disagree, and to respect each other's rights to speak and be heard, then efforts to address the past need not necessarily render it 'dead', but instead simply quieten its more divisive and threatening aspects. According to this understanding, transitional justice can be less ambitious, which – as the final section makes clear – fits with the overall argument of this book, namely, that transitional *should* be less ambitious, that it should be more cognisant of what it can realistically achieve and that it should not be considered as a tool to be applied to any context in which some desire a transition from authoritarianism and conflict to a more inclusive and democratic politics.

10.2 Conclusions: Transitional Justice as Political Performances

Performances seldom radically change perceptions that already exist in society; instead, they tend to reinforce them.

(Payne 2009: 240)

The idea that one can 'look backwards to reach forwards' rests in large part on an ability to provide an effective performance of change. However, as Leigh Payne has argued, audiences 'are not passive or uncritical consumers of a particular performance'. Instead, while 'the staging of the performance and the perpetrator's text may attempt to manipulate emotions, audiences bring to the performance their own understandings of the world and the place that this performance plays in it' (Payne 2009: 240). In turn, transitional justice mechanisms are easily undermined by technical shortcomings (such as limited finance, ill-considered mandates and poor leadership), but also by institutional environments (Bosire 2006); people's understandings of what has happened, is happening, and will likely happen; limited political will; concerted efforts to reinterpret their work and by the ways in which the past persists and possible futures infringe on the now. Moreover, the more transformative a mechanism seeks to be, the stronger will be the likely political backlash and limited nature of political will (Applebaum & Mawby 2016: 51). As a result, transitional justice efforts are not always helpful and can inadvertently (and sometimes intentionally) help to reinforce existing schisms and power relations, and be used to legitimise the status quo.

Kenya provides an excellent example of the difficulties of staging an effective performance of transition in the absence of substantive political change. The post-election violence ended with a power-sharing agreement and formation of a coalition government, which was characterised by a 'politics of collusion' that served to postpone conflict rather than to resolve it (Cheeseman & Tendi 2010: 203). In turn, while the 2010 Constitution was meant to be transformative, by the time Kenyans returned to the polls in 2017, there was clearly much continuity amidst change. National politics was still dominated by the same politicians or their sons as well as by shifting political alliances that were 'playing to win' (Hornsby 2012: 786). Ethnic identities remained politically salient (Lynch 2014a); public confidence in key institutions varied according to events and people's positionality (Harrington & Manji 2015; Shah 2015); police reforms had stalled (Osse 2016) and extra-judicial killings increased (Jones, Ramakrishnan & Wangui 2017; van Stapele 2016). Even the most substantive change – that of the devolution of significant power and resources to forty-seven new county governments – was associated with much continuity. Thus, while there had been a clear decentralisation of power and resources, and new governors were able to collectively protect themselves against the centre (Cheeseman, Lynch & Willis 2016), the central state had maintained a parallel administration in the form of the National Administration (Hassan 2015), leaders continued to mobilise support through patronage and the protection of community interests (Carrier & Kochore 2014; Chome 2015; Cornell & D'Arcy 2014; Willis &

Chome 2014), corruption had been localised (D'Arcy & Cornell 2016) and inter-communal tensions had been exacerbated in some areas (Cheeseman, Lynch & Willis 2016). In this context of continuity amidst change, it was perhaps unsurprising that transitional justice efforts met with a lack of political will, intransigence and direct opposition (Hansen 2013; Mueller 2014b), and that political elites, the media and general public did not readily accept the narratives presented and the transition staged.

Moreover, while transitional justice tends to describe 'crimes as belonging to the "past" in the chronological sense ... this is often more wish than reality' (Bevernage 2012: 86). In reality, and as highlighted in Chapter 6, the past is persistent and present in the ghosts of lives, loves and opportunities lost; in the continuous or repetitive nature of some harms; through the experientially rooted fears or popular angst regarding both imminent and more distant futures; the ways in which past violations can motivate future wrongs (either as a means to wreak revenge, protect against further harms, or to regain status and self-esteem) and through the ways in which past experiences shape narratives of injustice, which – due in large part to the pain, anger, fear, hatred and other emotions that they carry – can be politically useful and purposefully kept alive as a way to lay claims or to mobilise support.

The implication is that transitional justice mechanisms – as temporary bodies with restricted mandates – can only make a limited contribution to a shift in people's relationship with time even in relatively conducive political environments. This is important since the idea that one can 'look backwards to reach forwards' often downplays such complexities and converts the past's persistent, and the future's intrusive, nature into personalised trauma that can be addressed through Freudian-style talk therapy, punitive justice or acknowledgement. This is problematic as it encourages a tendency to focus on the individual or collective psyche and the need to deal with personal trauma through catharsis, forgiveness and reconciliation, to the relative neglect of power relations and contested futures.

The idea that transitional justice mechanisms can achieve truth, justice and reconciliation within a limited timeframe also often goes hand-in-hand with a sense that once the past has been 'confronted', it is obvious what a desirable shared future would look like. This is problematic not only because it is unrealistic, but because the notion of a limited transitional period, particularly when it is accompanied with the aim of national cohesion, can be used to facilitate a politicised assertion of closure, which excludes those who do not buy into the absence of the past, the newness of the present or the desirability of imagined futures.

The argument is not that the ideas or approaches of transitional justice should be abandoned. On the contrary, they can potentially make an important contribution to a sense of ending or change through both their tangible outcomes and performative effects. Instead, it is to call for greater recognition to be given to the extent to which transitional justice's constrained capacities are contingent upon persuasive performances and broader socio-economic, political and historic contexts; and for transitional justice to be both less ambitious in its aims and to guard against the promise of too rapid an assertion of closure. At one level, this is important in order to protect against an overemphasis on healing to the neglect of structures, and to manage expectations. However, if one adopts a political or agnostic notion of reconciliation, it is also important as a means to guard against the reinterpretation of a need to 'look backwards to reach forwards' as a means to insist that people trust others in order to protect and promote their interests, or to be united and cohesive, 'post-transition'.

Bibliography

Abrahamsen, R. (2000) *Disciplining Democracy: Development Discourse and Good Governance in Africa*. London: Zed Books.

Adhikari, Prakash & Wendy L. Hansen (2013) Reparations and reconciliation in the aftermath of civil war. *Journal of Human Rights* 12 (4): 423–446.

Africog (2007) *A Study of Commissions of Inquiries in Kenya*. Nairobi: Africog.

Africog (2008) *Commissions of Inquiry in Kenya: Seekers of Truth or Safety Valves*. Nairobi: Africog.

Africog (2009) *Mission Impossible? Implementing the Ndung'u Report*. Nairobi: Africog.

Africog/KPTJ (2013) *#Elections 2013: Deliberate Mismanagement? A Compilation of Published Opinions on the 2013 Elections*. Nairobi: Africog.

AI (2013) *Police Reform in Kenya: 'A Drop in the Ocean'*. AFR32/001/2013. London: Amnesty International.

AI (2014) *Crying for Justice – Victims Perspectives on Justice for the Post-Elections Violence in Kenya*. London: Amnesty International.

Alam, Mayesha (2014) *Women and Transitional Justice: Progress and Persistent Challenges in Retributive and Restorative Processes*. Basingstoke: Palgrave Macmillan.

Allen, Jonathan (1999) Balancing justice and social unity: Political theory and the idea of a Truth and Reconciliation Commission. *University of Toronto Law Journal* 49 (3): 315–353.

Allen, Tim (2006) *Trial Justice: The International Criminal Court and the Lord's Resistance Army*. London: Zed Books.

Allen, Tim (2008) Ritual (ab)use? Problems with traditional justice in northern Uganda. In Nicholas Waddell & Phil Clark (eds) *Courting Conflict? Justice, Peace and the ICC in Africa*. London: Royal African Society: 47–54.

Amran, Athman (10 August 2012) Report names Raila as poll chaos suspect, says Gachoka, *Standard* (Nairobi).

Anderson, David (2008) Kenya on the brink. *Prospect Magazine* 20: 142.

Anderson, David (2014) Remembering Wagalla: State violence in northern Kenya, 1962–1991. *Journal of Eastern African Studies* 8 (4): 658–676.

Anderson, David (2015) Guilty secrets: Deceit, denial, and the discovery of Kenya's 'migrated archive'. *History Workshop Journal* 80 (1): 142–160.

Anderson, David & Jacob McKnight (2015) Kenya at war: Al-Shabaab and its enemies in Eastern Africa. *African Affairs* 114 (454): 1–27.

Andrews, Molly (2003) Grand national narratives and the project of truth commissions: A comparative analysis. *Media, Culture and Society* 25 (1): 46–65.

Applebaum, A. & B. Mawby (2016) Accessing gender-responsive reparations in Kenya. In R. Warren & M. Alam (eds) *Women and Transitional Justice*. Occasional Paper Series. Washington, DC: Georgetown University's Institute for Women, Peace and Security: 35–51.

Apuuli, Kasaija Phillip (2011) Peace over justice: The Acholi Religious Leaders Peace Initiative (ARLPI) vs. the International Criminal Court (ICC) in Northern Uganda. *Studies in Ethnicity and Nationalism* 11 (1): 116–129.

Arendt, Hannah (1963) *Eichmann in Jerusalem: A Report on the Banality of Evil*. London: Viking Press.

Arora-Jonsson, Seema (2011) Virtue and vulnerability: Discourses on women, gender and climate change. *Global Environmental Change* 21: 744–751.

Arthur, Paige (2009) How 'transitions' reshaped human rights: A conceptual history of transitional justice. *Human Rights Quarterly* 31 (2): 321–367.

Article 19 (April 2016) Country report: Protest in Kenya 2015. www.article19.org/resources.php/resource/38331/en/country-report:-protest-in-kenya-2015 <last accessed 3 June 2016>.

Asaala, Evelyne O. (2015) Prosecuting the 2007 post election violence-related international crimes in Kenyan courts: Exposing the real challenges. In M. K. Mbondenyi, E. O. Asaala, T. Kabau, & A. Waris (eds) *Human Rights and Democratic Governance in Kenya: A Post-2007 Appraisal*. Pretoria: Pretoria University Law Press: 345–362.

Ashforth, Adam (1990a) Reckoning schemes of legitimation: On commissions of inquiry as power/knowledge forms. *Journal of Historical Sociology* 3 (1): 1–22.

Ashforth, Adam (1990b) *The Politics of Official Discourse in Twentieth-Century South Africa*. Oxford: Oxford University Press.

Asmar, Kader, Louise Asmal & Ronald Suresh Roberts (1997) *Reconciliation through Truth: A Reckoning of Apartheid's Criminal Governance*, 2nd edn. Oxford: James Currey.

Atieno-Odhiambo, E. S. (1987) The ideology of order. In Michael Schatzberg (ed) *The Political Economy of Kenya*. New York, NY: Praeger Publishers: 172–202.

Attafuah, Kenneth Agyemang (2009) A path to peace and justice: Ghana's National Reconciliation Commission in retrospect. In Chandra Lekha Sriram & Suren Pillay (eds) *Peace versus Justice? The Dilemma of Transitional Justice in Africa*. Scottsville: University of KwaZulu-Natal Press: 187–201.

Bachelard, Jerome (2010) The Anglo-Leasing corruption scandal in Kenya: The politics of international and domestic pressures and counter-pressures. *Review of African Political Economy* 37 (124): 187–200.

Backer, David (2010) Watching a bargain unravel? A panel study of victims' attitudes about transitional justice in Cape Town, South Africa. *International Journal of Transitional Justice* 4: 443–456.

Backer, David, Joseph Lahouchuc & James Long (2010) Kenya: Post-election violence addressed – Micro-level perspectives on transitional justice. *African Arguments*. 21 June. http://africanarguments.org/2010/06/21/addressing-the-post-election-violence-micro-level-perspectives-on-transitional-justice-in-kenya <last accessed 19 April 2016>.

Baines, Erin (2011) Gender, responsibility, and the grey zone: Considerations for transitional justice. *Journal of Human Rights* 10: 477–493.

Barkan, Joel (2013) Technology is not democracy. *Journal of Democracy* 24 (3): 156–165.

BBC News, 12 October 2013, 'African Union urges ICC to defer Uhuru Kenyatta case'. www.bbc.com/news/world-africa-24506006 <last accessed 22 August 2014>.

Beckmann, Nadine (2010) Markets for health, markets for sickness: The commodification of misery. In R. Van Dijk & M. Dekker (eds) *Health and Health in Africa: New Arenas and Emerging Markets*. Leiden: Brill Publishers: 201–227.

Bell, C. & C. O'Rourke (2007) Does feminism need a theory of transitional justice? An introductory essay. *International Journal of Transitional Justice* 1 (1): 23–44.

Benequista, N. (2015) Somwhere between truth and peace: Understanding the news coverage of Kenya's 2013 elections. In K. Njogu & P. W. Wekesa (eds) *Kenya's 2013 election: Stakes, practices and outcomes*. Nairobi: Twaweza Communications Ltd: 260–273.

Bensouda, Fatou (2014) Statement of the Prosecutor of the International Criminal Court, Fatou Bensouda, on the withdrawal of charges against Mr. Uhuru Muigai Kenyatta, 5 December. www.icc-cpi.int/en_menus/icc/press%20and%20media/press%20releases/Pages/otp-statement-05-12-2014-2.aspx <last accessed 23 March 2016>.

Berman, Berman (1990) *Control and Crisis in Colonial Kenya: The Dialectic of Domination*. London: James Currey.

Berman, Bruce & John Lonsdale (1992) *Unhappy Valley: Conflict in Kenya and Africa. Book 2: Violence and Ethnicity*. Oxford: James Currey.

Bevernage, B. (2012) *History, Memory and State-Sponsored Violence: Time and Justice*. Abingdon: Routledge.

Bhargava, Anurima (2002) Defining political crimes: A case study of the South African Truth and Reconciliation Commission. *Columbia Law Review* 102 (5): 1304–1339.

Bhatta, Gambhir (2001) Of geese and ganders: Mainstreaming gender in the context of sustainable human development. *Journal of Gender Studies* 10 (1): 17–32.

Bird, Edward & Zureida Garda (1997) Reporting the truth commission: Analysis of media coverage of the Truth and Reconciliation Commission of South Africa. *Gazette* 59 (4–5): 331–343.

Blommaert, Jan, Mary Bock & Kay McCormick (2006) Narrative inequality in the TRC hearings: On the hearability of hidden transcripts. *Journal of Language and Politics* 5 (1): 37–70.

Boesten, Jelke (2013) *Sexual Violence during War and Peace: Gender, Power and Postconflict Justice in Peru*. New York, NY: Palgrave Macmillan.

Boone, Catherine (2012) Land conflict and distributive politics in Kenya. *African Studies Review* 55 (1): 75–103.

Boraine, Alex (2000a) *A Country Unmasked: Inside South Africa's Truth and Reconciliation Commission*. Oxford: Oxford University Press.

Boraine, Alex (2000b) The language of potential. In Wilmot James & Linda van de Vijver (eds) *After the TRC: Reflections on Truth and Reconciliation in South Africa*. Claremont: David Philip Publishers Ltd: 73–81.

Borer, T. A. (2003) A taxonomy of victims and perpetrators: Human rights and reconciliation in South Africa. *Human Rights Quarterly* 25 (4): 1088–1116.

Borneman, John (2002) Reconciliation after ethnic cleansing: Listening, retribution, affiliation. *Public Culture* 14 (2): 281–304.

Bosco, David (2014) *Rough Justice: The International Criminal Court in a World of Power Politics*. Oxford: Oxford University Press.

Bosire, Lydiah (2006) *Overpromised, Underdelivered: Transitional Justice in Sub-Saharan Africa*. New York, NY: International Centre for Transitional Justice.

Bosire, Lydiah (2013) *Judicial Statecraft in Kenya and Uganda: Explaining Transitional Justice Choices in the Age of the International Criminal Court*. PhD dissertation, University of Oxford.

Bosire, Lydiah & Gabrielle Lynch (2014) Kenya's search for truth and justice: The role of civil society. *International Journal of Transitional Justice* 8 (2): 256–276.

Bowman, W. & J. D. Bowman (2016) Censorship or self-control? Hate speech, the state and the voter in the Kenyan election of 2013. *Journal of Modern African Studies* 54 (3): 495–531.

Bowman, W. & G. Githaiga (2015) Information technology, the state and the voter in the Kenyan election of 2013. In K. Njogu & P. W. Wekesa (eds) *Kenya's 2013 Election: Stakes, Practices and Outcomes*. Nairobi: Twaweza Communications Ltd: 274–293.

Bozzoli, Belinda (1998) Public ritual and private transition: The truth commission in Alexandra township, South Africa 1996. *African Studies* 57 (2): 167–195.

Brahm, Eric (2007) Uncovering the truth: Examining truth commission success and impact. *International Studies Perspectives* 8: 16–35.

Branch, Adam (2007) Uganda's civil war and the politics of ICC intervention. *Ethics and International Affairs* 21 (2): 179–198.

Branch, Adam (2014) The violence of peace: Ethnojustice in northern Uganda. *Development and Change* 45 (3): 608–630.

Branch, Daniel (2011) *Kenya: Between Hope and Despair, 1963–2011*. New Haven, CT: Yale University Press.

Branch, Daniel & Nic Cheeseman (2006) The politics of contol in Kenya: Understanding the bureaucratic-executive state, 1952–78. *Review of African Political Economy* 33 (107): 11–31.

Brassett, James & Nick Vaughan-Williams (2015) Security and the performative politics of resilience: Critical infrastructure protection and humanitarian emergency preparedness. *Security Dialogue* 46 (1): 32–50.

Brassett, James, Stuart Croft, & Nick Vaughan-Williams. (2013) Introduction: An agenda for resilience research in politics and international relations. *Politics* 33 (4): 221–228.

Brett, Sebastian, Louis Bickford, Liv Sevenko & Marcelo Rios (2007) *Memorialization and Democracy: State Policy and Civic Action*. New York, NY: ICTJ.

Brown, Stephen & Chandra Lekha Sriram (2012) The big fish won't fry themselves: Criminal accountability for post-election violence in Kenya. *African Affairs* 111 (443): 244–260.

Brown, Stephen & Roasalind Raddatz (2014) Dire consequences or empty threats? Western pressure for peace, justice and democracy in Kenya. *Journal of Eastern African Studies* 8 (1): 43–62.

Burbidge, Dominic (2014) 'Can someone get me outta this middle class zone?!' Pressures on middle class Kikuyu in Kenya's 2013 election. *Journal of Modern African Studies* 52 (2): 205–225.

Buss, Doris (2009) Rethinking 'rape as a weapon of war'. *Feminist Legal Studies* 17 (2): 145–163.

Butler, Judith (1990) *Gender Trouble: Feminism and the Subversion of Identity*. London: Routledge.

Capital FM (6 October 2014) Speech read by His Excellency Uhuru Kenyatta, C.G.H., President and Commander in Chief of the Defence Forces of the Republic of Kenya during the Special Sitting of Parliament on 6th October, 2014. www.capitalfm.co.ke/eblog/2014/10/06/ruto-the-acting-president-as-i-attend-icc-case/ <last accessed 14 June 2016>.

Carothers, T. (1999) *Aiding Democracy Abroad: The Learning Curve*. Washington, DC: Carnegie Endowment for International Peace.

Carranza, Ruben (2008) Plunder and pain: Should transitional justice engage with corruption and economic crimes? *International Journal of Transitional Justice* 2: 310–330.

Carrier, Neil & Hassan Kochore (2014) Navigating ethnicity and electoral politics in northern Kenya: The case of the 2013 election. *Journal of Eastern African Studies* 8 (1): 135–152.

Castillejo-Cuellar, Alejandro (2007) Knolwedge, experience, and South Africa's scenarios of forgiveness. *Radical History Review* 97: 11–42.

Cavende, G., K. Gray & K. Miller (2010) Enron's perp walk: Status degradation ceremonies as narrative. *Crime Media Culture* 6 (3): 251–266.

Chant, Sylvia (2006) Re-thinking the 'feminization of poverty' in relation to aggregate gender indices. *Journal of Human Development* 7 (2): 201–220.

Chapman, Audrey & Patrick Ball (2001) The truth of truth commissions: Comparative lessons from Haiti, South Africa, and Guatemala. *Human Rights Quarterly* 23: 1–43.

Charlesworth, Hilary (2005) Not waving but drowning: Gender mainstreaming and human rights in the United Nations. *Harvard Human Rights Journal* 18: 1–18.

Charlesworth, Hilary (2008) Are women peaceful? Reflections on the role of women in peace-building. *Feminist Legal Studies* 16 (3): 347–361.

Chawatama, Gertrude, Berhanu Dinka & Ronald C. Slye (2013) International Commission Dissent: Statement by Commissioners, The Final Report of the Truth, Justice & Reconciliation Commission of Kenya. http://digitalcommons.law.seattleu.edu/tjrc/8 <last accessed 18 April 2016>.

Cheeseman, Nic (2015) *Democracy in Africa: Successes, Failures, and the Struggle for Political Reform*. Cambridge: Cambridge University Press.

Cheeseman, Nic & Blessing-Miles Tendi (2010) Power-sharing in comparative perspective: the dynamics of 'unity government' in Kenya and Zimbabwe. *Journal of Modern African Studies* 48 (2): 203–229.

Cheeseman, Nic, Lynch, Gabrielle, & Justin Willis (2014) Democracy and its discontents: The Kenyan elections of 2013. *Journal of Eastern African Studies* 8 (1): 2–24.

Cheeseman, Nic, Lynch, Gabrielle, & Justin Willis (2016) Decentralization in Kenya: The governance of governors. *Journal of Modern African Studies* 54 (1): 1–35.

Cheeseman, Nic, Gabrielle Lynch & Justin Willis (2017) Voting for the devil you know: Kenya's 2017 election. *Review of African Political Economy* blog, http://roape.net/2017/08/14/voting-devil-know-kenyas-2017-election <last accessed 26 September 2017>.

Chege, Michael (2008) Kenya: back from the brink? *Journal of Democracy* 19 (4): 125–139.

Cherono, Stella (4 October 2016) TJRC proposes free access to public beaches. *Daily Nation* (Nairobi). www.nation.co.ke/news/TJRC-proposes-free-access-to-public-beaches/1056-3403870-icndp0z/index.html <last accessed 7 March 2018>.

Chome, Ngala (23 March 2013) Of demcoracy and the tyranny of numbers, Institute of African Studies Columbia University. www.ias.columbia.edu/blog/democracy-and-tyranny-numbers <last accessed 7 March 2018>.

Chome, Ngala (2015) 'Devolution is only for development'? Decentralization and elite vulnerability on the Kenyan coast. *Critical African Studies* 7 (3): 299–316.

Chua, Amy (2003) *World on Fire: How Exporting Free Market Democracy Breeds Ethnic Hatred and Global Instability*. London: Arrow Books.

Chuma, Aeneas & Ozonnia Ojielo (2012) Building a standing national capacity for conflict prevention and resolution in Kenya. *Journal of Peacebuilding & Development* 7 (3): 25–39.

Clark, Phil (2007) Hybridity, holism and 'traditional' justice: The case of the Gacaca Courts in post-genocide Rwanda. *George Washington International Law Review* 39 (4): 765–837.

Clark, Phil (2008) Law, politics and pragmatism: The ICC and case selection in the Democratic Republic of Congo and Uganad. In Nicholas Waddell & Phil Clark (eds) *Courting Conflict? Justice, Peace and the ICC in Africa*. London: Royal African Society: 37–46.

Clark, Phil (2013) Grappling in the Great Lakes: The challenges of international justice in Rwanda, the Democratic Republic of Congo and Uganda. In Brett Bowden, Hilary Charlesworth & Jeremy Farall (eds) *The Role of International Law in Rebuilding Societies after Conflict*. Cambridge: Cambridge University Press: 244–269.

Cohen, David William & E. S. Atieno Odhiambo (2004) *The Risks of Knowledge: Investigations into the Death of the Hon. Minister John Robert Ouko in Kenya, 1990*. Athens, OH: Ohio University Press.

Cole, Catherine (2007) Performance, transitional justice, and the law: South Africa's truth and reconciliation commission. *Theatre Journal* 59 (2): 167–187.

Cole, Catherine (2010) *Performing South Africa's Truth Commission: Stages of Transition*. Bloomington, IN: Indiana University Press.

Colvin, Christopher (2004) Ambivalent narrations: Pursuing the political through traumatic storytelling. *PoLAR: Political and Legal Anthropology Review* 27 (1): 72–89.

Comaroff, Jean & John L. Comaroff (2006) Law and disorder in the postcolony: An introduction. In Comaroff, Jean & John L. Comaroff (2006) *Law and Disorder in the Postcolony*. Chicago, IL: University of Chicago Press: 1–56.

Comaroff, John L. & Jean Comaroff (2009) *Ethnicity, Inc*. Chicago, IL: University of Chicago Press.

Cooper, Elizabeth (2014). Students, arson, and protest politics in Kenya: School fires as political action. *African Affairs* 113 (453): 583–600.

Cornel, Ernest (18 July 2017) Shun TJRC report, it will open old wounds, Ruto tells Coast voters. *The Star* (Nairobi).

Cornell, Agnes & Michelle D'Arcy (2014) Plus ça change? County-level politics in Kenya after devolution. *Journal of Eastern African Studies* 8 (1): 173–191.

Cornwall, Andrea (1997) Men, masculinity and 'gender in development'. *Gender and Development* 5 (2): 8–13.

Cornwall, A., Harrison, E., Whitehead, A. (2007) Gender myths and feminist fables: The struggle for interpretive power in gender and development. *Development and Change* 38 (1): 1–20.

Cramer, Chris (2003) *Homo economicus* goes to war: Methodological individualism, rational choice and the political economy of war. *World Development* 30: 1845–1864.

Crenzel, Emilio (2008) Argentina's National Commission on the Disappearance of Persons: Contributions to transitional justice. *International Journal of Transitional Justice* 2: 173–191.

Crocker, David (1998) Transitional Justice and International Civil Society: Toward a normative framework. *Constellations* 5 (4): 492–517.

Crocker, David (2002) Punishment, reconciliation, and democratic deliberation. *Buffalo Criminal Law Review* 5 (2): 509–549.

Croft, Stuart (2006) *Culture, Change and America's War on Terror*. Cambridge: Cambridge University Press.

D'Arcy, Michelle & Agnes Cornell (2016) Devolution and corruption in Kenya: Everyone's turn to eat? *African Affairs* 115 (459): 246–273.

Daily Nation (Nairobi) (3 September 2010) Civil society divided over truth team role.

Daily Nation (Nairobi) (11 June 2013) Judge rejects bid to block TJRC report.

Daily Nation (Nairobi) (16 September 2016) I have no apologies over Narok remarks, Raila says. http://allafrica.com/stories/201609160814.html <last accessed 26 September 2017>.

David, Roman (2014) International criminal tribunals and the perception of justice: The effect of the ICTY in Croatia. *International Journal of Transitional Justice* 8: 476–495.

De Gruchy, J. W. (2002) *Reconciliation: Restoring Justice*. London: SCM Press.

De Waal, Alex (2008) Darfur, the Court and Khartoum: The politics of state non-cooperation. In Nicholas Waddell & Phil Clark (eds) *Courting Conflict? Justice, Peace and the ICC in Africa*. London: Royal African Society: 29–36.

Deacon, Gregory (2015) Driving the devil out: Kenya's born-again election. *Journal of Religion in Africa* 45 (2): 200–220.

Deacon, Gregory (24 April 2016) Kenya: Thanking the Lord for power, control, and dropped charges at the ICC. *Democracy in Africa*. http://democracyinafrica.org/kenya-thank-the-lord-for-power-control-and-dropped-charges-at-the-icc/ <last accessed 26 September 2017>.

Deacon, Gregory, George Gona, Hassan Mwakimako & Justin Willis (2017) Preaching politics: Islam and Christianity on the Kenya coast. *Journal of Contemporary African Studies* 35 (2): 148–167.

Deacon, Gregory & Gabrielle Lynch (2013) Allowing Satan in? Moving toward a political economy of neo-Pentecostalism in Kenya. *Journal of Religion in Africa* 43: 108–130.

Derrida, Jacques (1996) *Archive Fever: A Freudian Impression*. Chicago, IL: University of Chicago Press.

Desrosiers, Marie-Eve & Susan Thomson (2011) Rhetorical legacies of leadership: projections of 'benevolent leadership' in pre- and post-genocide Rwanda. *Journal of Modern African Studies* 49 (3): 429–453.

Donald, Hafner & Elizabeth King (2007) Beyond traditional notions of transitional justice: How trials, truth commissions, and other tools for accountability can and should work together. *Boston College International and Comparative Law Review* 30: 91–109.

Duthie, Roger (2008) Toward a development-sensitive approach to transitional justice. *International Journal of Transitional Justice* 2 (3): 292–309.

El Bushra, Judy (2007) Feminism, gender, and women's peace activism. *Development and Change* 38 (1): 131–147.

El Gantri, R. (2015) Tunisia in transition: One year after the creation of the Truth and Dignity Commission. *ICTJ Briefing Paper*. www.ictj.org/publi

cation/tunisia-transition-one-year-after-creation-truth-dignity-commis sion <last accessed 17 April 2016>.

Elder, Claire, Susan Stigant & Jonas Claes (2014) *Elections and Violent Conflict in Kenya: Making Prevention Stick*. Washington, DC: United States Institute of Peace.

Enarson, Elaine (2012) *Women Confronting Disaster: From Vulnerability to Resilience*. Boulder, CO: Lynne Rienner.

Esterhuyse, Willie (2000) Truth as a trigger for transformation: from apartheid injustice to transformational justice. In Charles Villa-Vicencio & Wilhelm Verwoerd (eds) *Looking Back, Reaching Forward: Reflections on the Truth and Reconciliation Commission of South Africa*. Cape Town: University of Cape Town Press: 144–154.

Feldman, Allen (2003) Strange fruit: The South African Truth Commission and the demonic economies of violence. *Social Analysis* 46 (3): 234–265.

Ferguson, James (1990) *The Anti-Politics Machine: 'Development', Depoliticization, and Bureaucratic Power in Lesotho*. Minneapolis, MN: University of Minnesota Press.

Ferree, Karen E., Clark C. Gibson & James D. Long (2014) Voting behaviour and electoral irregularities in Kenya's 2013 elections. *Journal of Eastern African Studies* 8 (1): 153–172.

FIDH & KHRC (2017) Kenya's scorecard on security and justice: Broken promises and unfinished business. www.fidh.org/img/pdf/report_kenya _fidh_khrc.pdf <last accessed 26 September 2017>.

Fields, Sean (2011) Disappointed remains: Trauma, testimony, and reconciliation in post-apartheid South Africa. In D. Ritchie (ed) *The Oxford Handbook of Oral History*. New York, NY: Oxford University Press: 142–158.

Fishkin, James F. (2009) *When the People Speak: Deliberative Democracy and Public Consultation*. Oxford: Oxford University Press.

Fletcher, Laurel E. & Harvy M. Weinstein (2002) Violence and social repair: Rethinking the contribution of justice to reconciliation. *Human Rights Quarterly* 24 (3): 573–639.

Fontein, Joost (2009) Anticipating the tsunami: Rumours, planning and the arbitrary state in Zimbabwe. *Africa* 79 (3): 369.

Fontein, Joost (2014) Remaking the dead, uncertainty and the torque of human materials in Northern Zimbabwe. In F. Stepputat (ed) *Governing the Dead: Sovereignty and the Politics of Dead Bodies*. Manchester: Manchester University Press: 114–140.

Fontein, Joost (2015) *Remaking Mutirikwi: Landscape Water and Belonging in Southern Zimbabwe* Oxford: James Currey.

Fontein, Joost (2017) Epilogue: On the frontiers of time. In S. Jensen & O. Zenker (eds) *South African Homelands as Frontiers: Apartheid's Loose Ends in the Postcolonial Era*. London: Routledge: 163–172.

Forcey, L. (1994) Feminist perspectives on mothering and peace. In E. Glenn, G. Chang & L. Forcey (eds) *Mothering: Ideology, Experience and Agency*. New York, NY: Routledge: 355–376.

Foster, Don, Paul Haupt, & Marésa De Beer (2005) *The Theatre of Violence: Narratives of Protagonists in the South African Conflict*. Pretoria HSRC Press.

Fukuda-Parr, Sakiko (1999) What does feminization of poverty mean? It isn't just lack of income. *Feminist Economics* 5 (2): 99–103.

Fukuyama, Francis (1998) Women and the evolution of world politics. *Foreign Affairs* 77(5): 24–40.

Gachigua, Sammy Gakero (2014) Fuelling the violence: the print media in Kenya's volatile 2007 post-election violence. In Godwin Murunga, Duncan Okello & Anders Sjögren (eds) *Kenya: The Struggle for Constitutional Order*. London: Zed Books: 44–65.

Gachigua, Sammy Gakero (2015) The ICC and Kenya's 2013 elections: A perspective from Kenyan newspapers editorial cartoons. In K. Njogu & P. W. Wekesa (eds) *Kenya's 2013 Election: Stakes, Practices and Outcomes*. Nairobi: Twaweza Communications Ltd: 198–219.

Gachuhu, Roy (28 May 2010) Kiplagat digs in for battle in and out of TJRC. *Daily Nation* (Nairobi).

Galava, Denis (2015) From watchdogs to hostages of peace: The Kenyan media and the 2013 general election. In F. Otieno (ed) *New Constitution, Same Old Challenges: Reflections on Kenya's 2013 General Elections*. Nairobi: Society for International Development: 228–244.

Galtung, Johan (1969) Violence, peace, and peace research. *Journal of Peace Research* 6 (3): 167–191.

Gathumbi, Anne (2008) Preface. In Makokha, K. & O. Opondo (ed) *In the Shadow of Death: My Experience, My Trauma. Voices of Kenyan Women from Post-Election Violence*. Nairobi: African Woman and Child Feature Service: v.

Gibson, James (2002) Truth, justice, and reconciliation: Judging the fairness of amnesty in South Africa. *American Journal of Political Science* 46 (3): 540–556.

Gibson, James (2004) Overcoming apartheid: Can truth reconcile a divided nation? *Politikon* 31 (2): 129–155.

Gibson, James (2006) The contributions of truth to reconciliation: Lessons from South Africa. *Journal of Conflict Resolution* 50 (3): 409–432.

Gilligan, Chris (2006) Traumatised by peace? A critique of five assumptions in the theory and practice of conflict-related trauma policy in Northern Ireland. *Policy & Politics* 34 (2): 325–345.

Gitari, Christopher (2014) Lessons to be learned: An analysis of the final report of Kenya's Truth, Justice and Reconciliation Commission. ICTJ briefing. Nairobi: ICTJ. www.ictj.org/sites/default/files/ictj-briefing-kenya-tjrc-2014.pdf <last accessed 26 September 2017>.

Githongo, John (2010) Fear and loathing in Nairobi: The challenge of reconciliation in Kenya. *Foreign Affairs* 89 (4): 2–9.

Githongo, John (6 April 2013) Whither civil society. *The Star* (Nairobi).

Goetz, Anne Marie (2007) Political cleaners: Women as the new anti-corruption force? *Development and Change* 38 (1): 87–105.

Goldblatt, B. & S. Meintjes (1997) Dealing with the aftermath: Sexual violence and the Truth and Reconciliation Commission. *Agenda* 13 (36): 7–18.

Gordon, Avery F. (2008) *Ghostly Matters: Haunting and the Sociological Imagination*. Minneapolis, MN: University of Minnesota Press.

Govier, T. & W. Verwoerd (2002) Trust and the problem of national reconciliation. *Philosophy of the Social Sciences* 32: 178–205.

Govier, Trudy (2002) *Forgiveness and Revenge*. London: Routledge.

Graybill, Lyn (2001) The contribution of the truth and reconciliation commission toward the promotion of women's rights in South Africa. *Women's Studies International Forum* 24 (1): 1–10.

Graybill, Lyn (2002) *Truth and Reconciliation in South Africa: Miracle or Model?* London: Lynne Rienner.

Gready, Paul (2005) Analysis: Reconceptualising transitional justice: Embedded and distanced justice. *Conflict, Security and Development* 5 (1): 3–21.

Gready, Paul (2011) *The Era of Transitional Justice: The Aftermath of the Truth and Reconciliation in South Africa and Beyond*. Abingdon: Routledge.

Gready, Paul & Simon Robins (2014) From transitional to transformative justice: A new agenda for practice. *International Journal of Transitional Justice* 8 (3): 339–361.

Grunebaum, Heidi (2011) *Memorializing the Past: Everyday Life in South Africa after the Truth and Reconciliation Commission*. New Brunswick, NJ: Transaction Publishers.

Hamber, Brandon (1998a) Living with the legacy of impunity: Lessons for South Africa about truth, justice and crime in Brazil. *Latin American Report* 13 (2): 4–16.

Hamber, Brandon (1998b) The burdens of truth: An evaluation of the psychological support services and initiatives undertaken by the South

African Truth and Reconciliation Commission. *American Imago* 55 (1): 9–28.

Hamber, Brandon (1999) *The Burdens of Truth: An Evaluation of the Psychological Support Services and Initiatives Undertaken by the South African Truth and Reconciliation Commission*. Johannesburg: Centre for the Study of Violence & Reconciliation.

Hamber, Brandon (2002) 'Ere their story die': Truth, justice and reconciliation in South Africa. *Race and Class* 44 (1): 61–79.

Hamber, Brandon (2007) Masculinity and transitional justice: An exploratory essay. *International Journal of Transitional Justice* 1: 375–390.

Hamber, Brandon & Richard A. Wilson (2002) Symbolic closure through memory, reparation and revenge in post-conflict societies. *Journal of Human Rights* 1 (1): 35–53.

Hansard (18 November 2009) National Assembly Official Report. https://bo oks.google.co.ke/books?id=ovv7to_abxsc&pg=pp1&dq=18+november+2 009,+national+assembly+official+report.++kenya&hl=en&sa=x&ved=0a hukewiigkqa6azqahwsyrokhc6mabwq6aeiidab#v=onepage&q=18%20no vember%202009%2c%20national%20assembly%20official%20report .%20%20kenya&f=false <last accessed 26 September 2017>.

Hansen, Thomas Obel (2011) Transitional justice: Toward a differentiated theory. *Oregon Review of International Law* 13 (1): 1–54.

Hansen, Thomas Obel (2013) Kenya's power-sharing arrangement and its implications for transitional justice. *International Journal of Human Rights* 17 (2): 307–327.

Hansen, Obel Thomas & Chandra Lekha Sriram (2015) Fighting for justice (and survival): Kenyan civil society accountability strategies and their enemies. *International Journal of Transitional Justice* 9 (3): 407–427.

Harrington, John & Ambreena Manji (2015) Restoring Leviathan? The Kenyan supreme court, constitutional transformation and the presidential election of 2013. *Journal of Eastern African Studies* 9 (2): 175–192.

Harris, Brent (2002a) The archive, public history and the essential truth: The TRC reading of the past. In C. Hamilton, V. Harris, J. Taylor. M. Pickover, G. Reid & R. Saleh (eds) *Refiguring the Archive*. Cape Town: David Philip: 161–178.

Harris, Verne (2002b) The archival sliver: A perspective on the construction of social memory in archives and the transition from apartheid to democracy. In C. Hamilton, V. Harris, J. Taylor. M. Pickover, G. Reid & R. Saleh (eds) *Refiguring the Archive*. Cape Town: David Philip: 135–160.

Harris, J. Andrew (2012) 'Stain Removal': Measuring the Effect of Violence on Local Ethnic Demography in Kenya. Unpublished working paper. web.mit.edu/posner/www/wgape/harris_wgape.pdf <last accessed 26 September 2017>.

Hassan, Mai (2015) Continuity despite change: Kenya's new constitution and executive power. *Democratization* 22 (4): 587–609.

Haugerud, Angelique (1997) *The Culture of Politics in Modern Kenya*. Cambridge: Cambridge University Press.

Hayner, Priscilla (2011) *Unspeakable Truths: Transitional Justice and the Challenge of Truth Commissions*, 2nd edn. London: Routledge.

Hirsch, Alexander (2012) Introduction: The agon of reconciliation. In A. Hirsch (ed) *Theorizing Post-Conflict Reconciliation*. Abingdon: Routledge: 1–10.

Höhn, Sabine (2014) New start or false start? The ICC and electoral violence in Kenya. *Development and Change* 45 (3): 565–588.

Hoile, David (2014) *Justice Denied: The Reality of the International Criminal Court*. London: Africa Research Centre.

Horelt, M. (2012) Performing reconciliation: A performance approach to the analysis of political apologies. In N. Palmer, P. Clark & D. Granville (eds) *Critical Perspectives in Transitional Justice*. Cambridge: Intersentia: 347–370.

Hornsby, Charles (2012) *Kenya: A History since Independence*. London: IB Tauris.

Horowitz, Donald (2000) *Ethnic Groups in Conflict*. Updated edn. Berkeley, CA: University of California Press.

HRW (2011) *Turning Pebbles: Evading Accountability for Post-Election Violence in Kenya*. Washington, DC: HRW.

HRW (2013) *High Stakes: Political Violence and the 2013 Elections in Kenya*. Washington, DC: HRW.

HRW (2016) *'I Just Sit and Wait to Die': Reparations for Survivors of Kenya's 2007–2008 Post-Election Sexual Violence*. Washington, DC: HRW.

Hutchison, Yvette (2013) *South African Performance and Archives of Memory*. Manchester: Manchester University Press.

ICC (2010) Prosecutorial Strategy, 2009–2010, 1 February. www.icc-cpi.int/NR/rdonlyres/66A8DCDC-3650-4514-AA62-D229D1128F65/281506/OTPProsecutorialStrategy20092013.pdf <last accessed 7 March 2018>.

ICC (2015) Case Information Sheet. Situation in the Republic of Kenya: The Prosecutor v. Uhuru Muigai Kenyatta, March. www.icc-cpi.int/kenya/kenyatta/documents/kenyattaeng.pdf <last accessed 7 March 2018>.

ICC (2016) Case Information Sheet. Situation in the Republic of Kenya: The Prosecutor v. William Samoei Ruto and Joshua arap Sang, April. www.icc

-cpi.int/kenya/rutosang/documents/rutosangeng.pdf <last accessed 7 March 2018>.
ICG (2013) Kenya's 2013 Elections. Africa Report No. 197, 17 January. Brussels: Belgium. https://d2071andvip0wj.cloudfront.net/kenyas-2013-elections.pdf <last accessed 7 March 2018>.
Ichim, Irina (2008) *The Good, the Bad and the 'Other': Female Fighters and Transitional Justice*. Unpublished MA thesis, Institute of Commonwealth Studies, University of London.
ICJ-Kenya & KHRC (2012) *Elusive Justice: A Status Report on Victims of 2007–2008 Post-Election Violence in Kenya*. Nairobi: ICJ-Kenya & KHRC.
ICTJ (2009) What is transitional justice? www.ictj.org/sites/default/files/ictj-global-transitional-justice-2009-english.pdf <last accessed 26 September 2017>.
ICTJ/GiZ (October 2013) *Workshop Report: Safeguarding and Implementing the TJRC Report. A Workshop with Policy Makers and Stakeholders*. Workshop hosted by the International Centre for Transitional Justice and GiZ, Great Rift Valley Lodge, Naivasha, 10–11 October 2013. Copy shared with the author.
Ignatieff, M. (1996) Articles of faith. *Index on Censorship* 25 (5): 110–122.
Igreja, Victor Attafuah & Kenneth Agyemang (2009) The politics of peace, justice and healing in post-war Mozambique: 'Practices of rupture' by *Magamba* spirits and healers in Gorongosa. In Chandra Lekha Sriram & Suren Pillay (eds) *Peace versus Justice? The Dilemma of Transitional Justice in Africa*. Scottsville: University of KwaZulu-Natal Press: 277–300.
Ingelaere, Bert (2009) 'Does the truth pass across the fire without burning?' Locating the short circuit in Rwanda's Gacaca courts. *Journal of Modern African Studies* 47 (4): 507–528.
Ipsos Synovate (4 November 2011) Confirmation hearings boost support for ICC process. www.ipsos.co.ke/home/index.php/downloads <last accessed 7 March 2018>.
Jackson, R. (2005) *Writing the War on Terrorism: Language, Politics and Counter-Terrorism*. Manchester: Manchester University Press.
Jalloh, Charles Chernor (2011) Situation in the Republic of Kenya. *American Journal of International Law* 105 (3): 540–547.
Jones, Peris, Kavita Ramakrishnan & Kimari Wangui (2017) 'Only the people can defend this struggle': The politics of everyday extrajudicial killings and civil society in Mathare, Kenya. *Review of African Political Economy* 44 (154): 559–576.
Jubilee Party (2017) *Continuing Kenya's transformation, together: Jubilee manifesto 2017*. http://uhuruto2017.co.ke/jp-manifesto-compressed-web-version-12782.pdf <last accessed 29 September 2017>.

Kabaji, Egara (2008) Masculinity and ritual violence: A study of bullfighting among the Luhyia of western Kenya. In Egodi Uchendu (ed) *Masculinities in Contemporary Africa*. Dakar: CODESRIA: 34–53.

Kagwanja, Peter (2003) Facing Mount Kenya or facing Mecca? The Mungiki, ethnic violence and the politics of the Moi succession in Kenya, 1987–2002. *African Affairs* 102 (406): 25–49.

Kagwanja, Peter (2015) The geopolitics of international justice: ICC and Kenya's 2013 presidential election. In K. Njogu & P. W. Wekesa (eds) *Kenya's 2013 Election: Stakes, Practices and Outcomes*. Nairobi: Twaweza Communications Ltd: 144–161.

Kahora, Billy (2009) *The True Story of David Munyakei*. Nairobi: Kwani.

Kakah, Maureen (25 June 2015) President's kin loses bid to remove name from TJRC land report. *Nairobi News*. http://nairobinews.nation.co.ke/news/presidents-kin-loses-bid-to-remove-name-from-tjrc-land-report <last accessed 17 April 2016>.

Kanyinga, Karuti (2000) *Re-distribution from Above: The Politics of Land Rights and Squatting in Coastal Kenya*, vol. 115. Uppsala: Nordic Africa Institute.

Kanyinga, Karuti (2011) Stopping a conflagration: The response of Kenyan civil society to the post-2007 election violence. *Politikon* 38 (1): 85–109.

Kanyinga, Karuti (18 January 2015) National cohesion remains a dream. *Sunday Nation* (Nairobi).

Karanja, Samuel (9 September 2014) Githurai residents demand release of officer. *Daily Nation* (Nairobi).

Kasara, K. (2013) Separate and suspicious: Local social and political context and ethnic tolerance in Kenya. *Journal of Politics* 75 (4): 921–936.

Kelsall, Tim (2005) Truth, lies, ritual: Preliminary reflections on the Truth and Reconciliation Commission in Sierra Leone. *Human Rights Quarterly* 27 (2): 361–391.

Kendall, Sara (2014) 'UhuRuto' and other Leviathans: The International Criminal Court and the Kenyan political order. *African Journal of Legal Studies* 7: 399–427.

Kenya, Republic of (1934) *Kenya Land Commission: Evidence and Memoranda*. Nairobi: Government Printers.

Kenya, Republic of (1950) *Report of the Commission of Inquiry into the Affray at Kolloa, Baringo*. Nairobi: Government Printers.

Kenya, Republic of (1962) *Report of the Regional Boundaries Commission*. Nairobi: Government Printers.

Kenya, Republic of (1992) *Report of the Parliamentary Select Committee to Investigate Ethnic Clashes in Western and Other Parts of Kenya*. Nairobi: Government Printers.

Kenya, Republic of (1999) *Report of the Judicial Commission Appointed to Inquire into Tribal Clashes in Kenya*. Nairobi: Government Printers.

Kenya, Republic of (2000) *Report of the Presidential Commission of Inquiry into the Cult of Devil Worship in Kenya*. Nairobi: Government Printers.

Kenya, Republic of (2003) *Report of the Task Force on the Establishment of a Truth, Justice and Reconciliation Commission*. Nairobi: Government Printers.

Kenya, Republic of (2004) *Report of the Commission of Inquiry into the Illegal/Irregular Allocation of Public Land*, vols. 1–3. Nairobi: Government Printers.

Kenya, Republic of (2005) *Report of the Judicial Commission of Inquiry into the Goldenberg Affair*. Nairobi: Government Printers.

Kenya, Republic of (2008a) National Accord and Reconciliation Act. No. 4 of 2008. http://kenyalaw.org/kl/fileadmin/pdfdownloads/Acts/NationalAccordandReconciliationAct_No4of2008.pdf <last accessed 20 April 2016>.

Kenya, Republic of (2008b) *Report of the Commission of Inquiry into Post-Election Violence*. Nairobi: Government Printers.

Kenya, Republic of (2008c) *Report of the Independent Review Commission on the General Elections Held in Kenya on 27 December 2007*. Nairobi: Government Printers.

Kenya, Republic of (2008d) *The Truth Justice and Reconciliation Act, 2008*. Kenya Gazette Supplement, No. 84 (Acts No. 6), 2 December 2008. Nairobi: Government Printers.

Kenya, Republic of (2009) 2009 Population and Housing Census Results. www.knbs.or.ke/docs/PresentationbyMinisterforPlanningrevised.pdf <last accessed 7 March 2018>.

Kenyatta, Jomo (1961) *Facing Mount Kenya: The Tribal Life of the Gikuyu*. London: Mercury Books.

Kenyatta, Uhuru, 26 March 2015, State of the Nation Address to Parliament. www.the-star.co.ke/news/2015/03/26/president-uhuru-kenyatta-speech-during-state-of-the-nation-address-at_c1108742 <last accessed 7 March 2018>.

KHRC (2009) *Surviving after Torture: A Case Digest on the Struggle for Justice by Torture Survivors in Kenya*. Nairobi: KHRC.

KHRC (2011a) *Justice Delayed ... A Status Report on Historical Injustice in Kenya*. Nairobi: KHRC.

KHRC (2011b) *Lest We Forget: The Faces of Impunity in Kenya*. Nairobi: KHRC.

Kinyanjui, Sarah (2016) Gendering truth-seeking commissions: The Kenyan experience. In Sandra Cheldeloin & Martha Mutisi (eds) *Deconstructing*

Women, Peace and Security: A Critical Review of Approaches to Gender and Empowerment. Cape Town: HSRC Press: 151–168.

Kisia, Allan & Abigail Sum (27 May 2015) Raila Odinga calls for implementation of Truth Justice and Reconciliation Commission report. *Standard* (Nairobi).

KNCHR (2008) *On the Brink of the Precipice: A Human Rights Account of Kenya's Post-2007 Election Violence.* Nairobi: KNCHR.

KNCHR/ICTJ (June 2016) Report of a consultative forum to develop guidelines on the implementation of the TJRC recommendations and reparations. Serena Hotel, Mombasa, 19–22 June 2016. Copy shared with the author.

KNDR (June 2011) Annex 1: Kenya National Dialogue and Reconciliation Monitoring Project National Survey, June 2011. www.dialoguekenya.org/Monitoring/%28June%202011%29%2010TH%20Review%20Report%20Annex%201.pdf <last accessed 7 March 2018>.

Korir, Bishop Cornelius (2009) *Amani Mashinani (Peace at the Grassroots): Experiences of Community Peacebuilding in the North Rift Region of Kenya.* Eldoret: Catholic Diocese of Eldoret.

Krabill, R. (2001) Symbiosis: Mass media and the Truth and Reconciliation Commission of South Africa. *Media, Culture & Society* 23 (5): 567–585.

Kriger, N. (2006) From patriotic memories to 'patriotic history' in Zimbabwe, 1990–2005. *Third World Quarterly* 27 (6): 151–169.

Krog, Antjie (1999) *Country of My Skull.* London: Vintage.

Krog, Antjie (ed) (2013) *Conditional Tense: Memory and Vocabulary after the South African Truth and Reconciliation Commission.* London: Seagull Books.

Krog, Antjie, N. Mpolweni-Zantsi & K. Ratele (2013) Ways of knowing Mrs Konile. In A. Krog (ed) *Conditional Tense: Memory and Vocabulary after the South African Truth and Reconciliation Commission.* London: Seagull Books: 39–88.

Lambourne, Wendy (2009) Transitional justice and peacebuilding after mass violence. *International Justice of Transitional Justice* 3 (1): 28–48.

Lamin, Abdul Rahman (2003) Building peace through accountability in Sierra Leone: The Truth and Reconciliation Commission and the Special Court. *Journal of Asian and African Studies* 38 (2–3): 295–320.

Lanegran (2015) The Kenyan Truth, Justice and Reconciliation Commission: The importance of commissioners and their appointment process. *Transitional Justice Review* 1 (3): 41–71.

Lang, Britaa & Patrick Sakdapolrak (2015) Violent place-making: How Kenya's post-election violence transforms a workers' settlement at Lake Naivasha. *Political Geography* 45: 67–78.

Lang'at, Patrick & Bernard Namunane (17 September 2016) CORD leader plotting to split Jubilee Party, say Uhuru allies. *Daily Nation* (Nairobi).

Laplante, Lisa (2008) Transitional justice and peace building: Diagnosing and addressing the socioeconomic roots of violence through a human rights framework. *International Journal of Transitional Justice* 2 (3): 331–255.

Laplante, Lisa & Kelly Phenicie (2010) Media, trials and truth commissions: 'Mediating' reconciliation in Peru's transitional justice process. *International Journal of Transitional Justice* 4 (2): 207–229.

Laplante, Lisa & Kimberley Theidon, (2007) Truth with consequences: Justice and reparations in post-Truth Commission Peru. *Human Rights Quarterly* 29 (1): 228–250.

Lebaw, Bronwyn Anne (2008) The irreconcilable goals of transitional justice. *Human Rights Quarterly* 30 (1): 95–118.

Leclercq, Sidney (2017) Injustice through transitional justice? Subversion strategies in Burundi's peace process and postconflict developments. *International Journal of Transitional Justice* 11 (3): 525–544.

Lederach, John Paul (1997) *Building Peace: Sustainable Reconciliation in Divided Societies*. Washington, DC: United States Institute of Peace.

Leiby, Michele (2009) Digging in the archives: The promise and perils of primary documents. *Politics and Society* 37 (1): 75–99.

Lessa, Francesca (2011) Beyond transitional justice: Exploring continuities in human rights abuses in Argentina between 1976 and 2010. *Journal of Human Rights Practice* 3 (1): 24–48.

Levi, Primo (1986) *The Drowned and the Saved*. New York, NY: Summit Books.

Lindenmayer, Elisabeth & Jose Lianna Kaye (2009) *A Choice for Peace? The Story of Forty-One Days of Mediation in Kenya*. New York, NY: International Peace Institute.

Long, James D., Karuti Kanyinga, Karen E. Feree & Clark Gibson (2013) Choosing peace over democracy. *Journal of Democracy* 24 (3): 140–155.

Lu, C. (2002) Human wrongs and the tragedy of victimhood. *Ethics and International Affairs*. 16 (2): 109–117.

Lugano, Geoffrey (2017) Counter-shaming the International Criminal Court's intervention as neocolonial: Lessons from Kenya. *International Journal of Transitional Justice* 11 (1): 9–29.

Luke, Nancy (2005) Confronting the 'sugar daddy' stereotype: Age and economic asymmetries and risky sexual behaviour in urban Kenya. *International Family Planning Perspectives* 31 (1): 6–14

Lund, Giuliana (2003) 'Healing the nation': Medicolonial discourse and the state of emergency from apartheid to truth and reconciliation. *Cultural Critique* 54 (1): 88–119.

Lundy, Patricia (2009) Exploring home-grown transitional justice and its dilemmas: A case study of the historical enquiries team, Northern Ireland. *International Journal of Transitional Justice* 3 (3): 321–340.

Lutz, Ellen & Kathryn Sikkink (2001) The justice cascade: The evolution and impact of foreign human rights trials in Latin America. *Chicago Journal of International Law* 2 (1): 1–33.

Ly, Sok-Kheang (2009) What need for a truth commission? www.genocide watch.org/images/Cambodia_09_06_xx_What_need_for_a_truth_comm ission.doc <last accessed 7 March 2018>.

Lynch, Gabrielle (2009) Durable solution, help or hindrance? The failings and unintended implications of relief and recovery efforts for Kenya's post-election IDPs. *Review of African Political Economy* 36 (122): 604–610.

Lynch, Gabrielle (2011a) Democratisation and 'Criminal' Violence in Kenya. In Hendrik Kraetzschmar and John Schwarzmantel (eds) *Democracy and Violence*. London: Routledge: 161–184.

Lynch, Gabrielle (2011b) *I Say to You: Ethnic Politics and the Kalenjin in Kenya*. Chicago, IL: University of Chicago Press.

Lynch, Gabrielle (2012a) Becoming indigenous in the pursuit of justice: The African Commission on Human and Peoples' Rights and the Endorois. *African Affairs* 111 (442): 24–45.

Lynch, Gabrielle (2012b) Samoei, Koitalel arap. In E. K. Akyeampong & H. L. Gates, Jr (eds) *Dictionary of African Biography*, vol. 5. Oxford: Oxford University Press: 261–262.

Lynch, Gabrielle (2014a) Electing the 'alliance of the accused': The success of the Jubilee Alliance in Kenya's Rift Valley Province. *Journal of Eastern African Studies* 8 (1): 93–11.

Lynch, Gabrielle (2014b) Non-judicial battles: Kenyan politics and the International Criminal Court. *Africa Policy Brief* no. 8. www.egmontinsti tute.be/papers/13/afr/APB8.pdf <last accessed 7 March 2018>.

Lynch, Gabrielle (8 November 2014c) Execution of truth commission proposal long overdue. *Saturday Naton* (Nairobi).

Lynch, Gabrielle (2015a) Bringing the Audience Back In: Kenya's Truth, Justice and Reconciliation Commission and the efficacy of public hearings. In S. Rai & J. Reinelt (eds) *The Grammar of Politics and Performance*. Abingdon: Routledge: 162–182.

Lynch, Gabrielle (2015b). Democratisation in trouble: The election syndrome and the return of guided democracies. *The Constitution: Journal of Constitutional Development* 15 (1): 1–22.

Lynch, Gabrielle (28 March 2015) What the ICC should learn from witness mess in Uhuru Hague case. *Saturday Naton* (Nairobi).

Lynch, Gabrielle (30 May 2015) Why ICC has lost victims' support. *Saturday Naton* (Nairobi).
Lynch, Gabrielle (12 December 2015) End killings in northern Kenya and adopt proposals in the TJRC report. *Saturday Nation* (Nairobi).
Lynch, Gabrielle (2016) What's in a name? The politics of naming ethnic groups in Kenya's Cherangany Hills. *Journal of Eastern African Studies* 10 (1): 208–227.
Lynch, Gabrielle (9 April 2016) The ICC and the paradox of state cooperation in conducting investigations, determining ruling. *East African* (Nairobi).
Lynch, Gabrielle (16 April 2016) Violence victims still searching for justice. *Saturday Nation* (Nairobi).
Lynch, Gabrielle (10 February 2018) Government response to NASA inappropriate as it polarises an already divided country. *Saturday Nation* (Nairobi).
Lynch, Gabrielle & M. Zgonec-Rozej (2013) The ICC Intervention in Kenya. Chatham House Programme Paper AFP/ILP 2013/01. www.chathamhouse.org/sites/default/files/public/Research/Africa/0213pp_icc_kenya.pdf <last accessed 7 March 2018>.
MacGinty, Roger (2008) Indigenous peace-making versus the liberal peace. *Cooperation and Conflict* 43 (2): 139–163.
Mahony, Chris (2010) *The Justice Sector Afterthought: Witness Protection in Africa*. Pretoria: Institute for Security Studies.
Maliti, Tom (31 July 2013) Two opinion polls show support for the ICC drops in Kenya. International Justice Monitor. www.ijmonitor.org/2013/07/two-opinion-polls-show-support-for-the-icc-drops-in-kenya <last accessed 7 March 2018>.
Maliti, Tom (9 April 2015) Kenyan president and chief justice apologize for past injustices. *International Justice Monitor*. www.ijmonitor.org/2015/04/kenyan-president-and-chief-justice-apologize-for-past-injustices <last accessed 7 March 2018>.
Malombe, Davis M. (2012) The politics of truth commissions in Africa: A case study of Kenya. In C. Dolan, N. Mncwabe & M. Okello (eds) *Where Law Meets Reality: Forging African Transitional Justice*. Cape Town: Pambazuka Press: 99–123.
Mamdani, Mahmood (2000) A diminished truth. In Wilmot James & Linda van de Vijver (eds) *After the TRC: Reflections on Truth and Reconciliation in South Africa*. Claremont: David Philip Publishers Ltd: 58–61.
Mamdani, Mahmood (2002) Amnesty or impunity? A preliminary critique of the Truth and Reconciliation Commission of South Africa. *Diacritics* 32 (3–4): 33–59.

Mamdani, Mahmood (2009) *Saviors and Survivors: Darfur, Politics, and the War on Terror*. New York, NY: Pantheon.

Manson, Katrina (1 March 2013) Odinga warns of potential unrest if poll is not fair. *Financial Times*. on.ft.com/xfu2zu <last accessed 19 April 2016>.

Marcoux, Alain (1998) The feminization of poverty: Claims, facts and data needs. *Population and Development Review* 24 (1): 131–139.

Marks, S. C. (2000) *Watching the Wind: Conflict Resolution during South Africa's Transformation to Democracy*. Washington, DC: United States Institute of Peace.

Maupeu, Herve (2014) Kenyan elections: The ICC, God and the 2013 Kenyan general elections. In C. Thibon, M. Fouere, M. Ndeda & S. Mwangi (eds) *Kenya's Past as Prologue: Voters, Violence and the 2013 General Election*. Nairobi: Twaweza Communications Ltd: 27–41.

Mazzei, Julie (2011) Finding shame in truth: The importance of public engagement in truth commissions. *Human Rights Quarterly* 33 (2): 431–452.

McCargo, Duncan (2010) Thailand's National Reconciliation Commission: A flawed response to the Southern Conflict. *Global Change, Peace and Security* 22 (1): 75–91.

McEachern, C. (2002) *Narratives of Nation Media, Memory and Representation in the Making of the New South Africa*. New York, NY: Nova Science Publishers Inc.

McRobie, Heather (2015) Will Tunisia's Truth and Dignity Commission heal the wounds of the authoritarian past? http://ohrh.law.ox.ac.uk/will-tunisias-truth-and-dignity-commission-heal-the-wounds-of-the-authoritarian-past <last accessed 19 April 2016>.

Meister, R. (2002) Human rights and the politics of victimhood. *Ethics and International Affairs* 16 (2): 91–108.

Menkel-Meadow, Carrie (2007) Restorative justice: What is it and does it work? *Annual Review of Law and Social Science* 3: 161–87.

Meredith, Martin (2001) *Coming to Terms: South Africa's Search for Truth*. Oxford: Public Affairs Ltd.

Meyer, Birgit (2004) 'Praise the Lord': Popular cinema and Pentecostalite style in Ghana's new public sphere. *American Ethnologist* 31 (1): 92–110.

Miguna, Miguna (2012) *Peeling Back the Mask: A Quest for Justice in Kenya*. London: Gilgamesh.

Millar, Gearoid (2010) Assessing local experiences of truth-telling in Sierra Leone: Getting to 'why' through a qualitative case study analysis. *International Journal of Transitional Justice* 4 (3): 477–496.

Miller, Zinaida (2008) Effects of invisibilty: In search of the 'economic' in transitional justice. *International Journal of Transitional Justice* 2: 266–291.

Minow, Martha (1998) *Between Vengeance and Forgiveness: Facing History after Genocide and Mass Violence*. Boson, MA: Beacon Press.

Misztal, Barbara (2011) Forgiveness and the construction of new conditions for a common life. *Contemporary Social Science* 6 (1): 39–53.

Mituallah, Winnie (2015) Negotiated democracy: A double-barrelled sword. In K. Njogu & P. W. Wekesa (eds) *Kenya's 2013 Election: Stakes, Practices and Outcomes*. Nairobi: Twaweza Communications Ltd: 344–361.

Moon, Claire (2004) Prelapsarian state: Forgiveness and reconciliation in transitional justice. *International Journal for the Semiotics of Law* 17 (2): 185–197.

Moon, Claire (2012) 'Who'll pay reparations on my soul?': Compensation, social control and social suffering. *Social and Legal Studies* 21 (2): 187–199.

Moses, A. Dirk (2011) Genocide and the terror of history. *Parallax* 17 (4): 90–108.

Moss, Natalie & Alasdair O'Hare (2014) Staging democracy: Kenya's televised presidential debates. *Journal of Eastern African Studies* 8 (1): 78–92.

Motsemme, N. (2004) The mute always speak: On women's silences at the Truth and Reconciliation Commission. *Current Sociology* 52 (5): 909–932.

Mouffe, C. (2000) *The Democratic Paradox*. London: Verso.

Mueller, Susanne (2014a) Kenya and the International Criminal Court (ICC) politics, the election and the law. *Journal of Eastern African Studies* 8 (1): 25–42.

Mueller, Susanne (2014b) The resilience of the past: Government and opposition in Kenya. *Canadian Journal of African Studies* 48 (2): 333–352.

Munn, N. D. (1992) The cultural anthropology of time: A critical essay. *Annual Review of Anthropology* 21: 93–123.

Muriithi, Angela Githitho & Georgina Page (2014) *What Was the Role of the Debate Programme Sema Kenya (Kenya Speaks) in the Kenyan Election 2013?* Research Report Issue 5. London: BBC Media Action. http://dataportal.bbcmediaaction.org/site/assets/uploads/2016/11/Sema-Kenya-Research-Report.pdf <last accessed 7 March 2018>.

Murunga, Godwin and Shadrack W. Nasong'o (2007) *Kenya: The Struggle for Democracy*. London: Zed Books.

Murunga, Godwin, Duncan Okello and Anders Sjögren (eds) (2014) *Kenya: The Struggle for a New Constitutional Order*. London: Zed Books.

Musila, Godfrey (2009) Options for transitional justice in Kenya: Autonomy and the challenge of external prescriptions. *International Journal of Transitional Justice* 3 (3): 445–464.

Mutahi, Patrick (2005) Political violence in the elections. In Herve Maupeu, Musambayi Katumanga and Winnie Mitullah (eds) *The Moi Succession: The 2002 Elections in Kenya*. Nairobi: Transafrica Press: 69–96.

Muthoni, Kamau (20 September 2016) ICC refers Kenya to assembly of states parties. *Standard* (Nairobi).

Mutoko, Caroline (18 November 2013) Uhuru ditch the monkey on your back. *The Star* (Nairobi).

Mutongi, Kenda (1999) 'Worries of the heart': Widowed mothers, daughters and masculinities in Maragoli, western Kenya, 1040–60. *Journal of African History* 40 (1): 67–86.

Mutua, Makau (15 April 2003) Truth commission needed. *Daily Nation* (Nairobi).

Mutua, Makau (2008) *Kenya's Quest for Democracy: Taming Leviathan*. Kampala: Fountain Publishers.

Mwangi, Oscar Gakuo (2015) Don't be vague bash The Hague: Votes and legitimacy in Kenya's 2013 elections. *Commonwealth and Comparative Politics* 53 (4): 381–400.

NASA (2017) A strong nation: National Super Alliance coalition manifesto 2017. https://nasacoalition.com/nasa-coalition-manifesto.pdf <last accessed 7 March 2018>.

NCIC (2013) *National Cohesion and Integration Commission Annual Report, 2011–2012*. Nairobi: NCIC.

Ndonga, Simon (31 October 2013) ICC witness procurement, coaching must be exposed – Matsanga. *Capital FM* www.capitalfm.co.ke/news/2013/10/icc-witness-procurement-coaching-must-be-exposed-matsanga <last accessed 7 March 2018>.

Ndonga, Wambui (23 May 2013) Kiplagat doubts TJRC report will pass test of time. *Capital FM*. www.capitalfm.co.ke/news/2013/05/kiplagat-doubts-tjrc-report-will-pass-test-of-time <last accessed 7 March 2018>.

NEP Journal (30 April 2014) Wajir residents deface Wagalla massacre monument in protest of 'Qorahey' fencing. http://nepjournal.com/899 <last accessed 7 March 2018>.

Nesiah, Vasuki (2006) *Truth Commissions and Gender: Principles, Policies, and Procedures*. New York, NY: International Centre for Transitional Justice.

Newell, Stephanie (1997) Making up their own minds: Readers, interpretations and the difference of view in Ghanaian popular narratives. *Africa* 67 (3): 389–405.

Nichols, Lionel (2015) *The International Criminal Court and the End of Impunity in Kenya*. New York, NY: Springer.

Njenga, Bishop (Rtd) Peter (4 April 2012) Stop demonizing Gema: We only told ICC to be sensitive to local politics. *Daily Nation* (Nairobi).

Nordstrom, Peter (2013) Gender and reconciliation in the new Kenya. Institute of Justice and Reconciliation, policy brief no. 13. http://www.ijr.org.za/publications/pb13.php <last accessed 25 April 2016>.

Nyairo, Joyce (2015) The circus comes to town: Performance, religion and exchange in political party campaigns. In K. Njogu & P. W. Wekesa (eds) *Kenya's 2013 Election: Stakes, Practices and Outcomes*. Nairobi: Twaweza Communications Ltd: 124–143.

Ocampo, L. M (2009) ICC Prosecutor: Kenya can be an example to the world. Press release 18 September, www.icc-cpi.int/en_menus/icc/situations%20and%20cases/situations/situation%20icc%200109/press%20releases/Pages/pr452.aspx <last accessed 22 August 2014>.

Oketch, Willis (11 May 2013) Tough questions as Tana Delta clashes report gathers dust. *Standard* (Nairobi).

Olckers, Ilze (1996) Gender-neutral truth: A reality shamefully distorted. *Agenda* 12 (31): 61–67.

Oloo, Adams (2015) The triumph of ethnic identity over ideology in the 2013 general election in Kenya. In K. Njogu & P. W. Wekesa (eds) *Kenya's 2013 Election: Stakes, Practices and Outcomes*. Nairobi: Twaweza Communications Ltd: 48–63.

Omondi, Charles (21 May 2013) Kenya's president receives TJRC report, *Africa Review*. www.africareview.com/News/President-Kenyatta-receives-TJRC-report/-/979180/1859070/-/44g0b8/-/index.html%20%3C19%20August%202015%3E <last accessed 26 April 2016>.

Omwenga, Samuel (16 February 2012) Uhuru and Ruto sowing seeds of discord, *Pambazuka News*. www.pambazuka.org/taxonomy/term/6612 <last accessed 7 March 2018>.

Opalo, Kennedy (2013) Which way forward for Kenya's civil society? African Arguments, 28 May. http://africanarguments.org/2013/05/28/which-way-forward-for-kenya%e2%80%99s-civil-society-%e2%80%93-by-kennedy-opalo <last accessed 7 March 2018>.

Orentlicher, Diane F. (1991) Settling accounts: The duty to prosecute human rights violations of a prior regime. *Yale Law Journal* 100 (8): 2537–2615.

Orr, Wendy (2000) *From Biko to Basson: Wendy Orr's Search for the Soul of South Africa as a Commissioner of the TRC*. Saxonwold: Contra.

Osiel, Mark (2000) *Mass Atrocity, Collective Memory, and the Law*. New Brunswick, NJ: Transaction Publishers.

Osse, Anneke (2016) Police reform in Kenya: A process of 'meddling through'. *Policing and Society* 26 (8): 907–924.

Ost, David (2004) Politics as the mobilization of anger: Emotions in movements and in power. *European Journal of Social Theory* 7 (2): 229–244.

Otieno, F. (ed) (2015) *New Constitution, Same Old Challenges: Reflections on Kenya's 2013 General Elections*. Nairobi: Society for International Development.

Owens, Ingrid, Glenda Wildschut, Wendy Orr & Pumla Goboda-Madikezela (1996) Stories of silence: Women, truth and reconciliation. *Agenda* 30: 66–72.

Owusu, Maxwell (1992) Democracy and Africa – A view from the village. *Journal of Modern African Studies* 30 (3): 369–396.

Paisley, Ian (16 March 2012) Peace must not be the victim of international justice. New York Times, www.nytimes.com/2012/03/17/opinion/peace-must-not-be-the-victim-of-international-justice.html <last accessed 7 March 2018>.

Pambazuka News (11 June 2013) Britain announces compensation for Mau Mau victims. Official government statement read by Foreign Secretary William Hague www.pambazuka.org/security-icts/britain-announces-compensation-mau-mau-victims <last accessed 7 March 2018>.

Paris, Roland (2002) International peacebuilding and the 'mission civilisatrice'. *Review of International Studies* 28 (4): 637–656.

Payne, Leigh (2004) In search of remorse: Confessions by perpetrators of past state violence. *Brown Journal of World Affairs* 11 (1): 115–125.

Payne, Leigh (2007) Unsettling accounts: Pereptrators' confessions and the media. Conference on Truth, Historic Memory and Mass Media, 28 November 2007. Bogota: Columbia. www.researchgate.net/publication/241383015_Unsettling_Accounts_Perpetrators'_Confessions_and_the_Media <last accessed 7 March 2018>.

Payne, Leigh (2008) *Unsettling Accounts: Neither Truth nor Reconciliation in Confessions of State Violence*. Durham, NC: Duke University Press.

Payne, Leigh (2009) Confessional performances: A methodological approach to studying perpetrators' testimonies. In Hugo van der Merwe, Victoria Baxter & Audrey R. Chapman (eds) *Assessing the Impact of Transitional Justice: Challenges for Empirical Research*. Washington, DC: United State Institute of Peace: 227–248.

Peskin, Victor (2005) Beyond Victor's justice? The challenge of prosecuting the winners at the international criminal tribunals for the former Yugoslavia and Rwanda. *Journal of Human Rights* 4 (2): 213–231.

Peskin, Victor (2008) *International Justice in Rwanda and the Balkans: Virtual Trials and the Struggle for State Cooperation*. Cambridge: Cambudge University Press.

Peskin, Victor (2009) Caution and confrontation in the International Criminal Court's pursuit of accountability in Uganda and Sudan. *Human Rights Quarterly* 31 (3): 655–691.

Peterson, Derek (2012) *Ethnic Patriotism and the East African Revivial: A History of Dissent, c. 1935–1972*. Cambridge: Cambridge University Press.

Posel, Deborah (1999) *The TRC Report: What Kind of History? What Kind of Truth? A Preliminary Exploration*. Working paper, University of the Witwatersrand http://wiredspace.wits.ac.za/bitstream/handle/10539/8046/HWS-341.pdf?sequence=1 <last accessed 7 March 2018>.

Posel, Deborah (2008) History as confession: The case of the South African Truth and Reconciliation Commission. *Public Culture* 20 (1): 119–141.

Pupavac, Vanessa (2001) Therapeutic governance: Psycho-social intervention and trauma risk management. *Disasters* 25 (4): 358–372.

Pykett, J., M. Saward & A. Schaefer (2010) Framing the good citizen. *British Journal of Politics and International Relations* 12 (4): 523–538.

Ranger, Terence (2004) Nationalist historiography, patriotic history and the history of the nation: The struggle over the past in Zimbabwe. *Journal of Southern African Studies* 30 (2): 215–234.

Rasmussen, Jacob (2010) Mungiki as youth movement: Revolution, gender and generational politics in Nairobi, Kenya. *Young* 18 (3): 301–319.

Rawls, John (1972) *A Theory of Justice*. Oxford: Clarendon.

Reinelt, J. & S. Rai (2015) Introduction. In S. Rai & J. Reinelt (eds) *The Grammar of Politics and Performance*. Abingdon: Routledge: 1–18.

Rieff, David (2016) *In Praise of Forgetting: Historical Memory and Its Ironies*. New Haven, CT: Yale University Press.

Robins, Simon (2011) *'To Live as Other Kenyans Do': A Study of the Reparative Demands of Kenyan Victims of Human Rights Violations*. New York, NY: ICTJ.

Robins, Simon (2014) The 2011 toilet wars in South Africa: Justice and transition between the exceptional and the everyday after apartheid. *Development and Change* 45 (3): 479–501.

Roht-Arriaza, Naomi (2006) The new landscape of transitional justice. In Naomi Roht-Arriza & Javier Mariecurrena (eds) *Transitional Justice in the Twenty-First Century*. Cambridge: Cambridge University Press: 1–16.

Roht-Arriaza, Naomi & Javier Mariezcurrena (eds) (2006) *Transitional Justice in the Twenty-First Century: Beyond Truth versus Justice*. Cambridge: Cambridge University Press.

Rolfe, B. (2005) Building an electronic repertoire of contention. *Social Movement Studies* 4 (1): 65–74.

Rosen, Jonathan (2015) Reporters, witnesses silenced 'one by one' with ICC link deadly in Kenya. 24 August 2015. http://america.aljazeera.com/articles/2015/8/24/kenyas-dark-path-to-justice.html <last accessed 16 April 2016>.

Ross, Fiona (2003a) *Bearing Witness: Women and the Truth and Reconciliation Commission in South Africa*. London: Pluto Press.

Ross, Fiona (2003b) On having voice and being heard: Some after-effects of testifying before the South African Truth and Reconciliation Commission. *Anthropological Theory* 3 (3): 325–341.

Roth, Kenneth (2014) Africa attacks the International Criminal Court, *The New York Review of Books*, 6 February Issue. www.nybooks.com/arti cles/archives/2014/feb/06/africa-attacks-international-criminal-court <last accessed 26 August 2014>.

Roy, Arundhati (1997) *The God of Small Things*. New Delhi: Penguin Books.

Ruddick, Sara (1989) *Maternal Thinking: Toward a Politics of Peace*. Boston, MA: Beacon Press.

Ruteere, Mutuma (2011) More than political tools: The police and post-election violence in Kenya. *African Security Review* 20 (4): 11–20.

Ruteere, M. & K. Wairuri (2015) Explaining and mitigating elections-related violence and human rights in Kenya. In K. Njogu & P. W. Wekesa (eds) *Kenya's 2013 Election: Stakes, Practices and Outcomes*. Nairobi: Twaweza Communications Ltd: 112–123.

Ryanga, Heri (2015) *Women and Conflict in Mt Elgon, Kenya: Rape as a Weapon of War*. Saarbrucken: LAP Lambert.

Sanders, Mark (2007) *Ambiguities of Witnessing: Law and Literature in the Time of a Truth Commission*. Stanford, CA: Stanford University Press.

Sankey, Diana (2014) Towards recognition of subsistence harms: Reassessing approaches to socioeconomic forms of violence in transitional justice. *International Journal of Transitional Justice* 8 (1): 121–140.

Sarkin, Jeremy (1996) The trials and tribulations of South Africa's Truth and Reconciliation Commission. *South African Journal on Human Rights* 12 (4): 617–640.

Sarkin, Jeremy (2001) The tension between justice and reconciliation in Rwanda: Politics, human rights, due process and the role of the Gacaca Courts in dealing with the genocide. *Journal of African Law* 45 (2): 143–172.

Schaap, Andrew (2003) *The Time of Reconciliation and the Space of Politics*. Paper for the Second Conference on Law, Time and Reconciliation, University of Tilburg, 22–23 May 2003, http://hdl.handle.net/11343/337 74 <last accessed 26 April 2016>.

Schaap, Andrew (2004) Political reconciliation through a struggle for recognition? *Social and Legal Studies* 13 (4): 523–540.

Schaap, Andrew (2006) Agonism in divided societies. *Philosophy and Social Criticism* 32: 255.

Schaap, Andrew (2008) Reconciliation as ideology and politics. *Constellations* 15 (2): 249–264.

Schabas, William A (2008) 'Complementarity in practice': Some uncomplimentary thoughts. *Criminal Law Forum* 19 (1): 5–33.

Sey, James (1998) Psychoanalysis and South Africa. *American Imago* 55 (1): 3–8.

Shah, Seema (2015) Free and fair? Citizens' assessments of the 2013 general election in Kenya. *Review of African Political Economy* 42 (143): 44–61.

Sharp, Dustin (2012) Interrograting the peripheries. The preoccupations of fourth generation transitional justice. *Harvard Human Rights Journal* 26: 149–178.

Shaw, Rosalind (2007) Memory frictions: Localizing the Truth and Reconciliation Commission in Sierra Leone. *International Journal of Transitional Justice* 1 (2): 183–207.

Shaw, Rosalind & Lars Waldorf (2010) Introduction: Localizing transitional justice. In R. Shaw and L. Waldorf with P. Hazan (eds) *Localizing Transitional Justice: Interventions and Priorities after Mass Violence*. Stanford: Stanford University Press: 3–26.

Sheekh, Nuur Mohamud & Jason Mosley (2012) Kenya: Tana Delta Violence – Is there worse to come. *African Arguments*, 6 November. http://africanarguments.org/2012/11/06/kenya-tana-delta-violence-%e2%80%93-is-there-worse-to-come-%e2%80%93-by-nuur-mohamud-sheekh-and-jason-mosley <last accessed 7 March 2018>.

Sheikh, S. Abdi (2007) *Blood on the Runway: The Wagalla Massacre of 1984*. Nairobi: Northern Publishing House.

Silberschmidt, M. (1999) *'Women Forget that Men Are the Masters': Gender Antagonism and Socio-economic Change in Kisii District, Kenya*. Stockholm: Elanders Gotab.

Silberschmidt, M. (2001) Disempowerment of men in rural and urban East Africa: Implications for male identity and sexual behavior. *World Development* 29 (4): 657–671.

Situma, Arthur (27 September 2015) Martha Karua 'fixed' Ruto at ICC, Kuria insists as he reveals names of 'coached' witnesses. *Sunday Nation* (Nairobi).

Slye, Ron (1997) Socio-economic rights and the South African transition: The role of the Truth and Reconciliation Commission. *Law, Democracy and Development* 1: 137–159.

Slye, Ron (1998/9) Apartheid as a crime against humanity: A submission to the South African Truth and Reconciliation Commission. *Michigan Journal of International Law* 20: 267–300.

Slye, Ron (2000) Amnesty, truth, and reconciliation: Reflections on the South African amnesty process. In Robert I. Rotberg and Dennis Thompson (eds) *Truth v. Justice: The Morality of Truth Commissions*. Princeton, NJ: Princeton University Press: 170–188.

Slye, Ron (2017) Putting the J into the TJRC: Kenya's Truth Justice and Reconciliation Commission. (Later published in Mia Smart and Karin van Marle (eds) *The Limits of Transition: The South African Truth and Reconciliation Commission 20 Years On*. Leiden: Brill: 282–307) https://

papers.ssrn.com/sol3/papers.cfm?abstract_id=2929768 <last accessed 7 March 2018>.

Slyomovics, Susan (2005) The argument from silence: Morocco's Truth Commission and women political prisoners. *Journal of Middle East Women's Studies* 1 (3): 73–95.

South Consulting (February 2009) The Kenya National Dialogue and Reconciliation (KNDR) Monitoring Project, Project Context and Summary of Findings. www.katibainstitute.org/Archives/images/Monitoring%20and%20Evaluation%20Report%20on%20the%20National%20Accord.pdf <last accessed 7 March 2018>.

South Consulting (October 2009) The Kenya National Dialogue and Reconciliation (KNDR) Monitoring Project, Status of Implementation of Agenda Items 1–4, Fourth Review Report. www.dialoguekenya.org/mreport.aspx <last accessed 7 March 2018>.

Southall, Roger (2005) The Ndungu Report: Land and graft in Kenya. *Review of African Political Economy* 32 (103): 142–151.

Spear, T. and R. Waller (eds) (1993) *Being Maasai: Ethnicity and Identity in East Africa*. London: James Currey.

Spronk, Rachel (2014) The idea of African men: Dealing with the cultural contradictions of sex in academia and in Kenya. *Culture, Health and Sexuality* 16 (5): 504–517.

Sriram, Chandra Lekha (2007) Justice as peace? Liberal peacebuilding and strategies of transitional justice. *Global Society* 21 (4): 579–591.

Stahn, C. (2001) Accommodating individual criminal responsibility and national reconciliation: The UN Commission for East Timor. *American Journal of International Law* 95 (4): 952–966.

Standard (Nairobi) (11 October 2009) Probe cash misuse allegations in Kazi Kwa Vijana.

Standard (Nairobi) (25 October 2009) Youth employment hopes dim as SH15b project backfires.

Standard (Nairobi) (2 December 2012) Rift voters jittery over Ruto-Uhuru deal.

Standard (Nairobi) (5 April 2016) Kenyans react to caning of protesting UoN students by anti-riot police after SONU elections.

Stanley, E. (2001) Evaluating the Truth and Reconciliation Commission. *Journal of Modern African Studies* 39(3): 525–546.

Stein, D. J. (1998) Psychiatric aspects of the Truth and Reconciliation Commission in South Africa. *British Journal of Psychiatry* 173 (6): 455–457.

Steinberg, Jonny (2010) Briefing: Liberia's experiment with transitional justice. *African Affairs* 109 (434): 135–144.

Steinberg, Jonny (2016) *A Man of Good Hope: One Man's Extraordinary Journey from Mogadishu to Tin Can Town*. London: Vintage.
Subotić, J. (2009) *Hijacked Justice: Dealing with the Past in the Balkans*. Ithaca, NY: Cornell University Press.
Summerfield, Derek (2002) Effects of war: Moral knowledge, revenge, reconciliation, and medicalised concepts of 'recovery'. *British Medical Journal* 325 (7352): 1105–1107.
Sunday Nation (Nairobi) (1 April 2012) Wamalwa defends his membership in G7.
Tambakaki, Paulina (2011) Agonism and the reconception of European citizenship. *British Journal of Politics and International Relations* 13 (4): 567–585.
Tarrow, S. (2011) *Power in Movement: Social Movements and Contentious Politics. Revised and Updated Third edn*. Cambridge: Cambridge University Press.
Taylor, Diana (2003) *The Archive and the Repertoire: Performing Cultural Memory in the Americas*. Durham, NC: Duke University Press.
Teitel, Ruti G. (2000) *Transitional Justice*. Oxford: Oxford University Press.
The Star (Nairobi) (8 February 2013) US warns of ICC consequences.
Theidon, Kimberly (2006) Justice in transition: The micropolitics of reconciliation in postwar Peru. *Journal of Conflict Resolution* 50 (3): 433–457.
Theidon, Kimberly (2007) Gender in transition: Common sense, women, and war. *Journal of Human Rights* 6 (4): 453–478.
Thomson, Susan (2011) The darker side of transitional justice: The power dynamics behind Rwanda's gacaca courts. *Africa* 81 (3): 373–390.
Thuku, Wahome (6 December 2014) President Uhuru Kenyatta off the hook, heat turns on Bensouda. *Standard* (Nairobi).
Tilly, Chris (1995) *Popular Contention in Great Britain, 1758–1834*. Abingdon: Routledge.
Tostensen, Arne (2009) Electoral mismanagement and post-election violence in Kenya – the Kriegler and Waki Commissions of Inquiry. *Nordisk Tidsskrift for Menneskerettigheter* 27 (4): 427–451.
TJRC (2013) *Report of the Truth, Justice and Reconciliation Commission*, vol. 1–5. Nairobi: TJRC.
TRC (1998) Report of the Truth and Reconciliation Commission, vol. 1. www.justice.gov.za/trc/report <last accessed 7 March 2018>.
Tripp, Aili (2001) Women's movements and challenges to neopatrimonial rule: Preliminary observations from Africa. *Development and Change* 32 (1): 33–54.
Tripp, Aili (2010) *Museveni's Uganda: Paradoxes of Power in a Hybrid Regime*. Boulder, CO: Lynne Rienner Publishers.

Trouillot, Michel-Rolph (2011) From 'Abortive rituals: Historical apologies in the global era'. In Jeffrey K. Olick, Vered Vinitzky-Seroussi & Daniel Levy (eds) *The Collective Memory Reader*. Oxford: Oxford University Press: 458–464.

Truth and Reconciliation Commission of Liberia (2009) Final Report. http://trcofliberia.org/reports/final-report <last accessed 7 March 2018>.

Tutu, Archbishop D. (1999) *No Future without Forgiveness*. London: Rider.

UN (2006) Rule of law tools for post-conflict states: Truth commissions. www.ohchr.org/Documents/Publications/RuleoflawTruthCommissionsen.pdf <last accessed 26 April 2016>.

UN (2010) *Guidance note of the Secretary-General: United Nations approach to transitional justice*. United Nations Rule of Law. www.unrol.org/files/tj_guidance_note_march_2010final.pdf <last accessed 7 March 2018>.

Uraia (2013) End term evaluation report for the Uchaguzi Bora Initiative, September 2013–October 2013. http://uraia.or.ke/wp-content/uploads/2016/06/UBI-Evaluation-Final-Report.pdf <last accessed 7 March 2018>.

Van Stapele, Naomi (2015) *Respectable 'Illegality': Gangs, Masculinities and Belonging in a Nairobi Ghetto*. PhD dissertation, University of Amsterdam.

Van Stapele, Naomi (2016) 'We are not Kenyans': Extra-judicial killings, manhood and citizenship in Mathare, a Nairobi ghetto. *Conflict, Security & Development* 16 (4): 301–325.

Verdoolaege, Annelies (2005) Media representations of the South African Truth and Reconciliation Commission and their commitment to reconciliation. *Journal of African Cultural Studies* 17 (2): 181–199.

Villa-Vicencio, Charles (2000) Getting on with life: A move towards reconciliation. In Charles Villa-Vicencio & Wilhelm Verwoerd (eds) *Looking Back, Reaching Forward: Reflections on the Truth and Reconciliation Commission of South Africa*. Cape Town: University of Cape Town Press: 199–209.

Villa-Vicencio, Charles & Wilhelm Verwoerd (2000) Introduction. In Charles Villa-Vicencio & Wilhelm Verwoerd (eds) *Looking Back, Reaching Forward: Reflections on the Truth and Reconciliation Commission of South Africa*. Cape Town: University of Cape Town Press: 199–209.

Vilmer, Jean-Baptiste (2016) The African Union and the International Criminal Court: Counteracting the crisis. *International Affairs* 92 (6): 1319–1342.

Volkan, Vamik (1997) *Blood Lines: From Ethnic Pride to Ethnic Terrorism*. Boulder, CO: Westview Press.

Wachira, George (2009) Transitional justice and the rule of law: Lessons from the Truth Commissions in Africa. *Wajibu* 24 (1): 1–8. https://www.swradioafrica.com/Documents/AfricaFiles070409.pdf <last accessed 7 March 2018>.

Wachira, George & Prsisca Kamungi (2010) *Noble Intentions, Nagging Dilemmas: In Search of Context-Responsive Truth Commissions in Africa.* Policy Brief. Nairobi: NPI-Africa and WANEP.

Wainaina, Ndung'u (29 January 2009) The Truth, Justice and Reconciliation Commission: A flawed law. *Pambazuka News.* www.pambazuka.org/governance/truth-justice-and-reconciliation-commission-flawed-law <last accessed 7 March 2018>.

Wainaina, B. (10 March 2013) Kenyans elected a president we felt could bring peace. *Guardian* (London).

Waldorf, Lars (2012) Anticipating the past: Transitional justice and socio-economic wrongs. *Social & Legal Studies* 21 (2): 171–186.

Wangusi, Nathan (25 October 2012) 2013 election will be a referendum on integrity. *Pambazuka News.* http://allafrica.com/stories/201210260806.html <last accessed 7 March 2018>.

Wanner, Thomas & Ben Wadham (2015) Men and masculinities in international development: 'Men-streaming' gender and development. *Development Policy Review* 33 (1): 15–32.

Wanyama, Henry (1 February 2014) 61% of Kenyans want ICC cases dropped – poll. *The Star* (Nairobi).

Wanyeki, Muthoni (2012) The International Criminal Court's Cases in Kenya: Origin and Impact. Institute for Security Studies Paper, no. 237. www.issafrica.org/uploads/Paper237.pdf <last accessed 26 April 2016>.

Wasserman, Herman & Jacinta Mwende Maweu (2014) The freedom to be silent? Market pressures on journalistic normative ideals at the Nation Media Group in Kenya. *Review of African Political Economy* 41 (142): 623–633.

Wendo, Nabea (2016) Ethnic stereotyping on Kenyan blog sites in the 2013 political elections: A spurious harbinger of ethnic discord. In D.O. Orwenjo (ed) *Political Discourse in Emergent, Fragile, and Failed Democracies.* Hershey, PA: IGI Global.

Williamson, Cecile Aptel (2006) Justice empowered or justice hampered: The International Criminal Court in Darfur. *African Security Review* 15 (1): 20–31.

Willis, Justin (2015) 'Peace and order are in the interest of every citizen': Elections, violence and state legitimacy in Kenya, 1957–74. *International Journal of African Historical Studies* 48 (1): 99–116.

Willis, Justin & Ngala Chome (2014) Marginalization and political participation on the Kenya coast: The 2013 elections. *Journal of Eastern African Studies* 8 (1): 115–134.

Wilson, Richard A. (2001) *The Politics of Truth and Reconciliation in South Africa: Legitimizing the Post-Apartheid State*. Cambridge: Cambridge University Press.

Wilson, Richard A. (2005) Judging history: The historical record of the International Criminal Tribunal for the Former Yugoslavia. *Human Rights Quarterly* 27 (3): 908–942.

Wilson, Richard A. (2007) Humanity's histories: Evaluating the historical accounts of international tribunals and truth commissions. *Politix* 80 (4): 31–58.

Wilson, Richard A. (2011) *Writing History in International Criminal Trials*. Cambridge: Cambridge University Press.

Wipper, Audrey (1975) The Maendeleo ya Wanawake movement: Some paradoxes and contradictions. *African Studies Review* 18 (3): 99–120.

Wohl, M., M. Hornsey & C. Philpot (2011) A critical review of official public apologies: Aims, pitfalls, and a staircase model of effectiveness. *Social Issues and Policy Review* 5 (1): 70–100.

Wolf, Tom (2015) From sinners to saints? The ICC and Jubilee's triumph in Kenya's 2013 election. In K. Njogu & P. W. Wekesa (eds) *Kenya's 2013 Election: Stakes, Practices and Outcomes*. Nairobi: Twaweza Communications Ltd: 162–197.

Wrong, Michela (2009) *It's Our Turn to Eat: The Story of a Kenyan Whistleblower*. London: Fourth Estate.

Wrong, Michela (11 March 2013) Indictee for president! *New York Times*. http://latitude.blogs.nytimes.com/2013/03/11/being-prosecuted-by-the-i-c-c-helped-uhuru-kenyattas-chances-in-kenyas-election/?_r=0 <last accessed 7 March 2018>.

Yoder, Jennifer A. (1999) Truth without reconciliation: An appraisal of the enguete commission on the SED dictatorship in Germany. *German Politics* 8 (3): 59–80.

Young, Sandra (2004) Narrative and healing in the hearings of the South African Truth and Reconciliation Commission. *Biography* 27 (1): 145–162.

Zalewski, Marysia (2010) 'I don't even know what gender is': A discussion of the connections between gender, gender mainstreaming and feminist theory. *Review of International Studies* 36 (1): 3–27.

Index

Acknowledgment, reparations versus, 270–271
Adversely mentioned persons (AMPs). *See also* Impunity
  overview, 247–248
  'amnesia' and, 228–229
  assertions of innocence by, 243–246
  confession, lack of, 225, 232–234
  denial of wrongfulness of acts by, 229–231
  disdain for TJRC by, 235
  elitism of, 237–242
  hearsay alleged by, 227–228
  lack of cooperation by, 234–235
  lack of incentive to testify, 247–248
  platform for, TJRC hearings as, 234–243
  public naming of, 222, 242
  questioning of sources by, 227–228
  rumour alleged by, 227–228
  in TJRC hearings, 134–135, 139–140, 222–225, 234–243
  transfer of responsibility by, 226–227
  use of term, 222
  victims, portrayal as, 229
African Commission on Human and People's Rights, 180
African Court, 180
African Union, 71
Africa Peace Forum, 237
Agonistic reconciliation, 280–281, 282, 286–289
Ali, Muhamed Hussein, 69–70, 73
al-Shabaab, 55–56, 164
Amnesia, 8, 228–229
Amnesty. *See* Impunity
AMPs. *See* Adversely mentioned persons (AMPs)
Anglo-Leasing Scandal, 240, 241–242

Annan, Kofi, 24, 113, 115
Argentina, truth commissions in, 126–127
Asiyo, Phoebe, 180, 208

Barazas (public meetings), 36
Bensouda, Fatou, 73–74
Benzien, Jeffrey, 154–155, 157–158, 218
Bill of Rights, 177
'Blood money', 270
Bomett, Lawrence, 125
Botha, P.W., 155
BPT Advisors, 71
Buke, Wafula, 120
Bulla Karatasi Massacre, 222, 236
Burundi, Rome Statute and, 89
Business, 44
Buthelezi, Mangosuthu, 99

Calata, Nomonde, 154–155, 157
Cambodia, transitional justice in, 15
Carson, Johnny, 83
Cathartic effect
  of TJRC, 252–253
  of TRC, 128–129
Catholic Justice and Peace Commission (CJPC), 38–39, 41, 121–122, 266
Central Bank of Kenya, 240
Chawatama, Gertrude, 101–103, 120
Chepyuk Settlement Scheme, 225, 232, 236–237
Children, focus of TJRC on, 162–163
China, Rome Statute and, 66
Christianity
  Neo-Pentecostalism, 46–47, 48–49, 266
  peacebuilding and, 46–47, 48–49
Churches, response to TJRC, 266

327

Civil society organisations (CSOs)
  Mt. Elgon Conflict and, 47–48
  neo-colonialism and, 83
  peacebuilding and, 36–37, 38–39, 42–43
  TJRC and, 113, 115, 116–117, 119–120, 121–122, 140–141, 192, 259, 261–263, 265–266, 268
  Wagalla Massacre and, 140–141, 261–262, 271
Civil Society Organizations Network, 121–122
Class, focus of TJRC on, 164–165
Coalition for Reform and Democracy (CORD)
  generally, 35
  Neo-Pentecostalism and, 47
  2013 election and, 31, 50, 52–54, 59
Cohesion, reconciliation as, 280–281, 282, 285–286
Commission of Inquiry into the Illegal/Irregular Allocation of Public Land, 108, 115
Commission of Inquiry into the Post-Election Violence
  generally, 79, 231
  ICC and, 81–82
  investigations by, 24–25, 67–69, 76–78
  procedures of, 106
  reports, 203, 244
Commissions of Inquiry, 105–111. *See also specific Commission*
Community mediators and conflict monitors, 38–39
Comprehensive Peace Agreement (Sudan), 237
Concerned Citizens for Peace (CCP), 113, 115
Confession by AMPs, lack of, 225, 232–234
Congo (Democratic Republic)
  ICC and, 65, 66–67
  transitional justice in, 14, 18
Constituency Development Fund, 235
Constitution (2010), 290
Constitution and Reform Education Consortium (CRECO), 122
Constitution of Kenya Review Act (2008), 25

Contentious coexistence, 280–281, 286–289
Continuing violations, 175–177
CORD. *See* Coalition for Reform and Democracy (CORD)
'Cradock Four', 154
CSOs. *See* Civil society organisations (CSOs)

Daaba, 176
Darfur, ICC and, 67
Data collection in TJRC, 170–173
de Klerk, F.W., 155, 218–219
Democratisation, transitional justice and, 13–19
Dialogue sessions, 40–41, 43
Dinka, Berhanu, 101–103
District Peace Committees, 36–39
Dolan, Gabriel, 110
DRC. *See* Congo (Democratic Republic)
du Preez, Max, 160

East Timor, transitional justice in, 15
Eichmann, Adolf, 61
Electoral Commission, 3
Elitism of AMPs, 237–242
Ethiopia, nationalism in, 30
'Evil society', 52, 83
Extra-judicial killings, 231

Faith-based organisations, 42–43
Farah, Ahmed Sheikh, 101–103
Federation of Women Lawyers (FIDA), 115
Feminenza (NGO), 47–48
Forgiveness, 253, 283–284
Fourth World Conference on Women, 186
Freud, Sigmund, 17

Gado (satirical cartoonist), 141–142
Gambia, Rome Statute and, 89
Gender
  neglect of masculinity, 185, 189–190
  reinforcement of traditional gender boundaries, 185
  stereotypes regarding, 211–213
  women (*See* Women)

Gender and Equality Commission, 197
Gender Violence Recovery Centre, 192
General Service Unit (GSU), 3, 231
Germany
   Organisation for International Cooperation (GIZ), 103, 223, 262, 271
   Study Commission for the Assessment of History and Consequences of the Socialist Unity Party Dictatorship in Germany, 126–127
Ghana, National Reconciliation Commission, 130
Goldenberg Scandal, 143, 240
Grace Agenda, 261–262
'Gugulethu Seven', 157, 158

Hague, William, 270–271
Hate speech, 39
Hayner, Priscilla, 127
Hearings. *See* Public hearings
Hearsay, 227–228
'Hijacked justice', 57–58
Human rights
   socio-economic effects of violations, 166, 167–168
   transitional justice and, 14

ICC. *See* International Criminal Court (ICC)
ICJ-Kenya, 262
Ideology of order, 55–56
IDP Network, 261–262
Implementation Committee, 198, 255–256
Impunity. *See also* Adversely mentioned persons (AMPs)
   overview, 220–221, 247–248
   'amnesia' and, 228–229
   confession, lack of, 225, 232–234
   denial of wrongfulness of acts and, 229–231
   ICC, effect of, 221
   limitations on, 222
   questioning of sources and, 227–228
   TJRC Act, effect of, 221
   transfer of responsibility and, 226–227
   TRC and, 218–220, 224
   victims, portrayal of AMPs as, 229
Independent Electoral and Boundaries Commission (IEBC), 51, 61–62
Independent Review Commission on the General Elections Held in Kenya on 27 December 2007, 24, 106
Internally displaced persons (IDPs), 273
International Centre for Policy and Conflict (ICPC), 122
International Centre for Transitional Justice (ICTJ), 262, 268
International Commission of Jurists (ICJ), 119–120, 122
International Criminal Court (ICC)
   generally, 5, 177, 251
   overview, 87–90
   Africa, focus on, 64–65
   African Union and, 71
   Ali and, 69–70, 73
   Common Legal Representatives, 71
   criticisms of, 66–67, 275–276
   Darfur and, 67
   DRC and, 65, 66–67
   ethnic differences in support for, 75–78, 79–83
   'hijacked justice' in, 57–58
   impunity, effect on, 221
   intimidation of witnesses in, 78
   Jubilee Alliance and, 25, 57, 88
   Kenyatta and, 35, 52, 53, 60, 69–70, 73–74, 87–90, 242
   Kosgey and, 69, 73
   murder of witnesses in, 240
   Muthaura and, 69–70, 73, 78
   neo-colonialism in, 65–66, 83–86
   'Ocampo Six', 71–73, 76–77
   Odinga and, 228
   ODM and, 69–70
   Office of the Prosecutor (OTP), 24–25, 57, 63, 67–71, 72, 73–74, 75–78, 79, 81, 87–88, 114
   PNU and, 69–70
   pragmatism in, 65–66
   Pre-Trial Chamber (PTC), 57, 70, 72–73
   public support for, 75–79
   research methodology regarding, 28
   Rome Statute, 63, 66, 83, 89
   Ruto and, 25, 35, 38, 52, 53, 60, 69, 73, 74, 87–90, 242

International Criminal Court (cont.)
  Sang and, 69, 73, 74
  Security Council and, 63, 66
  shaming, 62–64
  shortcomings of, 87–90
  Sudan and, 66
  TJRC, upstaging, 144–145
  transitional justice and, 14, 18
  Uganda and, 65, 66–67
  Victims Participation and Reparation Section, 71
  virtual trials, 62–64, 71, 74, 87
  witness tampering in, 77–78, 79
International criminal trials
  evaluations of, 61–63
  politics of performance in, 60–61
  shaming, 62–64
  virtual trials, 62–64
International Criminal Tribunal for the former Yugoslavia (ICTY), 62
International Organisation of Migration (IOM), 38–39
Interpreters at TJRC hearings, 136

Jubilee Alliance
  generally, 35, 82, 86–87, 228
  overview, 25
  creation of, 58–59
  Harmonised Manifesto, 49
  ICC and, 25, 57, 88
  neo-colonialism and, 84, 85–86
  Neo-Pentecostalism and, 47
  in office, 251
  on reconciliation, 280
  RJF and, 265
  TJRC and, 260–261, 266–267
  2013 election and, 31, 51, 52–54, 58–59, 67
Judicial Commission of Inquiry into Inter-Communal Violence in the Tana Delta, 108
Judiciary, response to TJRC, 261

KAMATUSA Meeting, 240–241
Kapondi, Fred, 223, 225, 226, 227, 229, 232, 235–236, 242–243
Kariuki, G.G., 119, 236, 242
Karuiki, J.M., 107–108
Kaul, Hans-Peter, 70, 72, 73

Kazi Kwa Vijana (KKV), 42
Kenya. *See specific topic*
Kenya African National Union (KANU), 58, 111, 122
Kenya Against Impunity (KAI), 122
Kenya Human Rights Commission (KHRC), 119–120, 122, 262
Kenya Kwanza Campaign, 45
Kenya National Archive, 258
Kenya National Commission of Human Rights (KNCHR)
  generally, 79, 119–120
  ICC and, 81–82
  investigations by, 67–68, 76–78
  public memorials and, 271
  RJF and, 265
  TJRC and, 115, 122, 258, 261
  Wagalla Massacre and, 140–141, 223
Kenyans for Peace, Truth, and Justice (KPTJ), 113, 122, 265
Kenya Post Office Savings Bank, 242
Kenya Red Cross, 41–42
Kenya Transitional Justice Network (KTJN), 261–262, 265
Kenyatta, Jomo
  Commissions of Inquiry and, 107–108
  land grabbing by, 257
  nationalism of, 56, 275
  repression under, 166
  trial of, 84
Kenyatta, Uhuru
  generally, 25, 42–43, 54, 61–62, 86
  ethnic differences in support for, 75–76
  extra-judicial killings and, 231
  in government, 55–56, 86
  ICC and, 35, 52, 53, 60, 69–70, 73, 87–90, 242
  Kibaki compared, 56
  Kikuyus and, 81
  neo-colonialism and, 83–85
  on reconciliation, 280
  RJF and, 251
  TJRC and, 96–97, 120, 249, 257, 259–260, 262–263
  2002 election and, 111
  2013 election and, 31, 50, 54, 58–59

Kibaki, Mwai
  generally, 3–4, 5, 79, 145, 163–164, 227, 238–239, 242–243
  Anglo-Leasing Scandal and, 241–242
  Commissions of Inquiry under, 107, 108
  ethnic differences in support for, 75–76
  Kalenjins and, 80
  Kenyatta compared, 56
  National Accord and, 23–24
  repression under, 166
  TJRC and, 95–96, 114, 238
  2002 election and, 111
  2013 election and, 31, 58, 67
Kihara, Jane, 224
Kilukumi, Kioko, 238–239
Kiplagat, Bethuel
  generally, 123, 241
  as AMP, 222, 238
  credibility crisis, 96–97, 101–103, 114–120, 121, 122
  TJRC and, 227–228, 249, 257–258
  Wagalla Massacre and, 115, 116, 117–119, 224–225, 237
Kisiero, Wilberforce, 232, 233
Kituo cha Sheria (CSO), 121–122
Koinange, Mbiyu, 107–108
Kosgey, Henry, 69, 73
Kriegler Commission. *See* Independent Review Commission on the General Elections Held in Kenya on 27 December 2007
Kuria, Moses, 78

Liberia, transitional justice in, 15
Local mechanisms in transitional justice, 15

Maendaleo ya Wanawake (MYW), 192
Mandate of TJRC, 100–101
Mandela, Nelson, 84, 95, 99, 100, 155, 158, 219
Mandela, Winnie, 155–157, 158, 219
Mandela United Football Club, 155–156
Matsanga, David, 77–78
Mau Mau Rebellion, 84, 270–271
Mau Mau Veterans Association, 261–262

Mbeki, Thabo, 159, 219
Media
  Al Jazeera, 140–141
  Citizen TV, 140–141
  Daily Nation (newspaper), 141–142
  Kenya Broadcasting Company (KBC), 3, 145
  Kenya Gazette, 258
  Kenya's Unheard Truth (television program), 141
  Kenya Television News (KTN), 140–141, 145
  Long Night's Journey into Day (documentary), 157
  Media Owners' Association (MOA), 45
  peacebuilding and, 44–45
  South African Broadcasting Company (SABC), 132, 133
  South African TRC, media coverage of, 129–131, 132–133
  TJRC, media coverage of, 140–142, 143–146
Ministry of Justice, 103–104, 115, 119, 120
Moeketsi, Stompie, 155–156
Moi, Daniel arap
  generally, 111, 228
  Commissions of Inquiry and, 107–108, 163–164
  denial of wrongfulness of acts by, 230
  Kiplagat and, 115
  nationalism of, 56, 275
  repression under, 166
Mt. Elgon Conflict
  generally, 235
  CSOs and, 47–48
  denial of responsibility for, 232
  TJRC hearings on, 118–119, 139–140, 171, 222, 223
  transfer of responsibility and, 226
  victims, portrayal of AMPs as, 229
  women and, 47–48, 162, 213
Mugo, Beth, 261
Muigai, Ngengi, 261
Multi-polar redress, 271–272
Mungiki (ethnic militia), 23, 69–71, 78, 124, 174, 231, 232–233
Munyakei, David, 240

Murungi, Betty, 101–103
Muslims, focus of TJRC on, 163–164
Musyoka, Kalonzo, 31, 259–260
Muthaura, Francis, 69–70, 73, 78
Mutua, Makau, 111, 112–113
Mutunga, Willy, 35, 261

National Accord, 23–26
The National Alliance (TNA), 42–43, 58
National Cohesion and Integration Commission (NCIC), 39, 43, 45, 125
National Council of Churches of Kenya (NCCK), 38–39
Nationalism, 30–31, 56, 275
National Land Commission (NLC), 35, 264, 269
National Police Service (NPS), 265
National Rainbow Coalition (NaRC), 111–112, 160–161, 166, 241–242
National Steering Committee on Peace-Building and Conflict Management (NSC), 36–37, 39
National Super Alliance (NASA), 260–261, 266–267
National Victim and Survivors Network (NVSN), 116–117, 119–120, 121–122, 259, 261–262, 265–266, 268
Ndege, Bernard, 174–175
Ndungu Commission, 108, 115
'Negative ethnicity', 166–167
'Negotiated democracy', 43
Neo-colonialism, 65–66, 83–86
Neo-Pentecostalism, 46–47, 48–49, 266
Ngugi, Kiriro wa, 259
Njenga, Maina, 124, 232–233
Ntimama, William ole, 260
Nuremberg Tribunal, 13, 60–61
Nyayo House
  public memorials and, 271
  reparations for, 269, 273
  TJRC hearings on, 180, 222, 239
  torture at, 135, 166, 233
Nyongo, Anyang, 82
Nyuandi, Patricia, 192
Nzokia Commission, 108

Obama, Barack, 82
Ocampo, Luis Moreno, 57–58, 68–69, 70, 79, 81–83
'Ocampo Six', 71–73, 76–77
Odinga, Oginga, 54
Odinga, Raila
  generally, 3, 61–62, 76–77, 79, 81, 259–260
  ethnic differences in support for, 75–76, 81–82
  ICC and, 228
  National Accord and, 23–24
  neo-colonialism and, 85–86
  TJRC and, 95–96, 260–261
  2013 election and, 31, 50, 53–54, 58–59, 67, 79
Ojienda, Tom, 101–103
Operation Urijani Mwema, 36
Orange Democratic Movement (ODM)
  generally, 3, 67, 76–77
  ICC and, 69–70
  National Accord and, 23–24, 25
  2013 election and, 50, 53–54, 58
Orkoiik (spiritual leaders), 223
Ouko, Robert, 107, 115, 117–118, 171

Panel of Eminent African Personalities, 24
Party of National Unity (PNU)
  generally, 3, 4, 67
  ethnic differences in support for, 75–76, 79
  ICC and, 69–70
  National Accord and, 23–24, 25
  2013 election and, 58
Peace animators, 38–39
Peacebuilding
  overview, 23–25, 30–33, 55–56
  absence of violence, peace as, 33–34
  barazas and, 36
  campaign for peaceful elections, 43–49
  Christianity and, 46–47, 48–49
  community mediators and conflict monitors, 38–39
  CSOs and, 36–37, 38–39, 42–43
  dialogue sessions and, 40–41, 43
  District Peace Committees and, 36–39
  hate speech and, 39
  ideology of order, 55–56

Index 333

media and, 44–45
nationalism and, 30–31
Neo-Pentecostalism and, 46–47, 48–49
peace animators, 38–39
peace messaging, 44–45
peace volunteers, 38–39
positive peace, 33–34
in practice, 35–43
suppression of issues resulting from, 51–52
therapy and, 47–49
transitional justice and, 13–19
unemployed youth and, 41–42
violence of peace, 49–54
Peace messaging, 44–45
PeaceNet (CSO), 38–39
Peace volunteers, 38–39
Peru
reparations in, 268
sexual violence in, 211
Truth and Reconciliation Commission, 103, 130, 187, 200, 202
Pinto, Pio Gama, 261
PNU. *See* Party of National Unity (PNU)
Political reconciliation, 280–281, 282, 286–289
Politicians, response to TJRC, 259–261
Positive peace, 33–34
Pragmatism, 65–66
Presidential Special Action Committee to Address Specific Concerns of the Muslim Community in Regard to Alleged Harassment and/or Discrimination in the Application/ Enforcement of the Law, 108, 163–164
Prosecution, reparations versus, 272–273
Psongoywo Manyiror Tirop, Jason, 223, 225, 226, 236–237, 242
Public apologies, 7–8
Public Finance Management Act (2012), 265
Public hearings
overview, 124–126
AMPs in, 134–135, 139–140, 222–225, 234–243

audience for, 146–148
conduct of, 135–137, 138
distractions regarding, 144–145
engagement and, 146–148
general public at, 137
interpreters at, 136
media areas, 137
media coverage of, 140–142, 143–146
on Mt. Elgon Conflict, 118–119, 139–140, 171, 222, 223
on Nyayo House, 180, 222, 239
'once-againness' in, 138
publicity, lack of, 135
seating at, 135–137
setting of, 135–137
on SLDF, 223, 235–237
social media and, 141
as theatre, 146–147
thematic hearings, 140
TRC (*See* South African Truth and Reconciliation Commission (TRC))
VIPs at, 135–136, 137
on Wagalla Massacre, 140–141, 171, 222–223, 238–239
witnesses in, 135–136, 138–139
women in, 139, 183–184, 194–197, 198–202
Public memorials, reparations versus, 271
Punitive justice, 14–15, 253–255

Racial minorities, focus on of TJRC on, 164
Rape, focus on, 187–188
Reconciliation
overview, 26, 277, 280–281
agonistic reconciliation, 280–281, 282, 286–289
as cohesion and unity, 280–281, 282, 285–286
as contentious coexistence, 280–281, 282, 286–289
defined, 279–280, 281–282
forgiveness and, 283–284
Jubilee Alliance on, 280
political reconciliation, 280–281, 282, 286–289
reparations and, 250

Reconciliation (cont.)
  as substantive friendship, 280–281, 282–285
  transitional justice and, 279, 289–292
  Uhuru Kenyatta on, 280
Religious minorities, focus of TJRC on, 163–164
Reparations
  overview, 251, 274
  acknowledgment versus, 270–271
  'blood money', 270
  failed promises regarding, 269
  Framework, 264–265
  lack of clarity regarding, 269
  limitations of, 268–270
  for Nyayo House, 269, 273
  in Peru, 268
  prioritisation of, 253–255, 267–269
  problems with, 267
  prosecution versus, 272–273
  public memorials versus, 271
  punitive justice versus, 253–255
  reconciliation and, 250
  restorative justice versus, 253–255
  retributive justice versus, 253–255
  RJF and, 251, 263–264, 265, 269
  in Sierra Leone, 268
  truth commissions and, 268
  for Wagalla Massacre, 269
Research methodology, 27–29
Restorative justice, 14–15, 253–255
Restorative Justice Fund (RJF), 251, 263–264, 265, 269
Retributive justice, 14–15, 253–255
Rome Statute, 66, 83, 89
Rumour, 227–228
Rural Women Peace Link (RWPL), 47–48
Ruto, William
  generally, 61–62, 78, 86, 241
  in government, 55–56, 86
  ICC and, 25, 35, 38, 52, 53, 60, 69, 73, 74, 87–90, 242
  Kalenjins and, 80
  neo-colonialism and, 84, 85–86
  reprieve, 86
  TJRC and, 96, 259–260
  2013 election and, 31, 58–59, 67
Rwanda, transitional justice in, 15

Sabaot Land Defence Force (SLDF)
  generally, 272
  denial of responsibility by, 232
  TJRC hearings on, 223, 235–237
  transfer of responsibility by, 226
  victims, portrayal of AMPs as, 229
  women and, 184, 201, 202, 210, 213
'Safe spaces' for women, 198–202
Samoei, Koitalel, 84
Sang, Joshua arap, 69, 73, 74, 86
Security Council, 63, 66
Serut, John, 223, 225, 226, 227, 229, 232, 235–236, 242
Sexual violence, 187–188, 193–194, 209–211
Shaming, 62–64
Sharawa Commission. *See* Presidential Special Action Committee to Address Specific Concerns of the Muslim Community in Regard to Alleged Harassment and/or Discrimination in the Application/Enforcement of the Law
Shava, Margaret, 101–103
Shifta War (1963–1967), 176
Sierra Leone
  reparations in, 268
  transitional justice in, 15
  Truth and Reconciliation Commission, 102, 130, 180, 216
Situatanga Farm, 115, 117–118, 222
SLDF. *See* Sabaot Land Defence Force (SLDF)
Slye, Ronald, 101–103, 120, 220, 252
Social media, TJRC hearings and, 141
Sonko, Mike, 82
South Africa
  African National Congress (ANC), 95, 99, 155, 157
  Inkatha Freedom Party, 99
  National Party, 155
  Rome Statute and, 89
  TRC (*See* South African Truth and Reconciliation Commission (TRC))
South African Truth and Reconciliation Commission (TRC)
  generally, 8, 12, 18–19, 102, 103, 126, 148
  overview, 98–100

Index   335

apartheid and, 158–160
cathartic effect of, 128–129
conditional amnesty and, 218–220
creation of, 95
criticisms of, 16, 99–100, 133,
    159–160
debate regarding, 128
as distraction, 129
impunity and, 218–220, 224
indicative moments of, 153–154
inspirational figures, impact of,
    131–132
as 'Kleenex Commission', 133
media coverage of, 129–131,
    132–133
meta-narrative of, 158–160
narrative of, 149–150, 152
'performance of change' and,
    133–134
as public ritual, 127–128
realpolitik and, 99
Reparations and Rehabilitation
    Committee, 99
restorative justice and, 15
secondary audience for, 128
sexual violence and, 210
TJRC compared, 26, 91–93, 95–97,
    149–150, 160–161, 166, 182, 224,
    253
transitional politics, impact of,
    131–132
Tutu and, 95, 97, 98, 100, 132
ubuntu and, 98
women and, 186–187
Statement takers, 104–105, 193,
    200–201
Substantive friendship, reconciliation
    as, 280–281, 282–285
Sudan
    Comprehensive Peace Agreement,
        237
    ICC and, 66

Technical Committee, 255
Terrorism, 86
Thematic hearings, 140, 193–194
Therapy, peacebuilding and, 47–49
TJRC. *See* Truth, Justice and
    Reconciliation Commission
    (TJRC)

TJRC Act (2008)
    generally, 113
    hearings under, 134–135
    implementation under, 105, 110,
        255, 256–257, 266–267
    impunity, effect on, 221
    mandate of TJRC, 100–101,
        161–162
    reports under, 258
    women under, 191
Tokyo Tribunal, 13
Transformative justice, 16
Transitional justice
    overview, 7–13, 275–277
    accountability and, 13–19
    backward-looking nature of, 7–11,
        14
    in Cambodia, 15
    continuities in, 8–9
    criticisms of, 11–12
    dangers of, 11
    democratisation and, 13–19
    in DRC, 14, 18
    in East Timor, 15
    'echoes' in, 9–10
    evolution of, 13–19
    expansion of, 17–18
    'ghosts' in, 8
    'hauntings' in, 8
    human rights and, 14
    ICC and, 14, 18
    individual versus structural focus of,
        17
    in Kenya, 22–27
    in Liberia, 15
    limitations of, 11–12, 18
    local mechanisms in, 15
    narratives in, 9–10
    operational shortcomings of, 11
    peacebuilding and, 13–19
    politics of performance and, 19–22,
        289–292
    punitive justice, 14–15
    reconciliation and, 279, 289–292
    restorative justice, 14–15
    retributive justice, 14–15
    in Rwanda, 15
    in Sierra Leone, 15
    transformative justice, 16
    in Tunisia, 15, 17–18

Transitional justice (cont.)
  in Uganda, 14, 18
  victim participation in, 15
  'visions' in, 9–10
  women in, 184
TRC. *See* South African Truth and Reconciliation Commission (TRC)
Troon, John, 107
Truth, Justice and Reconciliation Commission (TJRC)
  generally, 68–69
  overview, 95–97, 122–123
  amnesty and, 220–221 (*See also* Impunity)
  broad interpretation of mandate, 160–162
  cathartic effect of, 252–253
  children, focus on, 162–163
  churches, response of, 266
  class, focus on, 164–165
  Commissions of Inquiry compared, 110
  on continuing violations, 175–177
  creation of, 25–26, 111–114
  criticisms of, 276
  CSOs and, 113, 115, 116–117, 119–120, 121–122, 140–141, 192, 259, 261–263, 265–266, 268
  data collection, 170–173
  departments in, 104
  disinterest in, 142
  on disparity in suffering, 168
  distractions regarding, 144–145
  on fear of future injustices, 177–178
  forgiveness and, 253
  on 'ghosts' of past injustices, 174–175
  human rights violations, socio-economic effects of, 166, 167–168
  ICC upstaging, 144–145
  Implementation Committee, 198, 255–256
  importance of, 134–135
  impunity and (*See* Impunity)
  insufficiency of 'only talking', 252–253
  interpreters and, 136
  Jubilee Alliance and, 260–261, 266–267
  judiciary, response of, 261
  Kibaki and, 95–96, 114, 238
  Kiplagat and, 227–228, 249, 257–258
  KNCHR and, 115, 122, 258, 261
  land chapter, 257–258
  local justice and, 253
  mandate of, 100–101
  media coverage of, 140–142, 143–146
  members, 101–103
  Muslims and, 163–164
  narrative of, 149–152
  non-implementation, 257–267
  Odinga and, 95–96, 260–261
  ongoing suffering and, 151
  on past inciting future injustices, 178–179
  on past shaping narratives of injustice, 179–181
  placing blame, 168–169
  politicians, response of, 259–261
  problems with, 101
  public hearings (*See* Public hearings)
  purpose of, 134
  racial minorities, focus on, 164
  recommendations, 169–170, 249–251, 253–255, 256–257, 274
  reconciliation (*See* Reconciliation)
  religious minorities, focus on, 163–164
  reparations (*See* Reparations)
  reports, 35, 96–97, 105, 115, 120, 135, 151–152, 165–166, 170–173, 197–198, 249–251, 258
  research methodology regarding, 27–29
  Ruto and, 96, 259–260
  scepticism toward, 142
  selectively exclusive nature of, 150–151
  social media and, 141
  staff of, 103–105
  statement takers, 104–105
  Task Force, 111–114, 191
  Technical Committee, 255
  thematic hearings, 140, 193–194
  TRC compared, 26, 91–93, 95–97, 149–150, 160–161, 166, 182, 224, 253
  truth-telling function of, 252–253

Index   337

Uhuru Kenyatta and, 96–97, 120,
   249, 257, 259–260, 262–263
women, focus on (*See* Women)
Work Plan, 104
Truth be Told Network, 121–122
Truth commissions
  in Argentina, 126–127
  in Ghana, 130
  in Kenya (*See* Truth, Justice and
    Reconciliation Commission
    (TJRC))
  in Peru, 103, 130, 187, 200, 202
  reparations and, 268
  in Sierra Leone, 102, 130, 180, 216
  in South Africa (*See* South African
    Truth and Reconciliation
    Commission (TRC))
  in Tunisia, 17–18
  women and, 186–187
Truth-telling function of TJRC,
   252–253
Tunisia
  transitional justice in, 15, 17–18
  Truth and Dignity Commission,
    17–18
Turner, Christian, 83
Tutu, Desmond
  generally, 273
  on 'amnesia', 8
  'Cradock Four' and, 153–154
  TRC and, 95, 97, 98, 100, 132
  Winnie Mandela and, 156

Ubuntu (humanity), 98
Uchaguzi Bora Initiative, 44
Uganda
  ICC and, 65, 66–67
  Lord's Resistance Army, 66–67
  nationalism in, 30
  transitional justice in, 14, 18
Unemployed youth, 41–42
United Kingdom
  colonialism and, 166–167
  Mau Mau Rebellion and, 270–271
  neo-colonialism and, 83
United Nations Development
   Programme (UNDP), 38–39, 103
United Republican Party (URP), 58
United States
  nationalism in, 30

  neo-colonialism and, 83
  Rome Statute and, 66, 83
  War on Terror, 45–46
Unity, reconciliation as, 280–281, 282,
   285–286
University of Nairobi, 231
UN Women, 194
Uwaino Platform for Peace, 39

Violence
  generally, 4–6, 23
  of peace, 49–54
  sexual violence, 187–188, 193–194,
    209–211
Virtual trials, 62–64, 71, 74, 87

Wagalla Massacre
  generally, 152
  CSOs and, 140–141, 261–262, 271
  denial of responsibility for, 232
  denial of wrongfulness of, 229–230
  Kiplagat and, 115, 116, 117–119,
    224–225, 237
  KNCHR and, 140–141, 223
  public memorials and, 271
  reparations for, 269
  TJRC hearings on, 140–141, 171,
    222–223, 238–239
Wagalla Massacre Foundation,
   140–141, 261–262, 271
Waheire, Wachira, 120, 265–266
Wajir Registry, 171
Waki Commission. *See* Commission of
   Inquiry into the Post-Election
   Violence
Wamalwa, Eugene, 86
Wanjala, Tecla, 101–103
Witnesses
  bribery of, 240
  intimidation of, 78, 240
  murder of, 240
  tampering with, 77–78, 79
  in TJRC hearings, 135–136, 138–139
Women
  overview, 216–217
  criticism of TJRC approach to, 185,
    190
  focus on TJRC on, 162
  gender-balancing in TJRC, 192–193
  gender stereotypes and, 211–213

Women (cont.)
  implementation and monitoring mechanism, 198
  integrity of, 215–216
  neglect of masculinity and, 185, 189–190
  non-tribalism of, 207–209
  peacefulness of, 213–214
  rape, focus on, 187–188
  reinforcement of traditional gender boundaries, 185
  resilience of, 215–216
  responsibility, incorporation of stories into broader narrative of, 189
  'safe spaces' for, 198–202
  sexual violence and, 193–194, 209–211
  shared vulnerability of, 204–207
  silence of, 188–189
  SLDF and, 184, 201, 202, 210, 213
  statements by, 193, 200–201
  strength of, 215–216
  suffering of compared to men, 209–215
  thematic hearings, 193–194
  in TJRC hearings, 139, 183–184, 194–197, 198–202
  in TJRC report, 197–198
  tokenism regarding, 187–188
  in transitional justice, 184
  TRC and, 186–187
  truth commissions and, 186–187
  unique experience of repression by, 203–204
  victimhood, incorporation of stories into broader narrative of, 189
  violence committed by, 213–214
World Bank Inspection Panel, 180

Youth Enterprise Development Fund, 42

Zimbabwe, violence in, 89, 109
Zuma, Jacob, 159